INCEPTIONS

Inceptions

LITERARY BEGINNINGS AND CONTINGENCIES OF FORM

Kevin Ohi

FORDHAM UNIVERSITY PRESS   NEW YORK   2021

Fordham University Press gratefully acknowledges the Office of the Dean of the Morrissey College of Arts and Sciences at Boston College for publication support.

Visit us online at www.fordhampress.com.

Library of Congress Cataloging-in-Publication Data available online at https://catalog.loc.gov.

Printed in the United States of America

23 22 21   5 4 3 2 1

First edition

Contents

PART IV. SOLITUDE AND QUEER ORIGINS

Those masterful images because complete
Grew in pure mind but out of what began?
A mound of refuse or the sweepings of a street,
Old kettles, old bottles, and a broken can,
Old iron, old bones, old rags, that raving slut
Who keeps the till. Now that my ladder's gone
I must lie down where all the ladders start
In the foul rag and bone shop of the heart.
                    —W. B. YEATS, "THE CIRCUS ANIMALS' DESERTION"

Exordium

For this is action, this not being sure, this careless
Preparing, sowing the seeds crooked in the furrow,
Making ready to forget, and always coming back
To the mooring of starting out, that day so long ago.
                              —JOHN ASHBERY, "SOONEST MENDED"

Its weight the iceberg dares
Upon a shifting stage and stands and stares.
                    —ELIZABETH BISHOP, "THE IMAGINARY ICEBERG"

In "The End of the Poem," Giorgio Agamben pursues the startling implication of Jean-Claude Milner's thesis that poetry can be defined by the possibility of enjambment, the possibility of opposing form and meaning, sound and
sense, a syntactical limit and a phonological or formal one: the end of a sentence or phrase and the end of the line.[1] If poetry is thus defined by this possibility, of opposing "a metrical limit to a syntactical limit, . . . a prosodic pause
to a semantic pause" (Agamben, "End of the Poem," 109), it follows, Agamben concludes, "that the last verse of the poem is not a verse" (112). Because
the poem becomes formally coherent only at its end—it is a unit, Agamben
writes, "that finds its *principium individuationis* only at the point at which it
ends" (111)—and because the last line is the one line in a poem where enjambment is not possible, it further follows that the poem is defined by an element
that is not poetry, takes form only when it ceases to be a poem. "Poetry," he
writes, "lives only in the tension and difference (and hence also in the virtual
interference) between sound and sense, between the semiotic sphere and the

1

semantic sphere" (109). The end of the poem thus instantiates a crisis in which the poem both comes into being and disappears: "As if the poem as a formal structure would not and could not end, as if the possibility of the end were radically withdrawn from it, since the end would imply a poetic impossibility: the exact coincidence of sound and sense" (113). Agamben's essay traces the poetic institutions that derive from the poetic confrontation with the end; equally striking are the metrical and linguistic innovations that Daniel Heller-Roazen traces in the multilingual poetry of tenth-, eleventh-, and twelfth-century Andalusia, and the emergence of a "form without precedent and sequel in the history of literature"—a shift, at the end of the poem, into another voice, and another language (even a non- or double-language of one tongue translit-erated into another) (Heller-Roazen, "Speaking in Tongues," 106). The radi-cal experiments of poets a millennium ago body forth poetry's perpetual confrontation with its conditions of possibility, with the limitations and incite-ments of its form.

This book starts out from the intuition that there is an analogous crisis of inception. For any material form—any work of art, for example—and perhaps for any form of consciousness, inception marks a discontinuity analogous to what, in music, is called "onset distortion," which R. Murray Schafer, in *The Soundscape*, defines as the distortion in any sound that (as is familiar to any string or woodwind musician as a major technical problem) derives from the fact that both the emission of sound and our perception of it depend on physi-cal vibration. Because it must overcome inertia, the beginning of any sound production, as of any perception of sound, entails distortion:

> All sounds we hear are imperfect. For a sound to be totally free of onset
> distortion, it would have to have been initiated before our lifetime. If it
> were also continued after our death so that we knew no interruption in
> it, then we would comprehend it as being perfect. But a sound initi-
> ated before our birth, continued unabated and unchanging through-
> out our lifetime and extended beyond our death, would be perceived
> by us as—*silence*.[2]

The imperfection rooted in the physical nature of sound makes it perceptible to us; temporal and formal boundedness entails a distortion that makes ap-prehension inseparable from a deformation. And not merely beginnings we might empirically isolate: Onset distortion, and what I will call *inception*, is internal to any sound. When one bows a string instrument, for instance, the hair of the bow repeatedly catches and releases the string, causing a vibration that then resonates inside the instrument; the seemingly continuous sound is, in fact, discontinuous, a series of repeated onset distortions. (The vibration of the reed in a woodwind instrument could be conceptualized in a similar way.) Inception (for sound, to be caused by a physical vibration that must perforce begin) marks every created form with an exteriority it cannot comprise; its orig- ination makes sound deviate from itself even as it constitutes it as sound, makes it perceptible even as it dictates that all origins be impure, that no sound coincide with its beginning. Or, in other terms, to have a form is to see that form ruined from the start.[3]

Onset distortion or impure beginnings thus make manifest an inherent property of form as such. Such a possibility is all the more legible where the ambition toward monumental form is most marked: In great performances of Beethoven's Ninth Symphony, for instance, one feels, viscerally, the ominous threat underlying the monumental ambition—as the last movement invokes themes and motifs from the previous movements to unify and sublate them in its closing Schillerian ode, the ecstasy is hardly to be separated from an anxiety that those gathered threads might, at any moment, and within the triumphal ode itself, unravel, and leave the monumental edifice to shiver into fragments. The high-wire act of the "Grosse Fuge" (op. 133) likewise makes viscerally perceptible this tension between order and chaos. Or, to turn to a more serene and less self-consciously monumental composer, in the first act finale of *Don Giovanni*, the virtuoso juggling of time signatures (fa- mously, Mozart coordinates the pit orchestra with two on-stage ensembles, all playing in different time signatures)[4] could fall into chaos—and, in a sense, it does, as desire erupts again, with the shriek of the molested Zerlina and the unrepentant, world-dissolving defiance of Don Giovanni ("Se cadesse ancora il mondo,/Nulla mai temer mi fa" [Confused and caught up in the finale's "tempest," he asserts that he will not lose himself or be confounded, even "if the world yet crumbles. Nothing will make me afraid"]).[5] In his lec- tures on painting, Deleuze cites a remark from Paul Claudel (from the *Intro- duction to Dutch Painting*), suggesting that visual form is less the arrest than the perpetuation of such a process of dissolution: "la composition c'est une organisation en train de se défaire" (a composition is an organized system [structure] in the process of coming undone).[6] These examples are mere analogies; the topic here is not sound or music—nor is it painting or visual art. Yet the question, in each case, is, explicitly or not, creation, and the emer- gence of the work of art. These analogies make tangible forms' confrontation with the contingency that marks the fact of their having a beginning. In in- ception, and the potential it embodies, for any form, that it might have been otherwise, or not at all, it is possible to see making and unmaking coincide within the mechanism of creation. That mechanism is crucially at stake in the texts I examine in this book.

Beginnings—and the questions of inception that they raise—thus bring one into contact with the text's own conditions of possibility. This is a question, in the first place, of foundation; the self-reflexivity of any textual beginning bears witness to the self-grounding quality of literary fiction—its inability either to comprise its inception or to externalize it in an authorizing exteriority, an aspect of creation that the book will return to in terms such as *posit* and *fiat*. (Bishop's imaginary iceberg bodies forth this groundless positing—and is, to that degree, an emblem of inception; her poem's dire terms of death and shipwreck point to the uncanny consequences of such moorings of our startings out.) Reading can perhaps only mirror this fundamental groundlessness. The non-trivial self-reflexivity of the work of art I try to specify in theoretical readings of various theorists or philosophers (especially Giorgio Agamben) and in detailed readings of particular texts. Beginnings and endings alike make visible a coming-together, even a becoming-indistinct, of a formal coherence and its undoing; beginnings in literary texts are often self-conscious about the pressure this coincidence puts on foundation, perpetually raising the possibility that the work might disintegrate in the very fiat that gives it birth. The tenuousness registered by every starting out therefore links the question of beginning to the potentiality of literary creation: the capacity to not be sheltered, according to the Agambenian gloss of Aristotle, within every actualization— understood, therefore, as a kind of suspension, a capacity to not not-be. Thus, while beginnings raise any number of questions—practical or generic questions, for instance, that might be answered by careful formalist analysis of a representative corpus; or historico-epistemic questions, in which a given period might be shown to confront the conditions governing the emergence of its particular forms of thought; or philosophical questions about the relation of origins to what comes after them, or about the possibility of recovering or deducing origins from supervening conditions; and so on—and while the specificity of various writers or thinkers or even works could be brought into view through a detailed examination of their particular relation to beginning or the particular mode their beginnings take, this book explores a more limited, if also a more general, topic: ways that inception makes manifest the potentiality structural to literary creation.

Thus, the book charts the productive gap between *inception* and related but not synonymous terms: *beginning*, *birth*, and *origin*. Perhaps idiosyncratically, I use *inception* to mark an asynchronicity within beginnings, textual and existential—where foundation diverges from mere starting out. "The action of entering upon some undertaking, process, or stage of existence: origination, beginning, commencement," reads the definition in the *Oxford English Dictionary Online*—nearly synonyms, the latter three terms perhaps beg the question.[7] The more technical sense of "incepting," which (at one time) marked "the master's formal entrance upon, and commencement of, the function of a duly licensed teacher and his recognition" by others in the profession, registers the multiple temporal layers of inception. The lag even within pedagogico-bureaucratic structures of licensing mirrors more fundamental kinds of asynchronicity. *Inception* is privileged here for this sense of establishing a form, institution, or consciousness; *beginning*, in contrast, can have the more neutral sense of merely locating a first moment in time. In *birth* (at least its mammalian varieties) one perceives the ways that separation is crucial to beginning (indicatively, in this case, separation from a maternal body); leaving the shelter of another's body, the newborn comes into existence—one synchronous with neither its biological "viability" as a separate organism nor with its independent consciousness. (Whatever else one might say about it, the fraught question in abortion debates about the boundaries of human life underlines the stakes of this temporal indeterminacy.) Unlike *inception, birth* retains a reference to biological reproduction, however much the latter might be obscured by the term's figural acceptations. *Origin* covers still different terrain, linking a beginning to a source or a cause—my humble origins, or the origins of the French Revolution—and which can be either absolute (the origin of the universe) or relative (the origin of that year's fiscal crisis—an origin that could itself have an origin, or that could share the field with other, equally salient origins). If certain chapters take *origin* as a central term it is insofar as *origin* in particular uses and instances (and in the particular vocabularies of writers I discuss) draws closer to *inception*. In the movement among these various terms one can chart the consequences, for the texts examined here, of *inception:* confrontations with staggered or asynchronous beginnings, with the onset distortion of any starting out and the ways that founding distortion brings into view the grounds of possibility of literary creation.

Thus the beginning of the poem, no matter what its theme, makes manifest a crisis of inception inherent in creation; one could also say that the crises of inception I trace in various chapters make manifest the non-coincidence of *beginning* and *inception*, or of either of them and *birth*—as in forms, for instance, that are founded or instituted only after their beginning. (When a beginning escapes our cognition [as do the beginnings of our lives], the subsequent form lacks a certain boundedness and troubles a clear moment of inception.) This formal question of inception is visible—to choose one example among many possible others—in Ovid's play with meter: The first poem of the *Amores* begins with the same word as the *Aeneid* ("Arma") and feigns dactylic hexameter until Cupid "steals a foot" from every second line, creating the elegiac couplet that Ovid adapts from early Greek verse and that will come to be associated with love poetry. In the *Tristia*, he will knowingly link this "limping" line to the deprived, displaced state of exile, as if his earlier meter were an anticipation of future privation—adding another retrospective layer of significance to his meter, and thus rhyming, as it were, formal considerations within the particular poems with a movement legible only from a meta-level reflection on shifts in metrical form across an entire corpus. Between these, in *The Metamorphoses*, it is only at the end of the *second* line that the meter (dactylic hexameter) becomes apparent, as the poem, by thwarting our expectations of finding the elegiac couplets of the *Amores*, returns to the meter of the epic.[8]

In general, prosodists know the difficulty of establishing a meter with only one line—a second line (at least) is required to confirm the meter. As Joseph Brodsky remarks, "Remember: it is the second, and not the first, line that shows where your poem is to go metrically" (further remarking that "the second line is the line that introduces the rhyme scheme").[9] This is the retrospective structure that Ovid exploits; metrically, that is to say, the poem comes into being a line after its beginning. Even if one accurately foretells the meter from the first line, there can be no hypothesis at all until the first line is complete. The first line hovers in a metrical no-man's land until a pattern can be confirmed (or posited) after two full lines. If, as Brodsky notes, the rhyme scheme likewise begins with the second line, it, too, is a retrospective structure, requiring the completion of a larger formal unit (a couplet, a stanza, or the entire poem) before it can be conferred, in hindsight, on the lines we have read. In the non-coincidence of *beginning* and *inception*, we find that forms are founded in and through this fundamental contingency.

Thus, Hannah Arendt's claim that beginning, "before it becomes a historical event, is the supreme capacity of man; politically, it is identical with man's freedom,"[10] ought perhaps to be read in relation to this contingency. As she addresses the question of beginning in *The Human Condition*, action is linked to speech because, in speech, human beings realize their uniqueness and take the risk of appearing to one another—which, not to be confused with self-expression, is rather an avowing of the contingency of one's actions in a world where there are others, each unique yet equal and capable of action. Beginning corresponds to what Arendt calls "natality" and is the mode through which man's status as equal and unique appears:

> The fact that man is capable of action means that the unexpected can be expected from him, that he is able to perform what is infinitely improbable. And this again is possible only because each man is unique, so that with each birth something uniquely new comes into

the world. With respect to this somebody who is unique it can be truly said that nobody was there before. If action as beginning corresponds to the fact of birth, if it is the actualization of the human condition of natality, then speech corresponds to the fact of distinctness and is the actualization of the human condition of plurality, that is, of living as a distinct and unique being among equals.[11]

Action thus also confronts a fundamental contingency: The uniqueness of each human being, and his or her capacity to act, means that the outcome of every action is unpredictable and potentially infinite. What she calls forgiveness (as a form of action itself that does not simply repeat the received action) responds to that contingency and prevents the paralysis that would attend it. Likewise, promises attempt to contain that contingency by binding people together, and to their words. In a very different context, then (which we will find echoed, however, in James's account of revision, and Foucault's account of parrhēsia), Arendt suggests some of the ethical stakes of the potentiality of inception. In the beginning, all could have been otherwise. *Inceptions* describes ways this founding contingency remains within the completed form the beginning foretells.

Origin is perhaps more problematic than *beginning* (or even *birth*), precisely because it has been an explicit term of reference for many disparate writers, including those who subject it to critique—from Nietzsche to Foucault to Derrida to Edward Said (who chose *beginning* over *origin*).[12] I do not propose to offer a history of the term, to speculate why, in certain eras and for certain thinkers, it became problematic, or to attempt to clarify its different uses (its different meaning for Rousseau, for example, than for Darwin, or, for that matter, for Heidegger). Eschewing *origin* for *inception*, the attempt here is to delimit a narrower topic, turning, again, to questions of literary creation and literary form in the vicinity of textual beginnings. Once again, it is the friction between terms that matters; arguably, for James's New York Edition prefaces, as for Welty's "First Love," the conceptual movement of each text could be charted by tracing, in detail, the non-coincidence of *origin* and *inception*. (Such would be one way to summarize the structure of these chapters.) The foundation of text or psyche—emerging, originated—as it departs in significant ways from its origin is registered in both cases by the multiple, and in many ways irreconcilable, narratives of origination they offer: The boy's "first love" in Welty is both his dawning love for a man (Aaron Burr, in the story's startling and delightful premise) and for the parents he has lost; these paired losses bring the boy's consciousness into being. In James, origins are both conceptual movements and anecdotal occasions (occasions that bear no clear relation to the ideas they inspire) structuring the narratives, in the prefaces, of the genesis of the novels and tales. That James knowingly assimilates differing registers without rationalizing their relation, just as Welty mingles a linguistic structure of inception with origin stories (of subjectivity, of desire—these, in turn, not assimilated to one another) marks much of the interest of beginnings for these texts. This book often invokes *origin* when the formal abysses of inception appear in relation to epistemological or existential difficulties of beginnings, which are forced to presuppose an inception with which they cannot coincide: This is perhaps the rhythm of literary creation in Maurice Blanchot, the pursuit of what he repeatedly terms *origin*, which, perpetually to be sought, perpetually escapes one, a creation that has, at any given moment, always already begun. This hiatus marks any inception; the coming into being of any text, no matter what its theme, leads one to confront the difficulty that Augustine perceived in Genesis: What is before the beginning?[13] Whatever one might decide about the cosmos, human thought seems structurally to follow from something that precedes it; in Wordsworth's lines from the *Prelude*: "Not only general habits and desires, / But each most obvious and particular thought, / Not in a mystical and idle sense, / But in the words of reason deeply weigh'd, / Hath no beginning."[14]

This is also the belatedness that structures human consciousness and might be named, simply, *birth*. Finitude entails that our knowledge will be fractured—and constituted—by the impurity of having begun. As Adam says in Book VIII of *Paradise Lost*, "For Man to tell how human Life began / Is hard; for who himself beginning knew?"[15] (In that poem, Adam's narrative of emergence retells the creation that the Archangel has just narrated—and is itself subsequently doubled by Eve's narrative. In each case, one tells to someone who might have witnessed it the story of a beginning one's consciousness cannot comprise.) This is among the questions confronted in the deceptively simple play on words at the beginning of *David Copperfield*: "I am born," the text announces, drawing on the placard-style chapter titles of eighteenth-century fiction, but thereby introducing, from the outset, in a first-person, quasi-autobiographical text, a fracture between its voice and its autobiographical "subject." The opening's pun—"To begin my life with the beginning of my life," Dickens writes in the novel's second sentence—further draws out the gap between the life lived and the life written, and locates that gap at the origin of the text (the origin toward which the text, written, moves, at which it hopes to arrive): "Whether I shall turn out to be the hero of my own life, or whether that station will be held by anybody else, these pages must show."[16]

Discussing the correlation of verb tenses in French, Émile Benveniste takes issue with a common account of the relation between the *passé simple* and the *passé composé*—an account in which the two forms are largely redundant, the latter having begun, around the twelfth century, to displace the former, which, never spoken, remains, vestigial, in literary and historical writing. The two forms, on the contrary, cover different fields, he suggests, and their opposition corresponds to that between "history" and "discourse"; "discourse" assumes the speaker and hearer that "history," on the contrary, excludes (208).[17] The historical, he writes, "excludes every 'autobiographical' linguistic form"; historical language excludes the personal pronouns (*je* and *tu*) in favor of the non-person (*il*).[18] It is unsurprising, given this account, that the *passé simple* conventionally lacks a first-person form; in this historical form, Benveniste writes, "no one speaks" (208). It is striking therefore that a notable exception is *je naquis*: I was born. *Je naquis*, the logic suggests, likewise excludes a first-person perspective; the formulation in the first person enacts the belated structure of consciousness in the very choreographies of speech—for one can speak a perspective that one cannot perforce comprise.[19] Who himself beginning knew? "I am born," David Copperfield can write, but only in a chapter heading, and in a narrative present tense that is divided from the first-person voice (Dickens, 1). "The blank of my infancy," he says, otherwise (13), recalling Prospero's "dark backward and abyss of time."[20] Speaking of one's own birth, no one speaks; the ostensible anomaly recalls, within speech, the contingencies of inception.

Birth, we noted, names the non-coincidence of an organism's emergence into the world, its achievement of organic coherence, and the dawn of its organizing consciousness. It thus brings into focus another central tension in conceptions of beginning, which recur to the beginning or origin of the text, and to the beginning or origin of a life. (This structure is particularly explicit in James's considerations of autobiography and revision.) The ways that texts and forms of consciousness arrive belatedly to themselves are analogous but not identical; the analogy is a powerful one for each to take cognizance of its particular belatedness. For autobiographical and quasi-autobiographical texts (*David Copperfield*, for example, *The Prelude*, *À la recherche du temps perdu*, or even James's New York Edition Prefaces), the difference between these is a productive force for the work, and in question is the text's power to bring into being an explicitly textual self. (If Samuel Johnson's *Lives of the Poets* might be said to mark one of the beginnings of literary criticism in English, criticism, like the novel, is marked from its beginning by the blurred boundary between the textual and as it were biological or historical status of the poet's "life." Similar oscillations are visible in the history of the term *character*.) This book's exploration of inception repeatedly returns to this relation—privileging in its account of novelistic beginnings, for example, the question of character and, more generally, the ways that lives are taken up and transformed by texts.

This emphasis in the book emerges from its exploration of inception in relation to potentiality. At various moments, Agamben's linking of potentiality to dimensions that he marks as ethical takes the form of considering the work's relation to the life of its creator. The ethical dimensions of potentiality preoccupy *The Use of Bodies*, for example;[21] schematically, one might say that, at many moments in his writing, the ethical life is one that gives form to potentiality—which is also to say suspends itself within potentiality. If what that entails often remains elusive, it is clear that it is linked to his understanding of authorship; in essays such as "The Author as Gesture" in *Profanations* or "*Opus Alchymicum*" in *The Fire and the Tale*, this ethical preoccupation emerges in his characterization of authorship as an enigmatic suspension of life within the potentiality of the work. Thus framed, beginnings bring into view a further set of questions: the relation between registers that are often called "psychological"—character, identification, personhood—and those that are termed "formal"—the literary work read as a structure, as, at the limit, an impersonal form. The author as a psychologically determined person whose influence over the work might be illuminated by biographical criticism and the author as a function, as if created by the work, or destined to disappear there in the fading vitality that makes for literary immortality; character as psychological verisimilitude or locus of identification or character as one among other formal attributes of fiction; "voice" as the speech of a person, however distant or attenuated in immediacy and as the all-but-inhuman locus of the person's disappearance: a series of hinges, these, in which one traces the vicissitudes of the relation of life to art. In Henry James's consideration of the authorial life in the shadow of revision; in Eudora Welty's account of emerging desire and consciousness as they coalesce in relation to language turned to gesture; in *Robinson Crusoe*'s imagining of the inception of speech and sociality; in George Eliot's and Charles Dickens's exploration of character, as it emerges as if from an indeterminate ground and then continues to exert its influence on their novels; in the ways that retrospection leads Wallace Stevens to an arid, abstract, and profoundly moving consideration of embodied experience; in the various ways that solitude leads writers to think about an originary human relation to language or speech; in the question of how a work might confront the not-yet-formed, the potential identity of the proto-queer child: The central concerns of each chapter of the book could be rendered in the particular terms of potentiality and literary creation—and the encounter thus charted between life and literary form—that emerge from the consideration of inception.

For me, *queer* has long been a useful category for thinking about related questions. In *Innocence and Rapture, Henry James and the Queerness of Style,* and *Dead Letters Sent, queer* was a central term for my literary analyses, and for my explorations of innocence, style, and transmission (respectively), in part because it marked a hinge between ostensibly personal or psychological questions of sexuality, on the one hand, and impersonal, formal, aesthetic ones on the other.[22] The central analytic category of each book was defined in relation to queerness, and for each book non-normative forms of sexuality illuminated and were illuminated by ostensibly non-sexual literary questions. The relation here is different because the central argument is not focused on sexuality. *Queer* serves rather to index a particular structure of inception, a paradoxical recursivity of foundation whose relation to potentiality is charted throughout the book. The turn to "queer origins" at the end of the book is, in the first place, a further instance of the vexed relation, brought to the fore by the question of inception, between so-called psychological and formal or impersonal registers. Phrased this way, however, the identity category could have been anything else—and my reading of Baldwin, for instance, might have focused on the ways the story of growing up in the text encounters ideologies of race and class, or the geographical fractures in the American history of both. These important questions are not, nevertheless, the focus of the chapter. My particular interests and training and preoccupations lead me to privilege questions of sexuality, but my particular intellectual formation is, to my mind, beside the point, for it isn't the turn to this particular identity (and not some other) that is the signal question. Rather, *queer* names not a particular identity but a powerful way of conceptualizing the relation between the abstract formal properties of the work of art and the ostensibly psychological categories of identification, psychology, and experience—between "art" and "life."

Forms founded after they have begun; the non-coincidence of temporal and conceptual beginnings; the tension and interference among *inception, beginning, birth,* and *origin*: Read in relation to writing and literary creation, these have different meanings and pose different questions for different writers and texts. The structure of the book—along with its reliance on close reading and on theoretical models immanent to those readings—attempts to do justice to that particularity. Repeatedly, nevertheless, in the return to the conditions of possibility of the work, one encounters a common thread that I attempt, in various ways, to link to potentiality—in otherwise disparate writers from Ovid to Dickens to Stevens to Welty. What remains of language thus returned to potentiality is given striking and highly condensed form by Augustine's *Confessions*. In the account of time that follows upon his consideration of Creation (in Book XI), Augustine's effort to make time perceptible appears to turn on a curious operation: Moving first to an analogy between time and sound (we are asked to imagine a noise), his phenomenalization of time seems to depend on the voiding of semantic content in the recitation of a hymn by St. Ambrose—the very hymn, one recalls, that consoled him after the death of his mother.[23] Excerpted first, to a line, the hymn is then reduced to a sequence of long and short syllables—which can be measured (not absolutely, but in relation to each other: the long syllables are twice as long as the short) and therefore supply the "tick" and "tock" of phenomenal time.[24] For the North African Church father, this procedure makes silence measurable, and one might suggest that this small moment also enacts the larger movement of the *Confessions* itself: from the specifics of personal loss and desire to abstraction, the consideration of time and faith toward which the text moves. A becoming-impersonal of loss is made analogous to a voiding of semantics in favor of sound with a (relative) duration. In the phenomenalization of time, the meaning of the hymn is at once sustained and voided, reduced to the smallest, unmeaning units of mean- ingful language, just as the subject's losses and consolations alike vanish into the materiality of the language through which he knows his losses and their remediation in faith. (Augustine's writing, presenting as it does a patchwork of quotations from the Gospels, and especially from Psalms, arguably has a similar effect: at once embodying his voice's saturation in the words of faith and abstracting those words so that they become the building materials of other sentences, become almost [though never quite] sequences of mere sound.) Thus perceptible here is a form of inception that one might counterpoise against the Biblical Creation with which he begins.

Repeatedly, in the course of *Inceptions*, we will encounter language ab- stracted or purified of any specific content other than itself—in, for example, the persistence of stone in Ovid's rendering of the songs of Orpheus as they encrypt the poem's structure of metamorphosis as creation; in "gesture" in Agamben and Eudora Welty as it bodies forth language that is as if prior to content; in Adam's invocation of natural forms in his address to God in *Para- dise Lost* as it is echoed in Wordsworth and in later instances of poetic posit- ing; in the shifting figurations of embodiment in Wallace Stevens; or in the blank positing of character in Dickens's *Our Mutual Friend*: Origin and in- ception in these cases return, in different registers, and with different empha- ses, to the capacities and potentialities of literature and literary creation.

Critics have considered textual beginnings in various ways; the most exten- sive literature is in narratology, which, however, often considers the question in largely pragmatic or descriptive terms.[25] Rather than focusing on such prag- matic or descriptive questions, I attempt to bring to the fore quandaries of a different order—the ways that, in their inception, texts confront their own con- ditions of possibility. Because, understood in relation to writing and literary creation, it has different meanings and poses different questions for different writers and texts, the book's structure privileges this specificity. It does not, therefore, proceed chronologically; it does not seek to make a historical argument, or to offer a genealogy of its central terms—both of which might have dictated a chronological progression. Instead, it is hoped that its groupings and juxtapositions will illuminate its central concepts. I have also felt emboldened to be careless of chronology in part because inception precedes all chronology. History is one after-effect of the constitutive fracture of the beginning. Each grouping into which the chapters are divided builds on what comes before even as it circles back to the central question of inception—while the book's argument elaborates theoretical strands that are spelled out in the introduction and in the chapters on Welty and James, true to the logic of inception, each part, and each chapter, must found itself anew, repeatedly returning us to the potentiality of literary form.

Thus, each chapter of the book in a sense lays out its own theoretical framework—in the place of a global theory an introduction might have offered. The book's theoretical frameworks emerge out of the detailed readings of particular texts: in Henry James's New York Edition prefaces, Giorgio Agamben's concept of potentiality in relation to what James calls "revision"—and the relation it charts between the text's perpetual return to its conditions of possibility and a "life" subjected to the work of art; in Eudora Welty's "First Love," a theory of gesture, also drawn from Agamben, among others, that attempts to confront language in its bare capacity to signify, prior (as it were) to its signifying anything in particular, and the way that theory abuts the emergence of consciousness and desire in Welty's text; in Defoe's *Robinson Crusoe*, its narrative of language acquisition in relation to some of the formal peculiarities of the text; in George Eliot and Charles Dickens, and their self-conscious consideration of how novels begin and how they create characters, questions that bring into view difficulties (specific to the fictional project of each writer) of foundation; in Ovid and Wallace Stevens, more or (often) less explicit theories of origin, immanent in the texts themselves, that allow one to pose the question of how the rendering of origin inflects the consideration of embodiment and literary form; in poetic invocations (in Milton, Wordsworth, Oppen, Shakespeare, and others) of a poem's power to posit, and the ways that it runs up against the limits of human mortality; in James Baldwin, Carson McCullers, and Su Friedrich, the narration of queer incipience, which brings to the fore quandaries of sexual etiology in queer theory—and the latter's vexed relation to questions of sexual identity and sexual politics. Out of the detailed readings of these texts in relation to these theoretical frameworks, the book brings into view key aspects of literature's confrontation with inception.

Because each chapter provides its own framework, I do not attempt here to offer a systematic account of theories of beginning, inception or origin—but turn, instead, to a few texts where beginning raises the question of the conditions of possibility of the text, often in realms removed from the explicit concerns of the chapters that follow. Thus, for example, in "The Discourse of History," Roland Barthes responds to Benveniste's opposition between "discourse" and "history," pointing to the ways that historical writing is ruptured from within by its moment of enunciation—by, in other terms, its inception. Barthes turns at one point to the "organizing shifters"—the shifters through which the historian "organizes his own discourse, taking up the thread or modifying his approach in some way in the course of narration" (points of reference to his own discourse [as *enunciation*, or what the translator renders as "uttering"] as it structures the historical material, to, in other terms, the fact that the discourse was *composed*).[26] These shifters, Barthes asserts, have a "destructive effect . . . as far as the chronological time of the history is concerned. This is a question of the way historical discourse is inaugurated, of the place where we find in conjunction the beginning of the matter of the utterance and the *exordium* of the uttering" (9). Not dissimilar to the convergence marking the crisis of the end of the poem, that conjunction is a problem, Barthes suggests, because it marks the coalescence of two disjunctive times—of the utterance or the writing and of the historical time it would comprise or represent,[27] between the time of "discourse" and the time of "history." The two forms of inauguration he notes (the invocation that recalls the opening of the epic and the prefatory commentary that locates the written history itself as an object of prospective or retrospective commentary) thus signal a crisis of inception. Barthes does not dwell on it in this essay, but inception marks an irreparable internal fracture in the discourse of history that is indistinguishable from its conditions of possibility.

In his study of "narrative beginnings," A. D. Nuttall elaborates on the logic and consequences of a pair of claims by Ernst Robert Curtius about the Muses: that they disappear in modern poetry, and that they come (in a displacement he first sees in Prudentius) to be replaced in the traditional *invocatio* by the "poet's soul."[28] (Ovid, as we will see, has it both ways in the *Metamorphoses*, appearing to invoke his own spirit or consciousness before ceding that place to unnamed gods.) For Nuttall, then, the question of beginning is a question of inspiration and authority: the question, enacted in the proem or invocatio, of what allows the poet to begin speaking, of whose voice this is, and whether it can ground or institute itself. Although Nuttall (like Curtius) does not draw out this particular implication, the individual poetic voice would seem to emerge from the internalization of a foreign, impersonal voice—of a deity or deities that speak through one; the shift from oral to written poetry and the adaptation of classical models for Christian poetry—both of which he does dwell on—could be read as moments in that history of inspiration.[29] In Nuttall's argument, this question of grounding emerges in the tension between "natural" and "artificial" openings; rephrasing Horace's distinction between a beginning *ab ovo* and one *in medias res*, this is an opposition between an absolute or a relative beginning, one might say, or, in other terms, the beginning of the world as opposed to the self-consciously "formal" or limited (or therefore "artificial") beginning of a text.[30] These are among the tensions I hope to name with the term *inception*.

If the question of beginning leads, in various ways, to the question of voice—and to the relation of "life" to text, or how to conceptualize the shaping power of authorship—it also raises more general questions of form. In Nuttall's worrying of the distinction between the "literal" and the "figural" in Dante (among other places), one perceives that what is in question is the relation between the inside and the outside of the text.[31] The artificial beginning strives to touch the natural beginning; form seeks to reach its outside. *The Aeneid* circles back to the creation song of Iopas, the Carthaginian minstrel (*Aeneid*, Book I, ll.740ff; see Nuttall, 29); in Dante's *Commedia*, an "*in medias res* narrative opening is followed by a classical proemium" (the invocation of the Muses in Canto II of *Inferno*) (Nuttall, 57). Dante, circling back to the invocation in the second canto, then repeats the gesture nine times in the course of the *Commedia*.[32] Milton, beginning with the fall of the rebellious angels, circling back to the Creation and moving forward to the Fall of man, aims, it might be said, to make epic the place for "natural" beginnings; for Gordon Teskey, Milton, alone in the epic tradition, chooses to dwell within the origin.[33] Nuttall's account of the relation of texts to their "outsides" is not always clear; although he does not use these terms (and, from what I can gather from the book's now antiquated polemics, would demur from this characterization), his reconsideration of poetic originality links it to a potentiality inherent in language.[34]

This potentiality emerges from the dynamic relation between forms and "reality" that Nuttall takes from Frank Kermode's *The Sense of an Ending*. There, potentiality is the consequence of the formal, or what Nuttall calls the "artificial," dimension of texts; a pure merger with reality would be illegible chaos, while to forget that reality fundamentally escapes capture in a form is to risk an error that Kermode repeatedly links to fascism.[35] Kermode's thematic concern with "ending" as apocalypse—and the desire to install an image of eternity in time (or its predicted achievement, repeatedly falsified by life in the "middest")—links literary form to an oscillation between artifice and nature, a sustained "as if" in which the literary artifact maintains an illusion of merger with a reality that, nevertheless, it never achieves. In like terms, then, beginnings make manifest a gap between boundedness or form and the external "form" or reality that they ostensibly represent (make clear that literary form is not a mimetic category).[36]

This fact is "known" by the opening of John Shade's poem in Nabokov's *Pale Fire*, where the difficulties of tracking the relations (temporal, spatial, and logical) between representation and its "object" (to say nothing of those between the "I" and itself) come to the fore in the emergence of the poetic voice, constituted in an encounter of scarcely sublimated violence: "I was the shadow of the waxwing slain / By the false azure in the windowpane."[37] The text's abyssal metafictional play is condensed in those opening lines, where the lyric voice stakes its claims in a posthumous utterance that figures the imponderable inception of poetic speech; reflection of shadow and "Shade," its metafictional pyrotechnics appear there as questions of reference and textual grounding. The "hidden" story of Zembla ostensibly revealed by the commentary, like the more humdrum experience of alienation revealed "behind" it, in turn allegorizes large-scale displacements of history (the Russian Revolution and a century of exile) as a small-bore drama of literary criticism; the relation of the inside and the outside of a text, of language to history, is rendered in the nice terms of poem and "responsible" commentary, the limits of identification. The dire terms of criticism of the text certainly miss its pleasures by overstating the consequences of the fictional narrator's infractions of standards of academic criticism; Kinbote's own misreadings are perhaps to be deplored less than those of the novel's critics, for, in misreading, Kinbote grasps the stakes of reading, and more lucidly than those who animadvert on the consequences of his mistakes. The slain waxwing joins the jewelry from a grave that cuts its facets from within in Bishop's "Imaginary Iceberg."

That "form" is not mimetic would seem to follow from the fundamentally metaphorical acceptation of the term as it is applied to literary objects whose bounds cannot in any literal sense be comprised by a gaze. Although argued in a different register, the potentiality highlighted by Kermode (as the gap between form and formalization) is perhaps also what D. A. Miller calls the "narratable": "the instances of disequilibrium, suspense, and general insufficiency from which a given narrative appears to arise. The term is meant to cover the various incitements to narrative, as well as the dynamic ensuing from such incitements, and it is thus opposed to the 'nonnarratable' state of quiescence assumed by a novel before the beginning and supposedly recovered by it at the end."[38] The "perverse" way that novels by Austen, Eliot, and Stendhal are shown to be at odds with themselves points to this central dimension of literary form as it emerges in studies of closure and opening alike: The curious self-suspension of a foundation that simultaneously puts in question the form it institutes.[39]

Examining beginnings, J. Hillis Miller points to a similar aporia of foundation:

> The paradox of beginning is that one must have something solidly present and preexistent, some generative source or authority, on which the development of a new story may be based. That antecedent foundation needs in its turn some prior foundation, in an infinite regress. The novelist may be forced to go further and further back down the narrative line in an ever unsuccessful attempt to find something outside the line to which it may be firmly tied.[40]

What Hillis Miller puts in terms of authority could also be rephrased in terms of reference: The beginning makes clear that the novel cannot touch its outside. Noting that "the beginning is both inside and outside the narrative at once," he suggests that the need to explain the conditions underlying any opening "involves an infinite regress forbidding a writer ever to establish, except virtually and by a fictive 'as it were,' the firm antecedent foundation necessary to get the story going." "Inside" the story, the beginning looks "arbitrary" and can supply no origin, a bridge started "midspan" with no connection to the shore; "outside" the story, it is foreign to it, and cannot supply the needed littoral anchor. For Hillis Miller, narratives "cover over" the impossibility at the origin; they "cunningly [cover] a gap," "the impossibility of getting started." Hillis Miller emphasizes the sleight of hand, but such a structure is often explicit (if perhaps not always perceived), not waiting to be unveiled by the intrepid literary explicator (58–9). The founding gesture that he addresses is evoked by the term *posit*, which, like the word *fiat*, I have invoked but not yet explicitly thematized. "How does a speech act become a trope," writes Paul de Man, "a catachresis which then engenders in its turn the narrative sequence of an allegory? It can only be because we impose, in our turn, on the senseless power of positional language the authority of sense and of meaning. But this is radically inconsistent: language posits and language means (since it articulates) but language cannot posit meaning; it can only reiterate (or reflect) it in its reconfirmed falsehood."[41] My account invokes the deconstructive use of the term *posit* (and with it, the deconstructive account of the performative dimension of language) within the context of literary inception. A central term for the book, *posit* indexes some of the paradoxes of *inception*. The formal contingency of the work of art entails an inception that might appear, in multiple ways, arbitrary. The asynchronicity of its startings-out—forms that begin after they begin—and the way that that beginning appears as a formal decree that stops the recursive movement back toward *origin* and forward toward formal constitution also has consequences, as Hillis Miller notes, for textual authority. Positing is a linguistic act, and one that invokes a text's power to found itself and to reach its outside, that therefore likewise returns us to the shaping power of authorship and, again, the relation of art to life.

The most sustained consideration of *positing* occurs in Chapters 4, 5, and 8. But many readings in the book will recur to such moments of self-conscious fiat where texts as if call themselves into being. It is often explicit that there can be no proceeding other than on the text's own knowingly arbitrary or contingent decree; the question, perhaps, is where one goes from there. Hence, perhaps, the self-reflexivity that Niels Buch Leander notes of beginnings: "The beginning of a story, whether cosmological or literary, will then also have to be the story of a beginning, a phenomenon that John Barth deliberately plays on in the opening of his *Lost in the Funhouse* (1969): 'Once upon a time there was a story that began'" (Leander, 26). The self-reflexivity of any textual beginning bears witness to the self-grounding quality of literary fiction—its inability either to comprise its inception or to externalize it in an authorizing exteriority. This impotence (if it isn't rather fiction's greatest power) the book names by the term *posit*.

How is one to understand this self-reflexivity—a concept that has, perhaps, been trivialized by its ritualized invocation in recent years? Inception, I have suggested, brings one into contact with the text's own conditions of possibility. In my opening account of "The End of the Poem," I simplified its exposition in order to frame the striking logic that moves from the definition of poetic language as the at least virtual possibility of enjambment to the formal definition of poetry by an element that is not poetry. Between the opening account of enjambment and this conclusion, Agamben dwells on the "unrelated rhyme" in Provençal and Stilnovist poetry: a word that, not rhyming with end words in its own stanza, "nevertheless refers to a rhyme-fellow in the successive strophe and, therefore, does nothing more than bring metrical structure to the metastrophic level" (111). For Arnaut, Agamben notes, the unrelated rhyme "evolves almost naturally into word-rhyme, making possible the stupendous mechanism of the sestina"; this mechanism is compelling to Agamben because "word-rhyme is above all a point of undecidability between an essentially asemantic element (homophony) and an essentially semantic element (the word). The sestina is the poetic form that elevates the unrelated rhyme to the status of supreme compositional canon and seeks, so to speak, to incorporate the element of sound into the very lap of sense" (112).[42]

The unrelated rhyme returns then at the end of the essay when Agamben addresses Dante's suggestion that the last verses of the poem should "fall into silence" together with these rhymes (113–14). The alternatives for the end of the poem, it would seem, are equally catastrophes for poetic language as Agamben has defined it: a "mystical marriage of sound and sense," on the one hand, or their perpetual separation "without any possible contact, each eternally on its own side, like the two sexes in Vigny's poem"—an alternative that would "leave behind it only an empty space in which, according to Mallarmé's phrase, truly *rien n'aura lieu que le lieu*" (114). Noting that sound and sense are not "two series or lines in parallel flight," not "two substances but two intensities, two *tonoi* of the same linguistic substance" (114), Agamben turns to a specific instance—to the envoi of Dante's "Così nel mio parlar voglio esser aspro." The couplets that end the poem rhyme with this unrelated rhyme (the word *donna* [lady], the word "that names the supreme poetic intention") (115):

> This would mean that the poem falls by once again marking the opposition between the semiotic and the semantic, just as sound seems forever consigned to sense and sense returned forever to sound. The double intensity animating language does not die away in a final comprehension; instead it collapses into silence, so to speak, in an endless falling. The poem thus reveals the goal of its proud strategy: to let language finally communicate itself, without remaining unsaid in what is said. (115)

For language thus to speak itself is to return itself to its potentiality—the silence of the end of the poem meets here the onset distortion I term *inception*. Such is one formulation of the non-trivial self-reflexivity of the work of art that will emerge in the chapters that follow.

PART I
Potentiality and Gesture

1
Revision, Origin, and the Courage of Truth
Henry James's New York Edition Prefaces

For many, origins are suspect in part because they are, by definition, outside history. Outside it, they are also compromisingly inside it. As Gordon Teskey notes, in historical explanations, origins are inevitably provisional, having antecedents that make them "look like effects: the origin is always receding before us."[1] In Teskey's account of Milton's decision, unprecedented in epic poetry, to treat—and to abide within—the origin, the author of *Paradise Lost* confronts not a historical event but the grounds of history as such. The ethical dimension of the question of origins is perhaps to be found here, in the paradoxical topography of origination, and in what resists being thought in the grounds of possibility of language and history—in the structure, in other words, that this book terms *inception*. (This chapter takes *origin* as its central term because it is closer to the preoccupations that I chart in Henry James—and to avoid a repeated periphrastic reference translating into my own book's vocabulary what is more properly called *origin* in James.) The literary work's confrontation with inception returns to this moment of possibility—to what appears as two different forms of origin. In the beginning one finds a merger of two related but irreducible instances: the origin of the work, and of the mind that ostensibly thinks it—different origins, and curiously difficult to disentangle (because they often prove mutually originating). Origins and their structure of internal heterogeneity, instantiating a history, or a consciousness, to which they nevertheless remain exterior, rhyme with the writer's mutually originating relation to the work.

Origins and their internal heterogeneity are repeatedly confronted by James's late writing. Personal origins, to begin with: his return to America in *The American Scene* or to his younger years in the three volumes of the autobiography.

And the New York Edition prefaces: written for the reissue of (some) of his works, the prefaces, which arguably initiate criticism of the novel in English, are often framed by origin stories.[2] Straightforward anecdotal accounts of the origins of the works, however, are almost the exception in the prefaces, where, more often, the moment of origination is forgotten ("yielding to present research no dimmest responsive ghost of a traceable origin" [1206]), deliberately suppressed ("I recall with perfect ease the idea in which 'The Awkward Age' had its origin, but re-perusal gives me pause in respect to naming it. . . . I am half-moved to leave my small secret undivulged" [1120]), or lost in retrospect. "In the case of 'Broken Wings' (1900)," he writes, "I but see to-day the produced result—I fail to disinter again the buried germ" (1241). "Let it pass," he writes of the group of stories about the writer's life that includes "The Lesson of the Master," "that if I am so oddly unable to say here, at any point, 'what gave me my idea,' I must just a trifle freely have helped myself to it from hidden stores" (1232).

The germ, at other moments, is found to have been always there. Thus, of the *Tragic Muse*, standing before him "a poor fatherless and motherless, a sort of unregistered and unacknowledged birth," his "precious first moment of consciousness of the idea to which it was to give form" is present to him only as an "effect" of "some particular sharp impression or concussion": "What I make out from furthest back is that I must have had from still further back, must in fact practically have always had, the happy thought of some dramatic picture of the 'artist-life' and of the difficult terms on which it is at the best secured and enjoyed, the general question of its having to be not altogether easily paid for" (1103); as he says later, "my original perception of its [my subject's] value was quite lost in the mists of youth" (1105). Or, of "The Altar of the Dead": "I consult memory further to no effect; so that if I should seem to have lost every trace of 'how I came to think' of such a motive, didn't I, by a longer reach of reflexion, help myself back to the state of not having *had* to think of it? The idea embodied in this composition must in other words never have been so absent from my view as to call for an organized search. It was 'there'—it had always, or from ever so far back, been there . . ." (1246). Likewise with *The Wings of the Dove*: "I can scarce remember the time when the situation on which this long-drawn fiction mainly rests was not vividly present to me" (1287). "The first perceived gleam of the vital spark," he writes of "The Reverberator"; the origin is the perceiving of an origin that, presumably, precedes it (1194), so that, for example, "The Pupil" is recalled to have begun with the activation of an origin that, unnamed, is yet further back: "what it really comes to, no doubt, is that at a simple touch an old latent and dormant impression, a buried germ, implanted by experience and then forgotten, flashes to the surface as a fish, with a single 'squirm,' rises to the baited hook, and there meets instantly the vivifying ray" (1166). (This instance is also perhaps characteristic of a certain figural multivalence—as the seed becomes a fish, and the baited hook, not the instrument of a fish's death but a "vivifying ray"; the fish flies free of itself as tenor, in other terms, and, caught, enlivens the idea it represents.) The glimpsing of a character—Christopher Newman of *The American* "rose before" him "on a perfect day of the divine Paris spring, in the great gilded Salon Carré of the Louvre"—is a "germination," James notes in passing, that "is a process almost always untraceable" (1056). Earlier in that preface, James writes, "It had come to me, this happy, halting view of an interesting case, abruptly enough, some years before: I recall sharply the felicity of the first glimpse, though I forget the accident of thought that produced it. I recall that I was seated in an American 'horse-car' when I found myself, of a sudden, considering with enthusiasm, as the theme of a 'story,' the situation . . ." That situation poses questions that are, somehow, answered: "I remember well how, having entered the horse-car without a dream of it, I was presently to leave that vehicle in full possession of my answer" (1054). What is remembered is not so much the genesis as the moment when he noticed that it had occurred. "I shall not pretend to trace the steps and stages by which the imputability of a future to that young woman [Christina Light] . . . had for its prime effect to plant her in my little bookbinder's path" (1098), he writes in the preface to *The Princess Casamassima*, of the character who first appears in *Roderick Hudson*.

When narratives of inception do appear, they are, at a cursory glance, deceptively simple, and present parallel accounts: of what occasioned an idea or story and, more often, of where James wrote them (locations that are rarely, if ever, the "settings" of the resulting texts). These latter are usually cast as memories of composition that come back to James as he rereads his works, and that originating scene, inaccessible, of course, to a reader, because never depicted in the text, hovers there, to be seen by the author—much like, as we will see, the inevitable new term in the revised text. There is, to my mind, no systematic account of the relation between the narratives of compositional situations and those of the germs that form the minimal ideas providing plot or character or situation. Thus, in the preface to *The Portrait of a Lady*, James moves from his memories of writing in Venice to a discussion of the structuring role of character in the origination of a novel—to characters' "germinal property and authority" (1073). "There are pages of the book," he writes, "which, in the reading over, have seemed to make me see again the bristling curve of the wide Riva, the large colour-spots of the balconied houses and the repeated undulations of the little hunchbacked bridges, marked by the rise and drop

again, with the wave, of foreshortened clicking pedestrians. The Venetian foot-
fall and the Venetian cry . . . come in once more at the window, renewing
one's old impression of the delighted senses and the divided, frustrated mind"
(1070–1). The text, reread, calls back into view the scene of its creation—
albeit with typical complication (the pages "have *seemed* to make me see
again . . .")—and that recovered scene thwarts the composition that has, of
course, already occurred. At the time of composition, Venice embodies an
excess that thwarts efforts to write it—too rich, and too interesting, it figures,
as the limit case of the superabundant actual, the ways that the world exceeds
containment by a text. Too suggestive, it overwhelms and divides the mind:
Such places "are too rich in their own life and too charged with their own
meanings merely to help him out with a lame phrase; they draw him away
from his small question to their own greater ones; so that, after a little, he feels,
while thus yearning toward them in his difficulty, as if he were asking an army
of glorious veterans to help him arrest a peddler who had given him the wrong
change" (1070). The multiple layers of incommensurate exchanges (the wrong
change, the army of glorious veterans assigned a task demeaning to their
glory, the incommensurate relation of this incommensurability to the exchange it purports to figure) thus stand in for the relation between art and life
explored by these narratives of germination. (The writer in this figure is himself just such a dishonest peddler, exchanging Venice for its representation,
and leaving the reader shortchanged.) In a perhaps characteristic structure,
the apprehension of division is then unifying—or rather harmonizing; the
"divided, frustrated" mind, remembered, is harmonized by the remembering
mind—divided, therefore, between its present reading and its memory of the
past—which is also to say that one's divided attention turns out, in retrospect,
to have been productive: "one's book, and one's literary effort were to be better
for them. Strangely fertilizing, in the long run, does a wasted effort of attention often prove" (1071). The revising mind makes these discrepancies "fertilizing." In the unrationalized interplay between these different forms of
inception there is an implicit reckoning of the relation between life and art;
confounding the inside and the outside of the text, the parallel narratives of
origination figure that relation, and link it, I will suggest, to what James calls
revision.

    In the preface to *Portrait of a Lady*, the incommensurability of inside and
out appears in the second term of what I have called an "unrationalized" relation: Turning to the origin (in a different sense) of the text, the preface explores
the "germinal property and authority" of character—a discussion that, personifying character (giving it agency, and an originating power, over the mind

that ostensibly imagines it), seems in various ways to *de*personify the author. In the first place, the theory of fiction is given as a "quotation" from Ivan Turgenev—who sounds, in turn, remarkably like Henry James. (Turgenev, admired historical personage that he was, thus also appears as a personification of the "author's" voice.) Notably, the origin once more disappears; as James has Turgenev remark, "As for the origins of one's wind-blown germs themselves, who shall say, as you ask, where *they* come from? We have to go too far back, too far behind, to say. Isn't it all we can say that they come from every quarter of heaven, that they are *there* at almost any turn of the road?" (1072–3).

This question of character leads James to the famous "house of fiction"; responding to the question of the "morality" of the work of art, James asserts that a subject is "moral" or "immoral" according to whether it is "valid" or "genuine," or, in other terms, whether it is "sincere, the result of some direct impression or perception of life" (1074). That question links the (personified) author with the postulated, originating character insofar as the latter stands in for a locus of perception. The moral question turns out to be that of the richness of the "soil" of the author's sensibility, "its ability to 'grow' with due freshness and straightness any vision of life" (1074). What James then calls the "high price of the novel as a literary form" comes from that sensibility's individuality:

> its power not only, while preserving that form with closeness, to range through all the differences of the individual relation to its general subject-matter, all the varieties of outlook on life, of disposition to reflect and project, created by conditions that are never the same from man to man (or, so far as that goes, from man to woman), but positively to appear more true to its character in proportion as it strains, or tends to burst, with a latent extravagance, its mould. (1074–5)

The "high price of the novel as a literary form" marks its value rather than its cost; the possible equivocation is matched by the slippery assimilation of novelistic form to the more specific relation of generalized reality or experience to particular forms or angles of perception. The "character" that takes on generative force in the Turgenev "quotation" becomes here the defining "character" to which the novel might remain "true"; the "latent extravagance" marks a defining quality of internal difference, and the novel, a genre that coheres insofar as it differs from itself. The novel that "conserves" its "literary form" "with closeness" appears "more true to its character in proportion as it strains, or tends to burst, with a latent extravagance, its mould." I will note other figures that make difference into a principle of unification or coherence; for the moment, the novel's versatility, or its inner difference, is also quasi-personifying to the degree that the burst mold also evokes a statue stepping free of its shaping material and, Galatea-like, walking forth on its own (as Maggie Verver does in a famous metaphor in *The Golden Bowl*).[3] James's figure in the preface ties together the originating power of "character" as an equivocal personification (equivocal because the figure is both animating and de-animating, and because of the temporal loop that produces this "character" subsequent to the originating force it then embodies) and the novel as a high-priced form of perpetual self-reinvention.

Critics (myself included) have offered detailed considerations of the "house of fiction," which appears just after this; for the moment, I would emphasize the curious abstraction of that figure as it is set up by this framing. It isn't just that the "direct impression or perception of life" turns out to be mediated by the angle of view, or that the angle would seem to take priority (of genesis) over the "figure" who watches (as in Deleuze's account of Proust, it is the perspective that forms the subject rather than the other way around).[4] Nor is it only that the personified view falls uncannily short of full personification ("a figure with a pair of eyes, or at least with a field-glass," as he disorientingly phrases it).[5] It is also that in the framing account, as in the extended metaphor of the "house of fiction," James assimilates a particular fictional method (mediating views through a "center of consciousness") *within* a work to an account of the difference of authorial sensibility that shapes the work itself. The choice of subject and the specifics of literary form are "as nothing," he later writes, "without the posted presence of the watcher—without, in other words, the consciousness of the artist" (1075). In the allegory or figure here, that posted presence, of course, arrives on the scene after the house of fiction itself—to gaze out apertures, as James puts it, "pierced, or . . . still pierceable . . . by the need of the individual vision and by the pressure of the individual will." Perspective becomes a figure through which to render choices that might include the (putatively authorial) use of particular perspectives. The indeterminacy of inside and out (of the literary text) figures, and seems a consequence of, the recursive structure of literary inception, the disappearance of the origin in a self-reflexivity at once constitutive and secondary.

This account of literary form—in his summary, the author's "boundless freedom and his 'moral reference'"—is, he then suggests, "a long way round, however, for my word about my dim first move toward 'The Portrait'" (1075). That dim first move, the grasp of a single character ("an acquisition I had made, moreover, after a fashion not here to be retraced" [1075]), then raises the question of how the vivid character is "placed"—how the book containing the initiating presence of Isabel Archer comes to be generated:

> One could answer such a question beautifully, doubtless, if one could do so subtle, if not so monstrous, a thing as to write the history of the growth of one's imagination. One would describe then what, at a given time, had extraordinarily happened to it, and one would so, for instance, be in a position to tell, with an approach to clearness, how, under favour of occasion, it had been able to take over (take over straight from life) such and such a constituted, animated figure or form. The figure has to that extent, as you see, *been* placed—placed in the imagination that detains it, preserves, protects, enjoys it, conscious of its presence in the dusky, crowded, heterogeneous back-shop of the mind very much as a wary dealer in precious odds and ends, competent to make an "advance" on rare objects confided to him, is conscious of the rare little "piece" left in deposit by the reduced, mysterious lady of title or the speculative amateur, and which is already there to disclose its merit afresh as soon as a key shall have clicked in a cupboard-door. (1076)

The narrative progression of the preface ("the long way around") points once again to the intertwining of two forms of originating personification that are at the same time consequences of the forms they initiate or imagine: the character who instigates the novel's genesis and the authorial consciousness—or, rather, its retrospective narration, the "so subtle, if not so monstrous" project of writing "the history of the growth of one's imagination," an imagination that it seems is not, under normal conditions, able to say "what, at a given time, had extraordinarily happened to it." To add to the quandaries of origin, it is all the more difficult to differentiate the novel that contains the stray figure from the consciousness that imagines both insofar as the figure for the waiting idea derives from, or at least retells, a central episode in *The Golden Bowl*: Charlotte and the Prince's visit (later reenacted by Maggie) to the Bloomsbury shop containing the eponymous bowl, the visit that catalyzes the novel's plot and establishes its symbolic structure. To say only the least complicated thing about the relations thereby established, the novel would thus seem to be the "source" of the originating consciousness more than its result. As the preface continues, the "spacious house" still further confounds the novel (and its "organizing [of] an ado about Isabel Archer" [1077]) with the authorial consciousness that conceived it—and also with the many-windowed "house of fiction" itself. (It would also be easy to show the many ways that the novel's characterization passes through, is constituted by, described houses—the bifurcated house of Isabel's aunt in Albany; Gardencourt, the Touchetts' home in England, with its interior spilling warmly out on to its thoroughly domesticated lawn; Gilbert Osmond's two-faced, backward-facing citadel in Florence.)

When, therefore, the prefaces produce origin stories as (self-consciously) retrospective reconstructions, at issue is perhaps both the provisional quality of
the posited authorial consciousness and its dependence on the texts that it ostensibly creates. These origin narratives, then, are "revisions" in the sense that
rereading creates them, and the author is linked to the virtuality of events in
James's fiction. Hence, for example, the accounts give us what "must have"
occurred—a locution that recurs throughout the prefaces: "It was at any rate
under an admonition or two fished out of their depths that I must have tight-
ened my hold of the remedy afforded . . . It was for that I must have tried, I now
see, with such art as I could command" (1049).[6] Such markers of retrospective
construction could also be paired with those of mediation—"I seem" or "I seem
to myself"—and with the provisional or hypothetical status of much of the
fictional events in James's work, the "as if" that so often modifies descriptions
of action:[7]

> I seem to myself to have waked up one morning in possession of
> them—of Ralph Touchett and his parents, of Madame Merle, of
> Gilbert Osmond and his daughter and his sister, of Lord Warburton,
> Caspar Goodwood, and Miss Stackpole, the definite array of contribu-
> tions to Isabel Archer's history. . . . It was as if they had simply, by an
> impulse of their own, floated into my ken. (1081)

Authorial consciousness and germinating character alike are at once originating and self-consciously posited, lending a certain groundlessness to the figures of organic wholeness that describe the remembered emergence of the
texts. The retrospective gaze of revision provides the "fascination" for the author: "These are the fascinations of the fabulist's art, these lurking forces of
expansion, these necessities of upspringing in the seed, these beautiful deter-
minations, on the part of the idea entertained, to grow as tall as possible, to
push into the light and the air and thickly flower there; and quite as much,
these fine possibilities of recovering, from some good standpoint on the ground
gained, the intimate history of the business—of retracing and reconstructing
its steps and stages" (1072).

"These necessities of upspringing in the seed": James's term for origination is "germ," and the difficulty of locating an origin is echoed by the term's
multivalent figural resonances.[8] Seed and sprout, a sprouting or the germination that presages it, the germ's connection to what germinates can be direct (a
seed becoming a plant) or indirect (as a germ triggering an illness): thus the
author's consciousness or sensibility is the "richer soil" into which a seed is
transplanted (1074; 1140) and is, at other moments, an organism infected by a

"virus."[9] The results, cultivated or nurtured, can also be involuntarily caught. (How the mind nurtures the germs it encounters, he writes in the preface to *The Spoils of Poynton*, is "an enquiry upon which, I hasten to add, it is quite forbidden me here to embark" [1139].) "Germ," etymologically, is both the ovum (or ovary—in botany, the pistil that will be the fruit) and the sperm; fertilized and fertilizing, it, like the author's consciousness, both acts and is acted upon—thereby naming the indeterminate agency in "having" an idea. The metaphor is also spatially multivalent: Both seed and sprout, *germ* can name the seed that contains the sprout, what sprouts from the seed, and the embryonic plant contained within the seed. In the several prefaces where James emphasizes the "quite incalculable tendency of a mere grain of subject-matter to expand and develop and cover the ground when conditions happen to favour it," the "unforeseen principle of growth" (1120) that makes "projected . . . small things" into "comparative monsters," he exploits the non-resemblance between the seed and what it becomes. A germ is also, simply, a small amount of something; the inspired writer, James asserts, wants only the merest hint of inoculation—too much information, and it will cease to be suggestive.[10] And the term invokes the characteristically retrospective temporality of Jamesian thought—the essence, what an idea, under analysis, later boils down to, or its central grain. In James's disorienting terms in the preface to *The Ambassadors*, "nothing can exceed the closeness with which the whole fits again into its germ" (1305).

This inside-out structure emblematizes the way these origin stories are also readings of the prefaced texts—and emblematizes the complex relation of authorial life to work. To forget the germ of "The Beast in the Jungle" (as James claims to have done) is to locate the story's beginning in a repetition of Marcher's own initiating forgetfulness (Marcher has told May Bartram the central, structuring secret of his life—and then *forgotten* he has done so). Likewise for the repeated note of "failure" in the preface to *The Wings of the Dove*: The novel's realized aesthetic form in some sense *is* Milly Theale's foreshortened life, Kate Croy's baffled scheme, and Merton Densher's thwarted love—a realized form of potentiality, the paradoxical mode whereby the authorial life enters the work, and disappears there. The search for origins in the prefaces (ever-baffled but never to be called off) is the cipher for that authorial life, and is where James locates an ethics of reading.

Even at a cursory glance, James's texts valorize tact in approaching the author's life; the novelizations by Colm Toibin and David Lodge are, whatever their many virtues, also violations to the degree that they are, at their inception, deaf to the sensibility they presume to ventriloquize. One thinks of

"The Death of the Lion" or "The Aspern Papers" or "The Birthplace."[11] In each case, though, the question becomes more complex, and returns us to a rhythm of creation—evoking a similar rhythm in Blanchot—where writing seeks an origin that recedes from it, seeking a beginning and a dissolution it can never achieve.[12] The elusiveness of origin stories in the prefaces evokes this view—for they are playful in their supposed revelations and more often than not keep what they conceal. Hence, they raise the question of whether the origin, even if known to the author, can (or should) be shared. Writing of the "miracle" that led to "The Pupil," James remarks:

> But there are fifty things to say here; which indeed rush upon me within my present close limits in such a cloud as to demand much clearance. This is perhaps indeed but the aftersense of the assault made on my mind, as I perfectly recall, by every aspect of the original vision, which struck me as abounding in aspects. It lives again for me, this vision, as it first alighted; though the inimitable prime flutter, the air as of an ineffable sign made by the immediate beat of the wings of the poised figure of fancy that has just settled, is one of those guaran-tees of value that can never be re-captured. The sign has been made to the seer only—it is *his* queer affair; of which any report to others, not as yet involved, has but the same effect of flatness as attends, amid a group gathered under the canopy of night, any stray allusion to a shooting star. The miracle, since miracle it seems, is all for the candid exclaimer. (1165)

The miracle is identified as a story told to him by a doctor "in a very hot Ital-ian railway carriage," a narrative that suggested, obliquely, the story of Mor-gan Moreen and his family. The language of prophetic vision, however, is striking, though, if I am not wrong to think that there is no specific biblical or mythological reference in this beating of wings, there is, characteristically, a crossing of different figural contexts and registers. Most immediately, the fig-ure of poetic inspiration (one thinks of the beginning of *Paradise Lost* and the "advent'rous song/That with no middle flight intends to soar/Above th' Ao-nian mount while it pursues/Things unattempted yet in prose or rhyme,"[13] of depictions of the muses as winged women, and even of bird song as a figure for poetry) is as if literalized (a "figure of fancy," therefore, in more than one sense), and that register is combined with a (again, I think, vague) context of reference: "canopy of night" perhaps comes from Milton (*PL*, III.556–7), while the star that may or may not be a sign evokes Genesis[14] and Revelation (also perhaps recalled by the beat of wings in the dark), or perhaps the star that guides the Wise Men in Luke's Gospel (here, of course, a falling star). And so on: Jane Eyre hearing the beating of wings in the red room; Herod hearing the beating of the wings of the Angel of Death in Wilde's *Salomé*; moments in Ezekiel where the beating of wings is compared to the sound of a voice;[15] again in *Paradise Lost*, the visits of the archangels Raphael and Michael to the Garden; St Francis among the birds; the writing on the wall in the Book of Daniel; perhaps even the Annunciation or Morpheus, the wingèd god of dreams, or the abduction of Ganymede by Zeus. The originating vision leads one to a range of possible references—hardly personal, hardly discrete, and, further, almost generic literary topoi—suggesting, if one had to press for a point, that literature, like the figure of beating wings, has no beginning. Yet it also seems to posit an originary moment—as if that recursive movement into an infinite range of references could be located in a particular moment. And all of this is contained in a personal, anecdotal instant—the exclamation of small, private, ultimately incommunicable aesthetic pleasure at a natural wonder that will have passed before others' attention can be drawn to it, and one that is, moreover, at once deflated (by the possibly pathetic desire to point) and invested (as a stand-in for more uncommon pleasures).

Nevertheless, one exclaims aloud, and however elusive origins in the prefaces turn out to be, it also seems that the search for them is not to be dispensed with: "I call such remembered glimmers always precious, because without them comes no clear vision of what one may have intended, and without that vision no straight measure of what one may have succeeded in doing" (1103). The equivocally ironical tone—in, for instance, "the air as of an ineffable sign made by the immediate beat of the wings," with its jarring collision of registers (especially evident in the word *immediate*)—perhaps marks this ambivalence or doubled relation to the project of uncovering origins. The "immediate beat" underlines the tendentious (or possibly ironic) literalization, and is in contrast to the series of attenuations that mark the receding of the origin from us: the "prime flutter," inimitable, is made an "air," not, in turn, "of an ineffable sign" but "as of an ineffable sign," and the "prime flutter" itself names an anteriority that precedes what initially seems an unequivocal assertion of recovery: "It lives again for me, this vision, as it first alighted" (1165). That first alighting of the vision turns out to have a prehistory, and the seer's difficulty communicating what he has seen replays his previous difficulty in locating his vision's source.

Writing seeks to surmount the problem of the perceived shooting star by prolonging the miracle, or by producing another one, the writing, in other words, that, directly or indirectly, it inspires; that the exclamation must come too late for the perception to be shared links a cognitive structure of belatedness (the cognition that must lag behind what it perceives) to the problem of other minds—each mind keeps as a solitary prisoner its own dream of a world, and keeps locked within it the miracles it shelters. Each moment of perception, in those terms, replays the unfathomable moment of origination to which the mind, by dint of being one, ever arrives too late to witness.

The failure to find the biographical source ("a torment," James writes of Shakespeare, "scarcely to be borne" [1215])[16] is, like the putative aesthetic "failures" confessed in the prefaces, a mode of sustaining (perpetuating, but also enduring) this mode of creation. The successful artist, James suggests many times, disappears, and, like Milly Theale or John Marcher, or like Shakespeare in *The Tempest*, turns his back on us, and escapes. Thus, explaining another kind of "failure"—a failure to make Nick Dormer "as interesting as he was fondly intended to be"—the preface to *The Tragic Muse* suggests that the artist's success may entail his disappearance:

> I come upon a reason that affects me as singularly charming and touching and at which indeed I have already glanced. Any presentation of the artist *in triumph* must be flat in proportion as it really sticks to its subject—it can only smuggle in relief and variety. For, to put the matter in an image, all we then—in his triumph—see of the charm-compeller is the back he turns to us as he bends over his work. "His" triumph, decently, is but the triumph of what he produces, and that is another affair. His romance is the romance he himself projects; he eats the cake of the very rarest privilege, the most luscious baked in the oven of the gods—therefore he may n't "have" it, in the form of the privilege of the hero, at the same time. The privilege of the hero—that of the martyr or of the interesting and appealing and comparatively floundering *person*—places him in quite a different category, belongs to him only as the artist deluded, diverted, frustrated or vanquished; when the "amateur" in him gains, for our admiration or compassion or whatever, all that the expert has to do without. . . . The better part of him is locked too much away from us, and the part we see has to pass for—well, what it passes for, so lamentedly, among his friends and relatives. (1118)

The "comparatively floundering *person*": the curiosity of Toibin and Lodge is not a reading of the texts (may even, in my view, desecrate those texts—at least to the degree that that curiosity about the amateur is taken as interchangeable with a sounding of the "expert." Their admiration or compassion is, at any rate, an act of aggression, which might be what is most interesting about those books, and what lingers in one's sense of whose psychology, ultimately, is revealed). One might be led to think of John Marcher turning away from us (to lie, face

down, on the tomb of his friend) at the end of "The Beast in the Jungle," or of
Milly Theale turning her face to the wall. The turning away from us of the
successful artist is—as the Shakespearean echo makes clear—a disappearance
of the flesh, or a becoming-spirit of the body in art that is also an amorous
address: "When thou reviewest this, thou dost review/The very part was con-
secrate to thee:/The earth can have but earth, which is his due;/My spirit is
thine, the better part of me" (Sonnet 74).[17]

The prefaces' confessions of putative failures thus ask to be read as complex markers of authorial presence, even of his (vanishing) person. The discussion of bewilderment in the preface to *The Princess Casamassima*, or the
"failure" outlined by the preface to *The Wings of the Dove*, like other such moments, makes their confessions interchangeable with another sort of authorial
disappearance—into the potentiality of art. The "was to have been" that, in
the *Wings of the Dove* preface, describes various plans that fail to come to frui-
tion is, as I have noted elsewhere, a characteristic orientation of Jamesian
verbs: Suspending "happening" between two temporalities (one marking what
was to happen and then did happen, and another marking what was to happen but then didn't), this complex verbal form is often how the late novels express what occurs in them. Particularly striking in *The Ambassadors*, it marks
every novelistic happening with the shadow of Strether's belatedness; the late
novels are novels without plots because nothing happens—less in the colloquial sense (for, contrary to popular opinion, they are in fact eventful) than in
the sense that happening is suspended, rendered hypothetical or potential.
Writing in 1918, Virginia Woolf compares James to "a priest to whom a vision
of the divinity has been vouchsafed at last." She continues: "A glimpse of the
possibilities which in his view gather around every story and stretch away into
the distance beyond any sight save his own makes other people's achievements
seem empty and childish. One had almost rather read what he meant to do
than read what he actually did do."[18] What from one angle looks like failure
from another looks like the securing of potentiality, an ever-renewed possibility of beginning again. And, thus, too, if the Jamesian artist fails more often
than he succeeds, failure is also another name for the creative act—and one
where the "real" man is no more to be found or known than is the successful
artist, turning away from us.

Hence the proximity of the prefaces to the autobiography under the aegis
of what James calls revision: "The rate at which new readings, new conduc-
tors of sense interposed, to make any total sense at all right, became, to this
wonderful tune, the very record and mirror of the general adventure of one's
intelligence," he writes of *The Golden Bowl* (1335); in the preface to *The American*, it is the "joy of living over, as a chapter of experience, the particular

intellectual adventure" (1060). (As he says of the artist's freedom, "It may leave him weary and worn; but how, after his fashion, he will have lived!" [1061].) If the prefaces make revision a form of autobiography, *A Small Boy and Others* makes autobiography a kind of revision, reliving, even reanimating the past: "I retrace our steps to the start, for the pleasure, strangely mixed though it be, of feeling our small feet plant themselves afresh and artlessly stumble forward again" (6).[19] Reanimated, the authorial life, subject to revision, is potential or provisional: "My cases are of course given, so that economy of observation after the fact . . . becomes inspiring, not less than the amusement, or whatever it may be, of the question of what might happen, of what in point of fact did happen, to several very towny and domesticated little persons, who were confirmed in their towniness and fairly enriched in their sensibility, instead of being chucked into a scramble or exposed on breezy uplands under the she-wolf of competition and discipline" (177). The possible gap between "what might happen" and "what in point of fact did happen" is the mark of "revision" in the autobiography; the economy of observation after the fact returns the past to potentiality, and the "lapse of consciousness" with which *Small Boy* ends as if registers the corrosive effect of that potentiality on the consciousness whose emergence the text narrates.[20] Unlike Romulus, the consciousness eclipsed does reemerge for another volume; in the context of the autobiographies, moreover, to "lose" oneself is aesthetically generative.

James's central statement on revision is the preface to *The Golden Bowl*, which articulates a complex relation between revision and the authorial life. "To revise," he writes, "is to see, or to look over, again—which means in the case of a written thing neither more nor less than to re-read it" (1332). Rereading is not rewriting (a "task so difficult, and even so absurd, as to be impossible") because the new terms are already there: "the act of revision, the act of seeing it again, caused whatever I looked at on any page to flower before me as into the only terms that honorably expressed it." The "'revised' element in the present edition," he continues, "is accordingly these terms, . . . registered; so many close notes, as who should say, on the particular vision of the matter itself that experience had at last made the only possible one" (1332). To revise is thus to perceive potentiality—what might have been, but wasn't—as lingering presences in the ostensibly finished text; like James's visions of past compositional milieux, they impose themselves on his imagination as visions of the texts in potential. "The deviations and differences," he writes, "became . . . my very terms of cognition" (1330). The gap between old and new readings thus limns the history of the authorial life—becomes "the very record and mirror of the general adventure of one's intelligence" (1335):

> The interest of the question is attaching . . . because really half the
> artist's life seems involved in it—or doubtless, to speak more justly, the
> whole of his life intellectual. The "old" matter is there, re-accepted,
> re-tasted, exquisitely re-assimilated and re-enjoyed—believed in, to be
> brief, with the same "old" grateful faith . . . ; yet for due testimony, for
> re-assertion of value, perforating as by some strange and fine, some
> latent and gathered force, a myriad more adequate channels.

The reread text is at least double: The old matter, re-assimilated, reveals new
terms that impose themselves as inevitable. Various figures render this dou-
bleness: children or old people made presentable for company, garments re-
paired, properties renovated, new terms "looking over the heads" of older ones,
"alert winged creatures, perched on those diminished summits and aspir[ing]
to a clearer air" (1332–3). Thus to see the old and new is to retrace the growth
of the artist's taste, "to hold the silver clue to the whole labyrinth of his consciousness" (1333).

Discrepancies, and the relation to the productions of one's past dictated by
a shifting consciousness, make reading "a living affair" (1335), which will link
revision to "responsibility." That note is struck early in figures amply com-
mented on—by, for example, J. Hillis Miller[21]—where revision is the effort to
follow footprints after one's gait has changed:

> Anything, in short, I now reflect, must always have seemed to me
> better . . . than the mere muffled majesty of irresponsible "authorship."
> Beset constantly with the sense that the painter of the picture or
> the chanter of the ballad (whatever we may call him) can never be
> responsible *enough*, and for every inch of his surface and note of his
> song, I track my uncontrollable footsteps, right and left, after the fact,
> while they take their quick turn, even on stealthiest tiptoe, toward the
> point of view that, within the compass, will give me most instead of
> least to answer for. (1322–3)

This figure recurs throughout the preface, where revision raises the question
of whether "the march of my present attention coincides sufficiently with the
march of my original expression," whether the "imaginative steps" of the reader
he has become sink into the "very footprints" (1329) of the younger composer
he was, whether his current mind can trace "that so shifting and uneven character of the tracks of my original passage" (1334):

> It was, all sensibly, as if the clear matter being still there, even as a
> shining expanse of snow spread over a plain, my exploring tread, for
> application of it, had quite unlearned the old pace and found itself

naturally falling into another, which might sometimes indeed more or less agree with the original tracks, but might most often or very nearly, break the surface in other places. (1330)

The "spontaneity" of these "deviations and differences," matters, he asserts, "not of choice but of immediate and perfect necessity," is what is "predominantly interesting" (1330). He couldn't, he writes, "forecast these chances and changes and proportions; they could be shown for what they were as I went; criticism after the fact was to find in them arrests and surprises, emotions alike of disappointment and of elation: all of which means, obviously, that the whole thing was a *living* affair" (1335).

The repeated forgetting of germs in the prefaces is an index of belatedness, what I elsewhere suggest is the thematic marker of James's style: consciousness arrives too late to perceive the emergence of its own ideas. The asynchronicity of consciousness might be said to enter the prefaces through figural discrepancies (of seed and germ, for example); through revision, the authorial life unifies, in its disappearing shadow, those discrepancies. The *Golden Bowl* preface figures that very process—makes discrepancy harmonious by articulating figures of bodily movement (tracing his uncontrollable footsteps) with figures of vision (falling into a gait and seeing the tracks of one's footsteps over a plain of snow). The first difference, made into something seen, turns discrepancy into the mark of perspective. Hence the first line of the preface: "Among many matters thrown into relief by a refreshed acquaintance with 'The Golden Bowl' what perhaps most stands out for me is the still marked inveteracy of a certain indirect and oblique view of my presented action" (1322). Later, those terms evoke a coincidence of original and retrospective vision more possible with recent works, the reader's footsteps sinking "comfortably" into the author's, so that "his vision, superimposed on my own as an image in cut paper is applied to a sharp shadow on a wall, matches, at every point, without excess or deficiency" (1329). With the passage of time, coincidence gives way to discrepancy, and hence to "relief": "This truth throws into relief for me the very different dance that the taking in hand of my earlier productions was to lead me; the quite other kind of consciousness proceeding from *that* return" (1329). Throwing a discrepancy into relief, the retrospective gaze makes it a unified vision. The maneuver is all the more complex in that refracted vision is his method of narration—"the marked inveteracy of a certain indirect and oblique view of my presented action," the mediation through a "center of consciousness" that, as opposed to "an impersonal account of the affair in hand," presents "my account of somebody's impression of it," the impression of the author's "concrete deputy or delegate," the "convenient substitute or apologist for the creative power otherwise so veiled and disembodied" (1322). The authorial life could here be said to be the anthropomorphizing shadow of a disembodied form—an indirection of view. Revision—reading one's previous work in the light of one's current consciousness—has that authorial life "intervene" on the text in a way analogous to a certain indirect and oblique view of the presented action within the text.

Thus James moves from focalization to revision because revision, too, is an indirect view—of new terms mediated by old ones.[22] Moreover, I have simplified things; the preface's highly abstract opening suggests that in *The Golden Bowl*, the technique of an indirect view mediated by an unimplicated observer (typical of the shorter works) is paradoxically embodied by the central characters (whose vision is then described as refracted); the Prince and the Princess are at once characters and anthropomorphic mechanisms of narrative method. (One's sense of Lambert Strether's remove from "life" in *The Ambassadors* is perhaps shifted when read in this context.) The "mere muffled majesty of 'irresponsible' authorship" describes an unmediated, or perhaps "omniscient," narration; implication, and responsibility, come, in the first place, with focalization. Maggie and the Prince personify focalization, and turn mediated vision into "direct" contact, pulling the author "down into the arena" with "the real, the deeply involved and immersed and more or less bleeding participants" (1323). (In short, the involvement here is perspectival; his angle of view places the author in the fray.)

By the end of the preface, the language of responsibility shifts to a different register of implication. The final paragraph begins by asserting the salience of the literary "deed," established through the felt unity of our actions and our expressions. It is as if the freedom of our capacity for expression made it one with our actions, and therefore susceptible to, and worthy of, ethical consideration:[23]

> as the whole conduct of life consists of things done, which do other
> things in their turn, just so our behaviour and its fruits are essentially
> one and continuous and persistent and unquenchable, so the act has
> its way of abiding and showing and testifying, and so, among our acts,
> are no arbitrary, no senseless separations. . . . [W]ith any capability, we
> recognize betimes that to "put" things is very exactly and responsibly
> and interminably to do them. Our expression of them, and the terms
> on which we understand that, belong as nearly to our conduct and our
> life as every other feature of our freedom. (1340)

That analogy ("just so") becomes consequence ("so") perhaps enacts his assertion; the passage begins with likeness, and seems to give agency to likeness itself. The binding connection between "things done" and what "other things" those things "do," begins a chain of likeness formed by the asserted connection: consequence (our actions have consequences that ramify), linked by the verb *to do*; the link between our "behaviour and its fruits," asserted to be "essentially one and continuous and persistent and unquenchable"; and the link between our various acts, which makes writing and doing one. "Literary deeds" enjoy an advantage over "other acts": "their attachment and reference to us, however strained, needn't necessarily lapse." If the claim at the end of the paragraph initially seems unremarkable—that our writing and reading, our thought, are all parts of our conduct and our life—the way that, as ethical acts, they form features "of our freedom" (a central term for James's understanding of writing, beginning as early as "The Art of Fiction") is crucial to the closing claims of the preface. As is often the case in such climactic moments in James, the logic is perhaps less important than its enactment by the writing (the very exercise of the writer's freedom)—here, by analogy and resemblance, which perform or enact the very connection he claims.

Thus the preface—and the prefaces as a whole, for the second volume of *The Golden Bowl* is the last volume of the New York Edition—ends on this hortatory note:

> Our relation to them is essentially traceable, and in that fact abides . . .
> the incomparable luxury of the artist. . . . Not to *be* disconnected . . .
> he has but to feel that he is not; by his lightest touch the whole chain
> of relation and responsibility is reconstituted. Thus if he is always
> doing he can scarce, by his own measure, ever have done. . . . Our
> noted behaviour at large may show for ragged, because it perpetually
> escapes our control; we have again and again to consent to its appear-
> ing in undress—that is in no state to brook criticism. But on all the
> ground to which the pretension of performance by a series of exquisite
> laws may apply there reigns one sovereign truth—which decrees that,
> as art is nothing if not exemplary, care nothing if not active, finish
> nothing if not consistent, the proved error is the base apologetic deed,
> the helpless regret is the barren commentary, and "connexions" are
> employable for finer purposes than mere gaping contrition. (1340–41)

The claims at the end are built, in more than one way, on "connexion"—that, most immediately, linking us to our words—a joining together material or immaterial, physical or rhetorical. The word appears ten times in the preface (eleven if one includes "disconnexion"), most often as a synonym for context. The final paragraph makes the connections between words or ideas[24] into material, bodily, or tangible relations (evoking the group of meanings of the word that center on sex, intimacy, and family). That link is also enacted in the peroration's own connections—the rhetorical assimilations of parallel rhetorical forms, most immediately, but also the crossing of registers that assimilates words, actions, and emotional states, makes a deed "apologetic" and a "regret" a "commentary." "Traceable" explicitly evokes rereading, James's tracking of his footsteps—or the silhouette that later reading seeks to retrace. Tracing an outline or deciphering a trace, rereading asserts various forms of connection.

How is one to understand the "attachment and reference to us" that James asserts here? His claims evoke other moments in the late writing—for example, in "Is There a Life after Death?," which asserts that connections will not lapse, that death will not rupture the links among us because we are capable of thinking them in the first place.[25] The traceable relation is our relation to our words—our words as actions, and the ethical dimension, therefore, of what we say; at the end of the preface, that dimension turns on the claim that connection is, ultimately, our capacity to revise: not to be reduced to mere gaping contrition, not to reduce care to passivity, is to assert the claims of connection by seeing, perpetually, our words afresh. In my view, the claim of ostensibly personal responsibility needs to be read in the context of the prefaces' confessions of "failure," and James's rendering potential of the authorial life as it disappears into the text. That question in late James calls to mind Foucault's exploration, in his final seminars, of parrhēsia—a mode of truth-telling to be distinguished from others in ancient Greece and Rome. Couched as historical investigation—a systematic outline of this particular mode of veridiction—it is also a theory of speech acts, and one that, separating truth from propositional content, shifts attention toward the context of utterance, and most often, to a risk incurred by the speaker: One example is telling someone you love him, and the risk is an isolation whose ultimate horizon is social ostracism. (In my memory, this is not an example that Foucault himself cites; the more immediate context for parrhēsia is political.) For parrhēsia entails a relation; it takes place "between two partners" (fundamentally, between friends).[26] The term evolves in complex ways; in political speech, it is, initially, the honesty that the benevolent ruler (forestalling flattery) will allow or invite. (This is the primary focus of the exploration of the term in the 1982–83 course on "the government of self and others.") But it later becomes a mode of assuming a life: "I must be myself in what I say. . . . I do not content myself with telling you what I judge to be true. I tell this truth only inasmuch as it is in actual fact what I am myself; I am implicated in the truth of what I say," as Foucault puts it in a commentary on Seneca (247).[27] I find moving and compelling in these late texts the way his interest in parrhēsia and the "care of self" tends to escape containment in the genealogy of confession's production of docile subjects that motivates it.[28]

This is not merely, in other words, the familiar story of subjects produced by a discourse of truth about sex; Foucault's courage of truth meets Jamesian revision in what Agamben calls potentiality.[29] In *Il fuoco e il racconto,* Agamben suggests why the work cannot be finished—why, to echo the terms of the prefaces, no work fully realizes the author's intentions, fully actualizes what was to have been: "Is it not the case that every book contains a residue of potentiality, without which its reading and reception would be impossible? A work in which creative potentiality [*la potenza creativa*] were totally exhausted [*spenta*] would not be a work but the ashes and sepulcher of the work."[30] This has nothing to do with perfectionism, with an anecdotal sense that nothing is ever finished, or with academics' laborious cultivation of writer's block. It has rather to do with potentiality, with a capacity that remains sheltered, as potential, within the creative act that actualizes it, with the words that peer out, in James's image, above or beyond the words that one has written. "It is," Agamben continues, "perhaps only this hybrid creature, this non-place in which potentiality does not disappear but is preserved and, so to speak, dances in the act, that deserves the name of 'work'" (94).

Potentiality is thus the central term for Agamben's reading of Deleuze's late lecture on the act of creation. Agamben reminds us that all creation, for Deleuze, is an act of resistance—"to death, first of all, but also . . . to the paradigm of information media, through which power [*il potere*] is exercised in what he calls 'control societies'" (33/39). The elaboration of the concept of potentiality that comprises the bulk of Agamben's essay is a complementary explication of the act of creation as resistance. Deleuze's own account of Foucault in the seminar on his friend and fellow philosopher affirms this connection. In the seminar, which preceded by a year the lecture on creation, Deleuze devotes considerable time to resistance, which, he says, emerges in Foucault's thought between *Discipline and Punish* and *The History of Sexuality.* In the lecture of February 25, 1986, for example, Deleuze links "resistance" to a "beyond."[31] Resistance is not a term or a vector of force within the "disciplinary diagram" but that which escapes capture in it. So, if discipline (on the one hand) takes any group whatever and forces it to perform any task whatever and (on the other) cultivates, manages, fosters a population, resistance is not a counter-force to either procedure. Likewise, it is not a resistance "to" either knowledge or power, which Deleuze conceptualizes according to formal, molar forces (on the one hand) and informal (de-forming) or molecular forces on the other. It is rather what remains beyond, or unrealized within, that schematization. And, outlining Foucault's characterization of power in the first volume of the *History of Sexuality*, he suggests, invoking Kant, that resistance is not to be confused with either "spontaneity" or "receptivity," with either the "power to affect" or the "power to be affected." In Deleuze's rendering, resistance is primary; it precedes relations of force. Potentiality in Agamben's account of the 1987 lecture offers a way to gloss Deleuze's understanding of "resistance" as a "beyond" that is not a form of transcendence.[32] Or to frame the centrality of origins to James's account of revision.

As in Agamben's other writings on potentiality, creation cannot consist purely in the passing into act of what was potential. Potentiality is sustained in the work by a trembling between creation and decreation, necessity and contingency—by "revision." Thus, every "authentic" creative process is "intimately and emblematically suspended between two contradictory impulses: upsurge [*slancio*, which the French translator renders as *élan* (Agamben, *Le Feu et le recit*, 53)] and resistance, inspiration and critique" (43/48). Artistic capacity is lined with a fundamental incapacity that one might call resistance—a potential-not-to that is a resistance internal to potentiality or power that prevents its being "exhausted" in its actualization (48); revision is the cipher of the authorial life because it bodies forth this contradiction, the suspension within creation that Agamben links to the non-trivial self-reflexivity of great poetry. Such poetry "does not simply say what it says, but also the fact that it is saying it"—says "the potentiality and impotentiality to say it" (48/52–3). Such self-reflexivity does not mean that poetry is the "subject" of "poetry," or "thought," of "thought."[33] Rather, "the painting of painting means simply that painting (the potentiality of painting, the *pictura pingens*) is exposed and suspended [*è eposta e sospesa*] in the act of painting, just as the poetry of poetry means that language is exposed and suspended in the poem" (50/55 [translation modified]). What remains potential within thought makes thought possible; the work, subject to revision, lays bare what Agamben calls "materiality," language as such prior to any meaning.

In "Opus alchymicum," Agamben asks why the ethical project of the self's transformation needs to pass through an opus (a work)[34]—in spite of the great temptation to dispense with that seemingly unnecessary detour. In accounts of various such projects—including Rimbaud's famous renunciation of poetry, and Foucault's "souci de soi"—Agamben ultimately finds an answer in the structure of potentiality. A preliminary problem is logical or grammatical; the self is not a "subject" that can transform or work "on" itself: "The pronoun 'se,' the marker of reflexivity in Indo-European languages, lacks for this reason the nominative case. It presupposes a grammatical subject that reflects upon itself but that can never itself be in the position of subject. The self [sé], to the degree that it coincides with a reflexive relation, can never be a substance, or a substantive." "The idea of an ethical subject," therefore, "is a contradiction in terms."[35] This aporia, Agamben notes, menaces every effort to work on the self: "there is no subject prior to the relation to the self: the subject is this relation itself and not one of its terms" (132–3/136–7 [translation modified]).[36]

Hence the transformation of the self has to pass through an "opus," and hence I think James's characterization of revision might speak to the intimate question of why one writes—and, among other things, to the political invest-ments of queer theory. Queer theory, like many liberationist critical practices, asserts a connection to the world, even aspires to an alchemical power to coun-teract its injustices. In Sedgwick and others, this imperative often appears in the form of a guilty conscience about writing, which, bringing the prose alive, nevertheless deforms the thought. This is the tension between the "proto-gay" child and the gay person whose necessity in our immediate world we are (I would say justly) enjoined to avow.[37] It perhaps also marks Sedgwick's turn to shame and affect, which is formulated in her brilliant reading of James's prefaces—an account that might be better known to readers of queer theory than are the prefaces themselves.[38] On the one hand, shame allows Sedgwick to posit queer identity in the mode of its suspension: "Shame interests me po-litically, then, because it generates and legitimates the place of identity—the question of identity—at the origin of the impulse to the performative, but does so without giving that identity space the standing of an essence" (Sedg-wick, *Touching Feeling*, 64). On the other, the reading of the prefaces' "lexicon" is at least partly enabled by a reification of the authorial consciousness that the prefaces themselves put into question—or that they posit as a belated conse-quence of the writing itself. The positing of James's psychological reactions—to the failure of *Guy Domville* and the lackluster sales of the New York Edition, to the physiological experience of constipation—seem, like the generalizations about the "kinds" of persons whose personalities might vibrate to the key of shame, both true (because they resonate with experience and observation in profound ways) and false (because reductive of, most importantly, the relation between identity and writing explored by the prefaces' probing of origins). In-sofar as shame, in her account, begins with a dynamic of (albeit thwarted) recognition, the account is grounded in a supposedly identifiable, psychologi-cal, and—harsh to say—therefore banalizing context.

In other terms, for all its opening of disparate questions of affect, by begin-ning from shame (especially as it formulated by Tomkins) it makes recogni-tion (given or withheld) the primary mode of relation to the world. A more detailed reading of Sedgwick's argument might thus begin with her own essay's curious beginning: Sedgwick looks down at lower Manhattan and the site of the missing World Trade Center towers and feels *shame*. This leads her to the dynamic of withdrawn or missing recognition (indicatively, a mother's) that defines shame for Silvan Tomkins. Whatever one thinks about that derivation (as evocative as it may be as a description), it is also worth holding on to how strange the affect is for the occasion. A fundamental disorientation in one's world legible to many of us, I have to assume, who have had to find new ways to discover north and south in Manhattan, that unmooring could potentially lead one to feelings of shame, but it wouldn't obviously be shame for the *build-ings*. It seems to me that that movement relies on a transfer of survivor's guilt to a theatricalized sense of self-exposure that replays (replays as a further level of exposure) the unspeakable theatricalization of death in the spectacle of 9/11. The content of shame is withdrawn and becomes almost synonymous with a formal structure of insides made visible—as the insides of the towers them-selves were made visible—that can therefore render the very process of identifi-cation that would, in a meta-level recursion, structure the identification of affect with destroyed buildings in the first place. I'm not sure what good it does to call all of this "shame" and to submerge that vicarious identification (both with the dead and with the thrill of survival that Canetti diagnoses as the tri-umph of the last man standing,[39] which is surely the obscene basis, too, of many violent entertainment spectacles)—however canny and astute the label-ing of the complex "affect" there might be.[40] Or perhaps better, the naming of that feeling—naming it, specifically, as shame—regardless of how illuminating it might be as an illustration of unrelated movements in shame, closes off—both concretizes and abstracts—the complex drama she invokes by making it an identifiable (and, it may be, morally valorized) feeling.

That movement of abstraction is likewise visible, paradoxically, in the turn to the highly lurid thematics of fisting, which thus has a curiously sublimat-ing effect, since shame is made queer while as if euphemizing a more obvi-ous occasion for gay male shame: anal sex.[41] So the effect is, potentially, both a derealizing of gay specificity and a reifying of psychology. Privileging recog-nition, then, it further contains the various, loaded dynamics of vision and ex-posure in the invoked scenario. Arguably, this reifying of identity (combined with a despecification of homosexuality) has marked shame's career in queer theory; moreover, it has allowed critics, because they were saying something "true" to avoid the truth of the texts they read—and to take as given queer iden-tity precisely to the degree that, as a "subject" of constatation, it is presumed to be suspended. For some, it is not regrettable that criticism might thereby become a psychologistic, sociological, and largely descriptive enterprise. That turn perhaps brackets questions of identity that—by refusing to resolve them—previous instantiations of queer theory found so productive. Partly, this is a (justifiable) shift away from the closet as a governing trope for understanding sexuality, and therefore a muting of the largely epistemological questions that shaped that earlier theory. And yet the turn to shame and affect might also then short-circuit the passage through the work that I have tried to name by way of James's revision.

"It's not writing that is happy," says Foucault, in the context of elucidating the source of what he calls an "obligation to write," and the "absolution" it offers one; "it's the joy of existing that's attached to writing, which is slightly different."[42] In Agamben's gloss: "Happiness—the ethical task par excellence toward which all work on the self tends—is 'attached' to writing ['*sospesa' alla scrittura*], that is, becomes possible only through a creative practice. The care of the self necessarily passes through an *opus*, implies an ineluctable alchemy" (Agamben, *The Fire and the Tale*, 134/138 [translation modified]). Thus, for Agamben, the transformation of the self through the creative act is made possible only if it constitutes a relation to a potentiality not exhausted by the work. "We write," Foucault suggests, "to hide our face, to bury ourselves in our own writing"; what he goes on to describe as an attenuation of the self is never achieved—life can never be contained in the text, can never be made "thin" enough to become one with the line of writing (Foucault, *Speech Begins After Death*, 66, 67).[43] The poet-become-seer ("voyant," in Rimbaud's terms) contemplates language itself—"not the written opus but the potentiality of writing" (Agamben, *The Fire and the Tale*, 137/141), like James, confronting the new terms as they impose themselves on his vision, or tracing his uncontrollable footsteps across a plain of snow. Because, in Spinoza's terms, "potentiality is nothing other than the essence or nature of every being, inasmuch as it has the capacity to do something, contemplating this potentiality is the only possible access to *ethos*, to 'seity'" (137/141 [translation modified]).[44] The transformation of the self, which must pass through the work, also deactivates the work, and returns it to potentiality. "Truly poetic," Agamben writes, "is that form of life that, in the work, contemplates its own power to do and to not do and finds peace in it [*Veramente poetica è quella forma di vita che, nella propria opera, contempla la propria potenza di fare e di non fare e trova pace in essa*]" (137/141 [translation modified]). This is one way to read James's rendering of revision as autobiography, and of autobiography as revision: a life suspended in, maintained in perpetual relation to, the potentiality of the creative act by way of a work that, ever-to-be-revised, is thus perpetually unwritten, a life, and work, that consume themselves in the origin where language speaks itself.[45]

This structure of origin is allegorized by James's story "The Middle Years," whose title, in a well-known, but not for that the less cryptic, gesture, he borrowed for the final (unfinished) volume of his autobiography—and which derives, in the story, from the title of the main character's final book.[46] An ailing writer named Dencombe, receiving an advance copy of "The Middle Years," discovers that he has, at last, and belatedly, achieved clarity about his aesthetic project even as death threatens to make him unable to realize that vision. Just then, he meets a devoted young reader, Dr. Hugh. A fuller reading would dwell on, among many other things, that erotic relation, and the way that it is structured against the claims of the Countess, a wealthy and ailing woman who has hired him as a personal doctor—a relation then further circuited through the Countess's companion, Miss Vernham (and her desire for Dr. Hugh). Here, however, I will focus on the story's consideration of revision. It is not merely that Dencombe never stops revising, marking up (as James himself did) even published copies of his work. More crucially, the story explores what a life given over to revision might be. Notably, it begins with a caesura; Dencombe has completely forgotten his book. This caesura makes possible something like a literal experience of revision: he reads the text again and sees that it is good: "Everything came back to him, but came back with a wonder, came back above all with a high and magnificent beauty. He read his own prose, he turned his own leaves, and had as he sat there with the spring sunshine on the page an emotion peculiar and intense. His career was over, no doubt, but it was over, when all was said, with *that*" (81).

The encounter with Dr. Hugh makes him dream that "ebbing time" and "shrinking opportunity," his sense that "he hadn't done what he had wanted" (80), might be vanquished, makes him dream of a second chance whereby his discovery of his capacity could structure his life: "It came over him in the long quiet hours that only with 'The Middle Years' had he taken his flight; only on that day, visited by soundless processions, had he recognised his kingdom. He had had revelation of his range. What he dreaded was the idea that his reputation should stand on the unfinished. It wasn't with his past but with his future that it should properly be concerned. Illness and age rose before him like spectres with pitiless eyes: how was he to bribe such fates to give him the second chance? He had had the one chance that all men have—he had had the chance of life" (90–1). "I want another go," he later explains; "I want an extension" (95, 96).

It would be easy enough to read in the story a renunciation of the aesthetic life in favor of what might crudely be understood as erotic fulfillment. For the story ends with Dr. Hugh and Dencombe together, Dr. Hugh pronouncing him a "great success," "putting into his young voice the ring of a marriage-bell"

(105). Ironized or not, the offered erotic consummation as a substitute for the aesthetic life is turned down by the writer, who "taking this in," demurs: there are no second chances, except to the very degree that no first chance is ever fully realized. Consummation would, of course, entail a contradiction; only their shared passion for Dencombe's work urges them toward the literal consummation in which they might dispense with it. The more crucial point is that the fantasy of second chances is also the fantasy that work could be something other than "unfinished," that the aesthetic life could be complete. Dencombe's demurral—one of the most often quoted passages in James—is a comment on the authorial life suspended in revision: "A second chance— that's the delusion. There never was to be but one. We work in the dark—we do what we can—we give what we have. Our doubt is our passion and our passion is our task. The rest is the madness of art" (105).

The tones of ethical exhortation are unmistakable; also unmistakable is a rhetorical structure typical in James: It has all the appearance—all the sound, and, to read, all of the satisfactions—of formal closure, but that form con- ceals, or rather discloses, terms that prove unexpectedly elusive. The satisfy- ing closure comes from the series of repetitions—"We work in the dark—we do what we can—we give what we have"—followed by the (also ostensibly paral- lel) terms of a chiasmus, sealed by the certainty of the paired copula: "Our doubt is our passion and our passion is our task." Paraphrased, this might assert that doubt—not being certain of our aesthetic vocation, perhaps, or of writ- ing's purchase on the world—is what makes for our passion, and that that passion is our ethical imperative. I think, however, that we are meant to be struck by the unresolved heterogeneity of the terms—doubt, passion, passion, task, all linked by "is." This isn't—as it has often been understood—a claim for art's transcendence, and not only because art is put in a possibly ambiguous relation to "madness" (is the genitive objective or subjective; is all art mad, or just a part of it?), but because what is thus defined—doubt and passion, pas- sion and task—forms a totality that excludes art, or produces it as a remainder: "the rest is the madness of art." The satisfying formal closure, whatever it might actually mean, thus bears on everything that *isn't* the statement's pri- mary concern. The last claim links "art" to the unwritten; in context, "the rest" has been defined: the "pearl," Dencombe asserts, isn't the public's ad- miration; "the pearl is the unwritten—the pearl is the unalloyed, the *rest*, the lost!" (104). No doubt, too, James was thinking of *Hamlet*: "the rest is silence." The madness of art is what remains unsaid or unexpressed, consists, perhaps, in the gap between the formal closure of this peroration and its content. That gap, one might say, is life as revision, or as potentiality.

The search for origins might be understood as a search for transcendence, a desire to escape history in a return to an uncorrupted state. But as Teskey points out in Milton, there will be no postlapsarian return to Eden; Eden is "destroyed in the Flood, torn loose from its foundations and washed down the Euphrates to the Persian Gulf, where it is now: 'an island salt and bare,/The haunt of seals and orcs and sea-mews' clang.'"[47] In "The Middle Years," when Dencombe is confronted with what loyalty will cost his young friend, the blow—and the renunciation he resolves on, of nothing less than his "second chance"—evokes Genesis prior to creation: "Oh yes, after this Dencombe was certainly very ill. . . . [I]t was the sharpest shock to him to discover what was at stake for a penniless young man of fine parts. He sat trembling on his bench, staring at the waste of waters, feeling sick with the directness of the blow" (100).[48] The echo of the story's opening—"He sat and stared at the sea, which appeared all surface and twinkle, far shallower than the spirit of man. It was the abyss of human illusion that was the real, the tideless deep. He held his packet, which had come by book-post, unopened on his knee" (77–8)—is perhaps less important for the tone of near despondency that marks the baffling of his hopes than for the formal return to the beginning, with (moreover) its evocation of the unread, the unopened, the forgotten book. In that echo, the story intimates that there dwells, in the baffled hope of second chances, a perpetual return to potentiality in writing's search for its origins. Thus to step outside history is not to secure transcendence for the work of art but, by consigning it to revision, to make it what James calls "a living affair" (1335), structured by "onset distortion" and the imperfections of created beings; suspended within this return to the origin, the writer strives to hear the exhortations of truthful speech, and to bear the risks of its equivocal importunings.

2
"First Love"
Gesture and the Emergence of Desire in Eudora Welty

Eudora Welty's strange and beautiful story "First Love" is about the quandaries of inception, and, dwelling in what Kathryn Bond Stockton calls the "interval" of the queer child, it renders that interval from within, from the perspective of the proto-queer child, and with no resolution, no later "knowing" perspective, no glossing or explanatory narrative voice, to resolve the incipience by telling us what it becomes.[1] The story of a young deaf boy named Joel Mayes who falls in love with Aaron Burr, its central plot begins with Joel in Natchez, where he works at the inn cleaning boots, and it moves in two directions within that interval: forward in time toward Burr's trial for treason and his eventual escape from town, and backward, toward Joel's gradual recovery of the memory of the loss of his parents—or, in other terms, forward toward one form of dispossession (the loss of Burr) through which he will rejoin or realize a previous one, the loss of his parents, paired losses that will come to constitute his "first love." The story's title, even on an initial view, invites multiple interpretations, beginning with its mode of designation: Is the "first love" Joel's, or is the story *about* "first love"—such that the title's relation to Joel's story might take any number of more or less oblique forms?[2] Does "first" mean the love that is before, or the love that is more important than, all the others (the first or prime mover, or the First Lady)? What is the relation between chronology and logical priority? If the love, in whatever sense of "first," is Joel's, does "first love" refer to his love for Burr or to his love for his parents? Further, Joel's own story, about origins and emergence, is also a frontier narrative about the nation's origins, and it gestures, beyond that, to more primal beginnings.

The story encourages us to read the first love as Joel's and to regard his falling in love with Burr as an initiation that points, in turn, to a prior love: Aaron

Burr allows him to experience his love for his parents. At the end of the story, Joel follows the fleeing Burr (who is disguised—in a departure, several critics have noted, from Welty's historical sources—as a Native American, with feathers in his hair and some of Joel's boot polish smeared across his face) until, following his beloved orator, he is overtaken by the posse that pursues the reputedly treacherous statesman: "He did not know how far he had gone on the Liberty Road when the posse came riding up behind and passed him. He walked on. He saw that the bodies of the frozen birds had fallen out of the trees, and he fell down and wept for his father and mother, to whom he had not said good-bye."[3] "First Love" might thus be read to name both the first love he knew—for his parents—and the love that, in leading him away from them, allows him to know the earlier one. *Nachträglichkeit* or latency: the emergence of desire scrambles terms of temporal priority. Burr's masquerade as a Native American seems less disguise than pastiche; the addition of Joel's boot polish would seem to move us into the realm of the phantasmatico-allegorical, and his curious costume allows someone—Joel, the story, Burr—to replay the loss of his parents, identifying the object of love with the people who dispossessed him. Led out of the town, and following a man wearing a transparent "disguise" made of minimal, non-verisimilar signs of the victims of American expansion, Joel's coming of age is indistinguishable from an unmooring: "Joel would never know now the true course, or the true outcome of any dream: this was how he felt. But he walked on, in the frozen path into the wilderness, on and on. He did not see how he could ever go back and still be the boot-boy at the inn" (168). This sharp rupture of identity, Joel's queer becoming, as one might call it, does not, furthermore, coincide with itself in time, reenacting and harkening back to previous seductions. Burr is explicitly linked to Old Man McCaleb, the old man who "took him away when his parents vanished in the forest, were cut off from him, and in spite of his last backward look, dropped behind" (154). (Would Burr and Blennerhassett, he wonders, "take him each by the arm and drag him on further, through the leaves"? [157]; "He would allow Burr to take him with him wherever it was that he meant to go" [159].) The relation is enacted spatially or topographically; dropping behind Burr as his parents "dropped behind" him, he enacts his loss of them as their (and Burr's) loss of him, and the *dropping* further evokes the falling gesture at the story's end, leaving Joel to take the place, in turn, of the frozen birds fallen from the trees.

Temporally, Joel seems to meet himself coming and going, and the first-ness of first love seems to consist paradoxically in its pointing to something prior. And in fact Welty says so explicitly: "If love does a secret thing always, it is to reach backward, to a time that could not be known—for it makes a history of the sorrow and the dream it has contemplated in some instant of recognition" (165). In my understanding, love narrativizes an instant, and, in unfolding the realization that is also the sorrow of a dawning hope, it confronts the abyssal temporality of inception. ("Could" here is perhaps ambiguous, since it is unclear whether love allows one to know, finally, what previously could not be known, or whether love reaches back to an unknown that is gestured toward, or perhaps even reached, but not known.) The particular "instant" here seems to be Joel's realization that his beloved Burr is leaving, and it comes into focus as the moment before a loss: "This was Burr's last night: Joel knew that. This was the moment before he would ride away. Why would the heart break so at absence? Joel knew that it was because nothing had been told. The heart is secret even when the moment it dreamed of has come, a moment when there might have been a revelation" (165). The passage collocates two different movements: a temporal recession and an emergence of a self in its act of looking back. Thus, in a temporal recession (on the one hand), there is no first love (because love always points to a love that precedes it) and (on the other) all love is first love (for the same reason), while in an involution into a self, the response one does not receive from another installs a secret within oneself, constitutes a self, even as it renders it opaque to "oneself." Welty's phrasing in the first instance is curiously circular, and in multiple ways: The secret thing seems to be both the reaching back and the unknowable time to which it reaches back, and she suggests that the time is unknowable *because* of the very reaching back, because it makes a history. That history, in turn, is made of "the sorrow and the dream it has contemplated in some instant of recognition," but, according to what comes before, what is recognized is that the heart is secret—love does a secret thing, and the heart is secret; the "instant of recognition" houses not a "revelation" but a moment when a revelation "might have been."

The logico-temporal reflexivity—the burrowing backward that, groundlessly, turns up secrets that are at once the finding and what is found—is paired with the movement between self and object. "Why would the heart break so at absence? Joel knew it was because nothing had been told": at first, one reads this moment as detailing the anguish of separating from a beloved person without telling him of your love—he does not tell Burr he loves him, and does not tell his parents goodbye. And I think that is indeed the anguish here. Yet that the heart is secret then comes to mean its opacity to itself: It isn't that Joel did not reveal his heart to Burr so much as that his love makes his own heart a secret to him. Thus the isolation is more intimate, even, than thwarted desire. "A boy or a man could be so alone in his heart that he could not even ask a question," Welty writes just before this passage, and "the instant of recognition" makes Joel long to speak: "What Joel saw before him he had a terrible wish to speak out loud, but he would have had to find names for the places of the heart and the times for its shadowy and tragic events, and they seemed of great magnitude, heroic and terrible and splendid, like the legends of the mind. But for lack of a way to tell how much was known, the boundaries would lie between him and the others, all the others, until he died" (165). This is not, one should hasten to add, a pain that could be palliated, a yearning that could be answered, by any bathetic announcement of identity or any ostensibly cathartic naming of desire (which is never anything but frankly registered in the text); this is, rather, the intimate solitude of queer becoming, the silence at the heart of the recursive structures of inception laid bare by the story.

That structure can be made apparent by pursuing the logic of the story's initiations. Love is individuating, it seems, and it creates a longing for two forms of remediation whose possibility it simultaneously forecloses: knowledge and speech. It is perhaps uncertain whether this structuring yearning—which imagines that to speak or to know would be to find the form of a connection with others—is derived from the story's central seduction (where Joel, not knowing the plot, watches Burr and Blennerhassett, illumined in the lamplight of his room, speak words he cannot hear) or whether the scene proves so galvanizing because it activates a prior yearning. Likewise, love leads him to his parents, or his parents to his later love, because both lead to this epiphany of the boundaries to lie between him and the others, all the others, until he dies. One of the perplexing aspects of this desolating insight is the question of whether Joel *can* speak. We are told he is deaf, and several critics refer to him as "deaf-mute." But the story never makes clear whether Joel is able to speak, never places the "level" at which we are to understand his muteness, just as in the thwarted longing to speak, we are perhaps unsure whether Joel confronts love's inexpressibility or his own personal disability, whether "to speak" is literal or figurative. That it is more than a personal disability is suggested by the fact that Welty's own writing in this passage is punctuated by ellipses—as if the silence were entering the narrative voice. In a larger sense, then, the abyssal temporality of inception is not merely the "subject" of this story; or rather, as its subject, it enters into the very language of the text, leaving as its mark on the story this uncertainty, at any given moment, of its register of language—of whether its primal silence is Joel's or that of language itself.

There is further reason to think so. These questions lead us back to Joel's initial encounter with Burr. He falls in love with Burr because of a gesture:

> Then the gesture one of the men made in the air transfixed him where he waited.
>
> One of the two men lifted his right arm—a tense, yet gentle and easy motion—and made the dark wet cloak fall back. To Joel it was like the first movement he had ever seen, as if the world had been up to that night inanimate. It was like the signal to open some heavy gate or paddock, and it did open to his complete astonishment upon a panorama in his own head, about which he knew first of all that he would never be able to speak—it was nothing but brightness, as full as the brightness on which he had opened his eyes. Inside his room was still another interior, this meeting upon which all the light was turned, and within that was one more mystery, all that was being said. (157)

Burr's gesture seems to startle the world into appearing; the world's animation is Joel's, and the inanimate world retrospectively apparent to him, an intimation, in his awakening, of what had been lacking before. The awakening takes shape as a discovery of an inside; the passage asks to be read as an allegory of an interiority (Joel's) coming into being. It is striking, therefore, how elusive the spatial relations turn out to be: The gesture is like the signal to open a gate, which opens upon a panorama in his own head. The passage then turns, without transition, to a nested series of interiors located outside him: the inside of his room, the "inside" of the conversation as it is marked by the circle of lamplight, and, within that, the "mystery" of "all that was being said." It seems to me that the lack of transition in the middle of the passage leaves open two possible readings of the relation between the panorama and the series: It is uncertain whether the panorama *is* this series or *is like* it. (In other terms, one doesn't know whether this nested series he sees in his room is inside his head or whether it resembles the inside of his head.)

My intuition reading these lines is that the brightness of the panorama within him is sealed away from him and sealed within him just as the mystery of "all that is being said" is removed from his comprehension. His interior comes into being insofar as it can be compared to an exterior image. His deafness isn't just an attribute of his mind; it is his mind's inside. If that's the case, it would follow that the story *can't* establish the "empirical" status of Joel's deafness. Its sometimes equivocal representation of that sensory debility is perhaps signal (as when he longs to "speak," when he is "told" things, or "hears" them, the words may or may not be figural). Love calls us back to, or as if realizes, a deafness that is something other than a debility. Forming an interior, an "inside" of his subjectivity analogous to a room, or a circle of light in a dark room, love grants him this inside on the condition of excluding him from it.

To be able to speak of it would express that interiority, and, paradoxically, include him in it.

It is perhaps worth noting that, yet again, the originary moment turns out to be anticipated by something prior: the play of interiors here is set up by Burr and Blennerhassett's previous invasion of Joel's room—the room that before this "was excessively his own, as it would have been a stray kitten's that came to the same spot every night" (155). Stray kittens are, of course, homeless; that might be what makes a spot "excessively" their own. Thus, too, the gesture makes an interior after the "violation" has already done so (156). Yet the gesture might be read as originary in another register as well.[4] Why does one fall in love with gestures? In the *Abécédaire*, Gilles Deleuze's discussion of friendship and the charming gesture points to an impersonal form of affiliation: In friendship, one shares not an opinion but a language. Speaking specifically of Foucault's great charisma and the charming gestures in which he most felt it, Deleuze suggests that such gestures inspire a particular kind of acquisitiveness. "I want that to belong to me," he says; yet to my mind his terms evoke the desire to memorize a poem more than any wish to *be* or to *have* the beloved person.[5] A drive for neither possession nor identification, it seems to seek a more purely aesthetic acquisition. One wants the gesture inside one—but inside as another's, as one memorizes a poem less to appropriate it than in hopes of reading it more closely. (I mimic the beloved's gestures in order to marvel at them as his, but in my hands.) The gesture, in Deleuze's account, I have suggested elsewhere, thus offers a model for thinking about style.[6] It is both expressive (one loves a gesture, like a tone of voice, because it is, unmistakably, the beloved's own) and depersonalizing (it is not him—at least in fantasy, it is separable from him). Its appropriation is at once impersonal and charged with personal significance. Likewise, *style* marks what is, unmistakably, unforgettably, a person's own, but also where that personality dissolves itself, depersonalizes itself in speech or writing.[7] (I think this explains something of the intense yet impersonal affect generated by writers—or, say, by great musicians—why they can make me feel something very much like love for them even as I have no particular desire ever to meet them.)

This aspect of the gesture might be rooted in the fact that it is intimately expressive without having (in most cases) a specific semantic content. As Werner Hamacher writes, "Gesture is what remains of language after meaning is withdrawn from it, and it is gesture that withdraws from meaning. The rest of language—and so language itself, language irreducible to meaning—is gesture."[8] Giorgio Agamben writes that the gesture, for Max Kommerell, "is not an absolutely nonlinguistic element but, rather, something closely tied to language." A "forceful presence of language itself" that "is older and more originary than conceptual expression," linguistic gesture, according to the Kommerell of Agamben's account, is "the stratum of language that is not exhausted in communication and that captures language, so to speak, in its solitary moments."[9] Glossing Kommerell's claim that "speech is originary gesture," Agamben writes that "what is at issue in gesture is not so much a prelinguistic content as, so to speak, the other side of language, the muteness inherent in mankind's very capacity for language, its *speechless* dwelling in language."[10] Gesture voids semantic content insofar as it speaks language itself: "Precisely for this reason—insofar, that is, as gesture, having to express Being in language itself, strictly speaking has nothing to express and nothing to say other than what is said in language—gesture is always the gesture of being at a loss in language" (Agamben, "Kommerell," 78).[11] Thus, elsewhere, Agamben compares the gesture to the gag—something put in one's mouth to hinder speech, or an actor's improvisation masking a memory lapse or a failure to speak—concluding then, by way of Wittgenstein, that "every great philosophical text is the *gag* exhibiting language itself, being-in-language itself as a gigantic loss of memory, as an incurable speech defect."[12]

Thus to be at a loss in language in gesturing toward language's taking place also becomes a model for criticism. For Kommerell, Agamben writes, "Criticism is the reduction of works to the sphere of pure gesture," the sphere that "lies beyond psychology and, in a certain sense, beyond all interpretation. . . . Consigned to their supreme gesture, works live on, like creatures bathed in the light of the last day, surviving the ruin of their formal garment and their conceptual meaning" (Agamben, "Kommerell," 80). "Reduced to its speechless capacity for speech," Daniel Heller-Roazen writes of these terms of redemption, "the object of Agamben's criticism is, at last, saved. It is nothing other than its own potentiality for expression, and what it shows is simply the existence of language: that there exists a medium in which communication takes place, and that what is communicated in this medium is not one thing or another but, first of all, communicability itself" (Heller-Roazen, "Editor's Introduction," 23). Gesture is originary in another sense—marking not temporal beginnings or causality but a reflection on language's own taking place—and it is therefore the term Agamben uses to describe the author's emergence through his disappearance in or into the work.[13]

In "Speaking in Tongues," Heller-Roazen suggests other contexts for thinking about this originary dimension of gesture.[14] Beginning with Paul's warnings, in the first Epistle to the Corinthians, against speaking in tongues, or "glossolalia"—to speak not meaningless sounds but unknown words in a foreign tongue, words whose meanings one does not know, to speak words "not altogether without significance, but rather without definite significance," words that, "caught at a point between the total absence of signification and its full presence, . . . are meaningful and yet without determinate meaning" (92)—he turns to a central dimension of Agamben's thought: "Marking a point within significant speech that resists signification, glossolalia furnishes Agamben with a fundamental example for the singular 'experience of language' (*experimentum linguae*) that he has defined as the *motivum* of his thought: that of the 'fact that there is language,' that fact that language, before or beyond determinate meaning, takes place."[15] From this framing, Heller-Roazen moves on to some of the ways that theological and poetic imaginings of creation are forced to confront this taking place, which is both within and without language. He pairs two theological accounts of Creation—the place of Nothing in Anselm of Canterbury's *Proslogion* and its reverberations in later philosophy and the place of the silent Aleph in Jewish theological traditions—with linguistic innovations that lay bare the taking place of language as such, the crisis of the "end of the poem" that is thus also a confrontation with inception.[16]

Particularly evocative for "First Love" is the account of the *aleph*: a letter with "no proper phonetic value" that lacks even the "non-phonetic, 'articulatory' value of the *hamza* in classical Arabic," it serves, in "post-Biblical pronunciations" as "the silent support for the vowels it bears, deprived even of the non-sound, the interruption in sound, that it is thought to have once expressed" (Heller-Roazen, "Speaking in Tongues," 99–100). Excluded from the act of the creation of the world, the silent letter, in a series of contractions from the Talmudic tradition to a Maimonidian gloss on it to an eighteenth-century doctrine summarized by Gershom Scholem (where the aleph is all that Israel heard from Moses at Mount Sinai), nevertheless (or therefore) becomes the cipher of divine revelation: "The divine revelation is thus reduced, in a series of contractions of increasing intensity, to its most discrete element: we pass from the text of the Torah as a whole, . . . to the only text that was heard by all, the first two commandments, which are then said to be contained in a single word *anochi* and, finally, in the most extreme case, compressed into its initial *aleph*, which the *Book of Bahir*, at one point, defines precisely as 'the essence of the Ten Commandments.'" He continues:

> once the sound of revelation is understood as that of the *aleph*, its sense alters radically: the divine word ceases to be a "word," and its representations, even a letter, at least as long as one understands a letter to be the representation of a determinate phonetic value. Contracted into the blankness of an absolute beginning, revelation becomes a mere "cipher" in the sense of the Arabic etymon of the term, *sifr*, a "nothing," a "zero," the irreducibly written sign of a

meaningfulness without definite meaning. . . . Such is that most modest of "glossolalias," that bare "voice"—so minimal that it is not even one—from which all speech would spring. The *Aleph*, the medium of a mute "speaking in tongues" before all tongues, would then be the mark of the inception of speech in the suspension of speaking; it would be a name for silent speech, or spoken silence.[17]

Joel's silence, I would suggest, is the silence of the *aleph*, as the mark of "the inception of speech in the suspension of speaking," and the story's blank expanse of snow, "the blankness of an absolute beginning." Or rather, part of what makes Welty's story so enigmatic is the difficulty of distinguishing an anecdotal or psychological experience of silence from this primordial silence. That confrontation of registers is perhaps what the story figures as reading; it is also the recursive structure of Joel's "first love," the movement from Burr and the beloved gesture back toward his parents, and his emergence, through that return, as a subject of desire.

Thus Joel's initiating perception of the beautiful gesture occurs in a context in which language has become gestural. After a framing passage about Natchez, which ends with a dead man who, having frozen to death crouched inside a tree, is carried to town, the story introduces its protagonist:

> Joel Mayes, a deaf boy twelve years old, saw the man brought in and knew it was a dead man, but his eyes were for something else, something wonderful. He saw the breaths coming out of people's mouths, and his dark face, losing just now little of its softness, showed its secret desire. It was marvelous to him when the infinite designs of speech became visible in formations on the air, and he watched with awe that changed to tenderness whenever people met and passed in the road with an exchange of words. He walked alone, slowly through the silence, with the sturdy and yet dreamlike walk of the orphan, and let his own breath out through his lips, pushed it into the air, and whatever word it was took the shape of a tower. He was as pleased as if he had had a little conversation with someone. (154)

This beautiful image of words become visible asks to be read, I think, as at once an image of language made gestural and as an allegory of writing. If writing, too, is the "infinite designs of speech" made visible, here it is imagined as shape—as pure capacity to communicate. A little later, writing in a foreign tongue takes on a similar quality—of pure inscription: "He began to keep his candlestick carefully polished, he set it in the center of the puncheon table, and at night when it was lighted all the messages of love carved into it with a

knife in Spanish words, with a deep Spanish gouging, came out in black relief, for anyone to read who came knowing the language" (155–6). Both passages evoke Welty's own description of her love of the alphabet in *One Writer's
Beginnings*: "My love for the alphabet, which endures, grew out of reciting it
but, before that, out of seeing the letters on the page. In my own story books,
before I could read them for myself, I fell in love with various winding,
enchanted-looking initials drawn by Walter Crane at the heads of fairy tales. . . .
When the day came, years later, for me to see the Book of Kells, all the wiz-
ardry of letter, initial, and word swept over me a thousand times over, and the
illumination, the gold, seemed a part of the world's beauty and holiness that
had been there from the start."[18] For Joel, this image of visible speech is, like
Welty's gaze at the beauty of letters she cannot (yet) read, originating, and a
glimpse of the beginning of the world; this opening anticipates his falling in
love with Burr—contemplating language as gesture, his face is made to show
its "secret desire."

A deaf boy falls in love with a great orator—for the gestural charisma of his
speech, for an unheard language that, Welty writes, might have been "in another language, in which there was nothing but evocation."[19] It is worth holding on to the strangeness of this premise, and worth noting, too, how startling
it is to read this allegory of writing from a writer whose account of authorial
origins itself begins with a chapter called "Listening." "There has never been
a line read," Welty writes, "that I didn't *hear*" ("One Writer's Beginnings," 851,
italics in the original). The story's haunting beauty is in large part in the aural
beauty of the sentences, and Burr's charismatic gesture suggests the possibility of heard language apprehended, paradoxically, as a visual image.[20] The
power of Burr's gesture for Joel is rendered by non-semantic elements and
renders a vanishing of meaning into uninterpretable sound: consonance and
cadence, the iambic tetrameter of "and made the dark wet cloak fall back."
These effects of sound render the power of an image Joel *sees*, silently; hearing them, one sees language, drawing together Joel's deaf apprehension of the
world with the act of reading. To hear language merely seen is not paradoxical insofar as such might describe, simply, reading, but the aural beauty of
Welty's story figures writing as gesture insofar as it renders the pleasure of
reading and of significant sound in the absence of any communicated content. If I said earlier that Joel's silence is the silence of the aleph, that revelation is as if distributed across the language of the story as a whole. Welty's
language is perhaps always oracular; the characteristic gestural quality of her
prose is perhaps even more in evidence in this story, which thereby becomes
especially enigmatic, particularly in the difficulty of deciding, for any given
statement, how freighted with symbolic, figural, or allegorical significance it

is. Each sentence seems at once to display the most quotidian of actions and to bear witness, in cryptic hieroglyphs, to the creation of the world. That makes interpretation a vexed enterprise, and in fact one has the sense that the text is to be memorized rather than interpreted.

Hence Burr's beloved face, which is repeatedly called "a speaking face," is, in giving a face to the seductions of language, as if no face: "Always he talked, his talking was his appearance, as if there were no eyes, nose, or mouth to remember; in his face there was every subtlety and eloquence, and no features, no kindness, for there was no awareness whatever of the present" (159). Burr, given over to his own words, is left in an unawareness that is hardly even attributed to him, or that spills over to characterize his rapt observer ("there was no awareness whatever of the present"). A mirror of that absorption, Joel's deafness makes manifest, through the words he doesn't hear, the equivocal nature of the speech of this speaking face; to be in doubt of what Joel hears is to be suspended between that "speech," as a realized figure, and an incomplete figuration that makes manifest that such speech is to be conferred on it by the linguistic "figure."[21] One doesn't need the French pun, in other words, to think that, in the seductions of Burr's speaking face, one is gazing at the story's own language—in all the redoubtable charisma of its many enigmas.

That this story of first love moves toward an allegory of writing as gesture is suggested, moreover, by an echo in the opening description of Joel. "Whatever word it was took the shape of a tower," we read of Joel's breath visible in the air. This formulation of a suspension of meaning evokes the story's opening: "Whatever happened, it happened in extraordinary times, in a season of dreams, and in Natchez it was the bitterest winter of them all" (153). ("There was no awareness whatever," we might add, "of the present" [159].) The immediate reference is perhaps the obscurity of Aaron Burr's plot. We know little of it from the story, largely because it is focalized through Joel, who lacks crucial information.[22] That obscurity radiates outward to the historical context, itself obscure; critical accounts of the story repeatedly confess that it is finally unclear what the historical Burr was plotting with Blennerhassett and why. It is one of the curiosities of the story that it takes place on the border of history—a verifiable historical event, told obliquely, through a purely private, personal, and to a large extent unknowable point of view. More crucial than the details—and Burr's ineffectual dream of conquest is a belated shadow or parody of the nation's own origins—is the figuring of "historical fiction," of the disappearance of historical fact into fiction. For one is also tempted to read "whatever happened" as referring to the happenings of *the story*. "Whatever" suspends the certainty (and perhaps the importance) of both fictional and historical event, and the echo on the next page—"whatever word it was took the shape of a tower"—makes history and text alike a beautiful exhalation made visible by atmospheric conditions, transforming both to gesture.

This turn to gesture leaves us suspended, as it were, within the interval of the queer child—in which we find a series of inceptions where whatever developments they portend remain unrealized, pointing back, and recursively, to previous moments of inception. One of the difficulties of the story—especially if one wants to read it as detailing the realization of inception, of the central formative trauma of the loss of his parents—is that it is punctuated by series of gestures—all initiatory gestures, one might say. The memory of the loss of his parents comes back to him as a series of enigmatic images. Thus, Joel remembers his arrival in Natchez with Old Man McCaleb: "To the man who had saved his life Joel lifted the gentle almost indifferent face of the child who asked for nothing. Now he remembered the white gulls flying across the sky behind the old man's head" (155). Beyond the striking image, which reminds one of a famous sequence in Dreyer's *Passion of St. Joan* that Stanley Cavell calls "the fullest image of absolute isolation,"[23] what is perhaps most notable is the abrupt shift in perspective—looking at his upturned face, we suddenly see what he sees, behind McCaleb's head. That movement evokes for me another gestural moment, Joel's vision as he listens to the "sound" of the violin:

> And quite clearly, and altogether to his surprise, Joel saw a sight that
> he had nearly forgotten. Instead of the fire on the hearth, there was
> a mimosa tree in flower. It was in the little back field at his home
> in Virginia and his mother was leading him by the hand. Fragile,
> delicate, cloud-like it rose on its pale trunk and spread its long level
> arms. His mother pointed to it. Among the trembling leaves the
> feathery puffs of sweet bloom filled the tree like thousands of paradisi-
> cal birds all alighted at an instant. He had known in the story of the
> Princess Labam, for his mother had told it to him, how she was so
> radiant that she sat on the roof-top at night and lighted the city. It
> seemed to be the mimosa tree that lighted the garden, for its bright-
> ness and fragrance overlaid all the rest. Out of its graciousness this
> tree suffered their presence and shed its splendor upon him and his
> mother. His mother pointed again, and its scent swayed like the Asiatic
> princess moving up and down the pink steps of its branches. Then the
> vision was gone. (163–4)

As in the moment with Burr, his mother's gesture seems to open up a world of sensation; it is striking, too, that the mother is as if anticipated by the tree, her gesture of pointing mirroring the spreading of "its long level arms." Like the moment with Burr, the image is a vision of luminosity; in the Indian fairy tale, the Princess is "so radiant that she sat on the roof-top at night and lighted the city." The tree's shedding of its splendor over mother and child figures the protection, now lost, of his mother's sheltering arms, but it also calls him away from that shelter. The "mimosa tree that lighted the garden" takes the place of the Princess, whose mere name suffices to lead the Prince away from his parents—as Joel was led away, to the cane brake, the inn, and Burr. In the fairy tale, the Prince hears of the Princess from parrots he is startled to discover have the gift of speech; in Joel's mimosa tree vision, the birds take on a similar, albeit figurative, power, through an effect of paronomasia, a non-semantic echo that links their appearance to luminosity: the Princess "lighted" the city as the bloom filled the tree like a thousand birds "all alighted at an instant." Symmetrically, if his mother "told" this story, it can only have been through something like gesture.

Later in the story, Joel, gazing at the Mississippi River, as if stages the moment of inception as Burr's gesture startles the world into animation. This emergence in turn leads to a beautiful allegory of the origins of reading:

> In the idle mornings, in some morning need to go looking at the world, he wandered down to the Esplanade and stood under the trees which bent heavily over his head. He frowned out across the ice-covered racetrack and out upon the river. There was one hour when the river was the color of smoke, as if it were more a thing of the woods than an element and a power in itself. It seemed to belong to the woods, to be gentle and watched over, a tethered and grazing pet of the forest, and then when the light spread higher and color stained the world, the river would leap suddenly out of the shining ice around, into its full-grown torrent of life, and its strength and its churning passage held Joel watching over it like the spell unfolding by night in his room. If he could not speak to the river, and he could not, still he would try to read in the river's blue and violet skeins a working of the momentous event. (160)

The river's leaping into being seems to stand in for Joel's own awakening. "Watched over" by the woods, the river leaps "into its full-grown torrent of life," and its "strength and its churning passage held Joel watching over it"—as he is held watching over the conspirators' late-night colloquies. As in the earlier description of the luminous spectacle Burr presents, Joel seems to emerge here as simultaneously watching and watched over, and, as before, his inability to speak is formative:

It was like the signal to open some heavy gate or paddock, and it did open to his complete astonishment upon a panorama in his own head, about which he knew first of all that he would never be able to speak. (157)

What Joel saw before him he had a terrible wish to speak out loud, but he would have had to find names for the places of the heart and the times for its shadowy and tragic events, and they seemed of great magnitude, heroic and terrible and splendid, like the legends of the mind. But for lack of a way to tell how much was known, the boundaries would lie between him and the others, all the others, until he died. (165)

At the moment on the river, one is led to wonder—again—about the register in which to locate the muteness, about why he can't speak to the river (since his inability to speak makes him long to read).[24] In what register, in other words, does one understand the privation? Is it a physical or (as it were) metaphysical condition? One might conclude, for instance, that he cannot speak to the river because he is deaf and literally cannot speak, because it is a river, or because he is belated and lives at the dawning of a modern world in which the responsiveness of nature to human yearnings can no longer be taken for granted. (Such questions are not facetious or impertinent; the story's language in many ways leaves us at sea.) There is something of that difficulty in the confirmation of the hypothetical—"if he could not speak to the river, and he could not"—which at once confirms what was left implicit and unsettles in this confirmation the rhetorical assumptions of the hypothetical. The repetition would also seem to be motivated by sound or cadence, and, turning back on itself, the sentence as if suspends meaning in repeated sound. That repetition or involution, experienced as incapacity, leads to the desire to read. Making language gestural, this turning back turns on the register of language to which Joel insofar as he is deaf, must be insensible—except to the degree that language's sound can be "seen."

Notably, reading here, elicited, is also baffled. He tries to "read in the river's blue and violet skeins the working of the momentous event" (160). The result is an obscurity one might link to the gestural quality of the story's language: "It was hard to understand. Was any scheme a man had, however secret and intact, always broken upon by the very current of its working? One day, in anguish, he saw a raft torn apart in midstream and the men scattered from it. Then all that he felt move in his heart at the sight of the inscrutable river went out in hope for the two men and their genius that he sheltered" (160). The difficulty isn't simply in the highly condensed chain of association that moves from the image of shipwreck to the fate of Burr and Blennerhassett[25] (the one torn apart in the water and the others broken upon in their scheming) and from the solicitation of empathy at the sight of another's distress to the emotion Joel shelters for the two men in watching the late-night discussions in which they will henceforth seem vulnerable to intrusion. I think the difficulty is also in the word "current"—and one's uncertainty about its status as literal or figurative—whether it is the current of the river or the direction of or animating power behind a scheme. The difficulty is further compounded by the fact that *working* can mean "the restless movement of water" or the "straining of a ship, a vehicle, etc. so as to loosen the fittings," and that, in addition to "of moment, of great weight, consequence, or importance," *momentous* can also mean (in archaic use) "having motive force."[26] (In that pun, then, the restless movement of the water leads one to the current's "motive force.") Such questions recurrently (as it were) come up in the story—perhaps unsurprisingly, as language as gesture would also mark the vanishing point where literal and figurative registers can no longer be told apart. (The mother's pointing to the mimosa tree would be an instance of this.) Hence, just as he seeks to read in the river the working of the momentous event, he treats knowledge as though it were a concrete place: "one day he was driven to know everything" (161), but his effort to find out about the trial is baffled. "His head ached. . . . All his walking about was no use. Where did people learn things? Where did they go to find them? How far?" (163, ellipses in original). The reader might also wonder in what sense Joel "hears" the music Blennerhassett's wife plays on the violin ("At first he did not realize that he had heard the sounds of her song, the only thing he'd ever heard"). "Heard" by pain in his fingers, he knows the hearing from the silence that interrupts it: "Then all at once as she held the lifted bow still for a moment he gasped for breath at the interruption" (164). It seems that the deaf boy can "hear" because hearing consists in the registering of silence; his deafness is "hearing" in its pure state.

The gestural quality of the story's language makes for its haunting beauty; as I have noted, it also makes it difficult to decipher what is "happening" insofar as the line between literal and figural language is nearly impossible to trace. Is Joel deaf?[27] Are we to understand those moments in the story that seem to refer to his speaking or his comprehension as "merely" figurative?[28] (From the other side, Joel's muteness also joins something inherent in the plotting of those who apparently can speak. Watching the nocturnal scheming of Burr and Blennerhassett, Joel sees that "the breath of their speech was no simple thing like the candle's gleam between them. Joel saw them still only in profile, but he could see that the secret was endlessly complex, for in two nights it was apparent that it could never be all told" [158].) Joel's knowledge of Burr and Blennerhassett comes into being on its own; as in the current's motion and its recursive figuring of its own "motive force," the abyssal quality of the realization as if figures inception as such, and draws us back to the gestural quality of the story's language:

> It was while he was cleaning boots again that the identity of the men came to him all at once. Like part of his meditations, the names came into his mind. He ran out into the street with this knowledge rocking in his head . . . There was no one to inform him that the men were Aaron Burr and Harman Blennerhassett, but he knew. No one had pointed out to him any way that he might know which was which, but he knew that: it was Burr who had made the gesture. (158)

How Joel comes to know is not something one is permitted to ask: It is as if one were confronted, as with Joel's deafness itself, with the unspeaking grounds of the story. No one had pointed out to him any way that he might know. The sealed-in silence of Joel's ostensible "disability," like the room that is made an interior by the invading conspirators or the circle of lamplight in which they speak or the inscrutable inside of the scheme, broken in upon by its own working, provides the setting for the cryptic *ex nihilo* emergence of creation.

For that reason, the moment calls to mind a disorienting self-reflexivity in the story whereby many instances of figurative language seem to figure the story's own language, which makes the events of the story difficult to distinguish from the taking place of its language—a recursive structure that I suggest here is the story's rendering of the fathomless initiations, the abyssal temporalities, of the interval of queer becoming and inception. The mother's pointing to the mimosa tree, as if to point to the gesture of pointing itself, comes to mind, as does the density and recursivity of the story's figurative language. For example, if Joel, falling down at the story's end to weep for the parents he had not told goodbye, reenacts the falling of the frozen birds, these birds, recalling the frozen man carried from the tree at the beginning of the story, are also anticipated by frozen flower buds Burr picks up just before the end, as he stops to visit a woman on his way out of town:

> He saw him stop beside a tall camellia bush as solid as a tower and pick up one of the frozen buds which were shed all around it on the ground. For a moment he held it in the palm of his hand, and then he went on. Joel, following behind, did the same. He held the bud, and studied the burned edges of its fold by the pale half-light of the East. The bud came apart in his hand, its layers like small velvet shells, still iridescent, the shriveled flower inside. He held it tenderly and yet timidly, in a kind of shame, as though all disaster lay pitifully disclosed now to the eyes. (167)

The camellia bush, "solid as a tower," echoes the "tower" made by the condensing, frozen breath of speech ("whatever word it was") and thus seems another figure for the story's own language—which then, frozen in the bud, comes apart in his hand, the disclosure of all disaster. Strikingly, just before this description, Burr's interaction with the woman gives Joel a taste of sexual jealousy: "Joel felt a pain like a sting while she first merged with the dark figure and then drew back" (167). The moment echoes the gesture that led Joel to fall in love with Burr ("and made the dark wet cloak fall back"), as well as the sensation of "hearing" the sound of the violin: "Try as he might, he could not comprehend it, though it was so calculated. He had instead a sensation of pain, the ends of his fingers were stinging" (164). Several layers of involution seem, in turn, to become involved: the initiatory gesture that merges with the sense of exclusion and sexual jealousy; the "sting" that links hearing and desire; the figural link, made by the echo of birds and buds, between the story of sexual initiation and the story of the loss of his parents; and even the alliterative echo linking frozen buds and frozen birds (both fallen from the frozen trees, and as if frozen forms, moreover, of the live birds and blossoms of the mimosa-tree vision of his mother). Those falls, further, echo not only the framing of the story (with its "strange drugged fall of snow" [153]) but also the first appearance of Burr and Blennerhassett: waking in his room where "from the window a wild tossing illumination came, which he did not even identify at first as the falling of snow," Joel "found that at some moment outside his knowledge or consent two men had seemingly fallen from the clouds onto the two stools at his table" (156–7).

The falling down at the end thus echoes the *ex nihilo* creation at the story's heart, likewise encrypted in the beloved gesture (and let the dark wet cloak fall back), or in negative form, in a dog that, "felled" by McCaleb (155), teaches Joel the meaning of silence, and the link, across various contexts, is, as it were, gestural. The moment when the deaf boy "hears," like the scheme that is broken in upon, repeats the spatial and temporal relations as the scheming friends invade Joel's room: an inside (or a nested series of insides) is constituted through the violation that ruptures it, and a moment of inception comes into being by pointing to something prior. The layers of the story—different moments of figurative language; the story of Burr's plot and trial, and of his seduction of Joel; the story of the Indian raid and of Joel's loss of his parents; the question of inception and the question of desire—all seem, in various figurative relays, disorientingly to stand in for one another, and to enact what Leo Bersani calls "inaccurate replications," a micro- and macro-level registering of sameness that appears in a series of formal repetitions or rhymes.[29] In that hall of mirrors, language turns to gesture. There is no deciding between

Joel's love for Burr and his love for his parents; pointing to and enacting language as gesture, both signal fathomlessly beyond themselves to an abyssal moment of inception.

The effects of this self-reflexivity extend to the story's relation to historical reference, which likewise seems to merge, in disorienting ways, with the writing of the story itself: It is startling, and a little dizzying, to discover that an important book on the Aaron Burr conspiracy was published in 1903 by Walter Flavius McCaleb.[30] (In the broadest strokes, McCaleb takes issue with the canonical account by Henry Adams.[31] Where Adams sides with Jefferson, McCaleb sides with Burr.[32]) Reading both McCaleb and Adams, one is struck by the way the Burr conspiracy makes especially manifest the difficulties of writing history: The scheme is hard to track not only because the evidence is fragmentary and all the witnesses seem interested and compromised, but because, even when there is documentary evidence (in letters and journals), the specifics seem to change depending on whom Burr is (at any moment) soliciting for support. The lack of a clear metanarrative from which to coordinate the various versions may be part of the appeal for Welty's text. In any event, Old Man McCaleb plays a crucial role in the story—saving Joel and leading the survivors of the Indian raid to safety—and yet he remains a shadowy presence in the text, his character never being elaborated, and his significance for Joel in the town afterwards remaining mysterious. That this character, doubling the historian who traced the Burr conspiracy through "hitherto unused sources," might in some sense figure authorship and history, leads one to think that the history the story presents is inscrutable not because details are suppressed but because history itself comes to seem curiously groundless. It is as if the saving of Joel, and his initiation into the meaning of silence, were in some sense the writing of the history of the plot.

Why does Welty choose this obscure historical plot to work through questions about the inception of desire? Why the backdrop of this conspiracy for this redoubtable consideration of the interval of queer becoming? At the moment on the river, Joel seems to wonder something similar, and to ask, in oblique terms, about how to locate, within the abyssal temporality of the psyche, a moment of initiation. For Joel's psyche, and its opening up onto the world, doubles, but also in a paradoxical sense constitutes, the breaking of the scheme upon the very current of its working. I take the question to be whether any scheme tends by its nature to betray itself. In this context, moreover, "the very current of its working" might name, simply, talking. Burr's scheme is "broken upon by the very current of its working," ceases to be "secret" and "intact" because the scheme is spoken. The boy's witnessing is explicitly discounted as a possible source of anxiety; they know he cannot hear. Yet that witnessing also

seems to constitute the way the scheme is broken upon insofar as it makes visible nothing but the talking itself—the talking, that is, apart from the scheme,
apart from anything said. The obscure content of the scheme in this sense
really does not matter insofar as the content is, simply, its telling: the historical scheme, and, by extension, its quasi-parodic replaying of American conquest, becomes an instance of language as gesture.[33]

A hallucinatory moment in the story as if figures this transformation:
The flotilla that was to have consummated the plot (treasonous or not) is
sadly, and, for Joel, disorientingly, a diminished or deflated thing: "There
was no galley there. There were nine small flatboats tied to the shore. They
seemed so small and delicate that he was shocked and distressed, and looked
around at the faces of the others, who looked coolly back at him" (162). If
one perhaps hesitates for a moment about the deflation—whether it is an
effect of perspective (Joel is far away) or of diminished expectations (in this,
it is as if he came from the future, where we, too, might expect a storied plot
to come with more accouterments of recognizable grandeur)—the empirical sighting is dwarfed by its phantasmagorical anticipation, the much more
terrible sight that precedes it. This is the sight of the fallen trees that,
forming a flotilla that Joel initially mistakes for that of the rebels Burr is
thought to have incited, makes him feel "terror": "But then he saw that what
covered the river over was a chain of great perfect trees floating down, lying
on their sides in postures like slain giants and heroes of battle, black cedars
and stone-white sycamores, magnolias with their heavy leaves shining as if
they were in bloom, a long procession. Then it was terror that he felt" (162).
The river is, throughout the story, the hallucinatory stage of Joel's unconscious. Here, too, the fallen trees that mime—but dwarf—the actual rebellious flotilla are not just anxious anticipations of a hero's fall; they are also
ciphers, yet again, of the story's gestural language: the mimosa tree vision
turned to "mere" language ("leaves shining *as if* they were in bloom"), and
fallen, to join the fallen snow, the men fallen from the clouds, the fallen
frozen birds and buds, the boy fallen down to weep for his parents, to whom
he had not said goodbye, all as if writ large, and terribly, on the stage of personal
experience and history.

It is striking in this regard that the story signals the relation between his
love for Burr and the loss of his parents, among other ways, through an implicit parallel that turns on silence. First, we are told of "the day after his parents had left him, the day it had been necessary to hide from the Indians."
Old Man McCaleb leads the survivors into a dense cane break where Joel
learns the meaning of silence:[34]

There they crouched, and each one of them, man, woman, and child, had looked at all the others from a hiding place that seemed the least safe of all, watching in an eager wild instinct for any movement or betrayal. Crouched by his bush, Joel had cried; all his understanding would desert him suddenly and because he could not hear he could not see or touch or find a familiar thing in the world. He wept, and Old Man McCaleb first felled the excited dog with the blunt end of his axe, and then he turned a fierce face toward him and lifted the blade in the air, in a kind of ecstasy of protecting the silence they were keeping. Joel had made a sound. . . . He gasped and put his mouth quicker than thought against the earth. He took the leaves in his mouth. . . . In that long time of lying motionless with the men and women in the cane break he had learned what silence meant to other people. Through the danger he had felt acutely, even with horror, the nearness of his companions, speechless embrace of which he had had no warning, a powerful, crushing unity. (155, ellipses in original)

Later in the story, Joel replays the scene with Burr. If in the first scene, the danger creates "a powerful, crushing unity," a "speechless embrace," the second scene occurs after Joel's epiphanic discovery of how love isolates him: "But for lack of a way to tell how much was known, the boundaries would lie between him and the others, all the others, until he died" (165). Alone with Burr for the first time, Joel watches over the sleeping Burr, and love pares away even the words the boy has tried to guess: "He looked at the sleeping face of Burr, and the time and the place left him, and all that Burr had said that he had tried to guess left him too—he knew nothing in the world except the sleeping face" (164). Burr, who has lain down on the table where dead men are laid out, then begins to "toss his head and cry out":

Joel was afraid of these words, and afraid that eavesdroppers might listen to them. Whatever words they were, they were being taken by some force out of his dream. In horror, Joel put out his hand. He could never in his life have laid it across the mouth of Aaron Burr, but he thrust it into Burr's spread-out fingers. The fingers closed and did not yield; the clasp grew so fierce that it hurt his hand, but he saw that the words had stopped.

As if a silent love had showed him whatever new thing he would ever be able to learn, Joel had some wisdom in his fingers now which only this long month could have brought. He knew with what gentleness to hold the burning hand. With the gravity of his very soul he

> received the furious presence of this man's dream. At last Burr drew
> his arm back beside his quiet head. And his hand hung like a child's in
> sleep, released in oblivion. (165)

Lay your sleeping head, my love / Human on my faithless arm. Or: father, can't
you see I'm burning? In this remarkable displacement downward, a hand is
exchanged for a mouth. The consummation of Joel's desire not only replays
the disappearance of his parents; it also transforms the loss of meaning caused
by his deafness into something like gesture. Words are transformed to the pressure of a hand. The sexual consummation enacts, moreover, the seduction
that Joel found in Burr's "speaking face," and literalizes its beautiful, abstract
rendering of what it feels like to be in love: "Looking up from the floor at his
speaking face, Joel knew all at once some secret of temptation and an anguish that would reach out after it like a closing hand. He would allow Burr to
take him with him wherever it was that he meant to go" (159). Reaching out
"like a closing hand," the anguish is localized in a gesture that, a literalization, is also an embodied figure of speech—uniting, thereby, the story's narrative of emerging desire with the self-reflexive drama of its oracular language.
"Whatever words they were" shifts from the words he fails to understand to
the words whose meaning is suspended in this anguished yearning of a reaching out, and carries us back to the words of the story themselves, suspended,
along with the story's historical reference, in a language become gestural, in
the story's luminous images of sound become visible. That transformation
makes for the consummation, as it makes, perhaps, for the initiation, which,
having already occurred, is ever yet to come. The queerness of inception—
the interval in which we are all suspended to the degree that we cannot originate ourselves—is, for this story, that of writing as such, made visible in a deaf
boy's "first love."

PART II

Novels and the Beginnings of Character

3

Robinson Crusoe and the Inception of Speech

We live in an old chaos of the sun,
Or old dependency of day and night,
Or island solitude, unsponsored, free,
Of that wide water, inescapable.
—WALLACE STEVENS, "SUNDAY MORNING"

Islands are either from before or for after humankind. . . . Dreaming
of islands—whether with joy or in fear, it doesn't matter—is dreaming
of pulling away, of being already separate, far from any continent, of
being lost and alone—or it is dreaming of starting from scratch, recreat-
ing, beginning anew. Some islands drifted away from the continent,
but the island is also that toward which one drifts; other islands originated in the ocean, but the *island is also the origin*, radical and
absolute.
—GILLES DELEUZE, "DESERT ISLANDS"

In Jorge Luis Borges's 1943 story "The Secret Miracle," a writer condemned to
death by the Nazis is granted a year's reprieve in which to complete his play:
"He had asked God for an entire year in which to finish his work; God in His
omnipotence had granted him a year. God had performed for him a secret
miracle: the German bullet would kill him, at the determined hour, but in
Hladick's mind a year would pass between the order to fire and the discharge
of the rifles. From perplexity Hladik moved to stupor, from stupor to resignation, from resignation to sudden gratitude."[1] The suspended time of writing—
"the physical universe stopped" (161)—is tied here to life's "indefinite reprieve"

made definite, and one is then confronted with an allegory of writing.[2] The secret miracle allows writing to coincide with its vanishing; in this story, writing's origin merges with its end, and opens up on to a radical solitude. The play, completed, is completed for Hladik alone: "He completed his play; only a single epithet was left to be decided upon now. He found it; the drop of water rolled down his cheek. He began a maddened cry, and the fourfold volley felled him. Jaromir Hladik died on the twenty-ninth of March, at 9:02 A.M." (162).

"A boy or a man could be so alone in his heart that he could not even ask a question," writes Eudora Welty in "First Love";[3] the solitude in that story, I suggest in the previous chapter, marks a confrontation with a silence at the heart of speech, an originary zone named by gesture. The English novel—in some accounts of it—begins with a man in "solitary residence" (176) on an "island of solitariness" (191), with what Robinson Crusoe calls "a melancholy relation of a scene of silent life."[4] A novel of striving, of an adventure determined, as we are repeatedly told, by his perverse unwillingness to abide in his station in life, it is structured—however one reads the consequences for inwardness or psychology in the tradition of the novel, and in spite of the many ways that the text is about the structuring of social relations, most notably as they are underpinned by slavery—by this stripping away of "human society": "I whose only affliction was, that I seem'd banish'd from human society, that I was alone, circumscrib'd by the boundless ocean, cut off from mankind, and condemn'd to what I call'd silent life; that I was as one who Heaven thought not worthy to be number'd among the living, or to appear among the rest of his creatures" (152).

Robinson Crusoe might be an unlikely place to locate a beginning for the psychological novel—whose initiations are more obviously at home in the epistolary enthusiasms of Richardson's deprecated heroines, in Fielding's parody of them, or even, for that matter, in *Moll Flanders.*[5] There would be many ways to tell the story, but one is perhaps uncertain about causality: because the concern with interiority arises in tandem with other questions (female virtue and chastity above all), one is unsure which is initiating, the "formal" question of representation, or the social pressures it shapes and to which it responds. If one is struck, reading in the eighteenth- and nineteenth-century English novel, by the way that female virtue and chastity form an almost neutral—not unseen, of course, but formal—background to its aesthetic innovations (one thinks of the liturgy of the mass), the problem of virtue is, arguably, an epiphenomenon of a technical innovation in the representation of interiority. (Certainly in *Tom Jones*, as at moments in the Mozart-Da Ponte operas, one has the sense of creators who were playfully aware of the liturgical quality of the ideology, and therefore used it as a stable framework for the aesthetic innovations that interested them.) Without denying, of course, the various, often contradictory ideological investments in policing female desire and behavior, the question of virtue has, as it were, the virtue of making it necessary to represent consciousness. Fielding's innovation in *Shamela* is, among other things, to show the shaping power of perspective; to distinguish between Pamela and Shamela requires narrative intervention—a framing that can make visible the intentions behind the act. Clarissa Harlowe herself knows that it is only by her intentions that her actions can be distinguished as virtuous: "Tell me truly if your unforced heart does not despise me?—It must! For your mind and mine were ever *one*; and I despise *myself!*—and well I may: for could the giddiest and most inconsiderate girl in England have done worse than I shall appear to have done in the eye of the world?"[6] Once intention matters more than act, interiority arises so that behavior might be judged in light other than that of the "eye of the world." Interiority and motive are also thereby constituted as unseen, as lying beyond appearances.

Robinson Crusoe is, markedly, removed from any such privacies—except, of course, in the form of the island itself, where that interiority is as if exteriorized, projected outward as the ur-form of the social. "There are no sunsets and no sunrises," wrote Virginia Woolf of the text; "there is no solitude and no soul. There is, on the contrary, staring us full in the face, nothing but a large earthenware pot."[7] The humor derives, no doubt, not only from its rendering of Defoe's clumsy writing and construction, and, one supposes, from its highlighting of the crude faculties that workmanship may be understood to address (the pot is large and earthenware), but also from the suspended anthropomorphism: the "staring," that, albeit "full in the face," is pointedly not the "staring" of a conscious, much less an intelligent, face. That blank stare refuses any solicitation that we might want to put to it, and thus also thwarts identification, as it itself (qua pot) has an inside but no interiority.[8] Thus there is a long tradition of reading the novel in relation to material conditions; to find oneself gazing at "nothing but a large earthenware pot" could also describe one's experience of reading many of the novel's descendants in the realist tradition. I would suggest, however, that it is the almost formal quality of psychology in *Robinson Crusoe* that makes it promising for an investigation of psychological inception—the inception, that is, of the novel genre, and, in this novel, its understanding of the coming into being of psychology.

Woolf's provocative claim that there is no "solitude" in the novel must mean, among other things, that there is no consciousness there to register the experience of it. For it is striking how little the novel seems to be concerned, in fact, with inwardness, which seems to spring from a belated discovery of social needs—it, too, an empty form, like the footprint the marooned islander will find in the sand. If one might nevertheless see the novel as a beginning of the psychological novel, it is unlike other beginnings—in Richardson, for example, or in *Moll Flanders*—in its unconcern with psychological verisimilitude. "Other castaways in the past," notes Ian Watt, "including Defoe's main model, Alexander Selkirk, were reduced to an extremely primitive condition, and in the space of a few years. Harassed by fear, dogged by ecological degradation, they sank more and more to the level of animals: in some authentic cases they forgot the use of speech, went mad, or died of inanition."[9] To the degree that the novel is concerned with inwardness, it is concerned with its formal positing rather than with its content: At the origin of the English psychological novel, it is as if aware of itself as that origin, and seems less concerned with interiority than with the punctuation that produces it. Defoe's novel produces psychological interiority as a by-product of a formal rhythm: the stripping-away of social bonds is followed by the rebuilding of social institutions and is thus a necessary step in the retrospective imagining of their origin.

There would be various ways to render the novel's systolic-diastolic or centripetal-centrifugal rhythm, which is legible, page by page, in the non-homogenous time, the text's often unmarked movement among different time-scales, sometimes laboring for paragraphs over a few minutes or hours and sometimes skipping over years in less than a sentence. That rhythm might be taken as a marker of the text's rendering of the layered time of inception— its narrative of origin (which, paradoxically, precedes or produces that origin): Enacting Descartes's *Meditations* (leading us to the island as a figure for the solitary mind), the text produces an originary solitude by working backwards from bourgeois sociability, and outwards from the metropole, shipwrecking Crusoe (twice) in order to imagine the inception less, however, of knowledge (as in Descartes), than of civic society. (At the origin of the English novel, realism is hardly to be told from an allegory of inception.) That Crusoe does not in fact start from scratch also marks the novel's concern with what comes before this imagined inception—the island, and the wrecked ship, provides him, as others have pointed out, with an astonishing number of objects necessary for his survival. "Everything is taken from the ship. Nothing is invented," remarks Gilles Deleuze, who also adds that "one can hardly imagine a more boring novel";[10] this is, as he suggests, an imagining of the self-constitution of bourgeois order, with all its tedious proprieties and far from innocuous forms of oppression. ("Any healthy reader," Deleuze writes, "would dream of seeing Friday finally eat Robinson.")[11]

I would dwell, however, on the exorbitance of the self-constitution. The rhythm of diastole and systole can be felt in the text's strange redundancies, starting with the double shipwreck, and what look like structural lapses: most notably, the movement, early in the novel, between the journal and the nar-

rated text that contains it, a (at first sight) perplexing doubling of the narrative
voice. The unmarked seams where the journal is interrupted by the narrator,
who returns us, unexpectedly, to the journal (sometimes leading one to wonder when we left it), with intruding commentary on (and marked moments of
ellipsis in the rendering of) that journal, seem to split the narrative voice from
itself. As if a proto-form of the text, the journal both is and is not contained by
the narrative that both represents it and in some sense is it, blurring the line
between the narrating voice and the narrated character, and the temporal relation between events and their telling. Those blurrings are enacted when the
journal continues after Crusoe has run out of paper and ink, literalizing in
the text a curiously disembodied form of writing. The conceit is, of course,
that the novel is narrated after the rescue, but when that conceit then produces
multiple redundancies (where the same events are told, more—or often less—
consistently, and with various contrasts of contraction and dilation), the narrative's folding back on itself starts to seem the point. The plot, in this way,
seems at every moment to enact the structurally redundant return to the (always belated) staging of origination. Crusoe's return to the island at the end
of the text (to see how things are going in the state he founded) is another instance of such redundancy, and the (coherence-defying) adventure with
starving wolves in snowy Europe moves the island to Europe—and therefore
makes explicit, in a repetition that is also a formal rupture (and geographical
superimposition), the structure of the book, where the colonizing explorer
heads out to discover an island that stands in for an imagined origin of what
he left behind. My interest is not so much in the politico-historical narrative
that could be wrought from that as in its relation to the almost contentless psychology that appears as a cipher of psychological inception. Just as the sea
seems to invade the land, and, in that deterritorialized episode in Europe, the
trials of the New World to appear in the Old, the difficulty of perceiving the
boundary of the journal makes it hard to contain the present tense of solitude
that threatens to overtake the text as a whole.

It is striking that, unlike the real-life models who quickly went mad (from
a diet of raw tortoise, for example [Watt, 297]), Crusoe seems almost not to
feel isolation or loneliness until his twenty-third year on the island, when he
sees the shipwreck that he thinks is without survivors:

> I cannot explain, by any possible energy of words, what a strange
> longing or hankering of desires I felt in my soul upon this sight;
> breaking out sometimes thus; O that there had been but one or two;
> nay, or but one soul sav'd out of this ship, to have escap'd to me, that
> I might but have had one companion, one fellow-creature to have

> spoken to me, and to have convers'd with! In all the time of my solitary
> life, I never felt so earnest, so strong a desire after the society of my
> fellow-creatures, or so deep a regret at the want of it.
>
> There are some secret moving springs in the affections, which
> when they are set a going by some object in view, or be it some object,
> though not in view, yet render'd present to the mind by the power of
> imagination, that motion carries out the soul by its impetuosity to such
> violent eager embracings of the object, that the absence of it is
> insupportable. (183)

The word that the Crusoe of Elizabeth Bishop's "Crusoe in England" forgets
when he attempts to cite Wordsworth is *solitude*.[12] Curiously, Crusoe seems to
think that a desire for human company requires explanation (which isn't to say
that it does not); leaving that explanation to the "Naturalists," he says it was
"doubtless the effect of ardent wishes, and of strong Ideas form'd in my mind"
(184). (From the shipwreck, he finds only the corpse of a drowned boy—with
some money and a pipe in his pocket.) It is also striking that the object in view
(the ship) is not the one that sets the affections in motion; the ship, rather, embodies the absence of the instigating object. For the "object" of the soul's eager
embrace is not the ship but the human company it might have brought Crusoe.
The viewed shipwreck then becomes a figure for the imagination—instigating
because of what it does not deliver. The alternation between external and internal stimuli (between a desired object, on the one hand, and the imagination of
such an object, on the other) becomes indeterminate to the degree that the internal stimuli are made visible externally. And that indeterminacy is also a form
of self-reflexivity: The shipwreck he witnesses brings home to him his solitude in
part, one suspects, because it allows him to witness, belatedly, his own shipwreck, and to cognize his posthumous state on the island. Viewing a belated
figure for the origin of his marooned state calls into being the internal faculty
that imagines it, and crystalizes the desire for company he will have wanted all
along. By the middle of the nineteenth century, when David Copperfield witnesses, helplessly from the shore, the shipwreck in which both Steerforth and
Ham (trying to save him) perish, the moment seems an inherited set-piece in
the imagining of the origins of sympathy and moral responsibility; in *The Tempest*, Prospero stages such a shipwreck for Miranda and allows us to witness, as
if spontaneously, the faculty of sympathy called forth by the spectacle that she
herself knows to be staged. A hundred and thirty years before *David Copperfield*, Robinson Crusoe appears to play all the parts—victim and witness
alike—apparently dispensing with others in this generative social drama, and
producing sympathy in the once again echoing recursivity of his solitude.

Leaving aside the longing for escape that emerges, and his strange, repellent plan to effect it ("I made this conclusion, that my only way to go about an attempt for an escape, was, if possible, to get a savage into my possession" [194]), as well as the idyll with Friday that follows from it, I would stress the relation between solitude and a confrontation with writing—staged here as the outbreak of his soul's speech occasioned by the externalized view of his predicament: "O that there had been but one or two; nay, or but one soul sav'd out of this ship, to have escap'd to me, that I might but have had one companion, one fellow-creature to have spoken to me, and to have convers'd with!" (183). This is the longing of the solitary man in the text; as he says of the dog that kept him company for many years, "I only wanted to have him talk to me, but that he would not do" (61). The conversation that finally does arrive (though not with the dog) replays the redoubling of those early moments where the journal and the narrative overlap. "Particularly said I aloud, (tho' to my self)," he remarks (47) (and implicitly narrates the remark, to us, and later): that comment could gloss both the journal and the way that speech comes into being in the text. Again as if allegorizing quandaries of inception, the text repeatedly has Crusoe confront speech that turns out to be his own: as hallucination, dream, or, more literally, words that he has taught, first to the parrot and then to Friday.

For Rousseau in *Emilius et Sophia, Robinson Crusoe* "affords a complete treatise on natural history" and would, in his new system of education, be the first book (albeit "cleared of its rubbish") given to Emilius to read: "the most certain method for him to raise himself above vulgar prejudices and to form his judgment on the actual relations of things, is to take on himself the character of such a solitary adventurer, and to judge of every thing about him, as a man in such circumstances would, by its real utility."[13] For Coleridge, too, the text was formative: "The writer who makes me sympathise with his presentations with the *whole* of my being, . . . ; and again, he who makes me forget my *specific* class, character, and circumstances, raises me into the universal man. Now this is De Foe's excellence. You become a man while you read."[14] The appeal for Rousseau is no doubt the possibility of remaking the social from the ground up; in Coleridge, too, the formation imagined is a kind of reworking of social determinants, a "raising" into the "universal man," where the emphasis is perhaps less on becoming a *man* than on becoming *a* man.

The pedagogical interludes in *Robinson Crusoe* confront inception in another, related, way: in them, the text imagines the inception of human speech. Friday's learning of English is one of the drastically telescoped episodes in the novel. The new companions begin with an exchange of gestures remarkably immune from misunderstanding. Friday

made all the signs to me of subjection, servitude, and submission
imaginable, to let me know how, he would serve me as long as he liv'd;
I understood him in many things, and let him know, I was very pleas'd
with him; in a little time I began to speak to him, and teach him to
speak to me; and first, I made him know his name should be *Friday*,
which was the day I sav'd his life; I call'd him so for the memory of the
time; I likewise taught him to say *Master*, and I then let him know, that
was to be my Name; I likewise taught him to say, *Yes*, and *No*, and to
know the meaning of them . . . (201)

Characteristically, the novel returns to this instruction a few pages later, offering another highly telescoped account of Friday's education (which is then
followed by startlingly complex discussions—of the history of the warfare
among different "cannibal" groups, and of Crusoe and Friday's theological
debates):

I was greatly delighted with him, and made it my business to teach
him every thing that was proper to make him useful, handy, and
helpful; but especially to make him speak, and understand me when
I spake, and he was the aptest scholar that ever was, and particularly
was so merry, so constantly diligent, and so pleased, when he could
but understand me, or make me understand him, that it was very
pleasant to me to talk to him . . . (205)

Whatever one might say about Defoe's version of Caliban (Friday's profit on it
not knowing how to curse but, it seems, how to debate questions of divine providence), or about how it responds to the period's understanding of language
acquisition, the narrative telescoping does not consist only in the narrative
compression in these two moments. The doubling also returns us to the text's
tendency to produce redundant accounts of origin or inception, and they invoke other moments that point, in turn, to the self-grounding quality of inception in the text.[15]

The teaching of Friday recalls an earlier pedagogical scene:

all the while I was at work, I diverted myself with talking to my parrot,
and teaching him to speak, and I quickly learn'd him to know his own
name, and at last to speak it out pretty loud POLL, which was the first
word I ever heard spoken in the Island by any Mouth but my own. (116)

These words are only minimally (or perhaps only literally) spoken by any mouth
but his own, and indeed, later in the text, he is seemingly taken in by his own
ventriloquism:

But judge you, if you can, that read my story, what a surprise I must be in, when I was wak'd out of my sleep by a voice calling me by my name several times, *Robin, Robin, Robin Crusoe*, poor *Robin Crusoe*, where are you *Robin Crusoe*? Where are you? Where have you been?

I was so dead asleep at first, being fatigu'd with rowing, or paddling, as it is call'd, the first part of the day, and with walking the latter part, that I did not wake thoroughly, but dozing between sleeping and waking, thought I dream'd that some body spoke to me: But as the voice continued to repeat *Robin Crusoe, Robin Crusoe*, at last I began to wake more perfectly, and was at first dreadfully frighted, and stared up in the utmost consternation: But no sooner were my eyes open, but I saw my *Poll* sitting on the top of the hedge; and immediately knew that it was he that spoke to me; for just in such bemoaning language had I used to talk to him, and teaching him; and he had learn'd it so perfectly, that he would sit upon my finger, and lay his bill close to my face, and cry, *Poor* Robin Crusoe, *Where are you? Where have you been? How come you here?* And such things as I had taught him. . . . holding out my Hand, and calling him by his name *Poll*, the sociable creature came to me, and sat upon my thumb, as he used to do, and continu'd talking to me, *Poor* Robin Crusoe, and *how did I come here?* and *where had I been?* just as if he had been overjoy'd to see me again; and so I carry'd him home along with me. (138–9)

In the echoing back of Crusoe's own words in the voice of another, the quasi-allegorical dimensions are perhaps unavoidable; as with the episode with Friday later, such a moment seems to raise the question of how to move from "one" to "two" (or more), how to derive sociality or even communication from solitude—in terms that do not make the latter terms seem like delusion, hallucination, or solipsism. His "teaching" of Poll seems to consist in his talking to himself; Poll in this sense makes this difficulty, and the attendant self-reflexive return, a figure for the reader, speaking over Crusoe's words, uttered to himself. (The nickname might make those words Poll's own, or in any event anticipates an avian self-recognition—leading one to wonder, perhaps, which words are originary, "Robin's" or the parrot's. Or, likewise, then, those of Robin or of the reader who is figured in this exchange.) Among many other things, striking at the end of the passage is the knowing way in which the shipwrecked hero allows himself to be taken in: Hearing the bird speaking his own words of self-pity, "just *as if* he had been overjoy'd to see me again," Crusoe accepts the parrot's simulacrum of sociability ("and so I carry'd him home along with me"). The factitious, or in any event quasi-parodic, founding of sociality is no doubt figured here. In terms of character psychology, the moment says less about Crusoe's psychology than about character as such: It is as if the content of Crusoe's psychology simply were the self-grounding quality of its instantiation. ("Even though I knew it was the parrot," Crusoe remarks, "and that indeed it could be no body else, it was a good while before I could compose myself" [139].) The hallucinatory moment with the parrot figures that self-grounding, and the exteriorization of consciousness it establishes.

As is typical for the text, the episode is repeated in different form; later, Crusoe peers into a cave:

> looking farther into the place, and which was perfectly dark, I saw two broad shining eyes of some creature, whether devil or man I knew not, which twinkl'd like two stars, the dim light from the cave's mouth shining directly in and making the reflection . . . I had not gone three Steps in, but I was almost as much frighted as I was before; for I heard a very loud sigh, like that of a man in some pain and it was follow'd by a broken noise, *as if* of words half express'd, and then a deep sigh again. (172–3)

"Just *as if* he had been overjoy'd to see me" and "a broken noise, *as if* of words." Interiority or motivation and language are posited as counterfactuals. In the latter case, too, these "words" are those of an animal: "I saw lying on the ground a most monstrous frightful old he-goat, just making his will, as we say, and gasping for life, and dying indeed of meer old age" (173). The caprine mimicry of speech, like its psittacine anticipation, presses on the boundary between words and their likenesses; the point is perhaps less the loneliness that would lead one to mistake animal noises for speech than the uncertainty of that boundary—and the arbitrary fiat at the origin separating noise from significant speech. That fiat cannot be glimpsed from within human speech; hence, perhaps, the parrot and goat. The self-conscious turn to figurative language ("just making his will, as we say") intensifies the earlier likenesses ("like two stars . . . like that of a man in some pain"), and it resonates in multiple registers: comparing one sort of preparation for dying (writing a will) to another (experiencing, or confronting it), it also makes that movement between the social or linguistic and the biological or bodily into a figure for the writing of animal life. At the same time, then, the figure of an animal writing also draws one's attention to the way that the human, too, slides away from language at death ("the poet essentially can't be concerned with the act of dying," Henry James writes).[16] In the instance of the goat, one perceives that the ostensible irony cuts both ways, and the ventriloquism is equivocal, in more than one way; it is not, perhaps, the goat who strives toward a world of writing and speech that he cannot comprise so much as it is that written word that cannot grasp the goat (looking into his eyes, we find only what we say). In still other terms, the text also confronts an ungraspable moment of inception. The self-conscious positing of speech makes the animal noises here at once an intermediate stage in the text's bringing-into-being of language and yet another instance where such language can be glimpsed only as already having been brought into being—grasped not *ab ovo*, but only *in medias res*.

The "second part of *Robinson Crusoe*," wrote Charles Dickens, "is perfectly contemptible, in the glaring defect that it exhibits the man who was 30 years on that desert island with no visible effect made on his character by that experience."[17] In terms Dickens would not use, the static quality of character makes visible an unfathomable formation or inception—and in this is not unrelated to the text's confounding imaginings of the origination of speech. The self-grounding quality of these moments also lead one to recall that Friday's appearance, too, is anticipated, and anticipated by a dream:

> I dream'd, that as I was going out in the morning as usual from my castle, I saw upon the shore, two *canoes*, and eleven savages coming to land, and that they brought with them another savage, who they were going to kill, in order to eat him; when on a sudden, the savage that they were going to kill, jumpt away, and ran for his life; and I thought in my sleep, that he came running into my little thick grove, before my fortification, to hide himself; and that I seeing him alone, and not perceiving that the other sought him that way, show'd my self to him, and smiling upon him, encourag'd him; that he kneel'd down to me, seeming to pray me to assist him; upon which I shew'd my Ladder, made him go up, and carry'd him into my cave, and he became my servant. (193–4)

That dream then comes true ("now I expected that part of my Dream was coming to pass" [197], Crusoe remarks); once again, the text combines solipsism with an exteriorization of consciousness. The founding of psychology and the founding of sociality seem equally problematic insofar as they anticipate one another, in a topography confounding inside and out. When Friday first speaks to him—"he spoke some words to me, and tho' I could not understand them, yet I thought they were pleasant to hear, for they were the first sound of a man's voice that I had heard, *my own excepted*, for above twenty-five years" (199, emphasis in original)—one would not be wrong to emphasize the appropriation that immediately occurs: "this my savage, *for so I call him now*" (199, emphasis in original). At the same time, that appropriation makes manifest a more abyssal movement, where the confounding of times (the events and their narration "now") is caught up in the difficulty of distinguishing projection from internalization, appropriation from expropriation. The text moves from one such moment to the next, and Friday's appearance is at once an impinging on Crusoe's unsponsored island solitude by an outside world and yet another form of projection or extension outward, extending circles that as if repeat each other: mind, house, fortification, island, and so on.

This is the context in which I would read the text's most famous moment, what Nigel Dennis calls "the most magical of all moments in fiction":[18]

> It happen'd one day about noon going towards my boat, I was exceedingly surpris'd with the print of a man's naked foot on the shore, which was very plain to be seen in the sand: I stood like one thunderstruck, or as if I had seen an apparition; I listen'd, I look'd round me, I could hear nothing, nor see any thing, I went up to a rising ground to look farther, I went up the shore and down the shore, but it was all one, I could see no other impression but that one, I went to it again to see if there were any more, and to observe if it might not be my fancy; but there was no room for that, for there was exactly the very print of a foot, toes, heel, and every part of a foot; how it came thither, I knew not, nor could in the least imagine. But after innumerable fluttering thoughts, like a man perfectly confus'd and out of myself, I came home to my fortification, not feeling, as we say, the ground I went on, but terrify'd to the last degree, looking behind me at every two or three steps, mistaking every bush and tree, and fancying every stump at a distance to be a man; nor is it possible to describe how many various shapes affrighted imagination represented things to me in, how many wild ideas were found every moment in my fancy, and what strange unaccountable whimsies came into my thoughts by the way. (149–50)

The footprint literalizes an "impression"—externalizes and renders palpable the impinging of the external world on the mind—and thereby at once produces a hallucination and dematerializes it: an "apparition," and, moreover, one it is only "as if" he had seen. That hallucinated sight then confounds the senses: "I listen'd, I look'd round me, I could hear nothing, nor see any thing." The welter of confused thoughts that follows describes Crusoe's panic at the threat another person might pose; it also repeats an initiatory moment of consciousness—imagination, fancy, and whimsy startled into action by the outside world. That quasi-psychological drama quickly becomes a social one. Crusoe will return to the print to measure it against his own foot; his thought that the footprint could be his own is not ratified, at least on the level of plot. In other ways, it feels as if the print were indeed his, which has a lot to do,

I think, with the moment's iconic status: Dennis's characterization of the moment as "magical" seems literally true, and the initiating moment of a condensed drama of social formation resembles magic. Seeming almost Crusoe's willful projection, it is also the moment where he registers, helplessly, the impingement of the world on his solitary consciousness. He cycles rapidly through a series of possible reactions to the existence of other people (agonism, self-destruction, flight and hiding, and then various forms of government, as if deducing the social from among other possibilities) before he is led to Friday—and, in an increasingly rapid exfoliation in the text, to the "founding" of a social order. The progression seems indubitable in the text (this moment is initiatory), even if the logic is far from clear. It seems, however, to follow from the externalized representation of an "impression" and the awakening of the fancy it catalyzes.

The Miltonic echoes of "thunderstruck" invoke the sense of being called to oneself, as Milton's rebellious angels are when, driven "thunderstruck" into "the wasteful deep" (VI:858, 862), they find themselves "astonished" (I:266) on the floor of the hell (astonished does not mean, as one might expect, "turned to stone"; it means, rather, "thunderstruck").[19] The hallucinatory image for Crusoe's own solitude, the footprint becomes the catalyst for the social world founded on the island. Like the dream-come-true of Friday, or the pitying words of Poll, the footprint at once bodies forth Crusoe's fears and embodies his psychological particularity as empty, as pure form. (That logic, as Hugh Kenner notes, implies a supplement: "He is to assume that the system of reality accessible to him contains one more man than he had previously surmised.")[20] The moment's power no doubt derives from its minimalism: a minimal sign of human presence (being just enough to be human), it registers an absence (where a foot was but is no longer). A single print, it does not describe motion (a gait, for instance, or tracks in a certain direction), and it shows neither motive nor history. It is as if Crusoe encounters his own initiating force in this minimal sign of human presence. Its ex nihilo appearance figures the self-generating quality of Crusoe's character and the world he inhabits, both within the novel and within the history of the genre to which (for some) it gives birth.

That *causa sui* fantasy is not an innocent one, of course; it would not be difficult to show, as indeed others have done, that the novel explicitly joins a Cartesian claim of epistemological self-sufficiency to a narrative justification for colonialism and slavery—thereby obscuring the contingent historical forces at work by casting them as inevitable, and sanctifying those historical outcomes by subordinating them to movement in which cognitive self-mastery extends outward to exert various forms of control over the world. (I am not certain that

I would share such a view—of Descartes, or of Defoe.) One might show, like-wise, the ways that the novel demystifies that link, exposing the ideological dimensions of an ostensibly neutral cognitive exercise. Here, however, I am more interested in the way that the alternatives seem undecidable in part because of the purely formal quality of the novel's figuring of inception, its staging of the emergence of character and psychology in solitude. If Crusoe encounters his own agency in that solitary footprint, it appears in a terrifyingly alienated, externalized, and blank form, where imperial power is hardly to be distinguished from helplessness.

The "scene of silent life" disappears into the social world founded by the protagonist's projection of voice; that world appears to be constituted by poor Robin's talking to himself—once again figuring, like the journal that doubles the narrative voice, the self-constitution, but also therefore the groundlessness, of this first-person text. The silence of that scene of silent life thus also dis-appears into the silence founding the text, the unfathomable moment of in-ception. Such is one way to understand the reading of *Robinson Crusoe* in J. M. Coetzee's *Foe* and its dual movement—toward, on the one hand, the silence of Friday, available to us only through Crusoe, and, on the other, toward a mise-en-abîme of writing. When, late in the novel, Foe speaks of the relation between silence and speech, one wonders, therefore, whether or not his terms are compensatory and redemptive, what it means, in other terms, to "speak" an unspoken word: "In every story there is a silence, some sight concealed, some word unspoken, I believe. Till we have spoken the unspoken we have not come to the heart of the story. I ask: Why was Friday drawn into such deadly peril, given that life on the island was without peril, and then saved."[21]

In one possible answer, to speak the word is to make what was unspoken spoken; Friday's experience becomes a story, and we find that it is the slave ship where his companions, and it may be his family, are entombed that he commemorates with flowers when Susan Barton sees him row out into the sea on a log. ("We must make Friday's silence speak, as well as the silence sur-rounding Friday" [142].) Naming the beginning or source might, in this model, be a form of compensation or healing. For Susan, at least initially, writing is, it seems, compensatory, offering the possibility of liberating Friday by reveal-ing his experience in language: "So, watching his hand grip the spade, watch-ing his eyes, I seek the first sign that he comprehends what I am attempting: . . . to build a bridge of words over which, when one day it is grown sturdy enough, he may cross to the time before Cruso, the time before he lost his tongue, when he lived immersed in the prattle of words as unthinking as a fish in water; from where he may by steps return, as far as he is able, to the world of words in which you, Mr Foe, and I, and other people live" (60). And she explains this to Friday (in words he may or may not understand) by way of a "similitude": "I say the desire for answering speech is like the desire for the embrace of, the embrace by, another being" (80). In this analogy, then, to speak, and to give words to silence, is to find a connection with others. This connection she ostensibly experiences with Foe when he kisses her, and she kisses him back—linking the mutual embrace of bodies and the speaking of silence.

In another version, however, it is in Friday that the silence "speaks," or bodies forth a resistance to its rendering in words, a story that is never verified, an experience that is never told—as figured by the mouth from which Susan looked away in terror but that returns in the crossing of eye and mouth in her discussion with Foe (Foe: "I said the heart of the story, . . . but I should have said the eye, the eye of the story. Friday rows his log of wood across the dark pupil—or the dead socket—of an eye staring up at him from the floor of the sea . . . To us he leaves the task of descending into that eye" [141]; Susan: "Or like a mouth . . . It is for us to open Friday's mouth and hear what it holds: silence, perhaps, or a roar, like the roar of a seashell held to the ear" [141–2]). When Friday appears at the end of the book, dressed in Foe's garments, wearing his wig, and holding his quill, dripping with ink (151), the appropriation of his life (predictable in a postcolonial rewriting of Defoe) merges with something unfathomable at the heart of writing, and his immersion in the "prattle of words" becomes something more like the imagined dive into the wreck, and into the historical grounds of the text, that never occurs: "But this is not a place of words. Each syllable, as it comes out, is caught and filled with water and diffused. This is a place where bodies are their own signs. It is the home of Friday" (157).

What does it mean for bodies to be their own signs? If bodies are their own signs, do they speak, or do they vanish into unfathomable silence? Speech as communion and sociality as the radical erasure of the subject: that alternation Jean-Claude Milner describes, in "Être Seul," in terms of the mathematical alternation of zero and one.[22] In his reading of the fort/da game of *Beyond the Pleasure Principle*, solitude is there, at the origin of speech. For Freud, he suggests, "The speaking being within the child depends on his solitude—not on a presence. To make it understood that the speaking being is alone from the moment he speaks, Freud shows that he speaks when, and because, he is alone. Wittgenstein, who argued that there is no private language, is refuted; Freud argues instead that there is nothing but private language" (147). The multiplicity that—in Milner's account of the relation of one to a multiplicity or a series—makes solitude impossible here enters into a structure of alternation, an alternation of mutual reciprocal annihilation that initially seems to constitute the drama of speech. "Two" as the instance of multiplicity becomes an alternation of one and zero, but what was an external agonism becomes the structure of the subject's relation to speech: "*Two* was the first of the numbers, according to the Greeks. Now, Freud didn't start out from *two*, but he engenders it from the one of solitude. Still more precisely, he engenders it starting out from *one* and *zero* [*il l'engendre à partir du un et du zero*], the *one* of the child left to itself and the zero of disappearances: that of the mother, that of the spool, that of the child itself" (147). The child takes in to itself those disappearances in its own emergence into speech. The alternation of mutual reciprocal annihilation is internalized, and becomes "the child's own annulling of itself" (*l'annulation de l'enfant par lui-même*") (148). Solitude thus becomes the cipher for the division of the subject as a speaking being:

> *Two*, recurrent through the course of the game, is neither more nor less than the interaction of a one and a zero. Is it a matter of *two* as a specific and distinct number? Rather, one here recognizes instead the minimal index of a teeming multiplicity. This multiplicity articulates itself with solitude in the form of indefinite alternation [*s'articule à la solitude dans la forme de l'alternance indéfinie*]. The alternation rests on the exchange between the positions of presence and absence. Child, spool, mother, phonemes, couplings abound; there are always two partners, but the child, as partner, never meets anything other than the absence of the other partner, with the result that *two* negates itself at the very moment of its constitution. From *zero* and *one*, *two* does not emerge as a realized number, but as emblem of the unlimited [*emblème de l'illimité*]. In the reciprocal alternation of absence and presence is located the cause: an impossible simultaneity—until, at the final stage, the child gives up being simultaneous with itself. The discovery by a speaking being of his being as a speaking being and the discovery of the incompossibility of self and itself are one and the same discovery. [*La découverte par un être parlant de son être d'être parlant et la découverte de l'incompossible de soi à soi font une seule et même découverte.*] (148)

Here is solitude, perhaps, without the "one"; this is a solitude of self-division, the paradoxical solitude of the speaking being.

Robinson Crusoe presents a myth of the origins of sociality—generates the social through the retrospective imagining of its destruction and rebirth. All the ways in which that isn't, somehow, a psychological drama, are legible in its exteriorized realism: the large earthenware pot that we are left gazing at, in lieu of a consciousness that would register the difference that solitude makes. To form the question in terms of such an opposition, Milner might be read as suggesting, belongs to the realm of the imaginary. (This would be the vision, too, underlying the idea that Susan Barton seems to posit in Coetzee's *Foe*, that the alienation depicted could be remediated by touch—remediated, pace Lacan, by a sexual relation.) In place of this imaginary alternation, Milner posits writing—allegorized in Blanchot's "The Death of the Last Writer," and acted out by the enfant in Freud's game of *fort/da*; writing, thus conceived, uncovers the essential solitude of the speaking being.[23] After the death of the last writer, Milner writes of Blanchot's text, there will be not silence but "murmur": "the writer, according to Blanchot, covers over this murmur. The writer's language prevails; or at least such is its design. It prevails no doubt because it feigns a semblance of order, because it makes the murmur, disordered in itself, appear to be rhythmical—just as drops of water, though governed by chance, come, with the rhythms of the sea prevailing, to organize themselves in waves and in sonorities [*Comme il arrive des gouttes d'eau, gouvernées par le hassard et qui pourtant, les rythmes de la mer l'emportant, s'organisent en vagues et en sonorités*]" (131).

At the end of the essay, Milner returns to Blanchot's "myth" of the last writer—"a name," Milner says, "for the speaking subject" (151)—who was caught up in a drama of alternating presence and absence. In Milner's narrating of this Blanchotian "allegory," ceasing to speak, one found one's place taken by another. Each speaker annulled the other in turn; this speaking being "was the only one to speak (speaking, was alone), for the first and last time [*il était seul à parler, pour la première et la dernière fois*]":

> As soon as he stopped, he heard the murmur; Blanchot thus desig-
> nates, unwittingly or unknowingly, the brute fact of the multiplicity
> of speaking beings. Now this murmuring annuls me, if ever I cease
> speaking. Or rather it would annul me, were I not dreaming of solitude
> [*si je ne rêvais pas la solitude*]. For solitude is the dream of someone who
> is not the only one to be alone [*qui n'est pas seul à être seul*]. Someone
> who, for that reason, is alone [*seul*] only when he speaks, because being
> alone [*être seul*] is only possible for a speaking being. Provided that, in
> speaking, he does not impose on himself the suspension of his own
> speaking. [*Encore faut-il que, parlant, il ne s'impose pas à lui-même le
> suspens de son propre parler.*] (151)

The alternation between annulment and multiplicity is thus the ground for articulating a paradoxical relation between the speaking subject and the social world of speech. "Constantly," writes Milner, "the speaking being speaks as if non-speakers (what I call things [*choses*]) spoke through his mouth. Or as if the murmur carried him away [*l'emportait*] from within his own speech. The murmur is others—others, transmuted into things" (151). This transmuting of others into things—which Milner here explicitly connects to what he elsewhere calls *la politique des choses*[24]—marks an agonistic relation characteristic of the imaginary. Other as image or thing: the mythology of solitude attempts to escape this structure through a myth or narrative that makes a decision of solitude. Evoking Rimbaud and Flaubert, Milner suggests, again, that this alterity is internal to the speaking subject: "Others and things: both are me. [*Les autres et les choses, c'est moi.*][25] Me, consumed by the murmur. The murmur that annuls me: I lose myself there by forming (asserting) myself as one [*Le murmure que m'annule, je m'y perds en m'affirmant comme un*]" (151–2).

Thus the writer rejects this form of self-assertion, and writing confronts an inception that is that of the subject's relation to speech:

> I have maintained that Blanchot, believing that he spoke of the last writer, spoke allegorically of every speaking being to the extent that he is and he speaks [*en tant qu'il est et qu'il parle*]. By a final withdrawal, joining so many others, I would argue that Blanchot, speaking of the speaking being, nevertheless also speaks of the writer. The experience (or experiment/practice) of the writer attests that the speaking being is possible [*L'écrivain attest, par l'experiénce, qu'être parlant, c'est possible*], if only for an instant—always suspended, but also always resumed. For the last writer is always also the first, and the only one [*le seul*], and alone [*seul*]. Like every speaking being. (152)

The solitude of the speaking being is thus, in a sense, the ground of his speaking, and is prior to any subjective "decision" or relation. We are marooned by the very faculty of speech that would ostensibly allow us to address another or others. From this solitude, Milner derives a paradoxical form of community. We have it, paradoxically, in common, that we are each of us alone: Such would seem to be the consolation for speaking subjects, who, replaying this originary solitude at the heart of speech, embody a suspended "one" between the zero and the many.

Early in Coetzee's *Foe*, Susan asks whether it is the fate of all storytellers to become "a body without substance": "Return to me the substance I have lost, Mr Foe: that is my entreaty" (51). The writer who becomes nothing but voice merges with Friday, who is voiceless, and for the body to become its own sign, the novel suggests, is less the transcending of the material means of communication than an encounter with it. It is an encounter, therefore, with the originary beyond which Borges's Hladik, for his suspended moment, might be said to live and which Welty's "First Love" explores through gesture and James encounters in revision—or which Defoe figures in the echoing words of a parrot, in the word-like exhalations of a dying goat, and in an empty footprint left in the sand.

4

The Clock Finger at Nought

Daniel Deronda and the Positing of Perspective

The first chapter of Book One ("The Spoiled Child") of *Daniel Deronda* begins with an epigraph:

> Man can do nothing without the make-believe of a beginning. Even
> Science, the strict measurer, is obliged to start with a make-believe
> unit, and must fix on a point in the stars' unceasing journey when his
> sidereal clock shall pretend that time is at Nought. His less accurate
> grandmother Poetry has always been understood to start in the middle;
> but on reflection it appears that her proceeding is not very different
> from his; since Science, too, reckons backwards as well as forwards,
> divides his unit into billions, and with his clock-finger at Nought really
> sets off *in medias res*. No retrospect will take us to the true beginning;
> and whether our prologue be in heaven or on earth, it is but a fraction
> of that all-presupposing fact with which our story sets out.[1]

The epigraph immediately raises the question of foundation: "the make-believe of a beginning" is at once the make-believe that there is a beginning and the make-believe that constitutes a beginning. It is itself the foundation that eludes it; its fiat, self-grounding and groundless. In question, then, is perhaps the logic of that claim, what can be thus be founded (given that logic), and the analogy (between science and poetry). Gesturing toward its own institution, the novel locates its inception as one in a series of potentially limitless instances of human activity (or what man can "do"); science would seem to be exemplary ("Even science . . .") in its freedom from constraint and its proximity to reality (it is more "accurate" than poetry), yet it, too, requires an anchor that turns out to be a form of human positing. The turn to measurement suggests that there is no beginning because one's cognition of it renders it inaccessible, because one cannot transcend the terms by which one would apprehend it. One moves, in other words, from the "make-believe of a beginning" to "a make-believe unit"; science (understood as a kind of empiricism)[2] is unable to comprise the grounds of its own possibility—the parallel terms suggest that the unit of measurement is science's beginning, and that its units can be only arbitrarily determined. (Every unit of measurement is arbitrary, even, or especially, when its basis is the human form—foot or fathom or finger's breadth [the latter also a "digit" or "dactyl"];[3] what observation cannot comprise is an exteriorized view of the whole whose boundedness makes observation possible, and which could then anchor the posited units.)[4]

Yet this seeming incapacity turns out to be foundational. Scientific rigor would in these terms be founded not on that posited global view, but on the very arbitrariness of its units. Science thus needs the "make-believe of a beginning"—not some specified relation to reality—to found its rigor; from this angle, too, it is formal rather than referential, and belongs to the realm of human making. (The sidereal clock does allow us to find objects in the sky even though it does not allow us to occupy an external perspective.) These quandaries of beginning might be read to suggest that cognition is a form and that "man" cannot escape his own cognition. Even if one might reach the grounds of that cognition, the beginning as such would elude one in the very perspective from which one grasped it. Yet that very illusiveness turns out to be foundational: the system of knowledge would seem to be founded on that blind spot. Realism, Eliot might be read to suggest, follows science in intensifying rather than transcending the predicament of inception. *Daniel Deronda* perhaps makes explicit that which structures *Middlemarch*, too, and might be read as wagering on the foundational power of this "make-believe" beginning, on the possibility of grounding knowledge on an arbitrarily determined unit—or, in the perhaps more familiar terms of "sympathy," of founding some form of global knowledge on multiple self-limiting perspectives.[5]

Implicitly, too, at stake here is not just the grounding of a form of knowledge but also the establishing of a text, and the fact that these statements appear in an epigraph is also, in itself, significant. *Epigraph* means to "write upon."[6] Literally, it is an inscription, and it originally referred to the inscriptions on buildings, tombs, and coins (*OED*). (While the word appears from the early seventeenth century as an imprint on a title page or a superscription on a book, the first attested use [in the *OED*] in its narrower modern acceptation is 1844, in Elizabeth Barrett Browning's *Sonnets from the Portuguese*.)[7] The word thus bears a not coincidental (I think) relation to the bestowal of *form* on literary objects: A book or essay becomes something with an outside upon which words or a motto can be inscribed—and therefore, by the same token, takes on an interior as well.[8] (Or rather, the epigraph figures it as such a structure with an outside.) The function of the epigraph—as a claim of authority, or an implicit guide for reading, or even as a complex form of ornament—marks in various other ways, too, the threshold of the text.[9] Genette includes epigraphs in the "paratext," along with prefaces, forewords, and other parts of the "apparatus" of a book (including the author's name);[10] Eliot's idiosyncratic practice of (often, though not always) composing her own epigraphs scrambles such distinctions, and makes it more problematic than is even usually the case to decide whether her epigraphs belong "inside" or "outside" the text.[11] Proliferating within a text (as they do in Eliot), they produce a series of bounded wholes (chapters, for example) even as the interpretative commerce (whatever one does with them) crosses (perhaps uncomfortably) the very boundaries thus established (all the more so in the case of Eliot). Her epigraphs also compound problems of authority and context raised by any epigraph taken from another text: a gesture of deference, the citation is also an appropriation, and truncated quotation dramatizes a difficulty of circumscribing the limit where an original text's meaning ceases to be relevant for the text at hand—or, on the contrary, retains its meaning, independent, that is, of the text to which it serves as a truncated motto.

An arbitrary gesture of delimitation is perhaps necessary before reading can begin. In her composing of her own epigraphs, it is as if Eliot sought to comprise that gesture. Her words serve as their own authority (even if, abyssally, that self-constituting authority contains an oblique citation of another's—Goethe's *Faust*, where the prologue of Part I is "in heaven" and, of Part II, "on earth").[12] If their formal function (outside of any specific, local question of interpretation) is to mark the threshold of the text—and thus to place the text in relation to an outside world (of other texts, of authority or its appropriation, of a larger world), Eliot's composition of her own epigraphs offers an allegory of realism that hyperbolizes the author's reach even as it diminishes it: On the one hand, it is perhaps characteristic (for Eliot) claim of narrative authority, asserting that there is no outside to the text (just as there is no other author to cite), that the author has composed it all. On the other hand, that very omnipresence also means that the text can *never* reach its outside—exceeding itself, it finds only itself, and it achieves merely the figuration of an external world. Raising questions that are prior to the interpretation of any text, that combination of omnipresent reach and impotent introversion, Eliot's epigraph suggests, founds the possibility of the text, and of interpreting it.

The claims of the epigraph prove to be as complex to chart as these protoformal dimensions of the epigraph itself. The analogies are difficult to paraphrase and emerge out of a dizzying series of crossings, which take shape as repeated forms. (These crossings are restatements of, and destabilizing puns on, the phrase "on reflection.") Science must begin as its less accurate grandmother does, *in medias res*; its placing of its clock-finger on "Nought" is, like the opening of a text, an arbitrary and founding limit from which to begin. By choosing a "clock," Eliot figures the figure's own self-reflexivity: The sidereal clock is at once a functioning system of measurement and the mechanism for "starting" that system. The clock, moreover, represents linear time (from beginning to end) by a circular movement; in this image, then, the measuring system repeatedly comes back to its own moment of foundation—thus figuring the repeated self-instantiation of the system itself. Linking science and poetry in a relation (poetry, the grandmother of science) throws in still another form of temporal relation, a mediated genetic transmission. The clock is also an abstract image superimposed on a flux of sense data, and thus figures cognition in its making sense of the world; science "measures" the world as time moves by on the face of a clock—so that, in turn, science's reckoning of its own grounds can be figured as a movement in time ("reckons backward as well as forward"). Moving backward (along a visual circuit that, in turn, represents time) can be equated with a moving toward a foundation; implicitly, too, such a correlation makes it possible for a synchronic image to comprise the diachronic, and for the diachronic to be read "back" from that image. The image forms another sort of unification as well, insofar as the stars viewed as the repository of transcendent (or one might say poetic) meaning ("heaven") are also the stars that are the object, par excellence, of scientific measurement. A "true" beginning is then implicitly rendered a whole—such that any arbitrary marking of "Nought" can become a "fraction" of that "all-presupposing fact with which our story sets out"; the space on the clock-dial represents a whole of which the starting point is a fraction. Thus does the clock in a sense comprise its own insufficiency—the whole of the clock face represents the whole of which, by representing it, it is only a fraction, while the fraction of the clock face that stands in for its "beginning" represents, in turn, that insufficiency or partialness, thus implying (but only implying) a whole that might comprise it. Finally, the unusual syntax of "all-presupposing fact" (one might expect "presupposing" to preface a necessary condition, and the syntax here appears to suggest that the fact itself is doing the presupposing, of an "all") leaves one in some doubt about where to locate the necessary presupposition. The various ways that all these relations both can and cannot be mapped, in turn, onto each other likewise figure the quandaries of inception. One finds, at various "levels," a repetition of the same difficulty, which is that of trying to comprise, in an image, two different forms or motions—which means that the interpretive problem of understanding the figural relays among the different moments in the passage repeats the quandary that each, individually, poses, even as that very repetition unsettles the hierarchy that would stabilize the meaning.[13]

The question of foundation is more than a general question of fiction or realism, for at play here, too, are questions of perspective that will be central to the novel. If there is a governing image, it is the sidereal clock.[14] That figure collocates a series of different relations, some of which we have begun to note already. A sidereal clock allows one to locate celestial objects because it coordinates two different movements: the rotation of the earth on its axis and its revolution around the sun (for that reason, it is about four minutes off from solar time, which considers only the rotation of the earth on its axis). In so doing, it also marks a reversal of perspective: The earth's movement appears as the movement of the stars. That apparently seamless motion, oriented around a pole star, in fact encrypts the coordination of two movements that might be said, abstractly, to mirror one another, on different scales and on different planes. The arbitrary founding of a whole that can then be made an object of knowledge is thus figured by a mechanism that allows one to deduce one's own movement from the observed movement of external objects. The arbitrary marking of "Nought," which attempts to figure or grasp the *nihilum* of creation *ex nihilo*, thus discloses a reckoning of movements that are not otherwise visible in themselves (as one gazes at the stars), and they allow one to calculate time (and make it visible) in the artificially established "units" of celestial bodies viewed according to the image of a clock. (The "clock" isn't the stars but an abstract grid placed over them that allows one to locate celestial objects in the sky—at a particular time, and from a particular place on earth.) The image of the sidereal clock also makes visible another sort of collocation: the "beginning" of logical priority (the grounding of "Science" as a system of measurement) with the "beginning" of temporal sequence. The image thus raises the hope that one could reach the former by reckoning "backwards as well as forwards" through time.

One highly abstract way to render the drama of *Daniel Deronda* would be to say that it involves treating questions of foundation as questions of perspective. Another complexity of the epigraph, then, is its figuring of the novel's structure, the two centers organizing the sidereal clock recalling the larger narrative structure of *Daniel Deronda*: the famously unstable organization around two centers (Gwendolen and Daniel) corresponding to the earth and sun, and the gradual shift from Gwendolen to Daniel, to a shift from a geocentric to a heliocentric solar system.[15] After the epigraph, we read the novel's famous opening:

> Was she beautiful or not beautiful? and what was the secret of form
> or expression which gave the dynamic quality to her glance? Was the
> good or the evil genius dominant in those beams? Probably the evil;
> else why was the effect that of unrest rather than of undisturbed
> charm? Why was the wish to look again felt as coercion and not as a
> longing which the whole being consents?
>
> She who raised these questions in Daniel Deronda's mind was
> occupied in gambling. (3)

I will not add to the voluminous commentary on these lines except to note that the locus of perspective is given only in the second paragraph—when the questions formulated at the beginning are retrospectively ascribed to Daniel Deronda's consciousness.[16] A novel largely about the determining power of perspective leaves its own initial perspective undetermined until a paragraph after it has begun—enacting, in prose, what Brodsky says about meter and the *second* line. What pulls one up there, it seems to me, is the sudden, retrospective attribution to a character of what initially seemed to be omniscient narration (posing questions that, retrospectively, are perhaps odd for a narrator to pose but which perhaps don't register that way until the second paragraph anchors them in a perceiving consciousness).

For Andrew H. Miller this opening is emblematic of certain potentialities in free indirect style and marks the novel's hesitant movement toward its own beginning:

> What indeed is the secret form or expression that gives dynamic quality
> to her glance—to Gwendolen's, to Eliot's? What makes her exemplary?
> Here, at least, it is the secret of free indirect discourse, which invites us to
> glance again, to find a perspective accommodating of our whole being,
> flesh and blood, even as it audaciously delays providing the reader with
> any understanding of the status and origins of the words we read. Are
> these questions—questions that suspend the present tense as they unfold,
> ward off both the arrival of past-tense narration and the passing of
> represented time itself—are these questions raised by the narrator or by a
> character as yet unknown to us? The wheel is spinning, and the ball,
> even, has been dropped, but all possibilities, red and black, remain: all the
> novel's numbers are still open. Beginning, *Deronda* defers its beginning, as
> if to ask again what it is to begin, but also to ask before whatever beginning
> it achieves, a coeval question: Who—or what—speaks these questions?[17]

The mobile play between narration and character—its indeterminacy of perspective—makes the question of beginning "coeval" with that of the question of who speaks. Explicitly, therefore, the novel's opening presents us with the coming-into-being of narration, perspective, character (as viewed, as viewing), and of a reader's view (performatively taken up by Miller in his knowing miming of the novel's own opening gestures).

The opening evokes omniscient narration because it behaves like stage-setting or an offering up for view the character we then expect to be the novel's protagonist (even as the title makes us think otherwise). Her displacement by Deronda at the beginning of the second paragraph drives a wedge between characters as they are seen and characters as they are seen through—or in other terms as objects and subjects of perception. There would be any number of ways to read the consequences of the retrospective structure of this displacement: The proximity to the epigraph leads one to imagine that the narrative posits Deronda as a way to place its clock finger at Nought. The obvious object of novelistic attention in this opening—Gwendolen, beautiful or not, whose ambiguous charms clearly recall the more hermeneutically stable beauty of Dorothea Brooke—perhaps distracts us from this other positing. Where we are led, retrospectively, to imagine that it is Daniel's consciousness that calls this quandary into being, the actual presentation of the narrative leads one to suspect the reverse procedure: a calling into being of consciousness by the perspective that it occupies. Character arrives belatedly to occupy its own perceptions, does not so much govern perspective as find itself generated by it. There is something self-consciously arbitrary about that emergence, as if the finger-mark of "Nought" landed on Deronda but could have landed anywhere else—but, one might almost say, for the visual composition of the conjured scene (Deronda and Gwendolen, each centering the novel's gaze both as object and as subject—as they confront each other, and the novel's focalization shifts back and forth between them). The arbitrary dimension is further emphasized by the visual echo that links fictional positing to chance, as the circular movement of the roulette wheel recalls the rotation of the sidereal clock—and is mimed, too, by the circular movement of perspective around the gambling parlor just after this. (As Miller implicitly notes, these echoes also draw us toward the novel's awareness, at the beginning, of its potentiality—"all the novel's numbers are still open.") The drama of Gwendolen's loss at the gambling table is measured in small units—recalling the image given by the epigraph for the units of that strict measurer, science: "Such a drama takes no long while to play out: development and catastrophe can often be measured by nothing clumsier than the moment-hand" (Eliot, *Daniel Deronda*, 7).[18]

Coming into being in this opening is character and narrative perspective. Alex Woloch links the novel's "late style"—its position after *Middlemarch*, and thus its supernumerary status after the totalizing achievement of that earlier text—to its exploration of character. Its series of virtuoso set-pieces embody for Woloch a narrative economy of excessive wholeness (thus, a redundant, fracturing repetition of multiple wholes)—a structural condition that then is played out in the doubling of main characters. In the harrowing suffering of Gwendolen, Woloch sees the felt experience of a structural separation of egotism and narrative sympathy (a coordination that, inversely, finds its supreme achievement, he suggests, in Austen's *Emma*). In a world that organizes itself according to Daniel's needs and desires (giving him Jewish origins, and Mirah, and, one might note, in Zionism a cause that is denied even the fish-out-of-historical-water, latter-day St. Theresa of a Dorothea Brooke), Gwendolen, for all of her charismatic egotism, begins a major character but ends a minor one. The constitution of perspective corresponds to a perhaps characteristic narrative movement in the text, encapsulated by Daniel's encounter with Mordecai on the Thames: Eliot, Woloch writes, "expands a single sentence in order to include the equivalent of a 360° movement that shows Daniel's apprehension of Mordecai's apprehension of himself." The "rigorously dramatized ambition" of that sentence strives "to effectuate a complete, and in fact bewildering, circuit of recognition, shifting Deronda from subject to object to incipient subject . . . once more."[19] This is the movement of the epigraph's sidereal clock, and of the roulette wheel; part of what is exorbitant about the novel is thus the way that it seems to endorse the self-generating quality of Deronda's emergence as a character. As a figure for the narration itself, it is pointedly more complex than narrative "omniscience"; comprising multiple views, it is, rather, a kind of oscillation, or rather a jamming together of a locus of perception with an object seen—as if one could view the rotating stars from the ground and from the projected clock-face at the same time.

It is also the movement of perspective in the virtuoso beginning of the novel—which coordinates spatial and temporal movements with a doubled narrative perspective. Repeatedly, and at different levels, the novel makes us feel as if we were sweeping around the clock-face and once more approaching the moment of "Nought"; the novel keeps deriving, or returning to, its own inception. If we are pulled up by the beginning of the second paragraph, it is notable that we are also liable to be fooled again. The third paragraph of the novel appears to launch us into an objective description that might stabilize the play of perspective in the two paragraphs that precede it: "It was near four o'clock on a September day, so that the atmosphere was well-brewed to a visible haze" (3). After two pages of description and a delimitation of various types of personages (within the narrow bounds of the society that has access to the gambling room), this apparently neutral description gives us, if not Deronda's thoughts, then the objects of his gaze: "Deronda's first thought when his eyes fell on this scene of dull-gas-poisoned absorption was . . ." (5).[20] Yet again, the "objective" view turns out to have been anchored—in Deronda's previously unmarked consciousness. We find, moreover, that, chronologically, the third paragraph occurs before the first and second; we have, unknowingly, been reckoning forward and backward, and are now approaching the beginning from behind: "But suddenly he felt the moment become dramatic. His attention was arrested by a young lady who, standing at an angle not far from him, was the last to whom his eyes travelled" (5). This woman turns out to be Gwendolen, and the thoughts occasioned, those of the novel's opening ("the inward debate which she raised in Deronda" [5]). The striking object of Deronda's attention would seem, despite the novel's arrestingly memorable opening lines, to need repeatedly to be derived. The first ostensible "action" of the novel, then, is to derive that beginning.

As one reads further into the novel, one discovers further chronological scrambling: As Irene Tucker notes, "the novel's opening episode . . . actually occurs chronologically well *after* Gwendolen's return to her family's residence at Offendene, although we are not likely to become aware of this narrative break until much later, when the flashback closes as the narrative returns to the moment of Gwendolen's arrival at Leubronn."[21] Moreover, if, as I have suggested, Deronda's consciousness seems to come into being as a result of the quandary this spectacle poses, Gwendolen in turn becomes, in this dramatic tautology, a consequence of the consciousness her mysterious presence excites. Her consciousness then emerges out of the consideration of her beauty; the narration of her actions as they appear to Deronda gradually becomes the narration of her actions as they seem *to her* to appear to him.[22] When their eyes meet ("But in the course of that survey her eyes met Deronda's, and instead of averting them as she would have desired to do, she was unpleasantly conscious that they were arrested—how long?" [6]) that exchange becomes explicit. The slightly unpleasant pedagogical relation that binds them together—on her side, with a desire for self-justification that shifts to a desire for self-improvement, and, on his, with a sense of deepening obligation whose expectations he is, ultimately, forced to disappoint—seems to follow as much from this drama of gazes as from the drama of the necklace. (The latter, in any event, explicates this exchange insofar as Deronda is posited as the unseen observer [invested, we come to learn, with narrative prestige] of her thereby "dramatic" body— initially privileged, increasingly to become merely an object, deprived of the investment that would make her interiority a matter of interest.)[23] Unrequited love (on her side) is, further, a consequence of this initial framing—and re-plays the various ways that this opening keeps starting again. (The departure from certain thematic expectations—given the structural privilege of the open-ing scene, one might indeed expect the relation of Daniel and Gwendolen to be *the* story of the text—can also be read as a consequence of a perspectival movement rooted in a shift in the constitution of character.)

Such play continues in the rest of the chapter, where, after a further narra-tive hiatus that takes us to the evening of the day at the roulette wheel, Gwen-dolen's view of Daniel alternates with a more generalized view of her (for "Gwendolen was much observed by the seated groups" [8]). (What is perhaps the apogee of Gwendolen's career in the novel—the archery scene—spells out her disastrous mistake: of thinking that narrative prestige follows from visual prominence, of thinking that to be the cynosure of all eyes guarantees a cor-responding attention, from the world, and from the novel, to one's interiority and one's desires.) The eye contact through which the narrative switches from Daniel to Gwendolen seems to promise an encounter that nevertheless fails to materialize in this chapter: "But Gwendolen did not make Deronda's ac-quaintance on this occasion. Mr Vandernoodt did not succeed in bringing him up to her that evening, and when she re-entered her own room she found a letter recalling her home" (10). The nested series of analogies in the epigraph are as if exfoliated in (the variously orbital movements of) this opening scene, and then in the narrative structure of the novel, which its movement approxi-mates. Woloch notes that that structure appears to endorse Gwendolen's ego-tism, returning again and again to the "affair of the necklace":

> But the narrative structure also, ironically, confirms Gwendolen's
> perspective, since this affair is *the* great set-piece of *Daniel Deronda*,
> locked into prominence by the astounding temporal organization of
> the novel, which snakes back twice toward its own beginning, each
> time newly revealed as a middle. In this way the famous commitment
> of *Daniel Deronda* to "set[ting] off *in medias res*" is also a way to hold
> the reader within the self-enclosed grip of the narrative structure,
> where the tensions between gain and loss, exclusion and inclusion, and
> the daring confusion of egotism and sympathy continue to reverberate.
> (Woloch, 176)

That "temporal organization" enacts, as narrative structure, the novel's disori-enting coordination of different registers: exemplification or image as it func-tions in cognition (in the epigraph), the movement of narrative perspective, the movement of narrative sympathy, the inner and outer circuits of charac-ters' visions and forms of self-regard, even the replication of the sidereal clock in the (visual, but also thematic and symbolic) appearance of the roulette wheel (as a spinning circle and a wheel of fortune). In that view, the epigraph of the first chapter is entirely overdetermined, and a certain self-reflexivity, writ large in the opening consideration of beginnings, represents the emergence and fate of character in the novel.

That emergence is perhaps figured by one of the stranger moments in the opening chapter. In the exfoliating movement of this chapter, the novel's gaze makes one circle around the gambling table before moving out into the wider room (to return, by the end, we noted, to Gwendolen's point of view):

> Round two long tables were gathered two serried crowds of human beings, all save one having their faces and attention bent on the tables. The one exception was a melancholy little boy, with his knees and calves simply in their natural clothing of epidermis, but for the rest of his person in a fancy dress. He alone had his face turned towards the doorway, and fixing on it the blank gaze of a bedizened child stationed as a masquerading advertisement on the platform of an itinerant show, stood close behind a lady deeply engaged at the roulette table. (Eliot, *Daniel Deronda*, 4)[24]

This child does not return to play any significant role in the novel (or any role at all, as far as I remember); a visitor, it might seem, from another register of novelistic representation (evoking the figure of Daniel Deronda we later see as a child reading in the grass just before reference to the Pope's "nephews" lays before him the mystery of his own parentage), his function seems to be that of securing both the closed circuit of the novel's perspective and the enclosed space of the realistic representation (gazing out the door, and inevitably evoking for me the open door at the back of Velasquez's *Las Meninas*).[25] Gazing outward, he becomes an advertisement for an unseen interior; he thus seems to advertise or embody character as such. "The blank gaze of a bedizened child": the child's gaze is literally exorbitant, and his denuded knees and calves seem to give us the embodied excess that emerges out of the circuit of perspective in the novel.

There would be many ways to trace what this blank gaze might portend in the course of Eliot's novel, which returns us, again and again, to questions of inception and origin: to begin with, Daniel's preoccupation with his parentage, and the resolution that the meeting with his mother gives to it, authorizing his tie to Mirah and Mordecai, and, through the Zionism he learns from Mordecai, to another world-historical project of origins constructed or rediscovered. The novel's rendering of the springs of Gwendolen's character—the delicate balance of nature and nurture that has produced her particular susceptibilities and limitations, given through the spiraling backward toward the sources that will have made her the spectacle Deronda sees in the novel's opening—presents a development that both progresses and stalls. Daniel Deronda's growth is, by contrast, more continuous, though it, too, proceeds through moments of revelation and of condensed realization that turn backward to seek a source. Zionism and his mother's quasi-renunciation of him are perhaps "lucky" forms of resolution insofar as they allow him to externalize these quandaries of origin. In Gwendolen, a narrative momentum of development stalls in what Woloch calls set pieces, not only because they tend to mark moments that pull the novel toward various loopings back, but also because these emblematic scenes (her appearance at the gaming table, the tableau vivant of her fright, her performance at the archery tournament, and so on), exactly as scenes, eschew development, and seem to arrive, fully formed, as originary. No retrospect will take us to the true beginning, and thus will the novel continue to derive its make-believe of a beginning, over and over again. In the next chapter, I turn to an even more explicit consideration of the groundless "positing" of character: *Our Mutual Friend*.

5

Proto-Reading and the Positing of Character in *Our Mutual Friend*

Continuing to reckon forwards and backwards, I turn now to the ex nihilo emergence of character in Dickens—particularly as it becomes the overarching concern of *Our Mutual Friend*. The openings of Dickens's novels, more generally, schematically isolate the elements that will form the texts. The repeated "it was" at the opening of *Tale of Two Cities*, like the near-total suppression of verbs in the noun phrases at the opening of *Bleak House*, might be read as separating setting or place from the other elements of fiction. Thus, pace Jesse Oak Taylor's compelling assertion of the fog's reality at the beginning of *Bleak House*, what is in question there is, rather, the figuration of the literal, even, therefore, the inaccessibility of place beyond the blank gesture of fictional positing.[1] The "real" fog one does not encounter, or finds only by way of this fictional fiat. (This is to demur from Taylor's literary reading, though not necessarily from the concomitant historical claims.) The beginning of the world is *fictional*: "London. Michaelmas Term lately over, and the Lord Chancellor sitting in Lincoln's Inn Hall. Implacable November weather. As much mud in the streets as if the waters had but newly retired from the face of the earth, and it would not be wonderful to meet a Megalosaurus, forty feet long or so, waddling like an elephantine lizard up Holborn Hill."[2] That Megalosaurus, out for a postdiluvian stroll, bodies forth a real that, cast in terms of expectations and semblance ("it would not be wonderful to meet" him), is a self-conscious effect of realism and its constitution of a fictional world; imagined, it is he who, in turn, calls forth the novel's first independent clause. It is therefore not an evasion to read the opening in the quite obviously allegorical register in which the fog and mud function for the text. The fog and mud are linked to all the paper produced by the legal proceeding but not, perhaps, according to a moralizing gloss in which a valorized real might be accessible outside the realms of chancery court. Rather, *Bleak House* cannot reach the real to the precise degree that it posits it; perhaps only spontaneous combustion can achieve the sublimation necessary for that contact. To that extent, what we encounter at the opening of *Bleak House* is not so much the London fog of indoor fires and small-scale industry as it is setting as such, the materiality not of the world but of the novel.

Likewise, *David Copperfield*'s wry doubling of "my life" (making homonyms of text and life in this opening chapter, entitled "I am born") raises the question of whether the speaking "I" will come into being, of the eventual convergence of narrating voice and the ostensibly autobiographical object of its reminiscence:[3] "Whether I shall turn out to be the hero of my own life, or whether that station will be held by anybody else, these pages must show. To begin my life with the beginning of my life, I record that I was born (as I have been informed and believe) on a Friday, at twelve o'clock at night."[4] The various ways that the rest of the chapter plays on questions of foresight and prophecy brings to the fore that generative but unstable doubling—figured, with an unsettling literality, by the caul that sticks to David's face. Thus, too, the play on names at the beginning of *Great Expectations*—"My father's family name being Pirrip, and my Christian name Philip, my infant tongue could make of both names nothing longer or more explicit than Pip. So, I called myself Pip, and came to be called Pip"—sets that declaration of self-making against the reading of tombstones that follows it, and the forcible manipulation of Pip's vulnerable infantine body as Magwitch (literally) turns his world upside-down.[5]

The novel that follows is in many ways structured between the poles hyperbolically formulated at the beginning (as they are perhaps hyperbolically imagined in the text): between a self-making that might stand utterly aloof from any determining contexts and a total susceptibility to being shaped by another's will. Estella's iconic place as an object of desire derives from her being so schematically an object, and she is recognizable as *the* object, therefore, to anyone who has ever been in love precisely to the degree that, an utterly improbable person, she seems, even in her willfulness and her refusal to desire Pip, to be defined as exclusively by that desire as she is formed by the monomaniacal designs of her benefactor. (It is perhaps only in their refusals to mirror us—in, precisely, what in them stubbornly escapes the terms of our desire—that our beloveds ever approach fidelity to us, temporary and contingent even then.) The thoroughgoing completeness of her formation by Miss Havisham clears a space for Pip's experiences of being manipulated, to make them part of a dialectic or a dynamic instead of being the utter undercutting of all his hopes; if a "gentleman" cannot afford to acknowledge the ways that he has been made, Pip attempts to choose his manipulator, and in the various ways that his expectations founder, perhaps discovers a new form of self-making: the recording of self-making's failure. Small wonder that Pip's adventure in *Bildung* begins in a cemetery, and with a reading of epitaphs. The voice that is brought into being as the telos of the first-person *Bildungsroman* cannot but be the death of the character who journeys toward becoming a voice, even as the permanent delay of that merger also marks that therefore never-realized character as stillborn.

As its title decrees, *Great Expectations* is a book about disappointment: Over and over, even the most trivial expectations (say, for instance, for a pork pie to end a holiday dinner) are baffled, or, arrived, contrive to disappoint—"My clothes were rather a disappointment, of course. Probably every new and eagerly expected garment ever put on since clothes came in, fell a trifle short of the wearer's expectation" [146]); so, too, with the larger hopes (Pip's, for Estella's love, or to secret Magwitch away before he can be recaptured). Precisely, however, to the degree that Pip the character never, in the space of narration, closes his asymptotic approach to the narrator he will someday have become (in this the novel is unlike the arresting final moments of *David Copperfield*), *Great Expectations* also keeps open a space where character, still in some respects to be formed, remains in potential, and, if resistant to the self's desire to establish itself, also undetermined by the actions and manipulations of others. (The novel's maniacally plotted symmetries perhaps locate the novel on both sides—in an implicit claim of fictional making, and a demonstration of lives permeable to others' schemes.) One wouldn't have to turn to the fact of the novel's two endings to see instated this double structure; even within the allegedly happy ending, "I saw no shadow of another parting from her" is "happy" to the degree that one takes yet another form of expectation for that expectation's realization (450). The past tense in "saw" hovers between two times: It could mean that he never (afterward) saw a shadow of another parting, or that he didn't (then) see a shadow that might (therefore) have descended on him, after all. Because Pip's approach to the narrator he will become remains asymptotic, to the degree that that expectation remains unbaffled, it also remains unrealized. Such therefore is both the joy and the unremitting sadness of a book whose perpetual thwarting of expectations—expectations that derive from that initial moment of self-positing—does not prevent it from continually eliciting them. Alive, one finds expectations as inescapable as is the realization that they are more or less irrelevant to the world, where, nevertheless, they serve as one's perhaps primary mode of finding oneself. To my mind, therefore, Pip's prolonged (and never fully achieved) starting out offers a redoubtable lesson in desire. He belongs with Dickens's other explorations of beginning because, disappointed and expecting, he is ever a proto-character.

A careful reading of the first chapter of *Our Mutual Friend* might show how it frames, in various ways and in various registers, not only the main plot, but most of the central questions, symbolic elements, themes, and even rhetorical maneuvers of the novel. Here, in no very systematic way, are some of the central interpretive questions legible there: What happens to human agency, desire, and identity after death—or how far does human agency extend, beyond physical proximity, beyond the body, beyond life itself? To what degree do those critical determinants of the human reside in the living body, and, if they are not there, where and how are they to be located? Are they malleable? At what moment does physical likeness shade over (if it does) into identity? Can one person assume another's identity, or put one on like clothes or a disguise? What are the constraints on social mobility? Is there some baseline nature that constrains that mobility, or are social conventions of place purely arbitrary? Is "character" innate or acquired? If innate, what are its sources? If acquired, how does one map the influences that shape it: material and social conditions, education, even esteem or desire? What duties does one owe one's relations, one's fellow human beings, or the dead? One could continue to multiply such questions, just as one could point to the symbolic importance of the river for the novel's structure, or to the resonances of the grotesque form of scavenging with which the text begins. All such questions and structures, however, are, in my view, secondary or supervenient to a more basic or originary question of inception itself. Posed at the beginning of the text is the question of the threshold of legibility or form, here, as a primordial emergence of character as such.[6] Once seen, this question inscribes itself at nearly every register of meaning in the text. *Our Mutual Friend*, read in these terms, is about nothing other than the question of literary inception.

Here is the opening of *Our Mutual Friend*:

> In these times of ours, though concerning the exact year there is no need to be precise, a boat of dirty and disreputable appearance, with two figures in it, floated on the Thames, between Southwark Bridge which is of iron, and London Bridge which is of stone, as an autumn evening was closing in.
>
> The figures in this boat were those of a strong man with ragged grizzled hair and a sun-browned face, and a dark girl of nineteen or twenty, sufficiently like him to be recognizable as his daughter. The girl rowed, pulling a pair of sculls very easily; the man, with the rudder-lines slack in his hands, and his hands loose in his waistband,

kept an eager look out. He had no net, hook, or line, and he could not be a fisherman; his boat had no cushion for a sitter, no paint, no inscription, no appliance beyond a rusty boathook and a coil of rope, and he could not be a waterman; his boat was too crazy and too small to take in cargo for delivery, and he could not be a lighterman or a river-carrier; there was no clue to what he looked for, but he looked for something, with a most intent and searching gaze.[7]

Whatever one might say about specific details (Southwark and London Bridges, for example, and their iron and stone, or the autumnal setting, or the place of the river in the era's imaginary), one of the most striking aspects of this opening is its pairing of negation and pure positing.[8] The first sentence establishes a temporal setting even as it withdraws from it any specificity, pointing to a contemporary world and a community of meaning ("these times of ours") while negating any particular content ("concerning the exact year there is no need to be precise")—a gesture that is picked up by the specified negation of the tools and accouterments and consequent trades that (the as yet unnamed) Gaffer does *not* practice. In those latter formulations, one perhaps expects a "so" ("and [*so*] he cannot be a fisherman"); the passage thus also seems to negate consequence, and perhaps even the consciousness that would put together these absences in a chain of consequence, as if "he cannot be a fisherman" were another element in a series of descriptors (all describing what isn't there to be seen). Such forms of negation are a persistent rhetorical structure in the book, forming part of its underlying syntax. Mr. Venus's (also weird, macabre) quasi-taxidermical profession is described in similar terms of negation. Or, likewise characteristic of a central structure of the novel are such descriptions as this one, of the river as Mortimer and Eugene watch with Riderhood, on the lookout, again, for Gaffer: "Not a ship's hull, with its rusty iron links of cable run out of the hawse-holes long discolored with the iron's rusty tears, but seemed to be there with a fell intention. Not a figure-head but had the menacing look of bursting forward to run them down. Not a sluice gate, or a painted scale upon a post or wall, showing the depth of water, but seemed to hint like the dreadfully facetious Wolf in bed in Grandmamma's cottage, 'That's to drown *you* in, my dears!' Not a lumbering black barge . . ." (*Our Mutual Friend*, 173). As at the beginning, the material specificity of realism—with its hulls and hawse-holes, its sluice gates and painted scales—is governed by negation, materialized as an exception or exclusion that constitutes a uniform whole.[9]

In another formulation characteristic of the novel, Gaffer (or the "strong man") looks for "something," and "with a most intent and searching gaze." The gaze is called into being before the object for which it might, retrospectively, appear to search. Here at the beginning, the seeming reticence is, of course, the novel's way of evoking the mystery (and the obscenity) of the trade plied by Gaffer, but that trade seems a consequence (again) of a more primary structure of positing. The novel's recurrent turn to indefinite pronouns holds a place for a posited object or person whose specificity or particularity is, simultaneously, withdrawn—leaving the trace, within the novel's very syntax, of this primordial structure of positing. (The eponymous "Man from Somewhere" of Book I, Chapter II, is both John Harmon and Veneering, along with, potentially, any number of others who might step in to take that, after all, nearly vacant, place.) Thus, in John Harmon's soliloquy in which he narrates the near-death experience at the center of the novel's plot: "It was only after a downward slide through something like a tube, and then a great noise and a sparkling and crackling as of fires, that the consciousness came upon me, 'This is John Harmon drowning! John Harmon, struggle for your life. John Harmon, call on Heaven and save yourself!' I think I cried it out in a great agony, and then a heavy horrid unintelligible something vanished, and it was I who was struggling alone there in the river" (363).

Looking for "something . . . with a most intent and searching gaze"; "a heavy horrid unintelligible something vanished, and it was I who was struggling alone there in the river" (13, 363). Gaffer is, of course, looking for corpses in the Thames. The "something" that he searches for will turn out to be a dead man, and the novel's primary objects of attention in this regard will be bodies, alive and dead. Rosemarie Bodenheimer has pointed out the nearly maniacal series of doublings in *Our Mutual Friend*. The departure here is the self-consciousness about this basic structural principle in all of his texts: "Dickens had spent his fiction-making career creating doubles, others, substitutes, and scapegoats," she writes, "but in this novel he seems to be writing *about* them. He's on to himself."[10] In the earlier novels, doubling serves, perhaps above all (she argues) to insulate middle-class characters from a guilt that is thereby projected onto lower-class and "overtly sexualized positions." Here, however, the doubling enacts a more disruptive or anarchic logic, and begins, in that very self-consciousness, to pose questions of legibility: "In *Our Mutual Friend*, however, the major male characters—like the self-doubled Dickens—seem to be overcome with the desire to fall, away from their earned or inherited status, away from the normative marriage plot and the fallen women who siphon off that plot's excess energy. Now Dickens begins to create doubles by fusion: they become inseparable, dependent, even identical" (168). The drive toward downward mobility evidenced here is perhaps the consequence of a structural clarity that becomes confused in the pressure of sheer repetition, a lapsing back into an undifferentiated state that throws into question an initial legibility of form.

I will return to how this doubling functions in specific instances—because it will turn out that all this doubling bears on the question, in a variety of modes and registers, of the emergence of character. For the moment, I would note, simply, that it is a generative structural principle for the novel. And thus the doubling of the bridges at the beginning, whatever (again) one might say about stone and wood and the rendering of historical time in the passage from one to the other, is important here for the otherwise blank positing of a crucial formal structure—which is to say, doubling as such. In the opening scene, a psychological structure emerges from a situation that threatens to overwhelm it with mirroring repetition: "She watched his face as earnestly as he watched the river. But, in the intensity of her look there was a touch of dread or horror" (13). (At the dinner at the Veneerings in Chapter II, an entire scene is described as what a mirror "reflects": "The great looking-glass above the sideboard, re-flects the table and the company. Reflects the new Veneering crest. . . . Re-flects Veneering . . . Reflects Mrs. Veneering . . . Reflects Podsnap . . Reflects Mrs. Podsnap" and so on [20–1]. One's slightly queasy feeling that one is some-how viewing the scene "backwards" corresponds to a deeper sense in which this underlying structure of reflection threatens to overwhelm realistic repre-sentation by returning it to the river at the beginning, and to this claustropho-bic but abyssal mirroring of gazes.) The object—the corpse that will be misidentified as John Harmon's—emerges out of this circuit of reflection, and, however one might explain the source of her intimated dread, the dread also arises from the uncanny sense in this text that, if you stare hard enough, you will discover a human form—and usually a dead human face.

In his consideration of beginnings (and endings), James Phelan articulates (as if in passing) the parameters of what he calls a "rhetorical" analysis of narrative:

> Rhetorical theory defines narrative as somebody telling somebody else on some occasion and for some purpose(s) that something happened. The theory further postulates that narrative is a form in which an implied author draws on or invents the appropriate textual and intertextual resources to convey a multi-leveled communication about the some-thing that happened to an implied audience.[11]

Such presuppositions allow for any number of intelligent and illuminating ob-servations about particular texts, but they are, nevertheless, presuppositions. The question of whether one ought thus to understand narrative as an implied scenario of address is a central question for narrative theory; I would side with Ann Banfield and those who challenge such a model of narrative in part because of what these assumptions obscure.[12] The self-consciousness of *Our*

Mutual Friend lies partly in the way that this visibility of incipient characterization renders explicit the otherwise inaccessible positing of this very scenario,
which the novel therefore refuses to let us take for granted. It is as if one could
read of "somebody telling somebody else on some occasion and for some
purpose(s) that something happened," without, that is, the specification of
those indefinite pronouns. Read this way, Phelan's definition is a pretty good
description of Beckett's fiction; I am trying to suggest that it's an implicit dimension of the novel genre as such. (I will return to these in greater detail,
but recall that in the most notable instances of direct address in *Our Mutual
Friend*, the novel addresses the dead, the inanimate, or [in, for instance, the
case of the little doll's dressmaker] those who wish that they were one or the
other.) In the novel's opening, at issue, perhaps above all, is the positing of "two
figures" and the question of whether they will (or will not) become not just
characters with names and identities, but legible human forms. Thus we find
the striking movement from "two figures" to "a strong man . . . and a dark girl,"
neither of whom accrues a name until he or she is addressed by another (Lizzie,
by her father, and Gaffer, first by Lizzie [as "father"] and then by Rogue Riderhood). This is the "figure" of John Harmon, too, struggling to be himself, in
the hallucinatory moments as he watches a man impersonating him anticipating his own struggle to survive: "The figure like myself was assailed," he
writes of the struggle before the attempted murder (363). If one of the difficulties in the novel is the sheer number of persons who can be called a "figure
like [himself]," that confusion is perhaps the consequence of the novel's repeated dealings in incipient persons.

   In this soliloquy, Bodenheimer notes, Harmon attempts to assemble himself out of the fragmented memories of the attempted murder. The logic of
that scene of quasi-soliloquy dooms the effort to a sort of failure ("Don't evade
it, John Harmon; don't evade it; think it out!" [*Our Mutual Friend*, 360])—which
recalls similar scenes of moral crisis where other characters attempt to come
to moral decisions by externalizing them in a monologue or dialogue. (This
is especially true of Bella, perhaps, though Wrayburn also reasons thus, if often in further externalized form, with Mortimer; Wrayburn takes this dimension further than any of the other characters, requiring Mortimer, and then
Jenny Wren ["an interpreter between this sentient world and the insensible
man" (720)], to speak his desire for him: even his marriage proposal to Lizzie
occurs by way of this redoubled proxy.) As Bodenheimer points out, the would-
be consolidating address also fragments Harmon into speaker and addressee:

> The speaking of this soliloquy seems designed to sew Harmon-Rokesmith
> together, minus the spooked and stuttering Julius Handford. But its

rhetoric keeps him in pieces. The narrating "I" is not John Harmon, but a voice in dialogue with somebody else he calls John Harmon, someone with whom he checks the accuracy of facts, or whom he warns against straying from his straight path of narrative. John Harmon is more spoken to than speaking, never more so than when he is drowning and someone—but who?—says "This is John Harmon drowning! John Harmon, struggle for your life!" The "This" would seem to be the body of John Harmon, not fully identical with the "I" who now "cried it aloud in great agony." It's as if John Harmon were being reintroduced to himself, in a recognition scene where a physical body and a capacity for speech and feeling converge, but do not fully merge. (Bodenheimer, 172)

It is worth spelling out a consequence that Bodenheimer leaves implicit. Noting earlier that "the most stunning formal feature of this novel" is the fact "that so much of what's important takes place in theatrical dialogue rather than in the familiar Dickensian self-performing narration" (166), Bodenheimer's essay suggests that this moment of self-fracturing address might mark the limit case of the narration as such. (It is the splitting occasioned by that address that allows Harmon to enjoin himself to recall what otherwise would be paradoxical—to recall his death: "I have no clue to the scene of my death" [*Our Mutual Friend*, 360].) Harmon's retrospective monologue in extremis as it intersects with these moments of ethical deliberation recalls Andrew Miller's brilliant discussion of Victorian casuistry, particularly as it is acted out in dramatic monologue, in relation to ethics and free indirect style.[13] Occasioned by its lurid premise, the novel here explores the consequences of its expropriating mode of address.[14]

The "theatrical dialogue" Bodenheimer notes emerges in the narration in other ways, too; I noted, for example, its recurring, at crucial moments, to forms of direct address, often to the dead or to inanimate objects. Hence, we read after Gaffer's body has been discovered:

Father, was that you calling me? Father! I thought I heard you call me twice before! Words never to be answered, those, upon the earth-side of the grave. The wind sweeps jeeringly over Father, whips him with the frayed ends of his dress and his jagged hair, tries to turn him where he lies stark on his back, and force his face towards the rising sun, that he may be shamed the more . . . Then in a rush, it cruelly taunts him. Father, was that you calling me? Was it you, the voiceless and the dead? Was it you, thus buffeted as you lie here in a heap? Was it you, thus baptized unto Death, with these flying impurities now flung upon your face? Why not speak, Father? Soaking into this filthy ground as

you lie here, is your own shape. Did you never see such a shape soaked
into your boat? Speak, Father. Speak to us, the winds, the only
listeners left you! (175)

The exchange here is complex; the words "spoken" at the beginning echo
Lizzie's, as she had called out to her father earlier in the evening (presumably
at the moment of his death). The text, giving voice to the "winds," has them
ventriloquize her; father and daughter, and the weary winds, are silent, but
the text's conferring of speech on the winds consigns Lizzie and her father to
two differentiated forms of silence. His is the muteness of death, and, hers, a
silence implicit in the quotation of her earlier speech that foregrounds her boot-
less imploring of the night and the wind. (She does not yet know he is dead;
that is the pathos here.) If she called out, it would be in vain—and already was
in vain, moreover, when she initially "heard" him. "Why not speak, Father":
the text's ironic question is the girl's earnest one. In both cases the address encounters the limit of death. In "Father," an as it were doubled vocative links
her (unheard) address to the text's ironizing of it. A possibly more benign version of this address appears in Jenny Wren's nevertheless fully thanatos-marked,
delusional imaginings of the "long bright slanting rows" of white-clad children
who called out to her: "'Who is this in pain! Who is this in pain!' And I used
to cry out, 'O my blessed children, it's poor me. Have pity on me. Take me up
and make me light!'" (238) (Or, in her creepier, crazier address on Riah's roof:
"Come up and be dead! Come up and be dead!" [280].) Jenny Wren (an alias,
too, like the names of so many in this book) as if short-circuits the address of
the dead to the winds posited earlier, and comprises that narrative circuit in
her relation to herself.

   We find a similar form of address in the revival of Riderhood, who, in what
is perhaps the novel's most famous scene, comes back to life after drowning.
Reduced to a mere "spark of life" (which Deleuze links to the impersonal force
animating "a life"), he gradually recovers the individuating marks of consciousness, and thereby loses the sympathy of those gathered around him—a thoroughly repellent person, it was only that impersonal "spark of life" beyond him
that held them in awe.[15] That incipient life force, which allows an identification with something beyond or before the individual, is linked to the text's
power of animating address: "If you are not gone for good, Mr Riderhood, it
would be something to know where you are hiding at present. This flabby lump
of mortality that we work so hard at with such patient perseverance, yields no
sign of you. If you are gone for good, Rogue, it is very solemn, and if you are
coming back, it is hardly less so" (*Our Mutual Friend*, 439). That address immediately precedes his revival: after a series of negations framed as a dialogue

between the doctor and himself ("Did that nostril twitch? No. This artificial respiration ceasing, do I feel any faint flutter under my hand upon the chest? No. Over and over again No. No."), the text exclaims, "See! A token of life! An indubitable token of life! The spark may smoulder and go out, or it may glow and expand, but see!" (440). Thus, when John Harmon turns, in his effort to remember (himself), his self-address attaches this narrative address to a character—and enacts the logic of the text's own effort to narrate the emergence of persons, which is most luridly displayed in the scene with drowned Riderhood. The novel's plot literalizes the effect of the split of that address, leaving Harmon between life and death: "So deeply engaged had the living-dead man been, in thus communing with himself, that he had regarded neither the wind nor the way, and had resisted the former as instinctively as he had pursued the latter" (367).

Harmon and Riderhood are only the most glaring instances of the novel's repeated concern with such liminal states. Wrayburn's long convalescence is likewise presented as a hovering between life and death—an experience that, moreover, gives him the chance to begin again, and to become the character that, before this, is becalmed, marooned in the doldrums of his whimsical inertia. Even the Boffins, when they discover that John Rokesmith is really John Harmon, both promptly lose consciousness—the awareness of the other serving to each as a motive for revival. When Bella (once unspoiled and taught to despise her avarice) isn't flashing her dimples, serving as a prop for her irritating baby, or earnestly applying herself to housework,[16] her pliant affection for her husband is displayed in a series of "mysterious disappearances"—"after that, [she] seemed to shrink to next to nothing in the clasp of his arms, partly because it was such a strong one on his part, and partly because there was such a yielding to it on hers . . . What he did was, once more to give her the appearance of vanishing as aforesaid" (595, 592, 593)—thus enacting physically what the mechanism of the plot does to her character. In these disappearances, whether she swoons or merely disappears from view, fully fathomed by his manly embrace, is often not clear to me; yet again, a description of a psychological state is difficult to distinguish from an externalized view marked by a particular perspective (she "disappears" into his consciousness and sense of things, but also from our view of her—because his body is in the way). Like Bella, the gradual numbness through which Betty Higden experiences the onset of death, itself like Mortimer's somnambulist journey home after the night watching on the river, reverses the more common movement in the text—its narration of incipient life, or the emergence of consciousness.

From Wegg's wooden leg to Mr. Venus's taxidermy and his assembly of "miscellaneous" skeletons (such as his never-completed French gentleman); from

Mr. Wilfer who awaits the money to buy a complete set of clothes to Charley Hexam, in whom "there was a curious mixture . . . of uncompleted savagery, and uncompleted civilization" (28); from Jenny Wren's magnificent hair, so discomfitingly fetishized and so notably (and one might even say cruelly) at odds with her misassembled body, to the prospective blushes that rule the social bearing of the Podsnaps; from the clasped hands and bent back of Mr. Riah to the prospective whiskers Fledgby perpetually fails to coax into evidence, the text inscribes at various levels, and in various registers, the kind of fragmentation of persons that Harmon experiences in the water—and in narrating the experience to himself—or an incomplete or mismatched assembly that embodies (as it were) persons not-yet formed or never fully to be formed. Likewise, we repeatedly find images of animation, or of characters' bodies rendered props for animation performed by others: the Lamills' ventriloquizing of the conversation of Miss Podsnap and Fledgby, for example; or Wegg's recurrent effort to manipulate Venus by giving voice to his "speaking countenance"; or, in the novel's unpleasant anti-Semitic subplot, Mr. Riah's being forced to serve as Fledgby's "mask," and to speak the stilted words expected of a stereotyped Jewish moneylender (true words in this case that will, by Fledgby's framing, be taken as disingenuous); or the outings of the diminutive dressmaker to the dolls, who makes unknowing society women the models for her dresses. (In case we miss the logic, Jenny returns to make her models "try on" the clothes she has made.)

The imperfect quality of both animation and assembly allows the text to hew close to the moment of emergence. The "bran-new" Veneerings enact, in the text's comic register, the drama of emergence and self-invention in the story of Harmon-Rokesmith and Riderhood. One recalls, too, how often in the text, persons ("figures" or "forms") emerge out of the darkness—"Venus, blowing his tea: his head and face peering out of the darkness" (88); John Rokesmith at the window as Venus and Wegg plot together at the Bower; the Inspector appearing out of the darkness, spookily already in the room with Rokesmith and Bella ("A twilight calm of happiness then succeeding to their radiant noon, they remained at peace, until a strange voice in the room startled them both. The room being by that time dark, the voice said, 'Don't let the lady be alarmed by my striking a light,' and immediately a match rattled, and glimmered in a hand" [740–1]); or the various nighttime visitors to the law offices of Mortimer and Wrayburn: "Lightwood, whose back was towards the door, turned his head, and there, in the darkness of the entry, stood a something in the likeness of a man: to whom he addressed the not irrelevant inquiry, 'Who the devil are you?'" (150). (In Dickens, as in Dostoyevsky, one is often made to feel how dark the world once was at night.)

What most often emerges from the dark—or from under the water—is a disembodied face. The night before the Boffins move out of the Bower, Mrs. Boffin repeatedly sees the faces of the dead:

> "Noddy, the faces of the old man and the two children are all over the house to-night."
>
> "My dear?" exclaimed Mr Boffin. But not without a certain uncomfortable sensation gliding down his back.
>
> "I know it must sound foolish, and yet it is so."
>
> "Where did you think you saw them?"
>
> "I don't know that I think I saw them anywhere. I felt them."
>
> "Touched them?"
>
> "No. Felt them in the air. I was sorting those things on the chest, and not thinking of the old man or the children, but singing to myself, when all in a moment I felt there was a face growing out of the dark."
>
> "What face?" asked her husband, looking about him.
>
> "For a moment it was the old man's, and then it got younger. For a moment it was both the children's, and then it got older. For a moment it was a strange face, and then it was all the faces."
>
> "And then it was gone?"
>
> "Yes; and then it was gone." [. . .]
>
> "No. I thought I'd try another room, and shake it off. I says to myself, 'I'll go and walk slowly up and down the old man's room three times, from end to end, and then I shall have conquered it.' I went in with the candle in my hand; but the moment I came near the bed, the air got thick with them."
>
> "With the faces?"
>
> "Yes, and I even felt that they were in the dark behind the side-door, and on the little staircase, floating away into the yard. Then, I called you." (190–1)

Tormented by Wrayburn, Headstone becomes one of these faces—at once defaced and made nothing but face:

> Looking like the hunted and not the hunter, baffled, worn, with the exhaustion of deferred hope and consuming hate and anger in his face, white-lipped, wild-eyed, draggle-haired, seamed with jealousy and anger, and torturing himself with the conviction that he showed it all and they exulted in it, he went by them in the dark, like a haggard head suspended in the air: so completely did the force of his expression cancel his figure. (534)

To have his figure canceled seems to mean that he has become disembodied (by the "force of expression" animating his face—the cancellation thus a literal "disfigurement," occasioned by what ostensibly enlivens it), and, indeed, just after this, he becomes a floating head: "So, the haggard head suspended in the air flitted across the road, like the spectre of one of the many heads erst hoisted upon neighbouring Temple Bar, and stopped before the watchman. . . . The haggard head floated up the dark staircase, and softly descended nearer to the floor outside the outer door of the chambers. . . . If Lightwood could have seen the face which kept him awake, staring and listening in the darkness outside the door as he spoke of it, he might have been less disposed to sleep, through the remainder of the night" (536–7). As Headstone's disfiguringly forceful expression suggests, this disarticulation of body parts also corresponds to an animation gone awry—to a body animated by passion unmodulated by conscious control.[17] The novel accounts for that structure in various psychologically acute ways. Yet such disembodiment (or intensification of face) floats free of psychology, so general a condition does it prove to be. A disarticulating figure (Venus calls his taxidermy "articulation," which thus also recalls Wegg's repeated invocation of his "speaking countenance"—itself a play on his fraudulent claims of literacy with Mr. Boffin as they "decline and fall" together), it is also an incipient form of animation. ("Decline and fall," in Wegg's rendering of Gibbon, literalizes "declension" and pulls reading closer, as it were, to his own body, which is inflected by its wooden leg.) At other moments, it takes on more benign forms of absorption or exaltation, as when, telling Jenny Wren of her love for Wrayburn, Lizzie forgets herself: "The face looking at the fire had become exalted and forgetful in the rapture of these words" (344).[18]

Yet it is also as if prior to that, and thus faces in the novel are often the objects of interrogation—standing in, sometimes, for a particular meaning, but, more often, for meaning as such. The "speaking countenance" makes this explicit; Wegg's quasi-literate efforts to read are part of the novel's fascination with the illiterate and sub-literate contemplation of the forms of meaningful language, and thus underline the place of faces as objects to be "read." One recalls a recurrent scenario in the novel, a choreographed circuit of scrutinized faces—enacted as various visitors come to the rooms of Wrayburn and Mortimer, for instance, or as people gather over the dying or the dead, or as Mrs. Wilfer communes with her grandeur:

> Mrs Wilfer's manner of receiving those viands was marked by petrified
> absence of mind; in which state, likewise, she partook of them,
> occasionally laying down her knife and fork, as saying within her own

spirit, "What is this I am doing?" and glaring at one or other of the party, as if in indignant search of information. A magnetic result of such glaring was, that the person glared at could not by any means successfully pretend to be ignorant of the fact: so that a bystander, without beholding Mrs Wilfer at all, must have known at whom she was glaring, by seeing her refracted from the countenance of the beglared one. (598–9)

Mrs. Wilfer here echoes John Harmon: "'This is John Harmon drowning! John Harmon, struggle for your life!'" (363); "What is this I am doing?" This expropriatingly reflexive circuit likewise recalls the moment with Lizzie and her father at the beginning of the novel and its refraction of gazes. The "petrified absence of mind" seems curiously to follow from it, however much it is rationalized in this instance by the comedy of her particular, and particularly unwarranted, self-regard. This comedy does not ultimately obscure what this "absence" of mind shares with the literal blankness and absence in the discovered corpses on the river. The Lammils, when alone, address not each other but an invisible third party, often called the skeleton in their closet.

The floating faces in the novel are, first and foremost, the faces of the dead or those feared to be dead, most often by drowning—those that Mrs. Boffin sees, or that, with Gaffer and Riderhood, we see emerge from beneath the surface of the water. The faces that Mrs. Boffin sees in the dark float—"Yes, and I even felt that they were in the dark behind the side-door, and on the little staircase, floating away into the yard. Then, I called you" (191)—and Lizzie's dramatic search for the man she will discover is Wrayburn is a search for a "floating," "drifting," or "bloody" face, just glimpsed on the surface of the water:[19]

Following the current with her eyes, she saw a bloody face turned up towards the moon, and drifting away.

Now, merciful Heaven be thanked for that old time, and grant, O Blessed Lord, that through thy wonderful workings it may turn to good at last! To whomsoever the drifting face belongs, be it man's or woman's, help my humble hands, Lord God, to raise it from death and restore it to some one to whom it must be dear! . . . Intently over her shoulder, without slackening speed, she looked ahead for the driving face. She passed the scene of the struggle—yonder it was, on her left, well over the boat's stern—she passed on her right, the end of the village street, a hilly street that almost dipped into the river; its sounds were growing faint again, and she slackened; looking as the boat drove, everywhere, everywhere, for the floating face. . . . She merely kept the

boat before the stream now, and rested on her oars, knowing well that
if the face were not soon visible, it had gone down, and she would
overshoot it. An untrained sight would never have seen by the moonlight what she saw at the length of a few strokes astern. She saw the
drowning figure rise to the surface, slightly struggle, and as if by
instinct turn over on its back to float. Just so had she first dimly seen
the face which she now dimly saw again. (683)

Lizzie's prayer resembles a poetic *invocatio*; her search for a face potentially
shifts into another register as it stands in for poetic invention (literally, and in
classical rhetoric, *invenire*, to come upon, to discover, to find). The recurrent
synecdoche also links Lizzie's search for the drowning man to the search she
does not yet realize she is undertaking—to recognize Wrayburn—and hence
gives to the rescue a redoubled sense: that, in saving him from drowning, she
will also as if reattach him to his erstwhile floating face, that the recognition
will confer upon him the identity that is under threat. (This scene thus presents a condensed version of Harmon-Rokesmith's effort to determine whether
Bella can "love [him] for [his] own sake" [366] and not for his money, or because
she was given him in his father's will; for all the unpleasant teaching of Bella,
it is finally her recognition that succeeds in realigning him with his name.) If
a face can be made to emerge from the blank context of the water, if Lizzie
can recognize Wrayburn by differentiating a face from other shapes in the wa-
tery void, he will live.
     Yet the keen eye that allows her to see him ("An untrained sight would never
have seen by the moonlight what she saw") has been trained by many hours on
the water searching for the dead; whether this mission is one of search and rescue or of recovery and scavenging might be said to depend on how one reads the
sought-for face. The search for a sign of life is also disfiguring to the degree that
the synecdoche reduces the wounded man to this isolated and significant body
part. Once she has, with preternatural strength, hauled her drowned lover
into her boat, she again gazes at his face: "She had so laid him there, as that she
might see his disfigured face; it was so much disfigured that his mother might
have covered it, but it was above and beyond disfigurement in her eyes" (684). It
is perhaps at least momentarily unclear what "above and beyond disfigurement"
means; if, ultimately, it seems that her love is such that his face cannot be disfigured in her eyes, his face, which his mother might have covered, also seems
thereby to float above itself. In his dying moments, Jenny's alcoholic father,
"Mr. Dolls," as Wrayburn christens him, confronts "a wall of faces, deformed
into all kinds of shapes through the agency of globular red bottles, green bottles,
blue bottles, and other coloured bottles. A ghastly light shining upon him that he

didn't need, the beast so furious but a few minutes gone, was quiet enough now, with a strange mysterious writing on his face, reflected from one of the great bottles, as if Death had marked him: 'Mine'" (712). Thus to be confronted by faces, and to have one's face written upon, is ambivalent in this novel, where the emergence of form and character so often shades into its vanishing. Summoned to the wedding of Eugene and Lizzie, Bella, covering for Rokesmith, who cannot meet Lightwood without exposing himself, decides to say that he has a swollen face that needs to be "lanced"—or "the face-ache," as Mrs. Milvey knowingly calls his strange attested condition (729).

People emerging out of the dark (or clutching each other in a murderous embrace) are often called "figures"; a figure is also a face, and, if Headstone's passion defaces him by making him nothing but face (when, later on, repressed passion makes blood erupt from his nose, the disfigurement literalizes his repeated failure to control his face), he enacts what deconstructive accounts of prosopopoeia—most notably, Cynthia Chase's, in "Giving a Face to a Name"— have taught us to see is the disfiguring potential of the proximity of figure and face.[20] (Wrayburn is "disfigured" by Headstone's attack, we are repeatedly told, though later we are reassured that "it was declared by the medical attendants that he might not be much disfigured by-and-by" [789]; the violence of the attack is perhaps not unrelated to this figural structure.)[21] "Figure is no less than our very face," as Chase writes (84); language disfigures us to the degree that it becomes visible that faces are *merely* figural. Headstone's name makes of him a walking catachresis (as his proposal to Lizzie, in, of all the most unpropitious, and also most unlikely, of romantic milieux, a cemetery, reminds us); the chip on his shoulder may be a consequence of his misrecognizing the particular way in which he is not fully a man.

Figure in *Our Mutual Friend* is often a face, if perhaps more often a body (or "shape") that thereby negates a face; it is also a form or outline on its way toward becoming significant—which thus marks an intermediate stage, for instance between mere shape or outline and a human form or face:

> Riderhood nodded, and the figure of the bargeman went its way along the soft turf by the side of the towing-path, keeping near the hedge and moving quickly. They had turned a point from which a long stretch of river was visible. A stranger to the scene might have been certain that here and there along the line of hedge a figure stood, watching the bargeman, and waiting for him to come up. So he himself had often believed at first, until his eyes became used to the posts, bearing the dagger that slew Wat Tyler, in the City of London shield. (*Our Mutual Friend*, 621–2)

In this hallucination, a visual outline literally wavers between person and sign. The positing of a "stranger" to view the scene allows the narrative to make the obscurity visible—and to narrate the sequence of apprehension ("so he himself had often believed at first"). Earlier in the text, as Mortimer, Wrayburn, and the policeman wait for Gaffer by the river in the dark (they will find him dead, tied to his boat, as if he had at last truly found the corpse he was looking for), shapes in the darkness likewise take on ambiguous human form: "The night was not so dark but that, besides the lights at bows and mastheads gliding to and fro, they could discern some shadowy bulk attached; and now and then a ghostly lighter with a large dark sail, like a warning arm, would start up very near them, pass on, and vanish" (168). Or, in another, similarly unsettling passage:

> With his Fortunatus's goblet ready in his hand, Mr Riderhood sat down on one side of the table before the fire, and the strange man on the other: Pleasant occupying a stool between the latter and the fireside. The background, composed of handkerchiefs, coats, shirts, hats, and other old articles "On Leaving," had a general dim resemblance to human listeners; especially where a shiny black sou'wester suit and hat hung, looking very like a clumsy mariner with his back to the company, who was so curious to overhear, that he paused for the purpose with his coat half pulled on, and his shoulders up to his ears in the uncompleted action. (352)

A hallucinated form, caught in mid-action, appears to listen; another of the novel's incipient or imperfectly animated forms, its listening posture (and incipient animation) evokes the reader, likewise eavesdropping on a scene at which he or she is only figurally present.

It is perhaps not surprising that faces in the text are often the objects of interpretive scrutiny—correctly to read them is to make manifest a community of interpretation (where, the grounds shared, the outcomes usually can be presumed to be, too), a subtlety of perception, or (and this is opposed to neither of the others) a subjugation to another's will that necessitates attentive scrutiny.[22] (Thus can Bradley Headstone read the fact of his fits—or the presence of Riderhood in the school—in the terrified countenances of his pupils; thus, too, do various happily and unhappily married couples commune: most notably, the Boffins and the Lammils, or the Wilfers, if one counts R.W.'s downright canine attention to the majestic face of his wife.) Perhaps more unexpected is the way that such interpretative questions return one to prior questions of articulation and voice, and to the emergence of a "figure" from a neutral ground. Bradley Headstone's monomaniacal fixation on Wrayburn and Lizzie is described as a fixed gaze at "two figures": "So slow were the schoolmaster's thoughts, and so indistinct his purposes when they were but tributary to the one absorbing purpose or rather when, like dark trees under a stormy sky, they only lined the long vista at the end of which he saw those two figures of Wrayburn and Lizzie on which his eyes were fixed—that at least a good half-mile was traversed before he spoke again" (540). The monomaniacal fixation on the lovers he will drive together is almost less striking here than the abstraction, the turning of human forms to the semblance of "dark trees under a stormy sky," lining a vista. More benignly, Miss Peecher's unrequited love for Bradley likewise involves a hypostatization: "For, oftentimes when school was not, and her calm leisure and calm little house were her own, Miss Peecher would commit to the confidential slate an imaginary description of how, upon a balmy evening at dusk, two figures might have been observed in the market-garden ground round the corner, of whom one, being a manly form, bent over the other, being a womanly form of short stature and some compactness, and breathed in a low voice the words, 'Emma Peecher, wilt thou be my own?'" (333–4). "Were copies to be written? In capital B's and H's most of the girls under Miss Peecher's tuition were half a year ahead of every other letter in the alphabet" (334): devotedly evoking him, Miss Peecher also reduces her beloved first to an outline seen at dusk, then to letters—and, then, more literally, to figures, as he also takes the form of mathematical exercises for the girls' slates.

In Bradley's case, his willful reading calls into being the sight he dreads: "I saw them walking side by side" (625). In a psychologically astute rendering of the self-destructive, morbid will of erotic jealousy (which here, cruelly, brings about the union it most fears), Bradley's pathological reading literalizes a movement elsewhere visible in the text. Just after he takes the signs by the river for human forms, the dagger on the sign (for the city of London) becomes for him like the dagger floating before Macbeth—and recalls the true object of his jealous passion. The threat there—to Wrayburn, above all—is also a literalization of the threat that figural animation poses to persons, and it erupts eventually in violence, destroying Headstone after it nearly kills Wrayburn. As the "recumbent figure," Riderhood's drowned body, is brought into the inn, Miss Abbey "started back at the sight of it. 'Why, good God!' said she, turning to her two companions, 'that's the very man who made the declaration we have just had in our hands. That's Riderhood!'" (438). Here, the exchange is all but explicit, the consigning of a will or declaration to paper animates and de-animates bodies. Riderhood's reduction to a pure spark of life corresponds to his becoming a declaration that might be held in one's hand and read. In Miss Peecher's more benign positing—benign possibly because it is thwarted—we find, as in all the sometimes tedious comedy of her "slate," a similar link between writing and a positing of the human that is animating—or the reverse.

For the "two figures" in both cases recall the "two figures" at the opening of the novel—a boat with two figures in it, floating between two bridges. The floating faces in the text, its quasi-animated, quasi-legible figures or forms, like its thematics of pedagogy or formation (from Mortimer's imitation of Eugene, to the lessons in reading offered various characters, to the more than unpleasant, nearly unreadably cruel education-cum-manipulation through which Bella is taught to value domestic virtues above the material means that she is not supposed to know sustains them) and like its various discourses of made persons (from class mobility to the literal assembly of bodies), inscribe in every plot and sub-plot, and in much of the text's figural language, the drama of uncertain identity and doubling (wills, disappearances, drownings, disguises) of the central plot of John Harmon and all his various aliases. Prior to that, though, all of these elements inscribe a more primordial drama, a moment of hesitation prior to signification. When Charley Hexam is said to be of a "curious mixture . . . of uncompleted savagery and uncompleted civilization," he also displays a kind of proto-reading:

> His voice was hoarse and coarse, and his face was coarse, and his stunted figure was coarse; but he was cleaner than other boys of his type; and his writing, though large and round, was good; and he glanced at the backs of the books, with an awakened curiosity that went below the binding. No one who can read, ever looks at a book, even unopened on a shelf, like one who cannot. (28)

The novel's repeated use of "reading" to describe a kind of scrutiny that isn't, literally, reading is not only a rendering of any hermeneutic activity by analogy to the reading of a book—as when, for example, because of the stories she "finds" there, fires are said to be Lizzie's "books," which she "reads," first to Charley, and then to Jenny. In both cases, and especially when Charley looks at the spines of books, the supposition of literacy allows them to "read" without reading anything in particular. And thus these scenes also evoke the recurrent gaze at "figures" or forms that are not yet meaningful.[23]

The novel's many faces belong to this register, this moment prior to meaning. Thus does Gaffer's exhaustive recall of the bodies he has found in the river take the form of his reciting of the placards of missing men he has found dead, delivering up the contents of the bills for Wrayburn and Lightwood without being able to read them:

"Now, here," moving the light to another similar placard, "*his* pockets was found empty, and turned inside out. And here," moving the light to another, "*her* pocket was found empty, and turned inside out. And so was this one's. And so was that one's. I can't read, nor I don't want to it, for I know 'em by their places on the wall. This one was a sailor, with two anchors and a flag and G. F. T. on his arm. Look and see if he warn't."

"Quite right."

"This one was the young woman in grey boots, and her linen marked with a cross. Look and see if she warn't."

"Quite right."

"This is him as had a nasty cut over the eye. This is them two young sisters what tied themselves together with a handkecher. This the drunken old chap, in a pair of list slippers and a nightcap, wot had offered—it afterwards come out—to make a hole in the water for a quartern of rum stood aforehand, and kept to his word for the first and last time in his life. They pretty well papers the room, you see; but I know 'em all. I'm scholar enough!" (31–2)

Known by their places on the wall, these significant signs are both read and not read by Gaffer. Evoking also Rokesmith/Harmon/Hanford's perusal of the bill that announces his death, and the bill advertising for Hanford, the proto-reading here is thus also tied to the logic linking death and drowning to becoming paper or being written.

We might then recall that the text's address to the dead Gaffer—enjoining him, with cutting irony, to speak, something he will never more achieve outside of that ironic invocation—invokes the perception of a shape: "Soaking into this filthy ground as you lie here, is your own shape. Did you never see such a shape soaked into your boat? Speak, Father." "Your own shape" would seem to be Gaffer's body, after death. To emphasize the exchange of places with his erstwhile sources of profit is perhaps less to the point than to note how the dead body becomes a mere "shape"—like the stain on the bottom of his boat in the first chapter: "Trusting to the girl's skill and making no use of the rudder, he eyed the coming tide with an absorbed attention. So the girl eyed him. But, it happened now, that a slant of light from the setting sun glanced into the bottom of the boat, and, touching a rotten stain there which bore some resemblance to the outline of a muffled human form, coloured it as though with diluted blood. This caught the girl's eye, and she shivered" (14). A shape emerges, again, from the closed circuit of their gazes. The obliquity of the description—bearing "some resemblance to the outline of a muffled human

form, coloured . . . as though with diluted blood"—links the attenuation of certainty in the fading of material forms (though faded by time, it *is* a stain left
by the impression of a body, and no doubt *is* colored by diluted human blood)
to the reader's perspective, a reader who does not yet know it is a bloody form
because he is still ignorant of Gaffer's macabre vocation. The text thus narrates that as it were propaedeutic view of the narrative events, and locates it as
the posited result of the crossing of attentive gazes: Gaffer's, at the water;
Lizzie's, at him; our own, at the two figures in the boat.

Thus, what is perhaps the governing image for *Our Mutual Friend* appears
at the end of Chapter I, as Gaffer "took a survey of what he had in tow":

> What he had in tow, lunged itself at him sometimes in an awful
> manner when the boat was checked, and sometimes seemed to try to
> wrench itself away, though for the most part it followed submissively. A
> neophyte might have fancied that the ripples passing over it were
> dreadfully like faint changes of expression on a sightless face; but
> Gaffer was no neophyte and had no fancies. (17)

These ripples return as Eugene strolls by the river in the moments before he
is attacked by Headstone: "The rippling of the river seemed to cause a corresponding stir in his uneasy reflections. He would have laid them asleep if he
could, but they were in movement, like the stream, and all tending one way
with a strong current. As the ripple under the moon broke unexpectedly now
and then, and palely flashed in a new shape and with a new sound, so parts of
his thoughts started, unbidden, from the rest, and revealed their wickedness"
(682). The rippling of water is the movement of our reflections, not to be laid
asleep, flashing forth new shapes and new sounds, like water lending expression to a dead face. Perspective lends the corpse—lunging, wrenching itself
away, or following submissively—the propulsive motion of the boat; we find a
perhaps similar uncertainty in our relation to figures that, animated or inert,
lend us life in turn, or leave us hanging, like an empty sou'wester suit, or a
figure that simply recedes back into the dark, unrealized. Neophytes (and
readers—the waterman scavenger is illiterate), we see what Gaffer does not in
the ripples of water passing over a sightless face, as if we might somehow read
the moment prior to our reading of a text: the uncertain animation of fictional
figures, the incipient meaning, lodged there in the mooring of our starting
out, inscribed in this text as the perpetually renewed drama of inception.

PART III
Our Stony Ancestry

6
Ovid and Orpheus

The act of writing begins with Orpheus's gaze, and that gaze is the
impulse of desire which shatters the song's destiny and concern,
and in that inspired and unconcerned decision reaches the origin,
consecrates the song. But Orpheus already needed the power of art
in order to descend to that instant. This means: one can only write
if one arrives at the instant towards which one can only move
through space opened up by the movement of writing. In order
to write one must already be writing. The essence of writing, the
difficulty of experience in the leap of inspiration also lie within
this contradiction.

— MAURICE BLANCHOT, "THE GAZE OF ORPHEUS"

Homer excelled in imagining what is great; Virgil in imagining what is
beautiful; Ovid in imagining what is new.

— JOSEPH ADDISON, *THE SPECTATOR* NO. 417

As is well known among classicists, Ovid's *Metamorphoses* becomes an object
of textual controversy as early as its second line.[1] For the detail in question,
the Loeb edition is representative of most modern editions:

In nova fert animus mutatas dicere formas
corpora; di, coeptis (nam vos mutastis et illas)
adspirate meis primaque ab origine mundi
ad mea perpetuum deducite tempora carmen![2]

In Allen Mandelbaum's translation:

> My soul would sing of metamorphoses.
> But since, o gods, you were the source of these
> bodies becoming other bodies, breathe
> your breath into my book of changes: may
> the song I sing be seamless as its way
> weaves from the world's beginning to our day.[3]

Or in Arthur Golding's:

> Of shapes transformde to bodies straunge, I purpose to entreate,
> Ye gods vouchsafe (for you are they ywrought this wondrous feate)
> To further this mine enterprise. And from the world begunne,
> Graunt that my verse may to my time, his course directly runne.[4]

Or, finally, in a literal, word-by-word translation:

> *Animus* my mind *fert* inclines [me] *dicere* to speak of *formas* forms
> *mutatas* changed *in nova corpora* into new bodies. *Dii* ye gods, (*nam*
> for *vos* you *mutastis et* also changed *illas* them;) *aspirate* breathe
> [propitious] *meis coeptis* on my undertakings; *deduciteque* and bring
> down *perpetuum carmen* an uninterrupted song *prima ab origine* from
> the first origin *mundi* of the world *ad mea tempora* to my own times.[5]

In question is the word *illas*, a plural feminine accusative pronoun. An 1894
edition by P. [Paul] Lejay[6] instead has *illa*, a neuter plural in the same case.
E. J. Kenney argued in 1976 for Lejay's reading, and others have followed suit,
expanding (and sometimes taking issue with) his reasons.[7] If the gods have
also changed "them" (*illa/illas*), the question is whether the referent is the
neuter *coeptis* (*illa*) or the feminine *formas* (*illas*), whether, on the one hand,
the gods also change the poet's undertakings or beginnings (one could render
coepta as *inceptions*)[8] or, on the other, whether they are responsible instead
for the metamorphosed forms described in the poem—the bodies of Daphne
and Niobe and their ilk.

   For Kenney (as for others), *illas* requires parsing the syntax as significantly,
and to his mind unacceptably, strained—in ways uncharacteristic of Ovid.[9] He
writes: "it is possible to keep 'illas' only, as Housman observed, if 'et' refers back
to 'mutastis': 'inspire me to tell of transformations, for you were also the cause of
them,' in Mr. Lee's reading."[10] William Anderson remarks that the parenthesis
has been "misunderstood" for "perhaps fifteen hundred years."[11] He continues:

> All our manuscripts, which go back to sources no later than the fifth
> or sixth century, give the reading *illas* for the final word of 2, which

means that the scribes understood the pronoun "them" to refer to the forms of line 1, not the "beginnings." So for centuries it was assumed that the parenthesis rather ineptly gave the gods credit for causing metamorphoses. However, Kenney (1976) and Kovacs (1987) show that the correct reading is neuter plural *illa*, to refer by the pronoun to *coeptis* ("beginnings").[12]

As R. J. Tarrant notes, the parenthesis occurs at a crucial moment for the poem's own form, the moment when the expected elegiac couplet (every second line of which would be a pentameter) reveals itself to be the hexameter of epic: "the words '*nam vos mutastis et illa*,' coming at the end of the second line, mark the point at which the meter reveals itself as hexameters rather than elegiacs." Ovid, he continues, "would then be neatly alluding to the fact that the *Metamorphoses* represented a departure from his customary elegiac poetry" (Tarrant, 351n35). As William Anderson notes, moreover, "What Ovid . . . made a caesura would normally, in his elegiac couplets have functioned as the break between the halves of the *pentameter*."[13] The drama of the metrical surprise thus remains, whether or not Ovid must be read (in *illa*) as explicitly referring to it. And the beginning of the poem is about thwarted expectations and reshaped beginnings in other ways as well. As has often been noted, "*In nova fert animus*" initially seems to complete a thought: As Kenney translates one's initial reading, "my inspiration carries (me) on to new things" (46), or, in Anderson's rendering, "My spirit takes me into new things" (Anderson, "Form Changed," 109).[14] It was also conventional for epics to begin with a noun specifying the principal theme ("Arma" ["arms," the *Aeneid*] or "μῆνιν" ["wrath," the *Iliad*]);[15] after its initial preposition, Ovid's epic might further lead one to expect an analogous noun (for example *nova* understood as a nominalized adjective, "new things"). The poem seems initially to invoke not the gods but its own originality.

Only as the poem continues (with a beautiful and startling instance of enjambment) do we understand that *nova* is an adjective modifying *corpora*; the implicit claim of originality ("here is a work the like of which the world has never seen" [Kenney, 46]) remains, perhaps, even as it is subject to a correction, or an implicit subordination (of *nova* to *corpora*, of Ovid's voice to the inspiring gods invoked in the proem). In the textual controversy, too, one almost wants to have it both ways: the hesitation between *illa* and *illas* itself enacts the exchange between Ovid's words and the shifting forms he depicts. In Kenney's account of the consequences of reading it as a moment of self-reference, "the implication . . . is that the *Metamorphoses* itself exists in consequence of a metamorphosis" (Kenney, 50). In the beginning, one might say, is metamorphosis, which is to say that, as in the level-jumping of self-reference, each moment of inception refers us to a prior one; there is no beginning, but only metamorphosis as a mode of perpetually sustained inception.

The markedly compressed proem (four lines—one might compare it to the eleven lines of the *Aeneid*'s opening invocation) as if installs its inception as the very matter of the poem. Repeatedly, of course, Ovid's poem gives us narratives of origins: where hyacinths come from (or why they look as they do), for instance, or the seasons, or cypress trees. (In several cases, Ovid gives several, conflicting, accounts of the same phenomenon.)[16] I would argue, however, that the poem is recurrently about inception in a larger sense; to return to one's inception might render, periphrastically, "metamorphosis" (and hence, also, by the logic of the poem, writing, singing, the creation of art). To that degree, metamorphosis, as the central movement of Ovid's text, embodies a paradox of inception: Each beginning points to something that came before it. That structure is inscribed in the larger movement of the text and is central to the famously exorbitant claim of immortality (*"vivam"*) with which it ends. ("I shall have life," in Mandelbaum's version [549], or "My lyfe shall everlastingly bee lengthened still by fame," in Golding's [404]; *vivam* could also be a subjunctive—"let me live" or "may I live.") Thus, the turn, after its opening invocation, to the creation of the world, points to a central concern of the poem, which begins with a world yet formless: "Before the sea and lands began to be, / before the sky had mantled every thing, / then all of nature's face was featureless— / what men call chaos." As the poet goes on to say, "no thing maintained its shape" (3). The giving of form that is creation is, however, hard to distinguish from the chaos it forms, and, when it returns fifteen books later in the speech from Pythagoras, this assertion becomes a claim for immortality: "For all things change, but no thing dies" (519); "in all this world, no thing can keep / its form. For all things flow; all things are born / to change their shapes" (520). Or:

> There is no thing that keeps its shape; for nature,
> the innovator, would forever draw
> forms out of other forms. In all this world—
> you can believe me—no thing ever dies.
> By birth we mean beginning to re-form,
> a thing's becoming other than it was;
> and death is but the end of the other state;
> one thing shifts here, another there;
> and yet the total of all things is permanent. (522–3)

The poem's concluding claim of immortality might thus be read as the poet's disappearance into the poem ("my book of changes," in Mandelbaum's

version [3]), into an ever-renewed inception, into the origin that precedes its
created world, and into metamorphosis itself—the perpetual birth that is
the re-forming of things.

If each metamorphosis recalls an inception that points, in turn, to something prior, each originary metamorphosis thus points also to itself, and therefore enacts, in each instance, the curiously self-grounding quality of the work
of art, the unfathomable beginning that is at once constitutive of the work and
utterly beyond it. It is no surprise, therefore, that Ovid's poem seems to have
trouble getting started, or, rather, seems to start by repeatedly starting again.[17]
(The poem's opening metrical feint, suspending one, until the second line,
between the dactylic hexameter of epic and the limping meter of the elegiac
couplet invented in the *Amores* in this sense moves this structure of inception
to the meta-level of the author's work.) As Deleuze remarks, cycles of creation
and destruction recur in origin myths—making clear that the second creation
or second birth is as crucial as the first. (The second origin, he goes on to say,
is perhaps even more important than the first, for it gives birth to the series.)[18]
In the *Metamorphoses*, after the prologue, the text opens with the beginning
of the world, its emergence out of formlessness, and from there it turns to the
origin of man—or, rather, to a series of origins. "May / the song I sing be seamless as its way / weaves from the world's beginning to our day" (3): if the song
be seamless, that seamlessness may come at the expense of a discontinuous
world.[19]

This rhythm of creation is also that of love, and of writing. In the beautiful
description of writing in the story of Byblis in Book IX, the love letter written
by the lovelorn nymph (enamored of her brother) takes shape as a series of era-
sures and redraftings:

And she begins to write,
composing words with care, though her hand shakes.
Her right hand grips the iron stylus, while
her left holds fast a slab of wax—as yet
untouched. And she, unsure, begins; she writes,
then cancels; traces letters, then repents;
corrects, is discontent, and then content;
picks up the tablets, lays them down; and when
they are at rest, she picks them up again.
She knows not what she wants; about to act,
she cancels her resolve. Upon her face
audacity is plain—but mixed with shame.
She has already written "sister" on

the tablet but decides to blot it out.

She cleans the wax and then inscribes these words: . . . (310)[20]

Recalling the poem's opening, this moment suggests that to write, and to create, is inevitably to revise, to begin by writing again.[21] Henry James's practice of revision, examined in Chapter 1, perhaps belongs in this tradition—its writing of potentiality is also an aesthetic practice of metamorphosis.

So, likewise, is the origin of man a series of draftings and redraftings.[22] After the creation of the world, "Then man was born" (5). The Creator is left indeterminate: "Either the Architect/of All, the author of the universe"—earlier identified as "whichever god it was" (4)—"in order to beget a better world/created man from seed divine—or else/Prometheus, son of Iapetus, made man/by mixing new-made earth with fresh rainwater" (6). "A muddled, indefinite account of human origins," as William Anderson writes (*Metamorphoses*, ed. Anderson, 152), here, as elsewhere, Ovid "muddles" things by presenting competing, contradictory accounts of origin. Whichever alternative ultimately determined it, this creation is presented as a transformation of the world: "So was the earth, which until then had been/so rough and indistinct, transformed: it wore/a thing unknown before—the human form" (6). In the fall that follows, the movement from a Golden Age to a Silver and then a Bronze, change emerges with duplicity, violence, and labor. Metamorphosis belongs to the fallen age; in the Golden age, there are no seasons, no agriculture, and no change. Though a world of plenty, the Golden Age is also a world without creation: There can be no emergence of "a thing unknown before." Thus, in the Bronze Age, "Men spread their sails before the wind,/whose ways the mariner had scarcely learned:/the wooden keels, which once had stood as trunks/upon the mountain slopes, now danced/upon the unfamiliar waves" (8). With exploration comes conquest, strife, and ambition; "not even heaven's heights/are safer than the earth" (9), and the Giants, vanquished in their presumptuous designs on Mount Olympus, provide yet another origin: the earth "gave their gore/new life: so that the Giants' race might not/be lost without a trace, she gave their shape/to humans whom she fashioned from that blood" (9).

Yet this is still not the beginning, or there is yet another beginning to come, for Jove resolves to "excise the malady/which can't be cured: mankind" (10), swearing that "a new race, one far different from the first,/emerging wondrously, would share the earth" (12). A flood that returns the world to formlessness ("Between the sea and land one cannot draw/distinctions: all is sea, but with no shore" [14]) sets the stage for another creation myth, a myth of antediluvian emergence in the story of Deucalion and Pyrrha. In their piety, these "last two exemplars," alone in "a wasteland where deep silence ruled, a bare/and desolate expanse" (17, 16) atone for the sacrilege of Lycaon (who most immediately inspires the rage of Jove), and they are told by Themis that they can repeople the earth if they cast the "bones/of the great mother" behind them. The son of Prometheus decodes the imperative, which at first seems sacrilegious (an imperative to dig up the bones of his mother), and he and Pyrrha realize that the bones in question are those of the earth, or stones. They

> Veil their heads, they both ungird their clothes;
> And they throw stones behind them as they go.
> And yes (if those of old did not attest
> the tale I tell you now, who could accept
> its truth?), the stones began to lose their hardness;
> they softened slowly and, in softening,
> changed form. Their mass grew greater and their nature
> more tender; one could see the dim beginning
> of human forms . . .
> And since the gods had willed it so, quite soon
> The stones the man had thrown were changed to men,
> And those the woman cast took women's forms.
> From this, our race is tough, tenacious; we
> Work hard—proof of our stony ancestry. (18–19)

Once again, the poem finds an origin for humankind in metamorphosis, also figured here by the softening of stones. For Frederick Ahl, moreover, this "re-generation of the human race by Deucalion and Pyrrha is based on an etymological wordplay" legible "long before Ovid's time."[23] He notes that "their actions, Apollodorus tells us (1.7.2), are reflected in the derivation of the word 'people' (LAoi) from 'stones' (LAes)" (Ahl, 104). (Examples of the reverse movement—from people to stones—occur, he notes, as early as *Iliad* 24.611 [Ahl, 105].) In Book I of the *Metamorphoses*, humankind, recreated, is followed by the animals, who are born spontaneously from the earth. From here, the poem itself finally gets going; the rest of Book I concerns itself largely with various myths of the birth of writing and art: Apollo and Daphne, Syrinx, and Io and Jove.[24] (As with the other books, the "inner" stories replay in various ways the framing action; in the case of Book I, the unifying thread is, fittingly, origins. The myths of the origin of writing and art link the birth of the text to the creation of the world it narrates just before this—what is as if serial creation in the opening of the text becomes a series of myths, not sequential this time [it doesn't matter whether any of the stories occur "before" any of the others], but as it were in parallel.)

The origin story of Deucalion and Pyrrha returns, more or less obliquely, at several moments in the course of the poem—as, for instance, when Jason repeats a similar gesture, casting snakes' teeth rather than stones, and causing warriors to spring from the earth: "so here, the likeness/of men, perfected in the pregnant earth,/sprang from the soil." Armed for battle, they attack Jason, who then reverses Deucalion's feat. Hurling a massive stone into their midst, he causes them to "rage against each other," and "the brothers/sprung from the earth met death in civil war" (214). Notably, too, it returns in Book XV in a simile that describes the wonder of a revived Hippolytus, who witnesses Egeria (her grief unassuaged by the story he has told of his own transformation) become the "waters of a cool, eternal spring":

> That prodigy astonished all the nymphs,
> Just as it stupefied Hippolytus—
> In fact his wonder was so great, it matched
> The wonder an Etruscan farmer felt
> When he, amid the fields, beheld a clod
> That seemed portentous—moving by itself,
> With no one budging it; and then it lost
> its earthly shape; it took on human form;
> and opening its newborn lips, it spoke
> of things that were to come. The natives called
> that augur Tages, and he was the first
> to teach the people of Etruria
> to read the future. (535)[25]

Whatever else it does, the simile leads one to recall, near the end of the poem, the story of Deucalion and Pyrrha at the beginning, and links that story to the "prophecies" at the very end, which promise that the poet shall have life.

Our stony ancestry appears in other ways in the text. Stones often appear to figure the falling silent that sometimes accompanies metamorphosis, the loss of human speech whereby the transformed body cedes its voice to the poem that describes the change. For instance, Battus, a farmer who would have betrayed Mercury (65–6); Aglauros, envious of her sister (70–1); Echo ("Her voice and bones are all that's left; and then/her voice alone: her bones, they say, were turned/to stone" [93]); those of the Theban women who dare to rebuke Juno, and who are thus denied the opportunity to follow Ino in her leap into the sea (131); Atlas, turned to stone (made into a mountain) by Perseus and Medusa's head (135); Niobe, bereft of the children she was so proud of, and made a stone that weeps (189); Lichas, hurled by Hercules as punishment for betrayal (296–7); a monstrous wolf in Book XI, changed to marble "as he held

fast a heifer he had ripped" (376); Hecuba, in grief, left "mute as stone, as stiff"
(451); Scylla (476); and Anxarete left, also in grief, "a stony form" (505). Likewise, coral, hardened by Medusa's head, embodies the change that comes from
the movement between elements: It "keeps that nature to this day;/the pliant
weed that sways beneath the waves,/above the surface stiffens into stone" (139).
And becoming-stone is made, in the final book, another in a series of instances
of the transformation to which all things are consigned: "And there's a river of
the Cicones/that turns to stone the guts of those who drink/its waters; anything its waters touch/is changed to marble" (525).

At a certain moment in the story of Perseus, this transformation moves as
if in reverse and points to this stony change's linking of desire and the aesthetic
animation expressed, in its most condensed form, by the poem's closing claim
of life. Here is Perseus and Andromeda, anticipating the story of Galatea and
Pygmalion:

> Andromeda was tied to a rough rock;
> And when he saw her, Perseus would have thought
> She was a marble statue, were it not
> For a light breeze that stirred her hair, and warm
> Tears trickling down her cheeks. He was struck dumb;
> A flame—its force was strange—swept through his limbs;
> Her beauty gripped him—he almost forgot
> To beat his wings, to keep his airborne course. (136 [iv: 663–85])

After he has vanquished Atlas by turning him to stone, Perseus, carrying the
head of Medusa, has this power, figuratively, turned against him—by, moreover, his desire for a woman who seems a marble statue. Frozen in the contemplation of a spectacle that mimics the power he has appropriated, he
presents an allegory of aesthetic capture: the beautiful woman who resembles
the work of art, or the work of art whose tiny, almost impalpable effects give it
the appearance of life, produces another reversal, the spectator himself "struck
dumb." Perseus thus allegorizes a structure implicit in the poem's movement
from Deucalion and Pyrrha to Tages: the poetic voice, coming into being, contemplates its inception, and, merging with its origin, falls silent. Notably,
then, "I shall live" or "I shall have life" (*vivam*) defers that life to a later moment that does not coincide with the poem, or with its writing, or even with
the mortal life of the poet himself.[26]

I will return to that possible implication of the poetic voice's confrontation
with (its) inception. First, however, I would dwell on a possibly more complex
echo of "our stony ancestry," the recurrent emergence of stone in Books X and
XI in the songs of Orpheus. Ovid, unlike the Virgil of the *Georgics*, recalls

the version of the ancient myth (given, for example, by Phanocles in his *Loves*, a Hellenistic [circa 425 B.C.E.] collection of homoerotic love stories)[27] in which Orpheus is the originator of love for boys. Renouncing women after the second death of Eurydice, "he was the one who taught/the Thracian men this practice: they bestow/their love on tender boys, and so enjoy/firstfruits, the brief springtime, the flowers of youth" (Ovid, *Metamorphoses*, 328).[28] In Ovid's time, Thrace was a tributary of Rome; it became a Roman province in 46 A.D. Whether or not Ovid presupposes a subsequent transmission to Rome from this once Persian domain, which, proverbial for effeminacy, was Hellenized before the Romans conquered it, is only one of many questions raised by this moment.[29] Such effeminacy would also include immoderate passion for women. Thus in Book VI of the poem, Ovid attributes the uncontrollable passion of the Thracian Tereus for Philomela, his wife's sister, in part to "an inborn tribal urge": "the flame of love/had taken Tereus, as if one had set/afire ripe grain, dry leaves, or a haystack./It's true she's fair, but he is also spurred/by venery, an inborn tribal urge./The vice inflaming him is both his own/and that dark fire which burns in Thracian souls" (195). Recent scholarship suggests that the Romans did not perceive desire for women and desire for boys as opposed—and certainly did not perceive them as opposites. According to Craig Williams, the crucial distinction for the Romans, as for the Greeks, was one of sexual roles, understood as gendered, no matter what the gender of the object.[30] An entire taxonomy is legible in Roman texts, he suggests; among the more fascinating revelations (for the non-specialist) is that Latin featured a series of verbs for sexual acts that differentiated not only among different orifices but between "active" and "passive" roles: If, just as in English, one could express the idea of being penetrated (for example) through a passive formulation (*to be fucked* as opposed to *to fuck*), Latin also had an active verb for the passive role in relation to each orifice.[31] To submit to penetration was not necessarily grammatically passive; it was conceived as actively done (at least potentially), and with strict consequences for gendered roles.

That, however, is a different thing from forming an identity. While it seems clear that some people preferred a particular gender, and even exclusively, for the structuring oppositions of the culture, the gender of one's desired object did not make anything like an identity. Rather, the crucial distinction is mapped along lines of penetration, and prohibition, in terms of objects, was centered not on gender but on social status: For the Roman citizen, sex with another citizen, male or female, youth or adult, was a problem. For the Romans, as for the Greeks, boys (teenaged boys) were a desirable category; unlike the Greeks, the Romans seem to have had no institution formalizing the erotic pursuit of citizen boys. The Greeks seem to have developed modes for citizen boys to take part in penetrative sex—as long as they were understood not to take pleasure in it, and as long as they received, as recompense, enlightenment or training in citizenship.[32] Williams shows, however, the Roman perception of teenaged boys as desirable was *not*, as some scholars have assumed, imported from the Greeks. For the Romans (again, like the Greeks), prohibition was centered on gender in another sense; to be penetrated was understood as incompatible with male identity. Williams repeatedly shows that social disapproval attends not sex with another man but the so-called passive position—and oral sex was "worse" than anal sex because the mouth was the organ of citizenship. Like the Greeks, then, to be penetrated (above all, to desire to be penetrated, for they understood that men, like women, were raped in war) disqualified one from citizenship. Williams's arguments are, of course, about the codification of sexual mores as they are legible in texts and other artifacts; no one would claim that such mores map perfectly onto everyone's experience of sexual desire.[33] In fact, it stands to reason that, given this ideological structure, the idea of being penetrated by another man must have exerted a powerful attraction for some, perhaps for many, men; the consequences of allowing that attraction to become visible were in most (though Williams also suggests not all) cases dire.

However that may be, Ovid's rendering of the Thracian "origin" of the desire for boys is thus more complex than it may initially appear—because the preference for boys is in no obvious way the "opposite" of an attraction for women, and because it is not a desire that, a priori, demands an explanation in a Roman context.[34] Williams repeatedly shows that desire for boys was presumed to be natural; or rather, since the natural would not have been at all the category it has become (for instance) for us, a desire for boys was simply taken as a given. Boys are "meant" to be anally penetrated, just as women are meant to be penetrated—vaginally, in the first place, but also orally and anally. Such acts were "natural" to the degree that anatomical possibilities aligned with social roles. In that regard, boys are a distinct gender from men, who are not "meant" to be penetrated. For Orpheus to turn to boys after the death of Eurydice is not to turn to a new "orientation" but to choose an alternative that would always, at least virtually, have been available to him. The forbearance would, in fact, have had much more to do with the field of women—that is, insofar as it singled out, in mourning her, one woman (Eurydice) among all others as alone desirable. It is only in the context of a later period that did organize desire according to an opposition between exclusive desires oriented toward specific genders that Orpheus's choice can appear foundational of an identity. Confronted by later commentators who return to Ovid's Orpheus, therefore, we face a multi-layered historical dilemma of (once again) lost inception, since Roman sexuality (to the degree that it can be taken as unified and consistent) is read through the lens of a later period's models of sexuality (including that period's understanding of the historicity— or ahistoricity—of sexuality). Whether framed in terms of approbation or reprobation, the later perception of Orpheus as originating a homoerotic tradition involves (to the degree that homoeroticism is understood as something like the "opposite" of desire for women) an anachronistic understanding of sexuality in Ovid's world. Ovid would not have understood this desire as "homoerotic"; the desire in question is for boys (not men, and not "same-sex" desire), and is not opposed to a desire for women.

That he did figure as such a source for later periods makes him a curiously elusive foundation for a desire that he himself could never have experienced. Critics note that Orpheus becomes an explicit touchstone for the fifteenth-century Florentine neo-Platonists (for instance) and that he lingers on in the Middle Ages, where, according to John Block Friedman, emphases on other aspects of the Orphic myth kept it alive for commentators in late antiquity and the Middle Ages: In early Christianity, he appears as an advocate of monotheism (and the pupil of Moses in an important Jewish forgery); later, in his role as psychopomp, he foretells Christ, becoming a composite figure in which Orphic iconography is understood to represent the savior; for Boethius and medieval commentaries on his *Consolation of Philosophy*, he is a moralized Orpheus who, as a couple with Eurydice, allegorizes complementary aspects of the human soul, reason and passion; with Eurydice again, in an account deriving from Fulgentius, he serves to form an allegory of the arts; and, most notably in *Sir Orfeo* and Henryson's *Orpheus and Eurydice*, the couple lives on in medieval romance.[35] For Arthur Golding, writing in his epistle, Book X embodies forms of illicit love, and the desire for boys falls under the seemingly more general name of incest: "The tenth booke chiefly dooth containe one kynd of argument / Reproving most prodigious lusts of such as have bene bent / To incest most unnaturall."[36] Still other historical questions emerge here that scholars have answered in diverse ways—namely, whether boy love was a distinct category in this later period, and how, therefore, the Ovidian passage might have sounded to Golding and other early modern readers.

For Friedman, the medieval tradition largely suppresses what he sees as the homoerotic dimensions of this origin tale in Ovid; for Bruce W. Holsinger, on the other hand, "the most startling aspect of the treatment of Orpheus in medieval mythographies is how often writers in the tradition in fact *fail* to elide Orpheus's homoerotic turn and obscure the original justification for the dismemberment of his body."[37] For Holsinger, the very efforts by certain writers to transform the homoerotic dimensions of the myth into Christian alle-

gory end up making that homoeroticism central to the moralizing accounts
that would leave it behind. Thus, for instance, even in the *Ovide moralisé*, if
the harp allegory though which the poet links the Orpheus story to Christ
produces a "thorough *psychological* fragmentation that recasts in Christian
terms the punitive dismemberment of the original, homoerotic Orpheus,"
that strategy, Holsinger suggests, also means that "Orpheus's homoerotic mu-
sicality directly inspires much of the poet's mythological creativity throughout this section of the *Ovide moralisé*" (319). "The energetic allegoresis
performed . . . throughout Book 10 highlights what is of course the motivating irony of medieval Christian mythography, a tradition of commentary that
depends upon and amplifies the various forms of eroticism it excoriates on the
literal level"; the poet, Holsinger concludes, "comes perilously close to locating
Christ himself as the quintessential Orphic sodomite, the savior who sings the
'New Song' luring young men into the faith" (320–1). Holsinger traces the
fate of what he sees as the homoerotic strand of the Orpheus story through
the medieval and early modern traditions—in Dante's *Purgatorio* (where homoeroticism, Holsinger suggests, serves as part of Dante's mode of negotiating
his relation to Virgil and antiquity [327–8]), for instance, and in Thomas
Heywood's use of John Lydgate[38]—concluding: "The fragmentation of his
legend and his body allows Orpheus to endure across the millennia as a continually revivified occasion for the musical practice of the flesh. Orpheus's
dissident musical *corpus*—despite punitive dismemberment in the *Metamorphoses*, centuries of denial or explicit vilification by poets and polemicists, and
anxious allegorical fragmentation at the hands of Christian mythographers—
ultimately survives" (343).[39]

Compelling as this narrative is, there is a major problem: There is no
"homoeroticism" to obscure or, on the contrary, to make explicit because this
simply isn't a category for the Romans. A question may be where, historically,
the category appears; before it can be submitted to the ideological work of
elision or explicitation (by Holsinger, or by the medieval texts he reads) it must
first be constructed as an anachronistic category. In other terms, the origin is
retrospective and in a sense self-reflexive; a later culture discovers its own
forms of sexuality and posits an origin for them in an anachronistic understanding of the Roman text. The homoerotic Orpheus illuminates the cul-
tures that look back to find him much more than he does the culture that
originated him. There would be a fascinating story to tell—by a writer with
different forms of competence than mine—about the fate of this homoerotic
Orpheus thus constituted after the era that Holsinger describes;[40] Mark Jordan's
fascinating account of the category of sodomy suggests that the reception
of Ovid was central to the complex "invention" of sodomy in Christian

theology.[41] Likewise, another reading might look to Orpheus for a more general origin myth—an alternative to Oedipus. One origin myth for desire for boys traces it to Oedipus's father, Laius, who, in exile from Thebes, kidnaps and rapes the beautiful son (Chrysippus) of his host, Pelops (Hubbard, *Homosexuality in Greece and Rome*, 78–9). This story, the subject of a lost play by Euripides, makes boy love central to the myriad unrelenting trials of Laius's family in the doomed generations that tread him down. Even so, Orpheus is in many ways a more appealing cultural originator:[42] Displacing the terms of family dynamics that so captivated Freud, the narrative produces not heterosexuality (or heterosexual neurosis) but (for the moderns) homosexuality. Against the futurity of Oedipus, Orpheus embodies a song of temporal suspension: Oedipus is structured by prophecy; Orpheus, by looking back.[43] And where, finally, Oedipus solidifies identity—for the mythic character who cannot elude his fate, as for the child who cannot evade its structuring complex—Orpheus disperses it, finding the origins of song in the inhabiting of disparate voices, even as his body, dismembered, sings in its very fragments, arriving at Lesbos to inspire that (for us) most fragmented of poets, Sappho.

In place of these larger claims, I would like to focus on the episode as it functions in the poem, on a form of suspension—figured by stone—that replays, in miniature, the structure of the poem as a whole. For Frederick Ahl, Orpheus's name encrypts a multilingual reference to metamorphosis and death. He is the example for one of the rules Ahl adduces for wordplay in Ovid and other classical poets (the rule that Greek words can retain their Greek meaning and become objects of bilingual wordplay in Latin).[44] In other ways, too, Orpheus is central to the poem. If the poem takes shape, as it were, between two abyssal moments of creation—the repeated origins of the beginning and "*vivam*" at the end—the tales of Book X appear between two deaths and between two descents into hell, and thus, among other things, explicitly link Orpheus's tales and terrestrial life. In this sense, it could also be said that the songs of Book X replay the journey out of hell with Eurydice and mark the interval between the escape and the inevitable return when Orpheus looks back. From the outset, Orpheus asks merely for an interval:

> For all of us are yours to rule by right;
> our stay above is brief; when that is done
> we all must—sooner, later—speed to one
> same dwelling place. We all shall take this way:
> our final home is here; the human race
> must here submit to your unending sway.
> She, too, will yet be yours when she has lived

in full the course of her allotted years.
I ask you only this: lend her to me. (326)

His songs, likewise, mark the momentary reprieve before our place knows us
no more; Samuel Croxall's eighteenth-century translation makes explicit, with
beautiful economy, that his final death is a return: "his ghost flies downward
to the Stygian shore / And knows the places it had seen before."[45] Or here is
Jack Spicer's condensed vision of that structure: "'Orpheus!' / He was at the entrance again / And a little three-headed dog was barking at him. / Later he
would remember all those dead voices / And call them Eurydice."[46]

Orpheus dies when his songs cannot be heard, when the shrieking of the
frenzied women drowns out the poet's voice, and its power to charm (until this
point, "even the stones / were held in thrall by Orpheus's tender tones," and,
hurled at him, "yield to the spell / of his enchanting voice and lyre" and fall harm-
lessly to the ground): "And so, at last, the stones were stained with blood, / the
blood of one whose voice could not be heard" (359). (Croxall's translation has
"Deafen'd stones.") Bloodied by stones, and finally torn apart by agricultural
tools left behind by the terrified farmers, Orpheus's death recalls the effect of
grief on him earlier. If the first death inspires the song that releases Eurydice
from the underworld, the second loss leaves Orpheus (momentarily) silent:

> And when that second death had struck his wife,
> the poet—stunned—was like the man whose fright
> on seeing Cerberus, three-headed hound
> enchained by Hercules, was so complete
> that he was not set free from fear until,
> his human nature gone, he had become
> a body totally transformed—to stone.
> Or one might liken Orpheus instead
> to Olenus, who took the blame himself
> for his Lethaea's arrogance when she—
> unfortunately—boasted of her beauty:
> Lethaea, you and he were once two hearts
> whom love had joined: but now you are two rocks
> that Ida holds on its well-watered slopes. (327–8)

If the falling silent of "one whose voice could not be heard" marks his death,
it also marks the moment when Orpheus enters into the songs he sings, when
he becomes, as the poem subsumes his voice, the final tale in his part of the
poem—the tale that he, in singing of baffled love, becomes. (There never was
a world for him except the one he sang and, singing, made.)

As Orpheus's head floats toward Lesbos,

. . . in your flow,
you, Hebrus, gathered in his head and lyre;
and (look! A thing of wonder) once your stream
had caught and carried them, the lyre began
to sound some mournful notes; the lifeless tongue,
too, murmured mournfully; and the response
that echoed from the shores was mournful, too. (361)

Orpheus continues to command a rapt nature, even in his disappearance, as the trees shed their leaves in grief, and the rivers swell with tears. This moment marks the becoming indistinct of Orpheus's charisma and the absorption it inspires. The tongue, murmuring, is yet "lifeless," and Orpheus, his soul returning again to the underworld, joins the mourning for his loss, and merges with his lyre, and with the "response that echoed from the shores." Origin and end become indistinct in this closing of a circuit of absorption, which makes the death of Orpheus a figure for the birth of poetry. The serpent that would bite his floating head, turned to stone by the intervening Phoebus, thus also figures the power of absorption that now unites Orpheus and the entranced world he seduced. The description of Orpheus's head as it floats downstream recalls moments earlier in the poem where a poetic voice is made indistinguishable from an automatism that arrives with death: the poet Ampycus, priest of Ceres, whose hand strikes his lyre as he falls, lifeless, in the bloodbath with which Perseus celebrates his nuptials ("the dying fingers brushed again/across the lyre's strings; that touch,/by chance, gave voice to sad and shadowed chords" [149]), and the severed tongue of Philomena, which continues to make inarticulate noise ("there, on the blood-red soil,/it murmurs" [199]).[47] In those exorbitant moments, absorption is as if separated from poet and reader alike, to be objectified in these riveting images of automatism—in moments, too, where poetic utterance merges with unmeaning sound, the murmuring of a lifeless tongue, the chance brushing of dying fingers on a lyre. Becoming stone returns the poetic voice to its origins, even as it figures both animation (of the world, of song) and absorption in the song of another.

The recursive turn whereby Orpheus's own story merges with the absorption he elicits from the world—his song turning back on itself to leave him rapt and originating—is also contained in the structure of address. The lines are at once about Orpheus and addressed to him: "The birds, in mourning, wept/o Orpheus—the throngs of savage beasts,/and rigid stones, and forests, too—all these/had often followed as you sang" (360). This doubled structure then extends to the river that holds him: "you, Hebrus, gathered in his head

and lyre; / and (look! A thing of wonder) . . ." (361). A not uncommon structure in the poem more generally, which often tells of those changed by turning to address them, here it marks the way that this recursive structure of address
is linked to the merger of origin and end, enacted as the poetic voice (foregrounded as such in these apostrophes) turns to meaningless murmur. The
stoniness that figures the falling-silent of the poetic voice also recalls the effect
of voice in the singer's first descent into the underworld:

> The bloodless shades shed tears; they heard his plea,
> the chant the Thracian had accompanied
> with chords upon his lyre. Tantalus
> no longer tried to catch the fleeing waves;
> Ixion's wheel stood still—entranced, amazed;
> the vultures did not prey on Tityus' liver;
> the Danaids left their urns; and Sisyphus,
> you sat upon your stone. (326)[48]

Orpheus embodies the structure of creation at the beginning of the text; just
as, in falling silent, the poet joins the rapt listeners he enthralls, the poem
makes becoming-stone indistinguishable from a kind of animation. Indeed,
Orpheus has both effects: Turning listeners as if to stone (and causing thrown
stones to accede, prematurely, to the force of gravity and lie still), he also animates the trees, which, in the beautiful opening of Book X, are called by his
song to uproot themselves and gather around the poet and his lyre. Likewise,
love in Ovid's poem is at once an animating, transforming force, and an im-
mobilizing, or even a lethal one: Recall, among many other examples, the stories of Apollo and Hyacinth, or of Cyparissus (where the boy's love for the stag
he inadvertently kills is doubled by Apollo's love for him, and his loss of the
boy in turning him into the tree that emblematizes grief). In still other terms,
this is also why the story of Galatea and Pygmalion belongs with the others in
Book X: to become stone in death or grief merges with the animation of stone
in art, the coming-to-life effected by art or love. Orpheus's death is his song.
Stone allows one to perceive this aspect of the suspension between two deaths—
those of Eurydice, and those of Orpheus, singing of tragic love after his return,
alone, from the underworld and before his final return to it—as the space of
metamorphosis, where the path out of hell is indistinguishable from the looking back that consigns Eurydice to it once and for all.

Another way to perceive this structure would be to focus on the different
forms of connection that unify the songs in Book X. As in the rest of the poem,
these connections are at once narrative, figural, and conceptual.[49] Thus, in
the story of Cyparissus at the beginning of Book X, the story of his becoming

a Cypress is narratively motivated: He is one of the trees that, lured by the Orphic song, gathers to listen to the poet sing. Figurally, the story's resolution links the boy with all the other arboreal transformations in the book, and elsewhere in the text: with Daphne, for example, or with Myrrha or the Bacchae. Conceptually, this is a story about intransigent grief (that of Cyparissus, but also that of Apollo): These stories of love, told in the space between Orpheus's two passages into the underworld, repeat the losses for which they also offer consolation. The path out, once again, is made difficult to distinguish from a looking back. That fact, too, makes for another form of conceptual unification: the tales repeatedly reenact, at this remove, the framing narrative of Orpheus and Eurydice, a redoublement that is further reeanacted here in Apollo's grief for his grieving beloved boy. To that extent, moreover, the impetus of metamorphosis links creative power—Apollo's, in this instance, to transform the boy into a tree, as an emblem for the ultimately poetic power of metamorphosis in the text—to the absorption it inspires. Apollo takes the place both of the poet who composes and the reader who contemplates these stories of grief and transformation. These forms of unification—metonymical and metaphorical—both propel the narrative (moving it, metonymically, from one transformation to the next, and linking the narrative in a progressive series) and stall it in repeated formulations of a central structure of metamorphosis.

As my earlier claims imply, it makes little sense to pit the desire for Eurydice against that for the boys who (for the course of Book X) are the focus of Orpheus's desire—except perhaps for an anachronistic view seeking to find or justify its own sexual ideologies in the Latin poem. Narratively, Ovid's poem might be read to privilege, on the one hand, the desire for Eurydice insofar as her loss would seem to be originary, and insofar as the poem gives us, in the coda Ovid adds to the story in Book XI, the couple's happy reunion as the ostensible resolution of the narrative. On the other hand, the narrative pleasure (which is also to say all of the stories that Orpheus sings of) is in the middle, in the suspension between, before resolution puts an end to songs and delay. If Orpheus's death, however, is his song, the turn away from Eurydice is perhaps not to be distinguished from the turn toward her.[50] Read in relation to the figuring of voice in this poem, this logic would also be one way to make sense of the long passage in Book X where Orpheus cedes his voice to Venus and where the parallel is explicit: Venus, speaking to Adonis, sits in the shade of the trees, just as Orpheus does for the singing of his songs, and her story, likewise, can delay but not prevent the death of the beautiful boy who does not heed her warning. The poetic voice, as it is figured in this book, comes into being with its disappearance, and with its transformation into another's, which is also to say that it enacts the logic of "I shall have life."[51]

Thus one might link Orpheus—and perhaps even the poet himself—to the plight of Echo, who in Book III, is doomed to speak only the words of others, as punishment, one notes, for so often telling tales designed to enable Jove's philandering by delaying Juno. She cannot initiate speech; as her name suggests, she can only echo it. "As soon as Juno had seen through that plot, / she menaced Echo: 'From now on you'll not / have much use of that voice that tricked me so' / The threat was followed by the fact. And Echo / can mime no more than the concluding sounds / of any words she's heard . . . she cannot begin / to speak: her nature has forbidden this; / and so she waits for what her state permits: / to catch the sounds that she can then give back / with her own voice" (91–2).[52] Thus consigned to secondary speech, to a speech whose beginning is, explicitly, exterior to it, she becomes herself the mode of further captivation: in her very desire, she is part of the mirror that entraps Narcissus by echoing back his words, along with his face's reflection in the pool. That the analogy therefore links Echo, Narcissus, Orpheus, and Ovid also suggests how perilous these echoes might be for a reader, who encounters, as it were, Orpheus's head floating toward Lesbos, with all its Medusa-like power to turn one to stone. (Notably, in Virgil's *Georgics*, Orpheus's severed head says "Eurydice," and the name is echoed by "the banks of the downward river Hebrus.")[53] The dispersion through which the poet is figured as consolidating himself is enacted not only by Orpheus's dismemberment at the end (his still murmuring head coming to reside at Lesbos) but also by the narrative profusion of this book. As Kaja Silverman writes, "Orpheus recounts so many consecutive stories that by the time we reach the end of Book X, we have forgotten all about him" (*Flesh of My Flesh*, 51).

The degree to which the turning toward Eurydice is difficult to distinguish from a turning away from her—a conflation that is in fact the literal result of Orpheus's own turning back, which consigns her to Hades—could also be said to structure the grief Orpheus's stories of love convey: The transformations in Ovid at once console and make permanent the grief they memorialize. The songs that make up the bulk of Book X might be read, that is, either as compensatory or as replaying the losses they describe, and, the book as a whole, therefore, as a transforming of loss into art or as an intransigent refusal to yield in the claims of grief (and hence as a repetition of his original looking back). That the intransigence of grief might be what, paradoxically, transcends it, could be said to be Percy Bysshe Shelley's emphasis in his rendering of the myth:

Then from the deep and overflowing spring
Of his eternal ever-moving grief

There rose to Heaven a sound of angry song.
'Tis as a mighty cataract that parts
Two sister rocks with waters swift and strong,
And casts itself with horrid roar and din
Adown a steep; from a perennial source
It ever flows and falls, and breaks the air
With loud and fierce, but most harmonious roar,
And as it falls casts up a vaporous spray
Which the sun clothes in hues of Iris light.
Thus the tempestuous torrent of his grief
Is clothed in sweetest sounds and varying words
Of poesy. Unlike all human works,
It never slackens, and through every change
Wisdom and beauty and the power divine
Of mighty poesy together dwell,
Mingling in sweet accord. (ll.70–87)[54]

The combination of opposites—the angry song whose sound rose to heaven is
"as a mighty cataract" that "casts itself/Adown a steep," and its "loud and
fierce . . . roar" is made "harmonious" in part because the cataract casts back
"up a vaporous spray" to catch the sun. The "eternal ever-moving grief" becomes the permanence of poetry when, the "horrid roar and din" as it were
transformed to "hues of Iris light" in the sun, the "tempestuous torrent of his
grief/Is clothed in sweetest sounds and varying words/Of poesy." Shelley's lines
are explicitly about metamorphosis: the grieving Orpheus turned to a cataract,
and the tumult of its fall, to a rainbow—whose very ineffability is made an emblem of permanence by taking on the qualities of the "perennial source,"
which is tied, in turn and silently, to the perennial light of the sun. Varying
words persist through every change as the figure here figures figuration as a
mode of metamorphosis—what Shelley's poem renders as clothing: the vaporous spray clothed in hues of Iris light and the tempestuous torrent of the young
man's grief clothed in sweetest sounds and varying words of poesy.

Shelley thus renders what is more or less explicit in Ovid's metamorphic
emblems of grief. For David Kovacs, if Tarrant is right to suggest that, evoked
in the parenthesis of the poem's second line is Ovid's own fresh undertaking
in meter (*illa* rather than *illas*)—and his turn from "light love poetry in elegiac couplets . . . [to] mythical narrative in hexameter"—the question is what
it means to say that the gods are responsible for this turn. Ovid's reference,
Kovacs claims, is to his banishment by Augustus: "the parenthesis in the proem
is meant to imply that his change of fortunes have wrought a change in the

kind of poetry he writes" (462). Ultimately, then, the shift in meter also signals Ovid's own entering into the metamorphosis he writes about, and metamorphosis, inside and outside the poem, becomes the agent of inception: the "*Metamorphoses* itself exists in consequence of a metamorphosis" (Kenney, 50). Orpheus's merger with the song he sings—his disappearance into the enchantment that turns listeners, rapt, to stone—is also a figure for Ovid's own disappearance into his text, into "them," *illas* or *illa*, forms, changed, or his own undertakings or inceptions, inspired. Kovacs writes:

> On another level proem and epilogue may suggest that Ovid has now become the poet he was fated to be, and that, just as so many of the heroes of his epic are changed into birds, beasts, trees, or flowers by the gods who have pity on the pain of their mortal existence, so the pain of Ovid's exile has changed him into a new kind of poet. And just as the heroes and heroines find relief from their mortal existence in the immortality and unchangeability of their non-human shape, so the poet's final metamorphosis into a "nomen indelebile" is his consolation for the irretrievable ruin of his ordinary human happiness. (Kovacs, 465)

Nothing retains its shape; "*vivam.*" A consolation, perhaps, but one that does not so much compensate a loss as make these shapes transformed to bodies strange emblems, paradoxically permanent in their metamorphic changes, of a founding loss. Thus in the poem the delicate beauty of the hyacinth flower consoles for the loss of the boy it memorializes by turning it to an emblem of poetic creation, but its stain recalls the blood spilled at his death and spells out a cry of grief that is permanently inscribed in the beauty that would sublate it.[55] By pairing (for instance) Galatea with Niobe, or Atlas with Andromeda, or the many figures who become trees with Adonis, who is born from one, the poem suggests that metamorphosis is reversible; more radically, it makes becoming stone difficult to distinguish from the softening of rock in animation and the birth of human form; dismemberment, from assembly; the consolations of art, from irremediable loss; the emergence of voice, from a falling silent; the escape from hell, from a turning back; origin, from end. The stony ancestry repeatedly evoked in the Orphic section of *The Metamorphoses* moves us, as often happens in this playful text, forward and backward, toward a "life" in the permanent metamorphoses of inception.

7

Wallace Stevens and the Temporalities of Inception and Embodiment

Hell is this:
The lack of anything but the eternal to look at
The expansiveness of salt
The lack of any bed but one's
Music to sleep in.

—JACK SPICER, "ORFEO"

Orpheus liked the glad personal quality
Of the things beneath the sky

—JOHN ASHBERY, "SYRINGA"

In the previous chapter, stones pointed to quandaries of inception in Ovid—where Orpheus, becoming one with the rapture he inspires and merging, finally, with Ovid's "book of changes," embodied a paradoxical origin that was metamorphosis itself. I turn now to another stone—to Stevens's "The Rock"—where one finds this enigmatic rewriting of the Promethean origin of man in Ovid and its retelling in the account of the Etruscan prophecies in the *Metamorphoses*:

The meeting at noon at the edge of the field seems like
An invention, and embrace between one desperate clod
And another in a fantastic consciousness,
In a queer assertion of humanity (525)[1]

I will return to the context of this assertion, and to some of the perplexities of the section as a whole. For the moment, I would note the reversal of perspective in the allusion—or perhaps unconscious echo—a reversal that evokes a crux in recent criticism of Stevens: Creation is imagined from the perspective of the created, the clods and not, for example, the startled farmer who witnesses their animation. Among other effects, this reversal locates consciousness "in" things.[2] To explore some of the stakes and consequences of that movement in relation to origins and inception, I will suggest that Stevens's imagining of origin in "The Rock" makes manifest a shift in his thinking about embodiment and temporality from the early to the late poems—from, for example, "Peter Quince at the Clavier," "Sunday Morning," and "The Idea of Order at Key West" to "The Rock."

A redoubtably abstract poet, Stevens also offers some of the most profound reflections on what it is to have a body, reflections that are often expressed in complex considerations of the relation of poetic representation to reality. "The Green Plant" displays, schematically almost, a movement legible in many of the poems of *The Rock* (the name Stevens gave to the final section of his *Collected Poems*), as well as some of that volume's recurrent concerns. The poem invokes an old, ultimately Platonic *topos* that opposes reality to its representation. In Shakespeare's Sonnet 98, for example, the boy's absence turns summer to mere representation, to "shadow," initially seeming to make the sonnet's own words at once compensatory and privative. Yet Shakespeare offers no alternative in presence beyond other forms of representation. (April is "proud-pied" and "dressed in all his trim," and to experience a world beyond shadow would be, it seems, to tell a summer's story, to wonder at the lily's white, to praise the deep vermillion in the rose, to create, in other terms, more "figures of delight.")[3] Platonic, one might say, because embodied existence cannot access reality beyond representation and cannot imagine that transcendent reality without representation; that predicament one might call "love." The conceit of Stevens's poem likewise links the coming of fall to an emptying of presence and meaning. Here are the second two stanzas:

> The effete vocabulary of summer
> No longer says anything.
> The brown at the bottom of red
> The orange far down in yellow,
>
> Are falsifications from the sun
> In a mirror, without heat,
> In a constant secondariness,
> A turning down toward finality—(*Collected Poems*, 506)

If "falsifications" and "constant secondariness"[4] draw an analogy between the coming of autumn and a fall into representation, made a reflection without heat, a decadent reflexivity where the "effete vocabulary of summer/No longer says anything," the analogy to mortality (if that is how to understand "finality," which it might not be) marks a second-order withdrawal, a further elaboration of secondariness that at once moralizes it and repeats it.

The poem then suddenly turns in the final stanza (in a gesture characteristic of the late poems) to an equivocal redemption:

> Except that a green plant glares, as you look
> At the legend of the maroon and olive forest,
> Glares, outside of the legend, with the barbarous green
> Of the harsh reality of which it is a part.

The problems of the previous stanza are resolved by fiat; the turn to the final stanza is conspicuously abrupt, and leaves open to question how to understand the relation between the "legend" and the green plant that "glares" outside of it, as well as that between the green plant and "the barbarous green/Of the harsh reality of which it is a part." The intrusion of reality is figured as a living presence that interrupts the fading away into legend, and yet the difficulty is not only, perhaps, the tonal question of why the reality is "harsh," and the green, "barbarous."[5] It is perhaps also the question of how to read "except," and why the relation between the plant and reality turns out to be so attenuated—the plant is linked to this reality by its glaring, and by the green it shares with the "barbarous green" of that harsh reality, and it is perhaps unclear whether it is the plant or the barbarous green that is a part of reality. Finally, the green plant shares with other figures in late Stevens a curious groundlessness: The figure appears so starkly and so suddenly that the tenor emerges in a pure positing that does without any clear relation to a vehicle.[6] (This characteristic alone points one to the centrality of "inception" to Stevens's poetics. His abstract figures repeatedly signal the poetic fiat that calls them into being.) Left uncertain whether meaning derives from any relation to an actual plant, one also seems to confront a plant, devoid of any poetic meaning: In the green plant, one confronts at once a purely poetic creation, a figment of the poet's power to posit, and an unmediated encounter with the real.[7] The claim of a poetic power of transcendence is difficult to distinguish from a radical destitution, a voiding of meaning in a pure material presence.

"The Rock," like other poems in the volume to which it lends its name, elaborates on the questions that emerge, schematically, in "The Green Plant," and it does so by pondering origins. That exploration presents a further layering of questions legible in earlier poems—in, for example, "Peter Quince at the Clavier" (*Collected Poems*, 89–92), which asserts, in highly condensed terms, the body's power to transcend itself by dwelling on its desiring and ephemeral nature, its power to transcend human finitude by coupling it with the capacity for sensuous evocation in poetic language.[8] The underlying axiom is stated at the beginning of the poem:

> Just as my fingers on these keys
> Make music, so the selfsame sounds
> On my spirit make a music, too.
>
> Music is feeling, then, not sound;
> And thus it is that what I feel,
> Here in this room, desiring you,
>
> Thinking of your blue-shadowed silk,
> Is music. (89–90)

The logic of the poem will depend on the identification of these two forms of music, on the analogy that makes aesthetic "feeling" a kind of physical action on a body, and therefore anchors the metaphysical, and hence the transcendence of mortality, in the body's finitude, and in its susceptibility to sense perception. That analogy is asserted in these opening lines, which perhaps leave in question the register in which they are to be understood. That register is determined by one's understanding of "just as": As an assertion of likeness, it becomes a metaphysical analogy (aesthetic apprehension can be comprehended on the model of sense perception, from which, however, it may differ in crucial ways), but as an assertion of identity, it becomes a more literal claim (aesthetic apprehension is a form of sense perception). The question of how to understand "just as," therefore, is in a sense the question of the poem. Stevens seems to make the latter, stronger claim, which then allows the "merely" physical to transcend itself: "Music is feeling, then, not sound." And vice versa: "And thus it is that what I feel, / Here in this room, desiring you . . . / Is music."

Playing on two different senses of "feel," the poem thus reduces almost to tautology a central tenet of aestheticist (and Romantic) aesthetics, and puts that aesthetic claim in the service of eroticism. It is, ultimately, a poem of seduction, and it joins (and plays on) a long series of such poems: Andrew Marvell's "To His Coy Mistress," for instance. Yet the claim is even stronger: Rather than conceding the ultimate power of "Time's wingèd chariot," and using the depredations of time to make the case to act now, Stevens's poem suggests that desire might overcome time itself.[9] Eroticism is made to enact the "just as" with which the poem begins; repeatedly, the poem's descriptions of desire make one hesitate about their status as figurative or literal. "The strain / Waked in the elders" (*Collected Poems*, 90) is both a force pulling on them (or an excessive demand on their strength) and the sound of music because music is desire. To feel "the basses of their beings throb" is at once to be affected to their very core by desire, and to suffer a painful state of erection (90). Likewise, in section II, is Susanna relaxing in a bath, or is she masturbating? How does one read her searching of "the touch of springs," and her finding of "concealed imaginings"? And "the dew / Of old devotions" is both a pastoralizing image that as it were sublimates desire and a lurid depiction of sexual arousal (90). The line between the abstract and the particular, the sublimated and the luridly concrete, has become indistinct.

The language is as if "literally" erotic insofar as the poem makes its case for seduction through the sensuous qualities of its language. More than that, taken at its word, the poem suggests that the sensuous qualities *are* its seductions. Apparent throughout the poem, these qualities are perhaps most conspicuous in sections III and IV, and are figured by a particularly arresting image:

> They wondered why Susanna cried
> Against the elders by her side;
> And as they whispered, the refrain
> Was like a willow swept by rain. (91)

It is perhaps difficult to describe what is so witching about this last couplet. In part an effect of the regularity of the iambic tetrameter, it is also, I think, a certain hesitation in the image itself: Does the refrain sound like rain whispering in a willow, or does the refrain sound like what a rainswept willow looks like? The possibility of the synesthesia thus figures, as sense perception, the crossing of registers that makes aesthetic perception a form of sense perception and eroticism. The water and willow together recall Ophelia's death in *Hamlet* ("There is a willow grows askaunt the brook")[10]—and its condensed expression of an abyssal mirroring, as Ophelia disappears into the lyrical utterance of Gertrude's speech. The synesthesia, in other terms, figures an aesthetic ideal where the idea would be immediately available to sense perception, and desire would be immanent in, and directly communicated by, a poem's music.[11]

The final section of the poem makes an explicit claim for the body's power to transcend death; death is recast as an aesthetic purification that makes the flesh the visible incarnation of an ideal:

> Beauty is momentary in the mind—
> The fitful tracing of a portal;
> But in the flesh it is immortal.
> The body dies; the body's beauty lives.
> So evenings die, in their green going,

A wave, interminably flowing.
So gardens die, their meek breath scenting
The cowl of winter, done repenting.
So maidens die, to the auroral
Celebration of a maiden's choral.
Susanna's music touched the bawdy strings
Of those white elders; but, escaping,
Left only Death's ironic scraping.
Now, in its immortality, it plays
On the clear viol of her memory,
And makes a constant sacrament of praise. (91–2)

Susanna's "escape" from the smitten elders (in Daniel 13) is made an escape from death itself—into an immortality where the physical has been identified with the impalpable, with music. Playing on the "clear viol of her memory," Susanna's "music . . . Makes a constant sacrament of praise." Made a sacrament— for the Anglican book of Common Prayer, an "outward and visible sign of an invisible reality" or "of an inward and spiritual grace"[12]—her "music" thus embodies an aesthetic ideal, and desire would seem to be what is left behind, a physical but intangible remainder, after the death of the body, the "wave" after evening's vanishing, or the "meek breath" of a faded garden. An exhalation of rot, that "meek breath" sublimates death; the lingering scent of flowers stands in for an attenuated presence and an aestheticization. The very transience of sensation is made a claim for its transcending of death, the body's very ephemerality therefore becoming what endures; this seems to be the sense in which beauty "in the flesh" is "immortal." Once again, too, the poem makes its claim in a figure of equivocal figurality, by a kind of pun: "the fitful tracing of a portal" is at once a crossing from the physical to the metaphysical and a description of masturbation.[13] As embodied, desirous, and ephemeral flesh, then, beauty is said to be immortal.

Evoking section one ("Just as . . ."), the fourth section is built on a series of parallels: "The body dies; the body's beauty lives" is explained or extended by analogies—"So evenings die . . . So gardens die . . . So maidens die." As is perhaps common in Stevens, what follows each of these parallel formulations is conspicuously not parallel: "in their green going . . . their meek breath scenting . . . to the auroral celebration." What differs is thus the remainder—the analogues to the body's beauty, the ineffable, attenuated presences that are as if the exhalations of a vanishing. Among other effects, the poem seems thereby to assert its power of unification—its power to produce a parallelism, to make us experience non-parallel elements as if they were drawn in parallel, enacting their status as material remainders in this non-parallel series. A conceptual parallel unifies them—if the "green going" of evening is like the as-if-light-saturated remains of day in the gloaming, what that image shares with the meek breath of expiring gardens, still scenting the winter, then colors, as it were, "the auroral/Celebration of a maiden's choral," leaving behind a song of praise that guards the body's beauty. The poem itself, then, is that song of praise. The claiming of a parallel formulation that isn't there thus enacts the purification or sublimation that turns the "bawdy strings" of the elders to the "clear viol of her memory."

As in the "sacrament of praise," there is perhaps a genitive ambiguity in "Susanna's music," an ambiguity emphasized by the narrative context of the poem. (Likewise, one might hesitate before concluding that it is one's desirous memory of Susanna that forms the "clear viol" and not her own memory that, remembering sensual pleasure, sublimates the lubricious gaze at her private pleasure.) It is unclear whether the "music" in question is her experience of her desirous body ("she sighed, for so much melody"), or a desire that she, as a spectacle, excites. "The sacrament of praise" evokes the "pizzicati of Hosanna" earlier in the poem, the "bawdy strings" of the elders touched (or plucked) by the sight of her body. Her escape, too, is equivocal, and one is unsure whether it is an escape from unwanted sexual advances or from mortality. The question is both a conceptual one—that of the particular claims that the poem makes for the transcendence of the body (through its sensations) by poetry—and of narrative framing or distance, and of the particular narrative related in the poem. Because the claim, ultimately, is for a poetic power of transcendence, that concatenation of registers is perhaps only to be expected. When we read figures in the poem as luridly sexual, we put ourselves in the position of the elders: Is the sexual desire there, in the poem or in Susanna, or do we, and the elders, see only our own desire? Likewise, the figure of masturbation itself admits of several readings: a literalization of the work's autonomy (the poem will remain whether we read it or not), it is also, potentially, a solicitation. The equivocal meaning of the sexual spectacle (if it is there)—is it an invitation, as the elders perhaps take it to be, or an indication that she, like the work of art, needs no one else to gratify her?—thus reenacts the uncertainly of registers that leaves one in doubt about the sexual specification in the first place.

Thus do the very terms in which the poem makes its claims for transcendence then seem to trouble those claims. *"All art constantly aspires to the condition of music,"* Pater writes; Stevens's poem appears to make aesthetic claims for bodies that have achieved that condition.[14] The figures in the poem that are simultaneously etherealized renderings of transcendence and lurid descriptions of desiring bodies, while embodying the poem's claims, perhaps make for complications similar to the poem's use of music. Music is at once the condition to which it aspires and the figures through which it reaches its aspiration, leaving one with a sense both of tautology and of an equivocating redoublement. In other terms, one is uncertain whether the poem makes these assertions or depicts the making of them, and whether it shares the perspective of its speaker. The persuasive power of these claims may depend on the poem's distancing of itself from them.

Desire in the poem is curiously distanced or vicarious: Our access to Susanna's bath time searchings is mediated by the lubricious elders, and their desire, by the speaker who describes it.[15] (When the lamp, uplifted, reveals her shame, we are made aware both of our implication in the desirous gaze at her and of our distance from the spectacle insofar as we merely read about the revealed shame and the desirable body that incarnates it.) If one believes that the poem itself is meant to seduce—or to depict an attempt at seduction—it is because of the second-person address at the beginning, and because of the poem's title: Shakespeare's Peter Quince would be the speaker whose fingers make music on "these keys." If the poem is an effort to seduce the "you" in "blue-shadowed silk," however, the story of Susanna in the Book of Daniel is a peculiar choice for a theme. The addressee is asked to identify with a highly unappealing desire for her, and to be seduced by the tale of its thwarting. (At the same time, it is not unastute, as a description of some of the self-thwarting movements of desire: I might not be alone in having tried, it need not be added unsuccessfully, a not dissimilar ruse.) The voyeurism described enacts the layering of perspective and voice; the speaker seems to count on a seductive power capable of unifying the music made by his fingers with "Susanna's music" at the end. And redoublement is a central theme from the beginning. "Just as my fingers on these keys/Make music, so the selfsame sounds/On my spirit make a music, too": the redundant insistence of "selfsame" and the pairing of "just as . . . so" with the (therefore also redundant) "too" suggest that the doubling may be as important as the parallel it enacts.

Such a redoublement has a precedent in *Midsummer Night's Dream*, where Peter Quince's play—a retelling of the story of Pyramus and Thisbe in Ovid— is comically inept ("This is the silliest stuff that ever I heard," says Hippolyta), in part because of an endearing credulity about the power of representation that, for example, leads the players to reassure the ladies that the depicted lion is no lion, but is, in fact, Snug the Joiner.[16] In Shakespeare's play, the effect is abyssal; the knowing audience of the play doubles the audience depicted within it ("Well moused, Lion"; "Moonshine and Lion are left to bury the dead" [V.i.268, 328]). When Puck delivers his epilogue, therefore, his unveiling of theatrical artifice echoes that of Peter Quince's players, whose making comic of Ovid's tragic story encapsulates the movement of Shakespeare's own play—which, further, is tied together at the end, by Quince and his company. The rhyming couplets in Stevens's sections III and IV evoke those of the wall—"the wittiest partition that ever I heard discourse," says Demetrius (V.i.166)—in Quince's Pyramus and Thisbe, and the couplets spoken by those star-crossed lovers as they speak to, and rhyme with, each other through it. The wall—in Ovid, and even more explicitly in Shakespeare—embodies the desire-fueling boundary or edge that Anne Carson explores in *Eros the Bittersweet*. The "fitful tracing of a portal" in Stevens is of equivocal figurality in yet another sense, as it seems to achieve its (figural) claim by literalizing this speaking wall. If one isn't sure whether the poem presents both an effort to seduce and an argument for the power of poetry as sense perception to transcend mortality (and for the mortal body to transcend itself by way of its own perceptions), or whether it depicts those arguments and therefore leaves open their power to persuade, the hesitation may be the poem's final way of making its claims: The body's seduction and the distanced reflection on it, immediate sense perception and its mediation by poetic language, are made indistinct.[17]

What is presented explicitly in terms of sexual desire in "Peter Quince at the Clavier" is given more neutral formulation in "Sunday Morning" (*Collected Poems*, 66–70). In a previous essay, I described my sense of the way the latter poem links the sensual dimension of poetic language—language not as meaningful but as a form, almost, of animal movement—to an experience of mortality as pure embodiment. That embodiment, moreover, is as it were dispersed across a landscape, a paradoxical internalization, as aesthetic rapture, of the dispersal of the self.[18] "I am content," says the woman in the poem, "when wakened birds, / Before they fly, test the reality / Of misty fields, by their sweet questionings" (68). These are perhaps what Wordsworth calls "those obstinate questionings / Of sense and outward things, / Fallings from us, vanishings"—those sense perceptions that, calling forth our sense of belatedness, recover, for the Romantic poet, something of childhood innocence in the realization of its loss.[19] The woman in "Sunday Morning" nevertheless yearns, in her contentment, for "some imperishable bliss" (68). She finds it in a beauty born of death. "Death is the mother of beauty": The poem articulates, as against religious observance, a form of transcendence found in poetic language—but as sound, as a rhythmical tattoo, consigning the mortal body to time (68, 69). For my earlier essay, that bodying forth of time linked the pleasure of poetic language to animal life and to a model of cinematic spectatorship it examined in terms of impersonality. In the final stanza, the poem is as it were divided between an explicit proposition—"she hears . . . / A voice that cries, 'The tomb in Palestine/Is not the porch of spirits lingering./It is the grave of Jesus, where he lay'"—and a series of images that do not so much make the claims for poetic transcendence as enact the voice's merger with an animal movement that might not be meaningful at all (70).

The paradoxically unifying division between the poetic voice and the animals that might embody it is enacted in the voice itself, in the positing of a voice that "she" hears (thereby in a sense hearing her own status as poetic proxy returning to her as a voice that cries). Such a structure is also visible in "The Idea of Order at Key West" in the poem's abstraction of voice (*Collected Poems*, 128–30): The "she" who walks between the poet and the sea embodies a "voice" that is at a remove from both the poet—who, to speak of order, turns away from her to address "Ramon Fernandez"—and the "constant cry, . . . Inhuman, of the veritable ocean" that, repeatedly, we are told, is to be distinguished from hers (130, 128). The idea of order at the poem's end emerges from a positing of voice that, not only at a remove from the poet's own and something more than mere "meaningless" sound is also (nevertheless) almost tautological. Her song says that she is the one who sings it:

> She was a single artificer of the world
> In which she sang. And when she sang, the sea,
> Whatever self it had, became the self
> That was her song, for she was the maker. Then we,
> As we beheld her striding there alone,
> Knew that there never was a world for her
> Except the one she sang and, singing, made. (129–30)

To my mind, the strange beauty of that last line derives not only from the metrical patterning but also from two non-parallel pairings, both semantico-morphological, but in different modes: "sang" and "singing" and "sang" and "made." The world is as if constituted in the non-coincidence of these two transformations, and in the attribution of a quality—emerging as isolated morphologically and by the punctuation—between two paired movements between subject and verb.

The "it" that "rose" and that is not "sound alone" is also said to be "more than that,/More even in her voice, and ours, among/The meaningless plungings of water and the wind," and that "more" is perhaps located, for this poem, in the sound of the language that describes merely what it isn't:

> If it was only the dark voice of the sea
> That rose, or even colored by many waves;
> If it was only the outer voice of sky

> And cloud, of the sunken coral water-walled,
> However clear, it would have been deep air,
> The heaving speech of air, a summer sound
> Repeated in a summer without end
> And sound alone. (129)[20]

A series of ineffable, all but imperceptible boundaries, between sky and cloud, or between coral and water, "the dark voice of the sea" becomes more than "deep air," more than "sound alone" because of the beauty of the words that evoke it. That sound is somehow both less and more than meaning, and it calls to mind the "body" of the water at the poem's opening:

> She sang beyond the genius of the sea.
> The water never formed to mind or voice,
> Like a body wholly body, fluttering
> Its empty sleeves. (128)

Does the water—as the image of the waves and sleeves enclosing no body might suggest—fail to cohere as a body, fail to become "like a body, wholly body," or does the water not form because it is merely a body, or "wholly body," whose sleeves are empty because it fails to reach a threshold of form that would make the merely bodily legible as something else? In this, the water is thus like the "she" of the poem, who both is and is not a physical presence.

That sense of supplementarity emerges at several moments in a syntactical indeterminacy where the crucial image is added paratactically, with the particular relation to what comes before it left unspecified.

> But it was more than that,
> More even than her voice, and ours, among
> The meaningless plungings of water and the wind,
> Theatrical distances, bronze shadows heaped
> On high horizons, mountainous atmospheres
> Of sky and sea. (129)

The structure of apposition is doubled, leaving uncertain whether the theatrical distances rename "meaningless plungings" or "more than that," even as the stanza also leaves open the possibility that the images aren't syntactically linked but present rather a series of images that condense the meaning or into which the meaning itself dissipates—images which therefore both do and do not complete a sentence, do and do not make a body, just as a wave makes indistinct a coalescence of form and its dispersion. Likewise, at the poem's end:

> Oh! Blessed rage for order, pale Ramon,
> The maker's raged to order words of the sea,
> Words of the fragrant portals, dimly-stared,
> And of ourselves and of our origins,
> In ghostlier demarcations, keener sounds. (130)

The "and" leaves unspecified the relations among "the fragrant portals," "ourselves," and "our origins," and the evocation of order emerges from a syntax more accretive than periodic. Likewise, the comparatives leave in question whether the demarcations are "ghostlier" than the sounds (and the sounds "keener" than the demarcations), or whether both are intensified by the rage for order, in comparison to what preceded that rage. And again, the order emerges from a supplementarity, or even a digressive quality difficult to distinguish from tautology—"enchanting night" calls one back to the poem's opening words: "she sang."

That sense of tautology is especially visible in the first question "we" are said to ask, which out of context (and maybe in context) is almost comical: "Whose spirit is this? We said, because we knew / It was the spirit that we sought and knew / That we should ask this often as she sang" (129). "The Idea of Order at Key West" is a difficult poem to remember accurately (for me, anyway) because the logic dictating the minute shifts in the assertions make the poem feel repetitive, and the parts leading up to the final address to Ramon Fernandez almost interchangeable. In caricature, the poem merely repeats a series of assertions: she is not the sea, she is the maker of her song, and something more and unspecified emerges from that noncoincidence. One's mind reading the poem, it seems to me, follows two tracks, one tracing a development that can more or less tenuously outline a conceptual movement toward an idea of order, and another in which a blank, repetitive utterance produces, in its very blankness, an order that is nothing other than the words of the poem itself. Even before that final address, then, the poem's repetitive language (most basically, think of the wave-like repetition of words and sounds—sea, sky, song, sang, summer, self, she, water, wind, and so on) enacts a pure meaningless positing through which meaning takes shape: like the surf's idiot insistence (which evoked for another poet a darkling plain swept by confused alarms of struggle and flight) these sounds become meaningful through the mere taking on of a tremulous cadence. Calling into view that barren positing, Stevens's poem confronts what I call "inception." That structure is visible, for instance, in the opening rendering of the waves: "and yet its mimic motion / Made constant cry, caused constantly a cry" (128). Or, similarly: "there never was a world for her / Except the one she sang and, singing, made" (130). The poem takes shape in the play between repetition and the proliferation of minimal distinctions.

The poem's multiplied drama of displaced voice—the sea, "she," the poet who addresses Ramon Fernandez—thus corresponds to a "beyond" within the idea of order: not just the remove that separates order from the idea of it, and not just the "rage" that perhaps separates the "maker" from the "idea," but also a recurrent shuttling between dispersion and tautology that, enacted syntactically, creates the sense of order and lies somewhere beyond the poem's meaning.[21] In the antepenultimate stanza, the poem renders a similar structure as a visual image: "It was her voice that made/The sky acutest at its vanishing./She measured to the hour its solitude" (129). These lines lead to the series of tautological assertions quoted earlier ("She was the single artificer . . ."). It may be that "she measured to the hour its solitude" means something like "she made one's solitude an attribute of the world by making it a quality of the hour, which is also to say made it perceptible as such," but I think it also is worth holding on to the unidiomatic quality of "measured to," to the fact that her presence therefore registers as an absence. The image preceding it seems to be about the establishment of perspective. If the sky is "acutest at its vanishing," it is perhaps because the world has become coherent as a spectacle when seen from a certain perspective, that of the viewer for whom the vanishing point would correspond with his own point of view "within" the picture—here, with the horizon, where the angle, in relation to the viewer, would be most "acute" (in other words a straight line). The idea of order is thus linked to the possibility that that viewer might be at once dispersed "in" the view and somehow there to witness his vanishing.

At the beginning of the poem, the water, I noted, both fails to be "like a body, wholly body," and fails to form to mind or voice to the degree that it *is* "like a body, wholly body." And when that body is said to be "fluttering its empty sleeves," it is both there and not there; an incomplete body bodies forth, as it were, the incomplete animation or meaningfulness of the merely bodily, and represents the bodily by failing to become a body. Put that way, the lines enact the wavering of personification in the poem—the various ways that persons or selves both do and do not come into being. One of the larger difficulties of the poem, it seems to me, is that of understanding the relation between the opening scenario and the closing discussion of "order"; more or less obliquely, that difficulty registers in one's uncertainty about whether the "she" who sings beyond the genius of the sea is actually there (whether the register is narrative or allegorical, to put it crudely), and about why the poem's claims about "the idea of order" requires the elaborate circuit of voices and variously redoubled forms of surrogacy:[22] Stevens's staging of a Romantic confrontation of poet and nature places a nameless "singer" between the poet and the sea, and, more than that, calls in Ramon Fernandez to have a discussion about her (a virtual conversation, or rather an address [tell me, if you know] about a virtual appearance). When the poem asserts that "The sea was not a mask. No more was she" (128), one perhaps does not need to have recourse to the word *prospopon* to feel that at stake is the question of personification; the "mask" that produces persons in the Greek drama is personifying to the degree that it posits a particular kind of meaning "behind" it: a person.

The curious abstraction of the poem's scenario is visible in this seeming assertion that "she" is not a personification—which could mean either that she is really there (is an actual person, not a figment of voice) or that whatever is animated or created by that figure of voice (later called a "self") ought not to be understood as a person. The "ever-hooded, tragic gestured sea" (129) is in this sense the empty form of a personification—like the body/not-a-body "fluttering its empty sleeves." "Whose spirit is this?" may or may not be a legitimate question (129); is she a "spirit" that can be said to belong to someone else? A similar rhythm can likewise be perceived in the speaker of the poem. The "we" that appears suddenly in stanza three recedes in the penultimate stanza, relinquishes its ostensible claims to universality as it is, in retrospect, specified as a particular two people (the speaker and Ramon Fernandez)—or, in other terms, "we" vacillates between a particular, localized locutionary context and a generalized, abstracted one, the context of poetic utterance itself, just as "she" at the beginning is both a woman walking by the sea and a figure of poetic voice. (Is Ramon "pale" because he, too, is both there and not there? Does he know, and is he even there to answer?) As one wonders about the relation between the "self" and the sea in the antepenultimate stanza, it is possible to miss the sudden appearance of that term (*self*), whose positing, therefore, seems as important as the relation of the sea to making (or, rather, a crucial part of rendering the articulation of that relation possible). If it isn't obvious that a sea would have a self, it is no more obvious how a self can be a song—that phrasing, in any event, brings into view, again, the question of whether poetic language can become, or confer, a form of personhood. More schematically, there are at least two "lines" in the poem—on the one hand, its questioning of whether the meaningless sounds of the sea will become ordered, and become poetic utterance, and, on the other, a more or less clandestine drama of voices and persons, posited and withdrawn. The profusion of voices in the poem is to that extent very much to the point. "The idea of order" and the "rage for order" both make order the cognitive or affective property of a consciousness; the vacillations and diffusions of voice in the poem thus suggest that the question of order is also in some way the question of whether that consciousness, voiced, will cohere in a person (in short, is she there, or is she a poetic figure, is the question).

The "Oh!" that begins the final stanza is at once a vocative (paired there-fore with the figure of address in "pale Ramon") and the interjection of a (mere) sound (holding a place in the iambic pentameter)—and it thus both is and is not a figure of voice. If the maker's "rage" is directed at "words" and not the sea itself, and to that extent never touches a sound that is not already a part of human meaning, and if, therefore, the sounds remain "keener" to the degree that the "demarcations," seen, are "ghostlier" because they are outside this realm of words, a question for the end of the poem is whether an apparent or formal parallelism indicates a substantive one. Does the series of (sometimes overlapping) parallel formulations—"Blessed rage for order . . . The maker's rage to order"; "words of the sea," "words of the fragrant portals," [words] "of ourselves"; "of ourselves and of our origins"; "ghostlier demarcations, keener sounds"—unify or only seem to unify its disparate registers (of sound and sense, form and content, spirit and body)? Thus, for example, the "And" that begins the penultimate line might admit of at least two possible readings: "words of the sea," "words of the fragrant portals, dimly starred," and words "of our-selves and of our origins" might be synonyms or (on the other hand) a series of possibly related but not synonymous elements.

"The Idea of Order at Key West" is, as even a cursory registering of its self-reflexivity suggests, about its own emergence as a poem; the way its logic tends to break down into constitutive elements—repeated sounds, emblem-atic gestures of positing, equivocal forms of personification that do and do not align with voice—evokes the elements of *Our Mutual Friend*, or the gestures of "First Love." It is a poem, in other terms, about emergence in a more radical sense, a poem about *inception*. Words "of ourselves and of our origins": the question of whether the sound of the sea will become meaning-ful, I noted, is linked, in various complex relays, to the layered and wavering emergence and eclipse of voice. The sudden appearance of "origins" at the end of the poem—and its making explicit of one's half-felt sense of a con-frontation, in facing the sea, with something primordial—ties that drama to the concern with origins throughout Stevens's corpus. "She made the sky acutest at its vanishing"; in question is perhaps whether anyone inhabits the perspective thus adumbrated. That image of perspective reappears in "The Rock" (*Collected Poems*, 525–8), but in a more disorienting, because more explicit, form:

The rock is the habitation of the whole,
Its strength and measure, that which is near, point A
In a perspective that begins again

At B: the origin of the mango's rind. (528)

The difficulty of image is not just its abstraction, and the different kinds of categories collocated: strength and measure, both perhaps qualities, though in different ways, and a visual image, perspective, ostensibly elaborating a relation of containment or belonging—and a paradoxical one where a "whole" can have a "habitation" (that, presumably, exceeds it). It is also in the double perspective—one that "begins again/At B."[23] It is as if one were asked to inhabit both one's perspective and the vanishing point that makes it one. It thus differs from the analogous moment in "The Idea of Order at Key West" by making explicit a potential there in the earlier poem's redoubling of voice and perspective; at this moment in "The Rock," wholeness emerges as the poem attempts to comprise a perspective that, because it is not "one," is impossible to inhabit.

This image of perspective comes from Part III of the poem (*"Forms of the Rock in a Night-Hymn"*). The first two sections set up the questions addressed here, which might be framed as responding to the concerns of the earlier poems. At first glance, the questions posed—here, most starkly, but throughout the volume to which the poem gives its name—are perhaps deceptively simple. "Peter Quince" and "Sunday Morning" both link poetic language and embodied pleasure (albeit in different ways, and with different particular complications); the sensual dimension of poetic sound, or "music," becomes, at the limit, the rationale for claiming a sort of immortality, achieved by, paradoxically, tying the formal qualities of poetry to the ineffability and ephemerality of the body's pleasure. For the earlier Stevens, I have noted, the analogy between poetic language and bodily existence allows him to find something of that imperishable bliss within the flesh, immortal in its very vanishing. "The Rock" leads one to wonder if that analogy still holds *"Seventy Years Later"* when the body is an old one, and whether, if it does hold, the analogy can still support the same kinds of claims. The arid beauty and often uncompromising austerity of language in Stevens's late verse, as well as its abstraction and (what perhaps amounts to the same thing) the indeterminate "motivation" or uncertain vehicles of his figurative language, suggest that poetic language, later on, is in a changed relation to the poet's experience of embodiment. Yet I think that change is not to be understood merely as the result of aging and the possibly changed relation to bodily pleasure that entails. The later poems work through more thoroughly difficulties left implicit in the earlier ones, and, in "The Rock," questions of origin, themselves raised by the poet's superannuation, provide the occasion for that reflection.

The opening of "The Rock" evokes a feeling of unreality introduced by the passage of time. Looking back *"Seventy Years Later,"* thought and even existence become impalpable, what the poem calls "an illusion":

It is an illusion that we were ever alive,
Lived in the houses of mothers, arranged ourselves
By our own motions in a freedom of air.

Regard the freedom of seventy years ago.
It is no longer air. The houses still stand,
Though they are rigid in rigid emptiness.

Even our shadows, their shadows, no longer remain.
The lives these lived in the mind are at an end.
They never were . . . The sounds of the guitar

Were not and are not. Absurd. The words spoken
Were not and are not. It is not to be believed. (525)

Intimated, it initially seems, is not just the uncanny sense of posthumeity that
the persistence of material things—rigid houses still standing—can inspire in
an ephemeral mind faced with the passage of time, but also the ephemerality
of thoughts and words and the productions of the mind because they are, as
productions, fastened to a dying animal—and therefore as fleeting as the sounds
of a guitar (or of the poem called "The Man with the Blue Guitar"). "Illusion,"
at least initially, places what is merely representation or thought—shadows, or
the lives of objects in the mind—on the side of what vanishes with the passage
of time, a negation that acts retrospectively, too: "they never were."

Yet the section moves from two directions simultaneously, both backward
from "Seventy Years Later," and forward from an origin or moment of inception, and the "illusion" that in the first movement produces a retrospective negation is recast in the second as a positing that makes existence self-generating
or autochthonous:

The meeting at noon at the edge of the field seems like

An invention, an embrace between one desperate clod
And another in a fantastic consciousness,
In a queer assertion of humanity:

A theorem proposed between the two—
Two figures in a nature of the sun,
In the sun's design of its own happiness (525)

The strains of desire through which similar questions are addressed in "Peter
Quince" have become highly abstracted; the "embrace" here seems a physical figure for a more abstract transaction, less a carnal encounter than a figure on the border of personification—which, if it gives birth to life, does so

only by way of a "queer assertion." The phrase "the nature of the sun" is, to my mind, obscure, at least in its meaning for the poem; "nature" can mean sexual desire or, in archaic uses, semen or genitals or menstrual discharge, but I suspect the sense here is rather of general physical constraints or power, vital needs or force, or the power to shape action—or even more generally, the world as it exists beneath the sun where nature (not God) governs causation.[24] I am not sure what authorizes readers—Helen Vendler, most notably—to take the "two clods" as figures for "man" and "wife,"[25] beyond a governing assumption that the poem is autobiographical.[26] To my mind, the abstraction is at least partly the point, and the rendering of parturition, or coupling, as "the meeting of two clods" at once places any bodily encounter at a level of materiality below the coherence of bodily forms and subordinates it to an abstract, and disembodied, positing. Not only memories, then, of Ovid, the clods, in that view, are instances of, and figures for, the positing I noted in "The Green Plant"—at once a purely poetic creation and a materiality beyond the reach of poetry, or language.

"The sun's design of its own happiness" emphasizes the autochthonous quality of that positing, the emergence of consciousness from mute materiality, from "clods." Taking the perspective of things, the poem, I noted, seems to derive consciousness from the earth of which bodies are made. This immanence takes the form of a groundless reflexivity that—queer assertion or theorem—is linked to the hypothetical nature of the poem's language, its "as if":

> As if nothingness contained a métier,
> A vital assumption, an impermanence
> In its permanent cold, an illusion so desired
>
> That the green leaves came and covered the high rock,
> That the lilacs came and bloomed, like a blindness cleaned,
> Exclaiming bright site, as it was satisfied,
>
> In a birth of sight. The blooming and the musk
> Were being alive, an incessant being alive,
> A particular of being, that gross universe. (526)

"Illusion" explicitly takes on a meaning different from mere falsehood and is tied to the mind's capacity to represent: a "sensuous perception of an external object, involving a false belief or conception: strictly distinguished from *hallucination*, but in general use often made to include it," and, hence, "the apparent perception of an external object when no such object is present, or of attributes of an object which do not exist."[27] In this positing, the material world seems a layering of qualities over an object that does not exist; the immateriality of poetic language becomes a cause of materiality and covers a nonexistence. (This is also the movement of the poem as a whole, which moves toward the derivation of its own origin, and as if seeks to produce the figure that, retrospectively, will have unified it.) That structure is perhaps nowhere more apparent than in the figure of the rock itself, which seems to emerge out of nothing, and which, while it invokes a figural structure that is relatively clear (green leaves and the blooming of lilacs covering the rock) nevertheless seems itself to be of an indeterminate figurality, which is also to say of an indeterminate solidity.

The difficulty in conceiving the materiality invoked here also emerges in the apparent contradictions: "an impermanence / In its permanent cold" or "the birth of sight" that leaves one uncertain whether "a blindness cleaned" is one that has been eliminated or one that has been made apparent, that leaves uncertain, therefore, whether the sight thus born sees anything other than its own blindness.[28] The complexity of the posited world is most apparent in the final sentence of the stanza—whose paratactic listing of phrases enacts a kind of positing. The redoubling with, as it were, ramifying specification, "were being alive, an incessant being alive," transforms *being* from a verb to a noun and gives it temporal extension, which leads then to the final line's bringing together of the particular and the general.[29] (The *particular* is defined by the *OED Online* as "that which is particular, as opposed to the general, universal, etc." and *gross*, as the general as opposed to the particular, the entire or the whole.)[30] To make sense of these lines, one follows a path of attribution, or a generating of the particular: For the particular being, the being that emerges from this "invention," the particular is all there is in the universe. Strikingly, moreover, the particularity that one might link to sense perception (particular qualities, for example) and embodiment (this body, which separates me from, but also gives me my only access to, the realm of ideas and forms) is seemingly equated with universality (made paradoxically particular by the demonstrative pronoun *that*) where sense perception is negated: *Gross* can mean material (as opposed to spiritual),[31] both "perceptible to the senses" and (following from a particular use in Matthew 13) lacking in delicacy of perception, or having dull faculties. (To those who would see with their eyes, hear with their ears, understand with their heart, and be converted, they, whose heart is waxed gross, might come to understand the parable.)[32] "A blindness cleaned" or "an embrace between one desperate clod / And another": The queer assertion of humanity, by projecting consciousness outward "into" things, makes sense perception and the insensate object of perception curiously indistinct.

The second section of the poem—*"The Poem as Icon"*—opens by asserting that "it is not enough to cover the rock with leaves" and seems thereby to seek something beyond representation, and beyond the groundless productions of the mind (526). Against (merely) "to cover," the poem juxtaposes "to cure," to be cured of the rock. Disconcertingly, one archaic meaning of "to cure" is "to cover";[33] for more current acceptations, the primary meaning—to be made well, to be cured, as of a disease, deriving from "the spiritual oversight of parishioners or laypeople: the office or function of curate"—is shadowed by its other meanings: to desiccate (for instance, meat), vulcanize (for instance, tires), or harden (for instance, concrete), or to clear land (for crops).[34] To be cured of the rock would also seem to draw one closer to it; this section of the poem, it seems, attempts to surpass the first section's mere "covering" of the rock by repeating it. It isn't just that the disconcertingly indeterminate quality of the metaphor is even more glaring in Part II—the rock and its covering leaves are at once material and pure abstraction, and the "grounding" of the figures is unclear, seeming to follow from pure assertion. It is also striking that the section makes its claim, once again, through hypothetical or conditional assertions, and through long chains of equivalence that verge on tautology: The cure, like the leaves, seems to emerge out of nothing, and by fiat.

That sense of tautology is evident in the opening of the section, and its repetition of the word *cure*:

It is not enough to cover the rock with leaves.
We must be cured of it by a cure of the ground
Or a cure of ourselves, that is equal to a cure

Of the ground, a cure beyond forgetfulness.

What follows, then, is doubly hypothetical:

And yet the leaves, if they broke into bud,
If they broke into bloom, if they bore fruit,

And if we ate the incipient colorings
Of their fresh culls might be a cure of the ground. (526)

The (again, highly abstract) claim seems to be that the covering leaves might become a cure if they could be internalized and integrated into an organic system (here represented as natural growth).[35] The literalizing of that internalization—"if we ate"—combined with the abstraction (or, as it were, the figural representation of abstraction) of what we might eat, "the incipient colorings/Of their fresh culls," again links the poem's act of representation to its making-visceral of something that remains intangible, and makes it present as at once incipient (an incipient quality, moreover, not an object) and a remainder, a fresh cull.

One of the difficulties of the poem, I noted, is that the figural logic of the rock itself is at once clear and opaque: The opacity is all in its self-generating positing, in the inception as it were, the *fiat* that asks a reader to accept its presupposed "grounds." Like other late poems, the abstraction perhaps derives from a refusal to elaborate on or rationalize the figure's vehicle, or to attempt to naturalize it as perceptible. Rather, the figures, concrete and ostensibly easy to visualize, often lack a "literal" motivation, and the relation to the figural meaning (also often relatively straightforward) is difficult to trace. The rock, in its barren solidity, as if offers a figure for that very characteristic of the late poetry. In the case of the rock, the rendering of the inception of voice or consciousness is a meta-poetic figure in another sense as well, for the rock is also a figure for tradition, or for American literature. As Theo Davis notes, the image of American literary tradition as a barren rock or desert was already conventional by 1835: "American literary nationalism focuses, it might be said, on the image of America as a barren rock, one which authors subject to a dual gesture: pasting interest onto it and uncovering a latent, innate interest within it."[36] The tautology out of which the poem evokes its own emergence leaves us suspended among various possible registers. As the poem moves toward the derivation, as it were, of itself, it is also reflecting on its relation to poetic tradition.

The cure thus emerges from another layer of mediation, where the mediation is asserted to grant a greater immediacy. If it is not enough to "cover the rock with leaves," what covers the rock becomes more than that when it takes on figural dimensions that coordinate natural growth and internalization with the seasons,[37] and give to "covering" the added dimension of clothing or adornment:

> The pearled chaplet of spring,
> The magnum wreath of summer, time's autumn snood,
>
> Its copy of the sun, these cover the rock.
> These leaves are the poem, the icon, and the man. (526–7)

The representative or secondary—clothing rather than body, covering rather than covered, copy rather than original—becomes the cure, a transformation enacted by the turn from relations built on likeness (leaves as chaplet, wreath, and snood) to synonymity (renaming them, simply, "these leaves"), to metaphor or identity: "These leaves are the poem, the icon, and the man." The poem thus asserts a more substantial relation through "fiction," and a positing of substantial identity: "the fiction of the leaves is the icon/Of the poem, the figuration of blessedness,/And the icon is the man" (527). The claim seems to be a more essential relation: an icon "is a sign which represents its object by virtue of having some character in common with the object: the colour of a colour-card as representing the colour of the object which it resembles is an icon, and a map as representing spatial relations is an icon." But it is also "an image, figure, or representation; a portrait; a picture, 'cut', or illustration in a book; esp. applied to the 'figures' of animals, plants, etc. in books of Natural History," and, in the rhetorical categories of Puttenham and others, a simile.[38] It is as if the turn from likeness to identity were grounded on a second-order figuring of likeness: the fiction of the leaves is the icon . . . and the icon is the man. "These leaves are the poem, the icon, and the man": The assertion of identity makes the poem an icon in all the senses mentioned. And the lines thus also figure the figural status of "the rock" itself—as "mere" materiality that somehow enables a pure groundless positing. The poem asserts (if one follows the literal claims made) that "These leaves . . . are more than leaves."

The lines that follow either elaborate on or restate this claim (depending on how one parses the syntax):

> They bud the whitest eye, the pallidest sprout,
> New senses in the engenderings of sense,
> The desire to be at the end of distances,
>
> The body quickened and the mind in root. (527)

"New senses in the engenderings of sense" condenses the perhaps central claim of the section, the linking of sense as meaning (which, layered, eliminates the barrenness of the rock by making it "a thousand things") and sense as embodied perception (which likewise covers the rock). Evoking the "blindness cleaned" of the previous section, the image, more than a little monstrous, of the leaves that "bud the whitest eye" locates sense perception "in" the world—here, in the non-seeing eye that a flower or a potato (for example) shares with the organ of sight by virtue of visual resemblance.[39] "The desire to be at the end of distances" then recasts that uncanny exteriorization in a more traditional image of sublimity—sense born from the desire to transcend itself, to move beyond its limitations, to comprise a perspective that is shaped by its finitude. "The body quickened and the mind in root" thus expresses the double movements that the section links to the making of meaning, and to its "cure"—a body coming to life and a mind located outside it, not "above" it, but "in root."

At the end of the second section, *The Poem as Icon,* then, the "cure" is announced: "This is the cure/Of leaves and of the ground and of ourselves./His words are both the icon and the man" (527). The ungrounded deictic pronoun (*this*) is conspicuous, referring, it seems, to the entire figural and symbolic elaboration that precedes it, and pointing, therefore, too, to the groundlessness: the poem produces a cure through its own language, roots its "meanings" in the fact that it asserts them. The syntax of the final line enacts this logic: There is no one to govern the possessive pronoun until "the man" appears at the end of the sentence, and he is brought into being by the copula, and by the equation of "his words" and "the icon" and "the man." As with "illusion" in the first section, the possibility that man can know nothing but his own representations is as it were surmounted by identifying him more closely with those representations themselves and then locating them outside of him in a world that—like the rock itself—is brought into being by his writing of it.

The final section of the poem—*"Forms of a Rock in a Night-Hymn"*—marks a shift of tone, a "hymn" to what the previous sections have created, and the poem ends by naming it: "Night's hymn of the rock, as in a vivid sleep" (528). The tone of the final lines is almost elegiac, and it occurs to me to hear an allusion to *Hamlet* ("For in that sleep of death, what dreams may come,/When we have shuffled off this mortal coil,/Must give us pause" [III.i.66–8]); the section speaks as if posthumously, from the sleep of death, and within its vivid dreams.[40] Before the dreams are vivid, they are "evil," and the beginning of the section seems initially to invoke a nightmare and even something like last judgment:

> The rock is a gray particular of man's life,
> The stone from which he rises, up—and—ho,
> The step to the bleaker depths of his descents . . .
>
> The rock is the stern particular of the air,
> The mirror of the planets, one by one,
> But through man's eye, their silent rhapsodist,
>
> Turquoise the rock, at odious evening bright
> With redness that sticks fast to evil dreams;
> The difficult rightness of half-risen day. (528, ellipsis in original)

Odious is used here in its literal or etymological sense of "exciting hatred"; the night might be hateful or repulsive to the degree that it evokes mortality. Otherwise, it is perhaps a slim thread on which to hang an assertion of the eschatological tone of the final section, but the word *odious* also appears at a crucial moment in Book IX of *Paradise Lost* when Eve, announcing to Adam that she has eaten from the tree of knowledge, asks him to join her. The uncommonly articulate snake, she says,

Reasoning to admiration and with me
Persuasively hath so prevailed that I
Have also tasted and have also found
Th' effects to correspond: opener mine eyes,
Dim erst, dilated spirits, ampler heart,
And growing up to godhead which for thee
Chiefly I sought, without thee can despise.
For bliss as thou hast part to me is bliss,
Tedious unshar'd with thee and odious soon.
Thou therefore also taste that equal lot
May join us, equal joy, as equal love,
Lest thou not tasting, different degree
Disjoin us and I then too late renounce
Deity for thee, when Fate will not permit.[41]

For Eve, the bliss that, unshared, is odious, is also hateful, as Adam knows, because it is the mark of the fall she would otherwise endure alone. The de-mystified reader—fallen, too, to register the double meaning—knows that bale and bliss are condensed, as it were, in a single word. In Stevens, knowledge seems to come at the cost of a different kind of fall, a secular one, into a different kind of knowledge, where the rising up and descending are not opposed but two sides of a kind of immanence. The parallel definitions of the rock—"the grey particular man's life" and "the stern particular of the air"—set up the topographies of the final stanzas and call to mind the exchanges at the end of section I, "A particular of being, that gross universe." The rising up that is also a step to "bleaker depths of his descents" is further echoed by the mirroring of earth and planets—and in the possible German pun—the mirroring of the planets by the stars (*Stern* as star). Out of this mirroring emerges—again, as if "groundlessly"—human perception: the shift marked by "But" introduces "man's eye" and makes the rock, once viewed, "turquoise." The transition is enacted syntactically; the parallelism is violated, but in the service of confirming an implied parallel in an inverted form: "The rock is . . . The rock is . . . Turquoise [is] the rock."[42]

The tentative redemption then is registered in the movement from "odious evening bright" to "half-risen day"; it is also possible to read, in "the difficult rightness of half-risen day," yet another form of interference between literal and figural registers. For one way to read this "difficult rightness" would be as a literalization, where, "half-risen," the day would have difficulty remaining upright.[43] As with some of the other figures, that interference makes the half-risen day at once unsettlingly concrete and difficult to visualize—more difficult to visualize as literal than as (dead) metaphor. (A similar question of register is perhaps raised by "sticks fast to evil dreams"; the figurative meaning is perhaps less obscure than the literal meaning that ostensibly generates it.) Evoking the status of gesture in Welty or of metamorphosis in Ovid, Stevens's language as if confronts its origins—and confronts what I have called "inception." Thus, the sense of mortality and passing time with which the poem begins has been transformed into language that is beyond (or prior to) visualization.

Indeed, the final four stanzas render the relation of poetry and thought to embodied perception and time through a paradoxical topography:

> The rock is the habitation of the whole,
> Its strength and measure, that which is near, point A
> In a perspective that begins again
>
> At B: the origin of the mango's rind.
> It is the rock where tranquil must adduce
> Its tranquil self, the main of things, the mind,
>
> The starting point of the human and the end,
> That in which space itself is contained, the gate
> To the enclosure, day, the things illumined
>
> By day, night and that which night illumines,
> Night and its midnight-minting fragrances,
> Night's hymn of the rock, as in vivid sleep. (528)

The poem spells out some of the complexities intuited by the earlier poems. The exteriorization of consciousness is, paradoxically, at the origin, as if the origin of the mind were, simply, its inability to originate itself. That structure leads to, or is formed by, a series of other reversals: a part that contains the whole of which it is a part, a perspective that constitutes itself by projecting itself outside itself, a container for space that is also the gate to the enclosure. Projected outward, sense perception is at once the "material" and the "object" of thought; it can thus be represented or objectified only in ungrounded figures—in their tautology and in their paradoxical topography, the unsettled relation between vehicles and tenors that makes Stevens's figures seem "abstract," even as they are concretely visualized, and, in that abstraction to figure a power of pure positing. Poetic language might be said to comprise the origin of the mind insofar as it renders thought unobjectifiable, or objectifiable only in and as such paradoxical topographies; by making tangible the ineffable groundlessness that is the origin of the mind it as if produces that origination. In this way does Stevens lead his reader to a confrontation with what I have called "inception." On the one hand, then, "It is the rock where tranquil must adduce / Its tranquil self": the repetition of tranquil emphasizes the purely self-grounding gesture whereby the tranquil self is brought "forward (verbally) for consideration" or cited by the very utterance that constitutes it.[44] As in "Sunday Morning," therefore, there is no beyond; the rock—or the mind or the self—is "The starting point of the human and the end." And, on the other hand, this immanence is rendered as an immersion in temporal existence where the "ground" is paradoxically both what is represented and the mode of representation: "day, the things illumined / By day, night and that which night illumines." And thus the "illusion" of the beginning (made into what night and day, equally "illumine") has become a "vivid sleep," recasting as transcendence the mortal predicament of temporal limitation.

Like "The Idea of Order at Key West," "The Rock," in closing, evokes the word *origin*. "The origin of the mango's rind" condenses something of the movement I have charted, between positing and figural abstraction, and between a minimally distinguished object of representation and a minimally evoked mode of representation. The poem presents a series of different progressions or figures: the clods that, as in the Etruscan prophecies, become human beings; the "covering" of the rock that is rendered as leaves, as clothing (thereby coordinating an opposition of vehicle to tenor with that of body to soul); the passing of seasons as a cycle, and as a gradual movement of covering; the relations among poem, icon, and man; a movement from blindness to "blindness cleaned," as if derived from the coming into being of appearances (so that "blindness cleaned" can mean both sight and the blindness of inhabiting primal appearances); the "particular" of a man's life in relation to the meaning that might be derived from it; and so on. The poem does not so much coordinate these various figural contexts (making them all cohere as expressions of a body's relation to something that transcends it, for example) as submit them to unification through a narrative of inception that runs in two directions at once (just as the poem, looking back from "seventy years later" will, in so doing, as if derive the poem as the condition of the experience that will have occurred). The movement from blindness to "a blindness cleaned" corresponds to a covering that is also a laying bare—a "cure" that is a covering of the rock and a desiccation that takes one "back" to primordial elements. The rocks that Deucalion and Pyrrha toss behind them create human beings; imagining the "rock," the poem returns to the inception of voice and consciousness and derives from that return a "ground" for that imagining itself—thus building on the American tradition while taking us back to something prior to it. The poem both is itself what covers the rock and, in producing its abstract figure, is the unification that, stripping away such covering, produces the figure of the rock itself as that which will unify the poem.

The chaplet, wreath, and snood; the leaves that cover the rock: The poem exploits a traditional instability in these figures insofar as their chiastic structure locates their central term on both sides of an opposition (clothing covers the body as the body covers the soul—leaving the body to stand in both for the soul and for the soul's inessential covering). Evoking the "incipient colorings" of the "fresh culls" we might eat earlier in the poem, the mango's rind is not only a visceral evocation of materiality. It also reverses the movement from inside out, from rock to leaves, so that the "inner" rock is identified with the "outer" rind, thus linking the reversal of perspective (from point A to point B) and the temporal horizon of existence (the starting point of the human and the end, and the view of life *"Seventy Years Later"*) to the imagining of immanence as a paradoxically objectified medium of thought inseparable from thought itself.[45] The "hymn of the rock," then, might be taken in both senses of the genitive—the hymn that is the rock and the hymn that is about the rock, insofar, that is, as the poem's account of inception tends to make these indistinguishable. The poem's beautiful final lines seem at once to elaborate that mutual relation of containment and, particularly in the serial syntax—which leaves in doubt the subordination or logical relations among elements—to make an excess, the beauty that emerges, groundlessly, from the constitution of sense perception. If one is perhaps unsure whether "vivid sleep" is sleep in which perception remains vivid (to the person asleep), or sleep that is made vivid (to someone else), that uncertainty reenacts the externalization of perception through which the poem links immanence and a paradoxical form of transcendence. (*Vivid* descends, of course, from *vivere* (to live), the verb of Ovid's *vivam*.) The uncertainty likewise raises the question of who "survives" at the end of the poem to contemplate what it has achieved; in that sense, the poem's final hymn transforms the death of the mortal body into a different kind of vanishing, where the speaking voice becomes a "silent rhapsodist," disappears into the non- or almost-person of the poem, into inception, the origin or hymn of the rock.

PART IV

Solitude and Queer Origins

8

"Epitaph, the Idiom of Man"

Imaginings of the Beginning

Our birth is but a sleep and a forgetting
—WILLIAM WORDSWORTH, "ODE: INTIMATIONS OF IMMORTALITY
FROM RECOLLECTIONS OF EARLY CHILDHOOD"

I was able to discern from these that the charm of each of them lay in
a sort of metamorphosis of the objects represented, analogous to what
in poetry we call metaphor, and that, if God the Father had created
things by naming them, it was by taking away their names or giving
them other names that Elstir created them anew.
—MARCEL PROUST, *WITHIN A BUDDING GROVE*

In the beginning, language confronts its boundaries: a "before" it can posit
but not imagine or inhabit and that likewise implies an "after" of its vanishing,
and the limits and extents of its power over an external world it would comprise in representation, shape through its influence, or, in the hyperbolic claims
of certain poets, even posit or bring into being. In considerations of inception
(of minds and subjects, of forms and works) writers confront the power—and
the impotence—of human speech. Birth and death—as limits to the power of
human making, and of the mind's ability to transcend its corporeality and its
finitude—like conception and initiation—as a limit or horizon of a subject's
autonomy—can be read as thematic markers or analogues to formal questions
of beginning or inception, and lead one, in otherwise disparate texts, to an
intuition of the ways this power and impotence are fundamentally linked. The
"formal" boundaries of the text as it is caught up in the temporalities of human
consciousness and desire, with their staggered initiations and becomings, their

latencies and precocities, all that is out of sync in human beginnings: In the most general terms, this is the question of *Inceptions*. The "outside" here is not context or history, but a striving, within language, beyond itself, to a fulcrum through which a text might move itself or imagine its own grounds, or to a possibility that language might shed its saying of anything in particular in order to say itself. *Inceptions* attempts to make that effort legible through a series of terms—gesture, for example, or potentiality, revision, or positing—and traces it through a series of thematic preoccupations, with initiation or incipience, or various forms of starting out. After the last chapter's consideration of inception in Stevens, and the self-positing of "The Rock," the current chapter considers what Eudora Welty calls the "frailty" of human speech. Starting from Welty's story "Circe," the chapter then traces a passage from Ovid as it is cited by Milton (at the crucial moment of Adam's telling of his awakening into life), and then by Wordsworth in the Immortality Ode. The chapter isolates a particular phrase in Wordsworth as an index of its paradoxical formulation of the power of human frailty—"there is" of poetic positing—and then traces some of its appearances in elegiac poetry: in George Oppen's "The Image of the Engine," read as a rewriting of the Immortality Ode, and then, briefly, in short poems by Mark Strand and Louise Glück. The chapter concludes by turning to the abyssal consideration of exteriority in a more monumental work in a different genre, albeit still in the mode of elegy: Gertrude's speech announcing Ophelia's death in Shakespeare's *Hamlet*.

The conceit of Eudora Welty's "Circe" is deceptively simple: She retells Odysseus's visit to Circe's island from the perspective of the goddess, thereby giving voice, and density of character, to one of the most charismatic figures in the *Odyssey*, whose importance for the epic perhaps lies in her causing one of the delays in Odysseus's return home that, like the hero's other trials, produces the poem.[1] If her charisma and allure fleshes out that structural place of delay by making it an object of desire—for the epic's crafty hero as, perhaps, for a reader—she is not, by that token, given much in the way of psychological motivation. The shift to a first-person narrative alters the story—the sexual relation between Odysseus and Circe, for example, and the patterning and rhythm of suspense (Circe having no investment in their escape, or in the completion of their voyage)—by altering the alignment of a reader's sympathy. A character precipitates out of the mix in the positing of a first-person voice; the narrative voice adumbrates a character, and one who is, among other things, very funny. The humor often derives from the story's quiet registering of her perspective, as when, for instance, she complains about all that the men take for granted after she turns them back to men ("more winsome than they could ever have been before"). The sailors, who have, the day before, been pigs, and who jokingly imitate "the sounds of pigs at each other's backs," eat "a god's breakfast" with "all, the very sausages, taken for granted" (534). The humor is, here as elsewhere, double-edged: Their obliviousness (to what is possibly cannibalism) is subordinated to her aggrieved sense of being taken for granted. Her charisma derives at least in part from an obliviousness in her that doubles theirs.

If Circe is made a character by a voice that speaks in the first person, that does not mean that she is personified or humanized. Characterized, she makes manifest the distance of her perspective from a human one; the arc of the story could be described as her coming to know the difference between her perspective and that of the men without, however, being able to understand their point of view. Outward signs can be interpreted—"reunions, it seems, are to be celebrated" (534)—but that Circe can never know human perspective from the inside means that the story's own manipulation of sympathy, produced as it is by the manipulation of perspective, limns the experience of a character unable to feel it. Ultimately, that sympathy is grounded in the "frailty" of human mortality (533). Early on, Circe complains that the men fail to appreciate the wonder of the transformation that turns them to pigs: "That moment of transformation—only the gods really like it! Men and beasts almost never take in enough of the wonder to justify the trouble" (531). The humor derives from her aggrieved sense that the men ought to appreciate that transformation and be as removed from their sense of loss as she is (she who sees "men and beasts" as equivalent). Her later use of the term (she calls the slain Elpenor "the transformed boy" [536]) signals her inability to register death as a difference that matters.

Circe does, however, come to know that she does not know something, and that knowledge is called a "torment." "Why keep it up, old woman?" she whispers to the moon: "I swayed, and was flung back in my torment. I believed that I lay in disgrace and my blood ran green, like the wand that breaks in two. My sight returned to me when I awoke in the pigsty, in the red and black aurora of flesh, and it was day" (536). The implicit exchange that puts her in the place of the men—transformed, as they were, to awaken in the pigsty—is a paradoxical form of identification with their mystification, which, in her case, prevents her from identifying with them, prevents her from comprehending mortality. In the final paragraph of the story:

> I stood on my rock and wished for grief. It would not come. Though I
> could shriek at the rising Moon, and she, so near, would wax or wane,
> there was still grief, that couldn't hear me—grief that cannot be round
> or plain or solid-bright or running on its track, where a curse could get

at it. It has no heavenly course; it is like mystery, and knows where to
hide itself. At last it does not even breathe. I cannot find the dusty
mouth of grief. I am sure now grief is a ghost—only a ghost in Hades,
where ungrateful Odysseus is going—waiting on him. (537)

The dusty mouth of grief is a ghost that cannot speak. In a striking reversal,
the intangible or impalpable figures what eludes her in embodiment and mortality; the grief that one knows by virtue of being consigned to a mortal body
becomes, for her, an essence without qualities, a mystery to her no less than
immortality is a mystery to men. The entire effect of the story is there, in the
non-symmetry of those two mysteries. "The dusty mouth of grief": naming at
once the voice and the source of grief, the (figural) body she cannot find is
the curse of a fallen humanity. "In the sweat of thy face shalt thou eat bread,
till thou return unto the ground; for out of it wast thou taken: for dust thou
art, and unto dust shalt thou return" (Genesis 3:19, Authorized King James
Version).

The dusty mouth of grief is also a mode of speech. Odysseus's absence,
which she is unable to grieve, is contrasted with the men's grief for Elpenor,
"the transformed boy":

> They all ran from the table as though a star had fallen. They stood or
> they crouched above Elpenor fallen in my yard, low-voiced now like
> conspirators—as indeed they were. They wept for Elpenor lying on his
> face, and for themselves, as *he* wept for them the day they came, when
> I had made them swine.
>
> He knelt and touched Elpenor, and like a lover lifted him; then
> each in turn held the transformed boy in his arms. They brushed the
> leaves from his face, and smoothed his red locks, which were still in
> their tangle from his brief attempts at love-making and from his
> too-sound sleep.
>
> I spoke from the door. "When you dig a grave for that one, and bury
> him in the lonely sand by the shadow of your fleeing ship, write on the
> stone, 'I died of love.'"
>
> I thought I spoke in epitaph—in the idiom of man. But when they
> heard me, they left Elpenor where he lay, and ran. (536)

"It was the blight man was born for/It is Margaret you mourn for," writes
Hopkins in "Spring and Fall."[2] In Hopkins, there is a double movement of
identification—the child Margaret's, with the transience she sees in "Golden-
grove unleaving," and the speaker's, with her, "who will weep and know why"—
with her, therefore, as another instance of that "blight" that proves the older

heart yet moved by the sights of transience that have it spare an unwonted sigh. A dramatic monologue, Hopkins's poem is as much about the speaker, and the equivocal projection onto youth of a desire to know its ruin, as it is about the girl's intimations of mortality; for the devout Jesuit poet, too, no doubt, the emphasis must also be on "spring," and on the irony, perhaps unregistered by that speaker, that "unleaving" is also the eternal life promised by redemption.[3] Like Wordsworth's "We Are Seven," the poem is a picture as much of the speaker's projections as it is of the child's innocent relation to mortality.[4] Margaret can mourn goldengrove because she herself is mortal; that structure of projection and identification, Circe perceives, perhaps extends to all human grief, which is to some extent always grief for oneself. Her immortality therefore prevents her from feeling the loss of another, leaves her to feel rather the loss of the possibility of loss. If this is the grief she cannot find for herself—an understanding of absence that would allow her to weep for him—it is also striking that, to the degree that we are to hear an echo of another fall (Lucifer, the fallen star of the morning, as he prefigures the fall of man) Elpenor's death at once evokes that Fall and negates it by literalizing it.

"Epitaph . . . the idiom of man": the suggestion seems to be that human language is nothing but epitaph, a marker of an absent voice, the ventriloquized speech of the dead. (Indeed, in the West, grave markers are the first entities to "say" *I*—a human voice is constituted through a subsequent appropriation.)[5] An earlier moment in the story suggests a way to understand some aspects of that speech:

> There exists a mortal mystery, that, if I knew where it was, I could crush like an island grape. Only frailty, it seems, can divine it—and I was not endowed with that property. They live by frailty! By the moment! I tell myself that it is only a mystery, and mystery is only uncertainty. (There is no mystery in magic! Men are swine: let it be said, and no sooner said than done.) Yet mortals alone can divine where it lies in each other, can find it and prick it in all its peril, with an instrument made of air. I swear that only to possess that one, trifling secret, I would willingly turn myself into a harmless dove for the rest of eternity! (533)

("Though ye have lien among the pots, *yet shall ye be* as the wings of a dove covered with silver, and her feathers with yellow gold" [Psalms 68:13].) Human frailty and "mystery" are tied not only to the punctuation of time by mortality, which thereby makes the "moment" perceptible ("His ship was a moment's gleam on a wave" [537]), but also to "an instrument made of air" that one is tempted to call human speech. Circe's parenthesis casts "mystery" as a linguistic impotence in contrast to her immediately effective speech—"Men are swine: let it be said, and no sooner said than done." Lacking "frailty," there is no gap in her speech separating it from its effectiveness in the world, and in her words, the jussive subjunctive evokes the creative power of the divine *fiat lux*. What her power rules out at this moment is metaphor, a mode of speech where "men are swine" would not mean that men literally were pigs. ("In the end, it takes phenomenal neatness of housekeeping to put it through the heads of men that they are swine" [531].) "The dusty mouth of grief" at the story's end is thus in a sense paradoxical; she cannot "find" it because her language literalizes it, makes it an actual mouth instead of a figure of speech. In giving voice to an immortal goddess, Welty's story finds in human "frailty" a paradoxical power born of impotence: human speech, or epitaph, the idiom of man.

Such a possibility is not unprecedented. One remembers that it is Adam, not God, who names the creatures of the earth (except himself), as if the power to name were in some sense a form of impotence, were a consequence of a speech from which the immediate effectiveness of the divine word has been withdrawn.[6] ("Only a god's word has no beginning or end," remarks Anne Carson in *Eros the Bittersweet*; that is Augustine's conclusion as well—and not just his, of course.)[7] In *Paradise Lost*, speech arrives to Adam as a form of address to the world, one that reaches out from a self that does not know itself:

> Myself I then perused and limb by limb
> Surveyed and sometimes went and sometimes ran
> With supple joints as lively vigor led.
> But who I was, or where, or from what cause
> Knew not. To speak I tried and forthwith spake:
> My tongue obeyed and readily could name
> Whate'er I saw. "Thou Sun," said I, "fair light,
> And thou enlightened Earth so fresh and gay,
> Ye hills and dales, ye rivers, woods, and plains,
> And ye that live and move, fair creatures, tell,
> Tell if ye saw how came I thus, how here." (*PL* VIII.267–77)[8]

"Not of myself," he concludes, and then is led to ask the world of his maker, "Tell me how I may know Him, how adore" (VIII.278, 280). When, a few lines later, Adam falls asleep, he thinks he is passing again into non-existence—"I thought/I then was passing to my former state/Insensible and forthwith to dissolve" (*PL* VIII.289–91): whatever the other reasons that God then comes to Adam in a dream, the revelation is constituted through a turning-inward that Adam initially finds indistinguishable from dissolution. (It is also as if Adam had to replay his creation, in reverse, in order to encounter God; his retelling to the Archangel likewise replays his various forms of address.) And Adam's discovery of his capacities is an intuition of his self-division: "To speak I tried and forthwith spake:/My tongue obeyed and readily could name/What'er I saw." The naming of the beasts then draws into stark contrast two modes of speech, God's, which calls the animals into being ("As thus He spake each bird and beast behold!" [*PL* VIII.349]), and Adam's, which names them ("I named them as they passed and understood their nature" [*PL* VIII.352–3]). God's calling forth of the animals seemingly answers Adam's earlier question by displaying the Creation that he awoke too late to witness. A secondary reading of God's creation, Adam's naming is a continuation of his questioning of the world about his origins. Structurally, the repetition of the story of Creation, told in Book VII and then retold by Adam in Book VIII, replays a common structure in tales of origin: One thinks of the multiplied accounts of Creation in, for example, Ovid's *Metamorphoses* or Plato's *Timaeus*. Or in Genesis. Deleuze notes that in creation myths "the formation of the world happens in two stages, in two periods of time, birth and re-birth" and that "the second is just as necessary and essential as the first."[9] Eve's subsequent narration of her awakening confirms the structure: for our first parents, one tells to someone who might have witnessed it the story of a beginning one's consciousness cannot comprise. Telling takes shape within a fundamental, founding impotence, bearing witness to one's staggered arrival at one's beginning, and the beginning of speech. Adam's turn to self-quotation enacts, as a structure of voice, the doubling of creation implicit in consciousness's belated arrival at its inception.

The asymmetrical structure of address is made explicit when Adam then asks the name of God—"'O by what name (for Thou above all these,/Above mankind or aught than mankind higher,/Surpassest far my naming) how may I/Adore Thee . . . ?'" [*PL* VIII.357–60]).[10] Adam's query as if vanishes into the fealty-attesting form of the rhetorical question (which may likewise disappear into anacoluthon, since the beginning, "O by what name" is not completed except insofar as it is absorbed by another question: "how may I/Adore Thee?" Seeming to suggest, by its posing, that there is no answer, it also thereby disappears into self-reflexivity). Adam then immediately moves on to a different question, and the juxtaposition leads one to think that the second is, if not synonymous with the first, then in some way a consequence of it:

> But with me
> I see not who partakes. In solitude,
> What happiness? Who can enjoy alone
> Or all enjoying what contentment find? (*PL* VIII.363–6)

It is not merely that Adam deduces his solitary state from seeing his exceptional place in Nature—above it, but also different ("They rejoice/Each with
their kind, lion with lioness,/So fitly them in pairs thou hast combined" [PL
VIII.392–4])—and not merely that the nature to whom he speaks cannot give
sufficient answer. It is also as if the confrontation with the limit of his power
to name ("O by what name . . . ?") makes manifest his solitude—the solitude
therefore of the speaking being that, by way of Jean-Claude Milner, we found
in *Robinson Crusoe*.

Indeed, the "Almighty" answers him with another question:

A nice and subtle happiness I see
Thou to thyself proposes in the choice
Of thy associates, Adam, and wilt taste
No pleasure, though in pleasure, solitary.
What think'st thou then of Me and this My state?
Seem I to thee sufficiently possessed
Of happiness, or not, who am alone
From all eternity? (*PL* VIII.398–406)[11]

As Adam answers on the next page, an infinite being cannot be solitary; only
imperfect beings need complements. The "nice and subtle happiness" suggests, moreover, that the Fall may be contained within that solitude itself, and
in the imagining of its remediation (in, perhaps, the proposing to oneself);
"subtle" is repeatedly the term used to describe the serpent, that "subtlest beast
of all the field" (for instance, *PL* IX.560; the source, ultimately, is Genesis:
"Now the serpent was more subtil than any beast of the field which the Lord
God had made" [Genesis 3:1]). Typically, Milton's terms shift meaning before
and after the Fall; words take on antithetical meanings in the poem's lexicon
even as the verbal echoes mark continuity and foreshadowing. Adam's subtlety
is here innocent, but he will weep and know why. For subtlety is expressed, of
course, in the serpent's speech, in the fact that he, alone of the beasts, talks.[12]
"Nice and subtle" enacts verbal subtlety; a not untypical form of Miltonic doubling, the pairing of near synonyms—like "thunderstruck" and "astonished,"
for example—adds emphasis even as it points to minimal, nearly ineffable distinctions. The colloquial use of "nice and" as a form of emphasis (nice and
easy, nice and slow) is not attested for another two centuries; the later acceptation would make redundant the pleonastic emphasis in God's remark. The
use of "nice" is also "subtle"; the immediate meaning is that of a fastidious or
minutely observed distinction (used in an ironic sense here)—an elegance and
scrupulosity that will be linked to a fine style (in dress, in writing, in conduct),
and to a fine discrimination in perception and thought. The irony is, no doubt,

in God's invoking of that refinement—and the word's associations with cultured or polite society—in the context of the, after all, simple society that Adam hopes to form with a single mate. (Once there are two rather than one, he seems to imply, it is but a short step to the refinements of the subtlest court.) Given the pleasure of being created, and, created, of the world he finds, Adam wants something nicer; the comment is directed at Adam's disregarding a pleasure that, without the refinement of added subtlety, will not, for the jaded, rise to the level of a pleasure. The niceness, however, is not just in the palate of the solitary man; it is also in the word's splitting into antithetical meanings: difficult to understand, requiring close consideration (minute and subtle), but also unimportant or trivial, even senseless; discriminating but also overly or pointlessly discriminating; respectable, virtuous, decent, proper, but also lascivious, wanton, silly, corrupt, foolish; shy and modest, but also overly so (tender and delicate), or, even more pointedly, cowardly and effeminate. God's ironic praise names the laudatory acceptations while covertly invoking the reprobative ones—a mode of speech that is, of course, itself a form of subtlety (a corruption there, however, perhaps only to the degree that, fallen ourselves, we as readers are subtle enough to see it).

The implication, in any event, would seem to be that the "happiness" Adam desires is too nice, too subtle, and that the yearning, which will lead to the Fall, and Man's greatest unhappiness, is a part of the subtlety of speech. Thus, in the final lines of the poem, Adam and Eve leave paradise: "The world was all before them, where to choose/Their place of rest, and Providence their guide./ They hand in hand with wand'ring steps and slow/Through Eden took their solitary way" (*PL* XII.646–9). In solitude, what happiness; who can enjoy alone, or all enjoying contentment find: the very need for complementarity expressed in Adam's initial speech to his creator contains the Fall—anticipates the "wandering" that throughout the poem constitutes the lexical foreshadowing of the causes and consequences of sin. After the Fall, Adam seeks solitude—in a gesture of the guilt that, for the poem, replays the infraction: "O might I here/ In solitude live savage in some glade/Obscured where highest woods impenetrable/To star or sunlight spread their umbrage broad/And brown as evening! Cover me ye pines,/Ye cedars, with innumerable boughs/Hide me where I may never see them more!" (*PL* IX.1084–90). If the seeds of the fall are to be found in Adam's yearning desire for company, this is not merely to suggest that it is through Eve's fault that man is destined to fall. The subtlety of speech that moves from happiness to enjoyment to contentment suggests the possibility not of recovered wholeness but of a solitude shared. In the poem's layered consideration of solitude and inception, one finds again the consequences of a fundamental, constitutive frailty of human beings who speak.

Adam's solitude thus points to a relation linking the frailty of human finitude, the Fall, and certain forms of speech: invocation, address, naming. (These
are registers of epitaph, the idiom of man.) This context suggests ways to understand the echo of Adam's initial awakening address ("Ye hills and dales, ye
rivers, woods, and plains") in the triumphant final section of Wordsworth's
Immortality Ode: "And O, ye Fountains, Meadows, Hills, and Groves/Forbode
not any severing of our loves!"[13] In Milton, Adam's words explicitly return, at
the end of his lament in Book X (words that are, perhaps, even closer to the
Immortality Ode): "O woods, O fountains, hillocks, dales and bow'rs,/With
other echo late I taught your shades to/To answer and resound far other song!"
(*PL* X.860–3). A similar address appears in Adam's lament, just after the fall,
in Book IX, "Cover me, ye pines,/Ye cedars." (His awakening speech is also
echoed in Book IX by Satan: "With what delight could I have walked thee
round/(If I could joy in aught) sweet interchange/Of hill and valley, rivers,
woods and plains,/Now land, now sea and shores with forest crowned,/Rocks,
dens, and caves!" [*PL* IX.14–18]. The potential or virtual vocative marks the
joy that Satan, fallen, cannot have.) The likely source for Milton's language is
the magical incantation of Medea in Golding's translation of Ovid's *Metamorphoses*: "Ye Ayres and windes: ye Elves of Hilles, of Brookes, of Woods
alone,/Of standing Lakes, and of the Night approche ye everychone"[14]—which
is echoed (cited) by Prospero in Shakespeare's *Tempest*: "Ye elves of hills,
brooks, standing lakes and groves,/And ye that on the sands with printless
foot/Do chase the ebbing Neptune . . ." (V.i.33–50).[15] The moment in *The Tempest* appears at the beginning of Act V, where Prospero, claiming even the
power to raise the dead ("graves at my command/Have waked their sleepers,
oped, and let 'em forth/By my so potent art"), invokes his exorbitant powers,
apparently to renounce them: "But this rough magic/I here abjure, and when
I have required/Some heavenly music—which even now I do— /To work mine
end upon their senses that/This airy charm is for, I'll break my staff,/Bury it
certain fathoms in the earth,/And deeper than did ever plummet sound/I'll
drown my book" (V.1.50–57). In Ovid, Medea's invocation appears as she gathers herbs for the potion that will rejuvenate Aeson—a rejuvenation that she
later counterfeits in her ploy to make Pelias's daughters stab him to death by
holding out the delusory promise of restoring his youth.

I have elsewhere dwelt on the complexities of Prospero's repeated gestures
of renunciation—and on some effects of Shakespeare's citation of Ovid.[16] In
Milton, Adam and Satan alike know that they do not recall their Creation,
but while Adam—"For Man to tell how human life began/Is hard: for who
himself beginning knew?" (*PL* VIII.250–1)—infers his status as created, for

Satan, that oblivion suggests self-making: "who saw / When this Creation was? Remember'st thou / Thy making while the Maker gave thee being? / We know no time when we were not as now, / Know none before us, self-begot, self-raised / By our own quick'ning power . . ." (*PL* V.856–61).[17] Yet Adam's questioning of the world hides a certain claim to self-making, too. Like Welty's Circe, Milton, recalling Ovid (and possibly Shakespeare), brings magic into contact with human finitude. Adam's address as he awakes to consciousness ("Ye hills and dales . . ."), which, in pondering his origins, bears witness to his "frailty," is also an incantation or invocation, and thus a claim of power. Given the Miltonic echo, the severing in Wordsworth seems all but inevitable, and, the poem's conclusion, all the more tendentious—or, rather, a function purely of poetic fiat and poetic will. Put another way, in each instance, the poet calls on nature to bear witness to, or to create, a power over life and death that is beyond nature;[18] for the later invocations, that power is lined with a registering of its impossibility. For Prospero, his power in many ways simply *is* his repeated gestures of renouncing it, as if that renunciation could encompass, and thereby transcend, human frailty and the limits of mortality; in Milton, the address to nature recalls that abjured magic, even in the claim that would set Adam above the beasts. The movement from Book VIII to Book X—the recurrence of the Medean invocation at Adam's waking first to his creation, and then, in lament, to his fall—suggests that Adam may, unlike Satan, register the mark, within his very speech, of his finitude as a created being; in writing these lines, the poet may, once again, be closer to the rebellious angel in the implicit claim of a power to comprise it. However that may be, Wordsworth then recalls, perhaps ironically, the initial context of rejuvenation; the gaze at childhood at once claims the fate of Aeson and consigns the aging poet to the mortality of Pelias. He also takes on something of Prospero's brand of magic; the layered references prove a way of sustaining the claim for poetic magic through the very gestures that would accede to its limits.

For Wordsworth finds redemption as if within the fall itself, within knowledge, but also within the fall from innocent immediacy, childhood "appareled in celestial light" (Wordsworth, 635). That movement in this famous poem is perhaps too well known to warrant another rehearsal: a fallen state is made its own consolation, and a self-consciousness about loss consoles the poet for the loss of an unmediated bliss that never knew itself as such. Knowing mortality, and the very self-consciousness that signals it, consoles one for the loss it entails—by putting one in contact, through that very fall, with "that immortal sea / Which brought us hither" (640). It is perhaps not surprising that the poem turns to figures of conferred or posited speech—and makes that speech remediation for the loss charted at the beginning ("there hath passed away a glory from the earth" [636]). The poem as if wills (paradoxically) a spontaneous utterance to compensate for the loss of remembered unmediated natural pleasure. The closing Adamic address is thus made the achievement of the poem (and hence is a kind of self-creation). The child is the father of the man: the poem returns to its epigraph (and poetic precursor) at the end, as if to gloss it, and the falling away that initially seems the result of thinking on the shaping power of those earlier days becomes a claim of poetic self-making. The Miltonic echo makes the fallen state of self-consciousness a version of the "primal sympathy" (640) it aims to recover (precisely, that is, because it is Adam's waking speech, and the closing stanza in Wordsworth becomes the announcement of a birth, and one doubled, like Adam's, as the retelling of that experience). At the same time, the self-consciously belated speech of the poet, in its thwarted effort to recover the glories of childhood, as it were cedes that recovery to the loss it was born for in order to make the speech itself its own reward.

A detailed reading of the poem might trace the uneven movements of its various moments of address. Thus, for instance, the willed "jollity" of the third stanza ("No more shall grief of mine the season wrong")—at this point in the poem, we are meant to feel the willfulness, and the strain, for the transmuting of loss is here yet merely willed—becomes a demand for speech: "Thou Child of Joy,/Shout round me, let me hear thy shouts, thou happy Shepherd-boy!" (636). The closing turn to a valorized self-consciousness is prepared by that continuity—the way that presence, loss, and recovery are all alike rendered as forms of speech, in relation to a nature that speaks and can be spoken to. With "And O, ye Fountains, Meadows, Hills, and Groves" (640), the poem's voice might be said to bring itself into being, to answer human lack with a posited address—a speaking epitaph, as Welty might have it, the idiom of man. The echoes of Ovid and Shakespeare suggest that this address is also an incantation, a claim of magic powers to which, moreover, the density of literary reference is not irrelevant. When, in the earlier stanza, Wordsworth addresses "thou happy Shepherd-boy," he invokes both an imagined child, one quite possibly gamboling about, in the bliss of unconscious wonder, and a long tradition of pastoral poetry stretching from Theocritus and Virgil to Wordsworth's own nature poetry. If, at this earlier moment, it perhaps strikes one as something of a problem—claiming unmediated, untutored joy in the guise of one of the most hoary of literary tropes—the closing incantation brings together literary tradition and the turn to redeemed self-consciousness claimed by the incantation itself. Exactly as hoary, and as fallen, then, can the redemptive magic recover the glory and freshness of the dream. "I love the Brooks which

down their channels fret" (640): perhaps the poem's most straightforward assertion of feeling, unmodulated by equivocation or distanced recollection or
description and unmediated by indirection or vicarity of voice, this speaking
of the poet's own emotion appears after he has buried his voice in precursors
whose writing he also appropriates.

Wordsworth's implicit quotation is also a reading of his precursors: Read in
the context of the Immortality Ode, Adam's awakening address to nature bears
the traces of the fall that Wordsworth will retell in the secular terms of self-
consciousness, and the incantations of Medea and Prospero seem to register
what Welty calls human "frailty," albeit in an equivocally celebratory mood.
Without pursuing a detailed reading of the poem, I would, by dwelling on
the ode's fourth stanza, suggest the outline of the claim of self-making that
emerges out of a poetic comprising of human frailty:

> Ye blessèd creatures, I have heard the call
>   Ye to each other make; I see
> The heavens laugh with you in your jubilee;
>   My heart is at your festival,
>   My head hath its coronal,
> The fullness of your bliss, I feel—I feel it all.
>   —Oh, evil day! if I were sullen
>   While Earth herself is adorning,
>   This sweet May morning,
>   And the Children are culling
>   On every side,
> In a thousand valleys far and wide,
> Fresh flowers; while the sun shines warm,
> And the Babe leaps up on his Mother's arm—
>   I hear, I hear, with joy I hear!
>   —But there's a Tree, of many, one,
> A single Field which I have looked upon,
> Both of them speak of something that is gone:
>   The Pansy at my feet
>   Doth the same tale repeat:
> Whither is fled the visionary gleam?
> Where is it now, the glory and the dream? (636–7)

The stanza enacts in various ways the uneven, starting-and-stopping motion
of the poem's movement toward redemption, and it is made explicit here that
a will to join in the fun is linked to a positing of voice: In the interpolated repetitions, for example ("I feel—I feel it all"; "I hear, I hear, with joy I hear!"), a

repetition of almost stuttering hesitancy (I *will* feel it all, a hesitancy that is picked up in the second thoughts later on ["Oh, evil day, if I were sullen"]) becomes a mimicking of a speaking voice. The hesitancy is already there at the opening of the stanza insofar as the immediacy is (only) that of immediate sense perception (I have heard, I see).

The falling away from the transcendence that (after all) will not arrive for another six stanzas gives that posited voice the form of an interruption: "But there's a Tree, of many, one, / A single Field which I have looked upon." The particularity of perception interferes with the transcendence—the specific history of the poet's individual perceptions will not be so easily sublimated. Read in the context of *Paradise Lost*, that "Tree, of many, one," no doubt evokes the one tree of many whose fruit is not to be tasted ("O sovereign, virtuous, precious of all trees / In Paradise" [*PL* IX.795–6]); only after the fact, with the "single Field which I have looked upon," does "of many, one" come to signal an individual experience rather than an allegorical reference that would submit that experience to the shape of human history (just as it also becomes clear that "of many, one" is a limiting rather than a unifying relation, one tree that resists assimilation rather than one tree that represents them all). If the stanza marks a hinge point for the poem, it is perhaps because the ostensible failure here will eventually become the empowering frailty of human speech—what the poet will come to "raise" his "song of thanks and praise," for "those obstinate questionings / Of sense and outward things, / Fallings from us, vanishings" (639). For another movement is legible in "There's a Tree, of many, one / A single Field which I have looked upon": what we might initially take to be a form of positing— "There's a Tree"—becomes instead something given, something there to be "looked upon."[19] At the same time, then, the mere finding of a natural spectacle can become a claim for human making; the moment thus condenses the gesture inherent in the invocations of Medea, Prospero, and the poem's close.

At this point in the poem, the speech that arrives speaks of loss: "Both of them speak of something that is gone." In the final two lines of the stanza, the voice of the poem merges with this elegiac voice of nature, giving voice to "The Pansy at my feet" that "Doth the same tale repeat": "Whither is fled the visionary gleam? / Where is it now, the glory and the dream?" (637). Speaking of loss, the ventriloquism of natural forms makes the poet's own voice seem ventriloquized. One question for the poem might be the degree to which the final stanzas manage to reverse the valence of what otherwise they could be said simply to repeat—the degree to which destitution spoken can be made its own reward, and a form of transcendence whose vanishing it concedes. In "The Image of the Engine," a poem that might be read as a response to Wordsworth's ode, George Oppen returns to this question: beginning from the "image of the engine"—the frail mortal body, made a "mere" machine, that, "when it stops, it stops"—it links that "machine involved with itself, a concentrated/Hot lump of a machine/Geared in the loose mechanics of the world" to the mind's power to console (or delude) itself with its own images: "will one imagine/Then because he can imagine/That squeezed from the cooling steel/There hovers in that moment, wraith-like and like a plume of steam, an aftermath,/A still and quiet angel of knowledge and of comprehension."[20] The "machine involved with itself" denotes both the "turning" of an engine (literally "involved," it is turned inward—*volvere* means to roll) and the island solitude, unsponsored, free, of the mortal body, unmoored from any existential guarantee beyond its own mechanism. Both in turn then become the self-reflexivity of the poem, its ungrounded self-involution, captured in the poem's repetitions: "A machine involved with itself, a concentrated/Hot lump of a machine/Geared in the loose mechanics of the world"; "When the thing stops,/Is stopped, . . . stopping, finally/Stopped"; "will one imagine/Then because he can imagine"; "wraith-like and like a plume of steam" (both recalling the opening "likely"). Turning language to repeated sounds, the syntax, literally "involved with itself," enacts the marooned state of the mortal body even as it marks a mimetic rendering of the engine's mechanism.

Ultimately, the poem (which, as if citing Wordsworth, likewise turns to children, but "beautiful bony children" of a dirty, rubble-filled city instead of Wordsworth's gamboling children of nature) will offer a similar form of consolation—not transcendence, but the desire for it: "But they will find/In flood, storm, ultimate mishap:/Earth, water, the tremendous/Surface, the heart thundering/Absolute desire" (42). Much of the power of the poem's ending derives from that paratactic structure, from the uncertainty we are left in about the relations among these posited images, which therefore return us to primal elements. "The tremendous/Surface" does not clearly refer to a finished form—it could be the surface of the body, or the surface of the earth, or the exterior as such, appearances as they greet us prior to any meaning (or prior to us). The parallelism—flood to earth, storm to water, ultimate mishap to tremendous surface—does not offer a clear path among unambiguous analogies but suggests an apocalyptic progression where the "ultimate mishap" is both mortality and the end of the world. These images, moreover, feel as if they "take place" nowhere, and the final phrases—"the heart thundering/Absolute desire"—thus paradoxically locate human yearning in a field cleared of human presence. (In question, too, is the relation between those two phrases, whether absolute desire is thundered by the heart, whether they are synonymous formulations, or whether they are parallel but not necessarily related elements in a series. More generally, the poem's tendency to isolate verbal action from clear syntactical governing by subjects both as it were dehumanizes the action and curiously intensifies the affect.)

As in the Immortality Ode, the middle reaches of the poem are taken up with something more like particularity. As at the end, though, much of the power of its initial evocation comes from certain grammatical indeterminacies:

> The machine stares out,
> Stares out
> With all its eyes
> Thru the glass
> With the ripple in it, past the sill
> Which is dusty—If there is someone
> In the garden!
> Outside, and so beautiful. (41)

The exclamation—"If there is someone/In the garden!"—links human presence to the particularity that has movingly been evoked by the rippled glass and the dusty sill, but it makes that presence a mere positing. It is thus as if that positing (rendered, moreover, in the form of "someone") were the equivalent of those particularities (the "if," that is, rather than the "someone"); the suspended syntax makes the positing the (suspended) content of an exclamation. The exclamation, which would appear to mimic a voice, in fact interrupts the syntax, making "Outside, and so beautiful" ambiguous—leading us to wonder whether someone is in the garden outside, or whether "outside" modifies the entire stanza, and whether, perhaps, it is exteriority itself (unmoored there in its equivocal reference, and therefore suspended, too, in its relation to any inside) that is so beautiful.

In the next stanza, a voice does appear, and in quotation marks: "'I want to ask if you remember/When we were happy!/As tho all travels/Ended untold, all embarkations/Foundered" (41). Our sense of this "I" is no doubt shifted by the hypothetical "someone" in the previous stanza; notably, moreover, the quotation is never closed, so the rest of the poem—and this utterance, too—both is and is not spoken, and by a voice that is therefore both of the poem and not, both cited, from outside, and identical with the poem's voice. (The quotation from Ecclesiastes that opens the final section of the poem—"*Also he has set the world/In their hearts*"—appears in italics rather than quotation marks, and may or may not be spoken by this earlier voice.) The fourth section of the poem offers another image for loss—once again, a highly particularized one that occurs as if nowhere:

On that water
Grey with morning
The gull will fold its wings
And sit. And with its two eyes
There as much as anything
Can watch a ship and all its hallways
And all companions sink. (41)

"That water" has the curious effect of localizing an absence, or of de-realizing the scene through the very concreteness of its gesture of pointing. Like the dusty sill and the "outside" we do and do not glimpse, the scene here is at once abstract and particularized. "That water," if it has a reference beyond the posited scene that follows, would seem to refer to the hypothetical at the end of section 3, to supply a scene for a supposition: "as tho . . . all embarkations / Foundered." It seems to me that one feels at once the power of that evoked scene—the impassive gull witnessing shipwreck, where the impassivity is compounded by the even (but therefore apathetic) bestowal of existence ("There as much as anything")—and feels that it is merely evoked, feels, in other terms, its arbitrary or contingent nature, its status as something that one imagines because he can imagine. The gull's "two eyes" echo the machine "with all its eyes" earlier, making explicit that the machine's consciousness has been projected outward (and is perhaps even more human insofar as the initial "all" suggests the machine might have more than two eyes). The uncanny effect is compounded by the realization that the entire image is as if a literalization of "companionship" in the previous section ("Even companionship / Ending"). The moving image of the loss of human connection turns out to be the sinking of a "companion ship," another engine, no doubt, not only because the ship itself is a machine but because language seems here to supply arbitrary connections that nevertheless have the power to move us. "Companionship" both forms a word and comes apart, marks the content of human yearning even as it shades into a paronomastic hallucination, an effect of contingency as language again turns to involved mechanism.

Will one imagine then because he can imagine? At issue for the poem is the mind's power to console itself, and possibly factitiously, a power to posit that overlaps with the perception of the particular, the obstinate questionings of sense and outward things. It is striking that the formulation that caught my attention in Wordsworth—"But there's a Tree, of many, one, / A single Field which I have looked upon"—is echoed in seemingly unrelated elegiac verse (as in, perhaps, Oppen's gull, "there as much as anything"). The first poem in Louise Glück's strange and beautiful collection *The Wild Iris* begins with these lines:

> At the end of my suffering
> there was a door.
>
> Hear me out: that which you call death
> I remember.[21]

The collection moves among a series of voices—the plants or flowers, the gardener, and something like God—and among other things it is part of a tradition, generally conceived, that, stretching from Virgil's *Eclogues*, includes the Immortality Ode. Glück's collection uncannily literalizes the conveying of voice in the address to nature in Ovid, Shakespeare, Milton, and Wordsworth; if Medea invokes the natural world in her spell, Glück's flowers appear to speak back. Again without proposing a detailed reading of the poem, which would take us far from the current argument, I would point simply to the convergence of an imagining of an emerging voice from beyond mortality or death—"You who do not remember/passage from the other world/I tell you I could speak again: whatever/returns from oblivion returns/to find a voice"—and a similar gesture of positing: "there was a door." Part of what's powerful about the image is, like the ship in Oppen, its bare, referential quality, as if, in its very abstraction, it could, devoid of other qualities, be concretely referred to—its status, in other words, as posited, but only posited.

In Mark Strand's "The New Year," section 6 of "Elegy for My Father," a voice repeatedly addresses an absent "you," as if to give a local habitation and a name to a particular absence: "nobody knows you."[22] Particularity instead accrues to all that "you" do not see and feel: "You do not see the rain falling and the man walking away,/the soiled wind blowing its ashes across the city./You do not see the sun dragging the moon like an echo." That evocation of loss then turns to an imagining of last days—"The meek are hauling their skins into heaven. . . . /It is over and nobody knows you"—where the linguistic gesture of positing appears again:

> There is starlight drifting on the black water.
> There are stones in the sea no one has seen.
> There is a shore and people are waiting.
> And nothing comes back. (77)

Recalling, no doubt, Gray's "Full many a gem of purest ray serene" that "The dark unfathomed caves of ocean bear,"[23] Strand's lines make explicit the gesture of positing within the evocation of that unwitnessed beauty: flowers in a sense brought into being by the positing of their unseen blush, such sights, unfathomed, are also not to be comprised, a coming together of poetic power and impotence that is evocative for the experience of grief. As in the equivocal conjuring magic in the invocations of Ovid, Milton, and Wordsworth, Strand's "there is," in its very power of evocation, makes manifest an absence. By the penultimate line of the poem, that link becomes explicit: "Because there is silence instead of a name." The perhaps more expected premise of the poem—the continuation of the world after the disappearance of the loved one—shades into something more unsettling as the evoked world takes on a curiously lunar, abstract particularity, and the loss, generalized, marks a vanishing of human presence. The power to posit appears then in the absence of any observer—and seems here almost causal, as if to say "there is" were to create a world after the disappearance of the human, to make indistinct a claim of a poetic power of creation and the desolating disappearance of the poet as anything but the voice that "speaks" the incantation.

Here is a final and more famous instance in which human finitude encounters a poetic power to posit, and with which we might conclude this consideration of speech, solitude, and inception—Gertrude's lament for Ophelia in Act IV, Scene 7 of *Hamlet*:

> There is a willow grows askaunt the brook,
> That shows his hoary leaves in the glassy stream;
> There with fantastic garlands did she make
> Of crow-flowers, nettles, daisies, and long purples
> That liberal shepherds give a grosser name,
> But our cull-cold maids do dead men's fingers call them:
> There, on the pendant boughs her crownet weeds
> Clamb'ring to hang, an envious sliver broke;
> When down her weedy trophies and herself
> Fell in the weeping brook. Her clothes spread wide;
> And mermaid-like awhile they bore her up:
> Which time she chaunted snatches of old lauds;
> As one incapable of her own distress,
> Or like a creature native and indued
> Unto that element: but long it could not be
> Till that her garments, heavy with their drink,
> Pull'd the poor wretch from her melodious lay
> To muddy death. (*Hamlet* IV.vii.166–83)[24]

This is one of the moments in the play when it seems to bump up against its own status as a text—if for no other reason that we here feel with particular intensity the tension between the lyrical lines and the characters (with psychology, motives, even extension in the world) they ostensibly represent. In one register, it would be reasonable to ask why, if Ophelia's death could be so minutely observed, did no one step in to fish her out of the drink? Why foreground, if only implicitly, their status as mere helpless observers? In tension, in other terms, is the play's rendering of probable action and the action's serving as the occasion for lyrical utterance.[25] (Laertes is stirred to vengeful action, but he is not troubled by Gertrude's inaction. The speech's function is surely foregrounded, too, insofar as its periphrastic opening [and lyricism] is explicitly at odds with the framing of the speech as informative.) One then recalls that the boundary between observation in the play (by characters) and observation of the play (by the audience) is a crucial, often undecidable question—and central to *Hamlet* in multiple ways. The institution of the soliloquy makes that difficulty particularly perceptible: the paradox of internal thoughts spoken aloud corresponds to a far from trivial uncertainty in the staging of the play about whether these words are overheard by other characters. In Mozart's operas, it is ever an important moment when a character, singing on stage, is "really" singing in the depicted action—think of Don Giovanni's "Deh vieni alla finestra," or Cherubino's "Voi che sapete che cosa è amor." The soliloquy leads one to ask, similarly, whether the speaking character "really" speaks, and hence introduces a division into the play's mimesis at its very foundations—and just at the moment when a character's interiority is most intimately displayed. Is, for example, the "To be or not to be" soliloquy overheard by Ophelia (and, beyond and watching her, Polonius and Claudius), and, if it is, does Hamlet know he is speaking aloud or know he is being observed? If he is heard (and knows he can be heard), what happens to the representation of thought? (The crux of "The Mousetrap" could be phrased in similar terms: Do the people on stage see what we see? Beyond that, Hamlet's worries about what in grief "passeth show" is also a worry about whether emotion can be represented, whether feelings, interiorities in a play can be believed [I.ii.85].) In the course of the play, one begins to suspect that Hamlet, that exemplar of solitary subjectivity, can never be alone for the simple but abyssal reason that he is in a play. Thus, when, to begin another soliloquy (at the end of Act II—"O, what a rogue and peasant slave am I!") he says, "Now I am alone," he as if speaks the fact of soliloquy itself, and thereby, in speaking, calls its solitude into question (II.ii.509, 508). The self-reflexive devices in the play mark Hamlet's response, which is to try to escape that structure by compounding it.

Such moments are perhaps not uncommon in theater. Proust writes humorously, for instance, of "certain scenes in Molière where two actors who have been delivering long soliloquies each on his own account, a few feet apart, are supposed not yet to have seen each other, and then suddenly catching sight of each other, cannot believe their eyes, break off what they are saying, and then simultaneously find their tongues again (the chorus meanwhile having kept the dialogue going) and fall into each other's arms."[26] Part of the reason to dwell on what is otherwise a trivial question (and the search for psychological motivation, not least for characters like Gertrude or Ophelia, perhaps inevitably hits the dead-end of the lyrical lines they occasion) is that, in *Hamlet*, the play's plot is repeatedly confounded with the question of primal inception, of utterance or representation as such. Taking Ophelia's action as an occasion for lyrical song, Gertrude enacts, in a clandestine way, the most prominent attribute of her more famous son. Read in the context of this study of beginning and inception, the notorious indecision of Hamlet could be rephrased as the curious difficulty of getting started—of starting anything, character, action, the play itself.[27] The exemplary literary character, Hamlet also isn't one, as his ostensibly internal predicaments ravel outward, to be acted out by others—others who therefore seem at once adjuncts to or devices enabling the expression of his psychological depths and more fully realized characters than he is. Ophelia enacts his desire and realizes his madness; Gertrude, his incestuous yearnings; Claudius, his parricidal wishes; Laertes, his filial piety and his revenge. Rosencrantz and Guildenstern die in his place, and, in the end, Horatio even speaks for him, as Fortinbras steps into his place on the throne. Hamlet may be the fullest character in modern literature because, not in spite, of this characterization-by-proxy, its projection "outward" of interiority. Because of this externalization, he is the most realized of literary characters but also among the most vacant, and the Oedipus complex seems more consequence than cause of its self-expropriating structure.

Thus, the dumb show followed by the play that repeats it enacts a fundamental structure—of doubling, self-reflexive displacement, and externalizing representation—through which the overheard soliloquy emblematizes the self-thwarting efforts of the subject to get started. The enigmatic moment with Gertrude belongs to this economy. One recalls Hamlet's famous speech to the players: Against those who would "split the ears of the groundlings, who for the most part are capable of nothing but inexplicable dumb shows and noise" (III.ii.10–12), he speaks of "the purpose of playing, whose end, both at the first and now, was and is, to hold as 'twere, the mirror up to nature" (III.ii.21–2). In Gertrude's narration of Ophelia's death, it is as though nature itself had obeyed that injunction: The willow that shows its hoary leaves in the glassy stream presents us with a primal instance of that mirroring (nature holding a mirror up to herself)—one where any intervening player disappears from the mirroring, and representation occurs as if in the absence of a human observer. That she can be seen but not saved points to the way that Ophelia disappears into the play's self-consciousness, or, in other terms, into a blank structure of "pure" theater—Hamlet's injunction obeyed, but as if in the absence of any content (or any concrete theater). Hence, perhaps, the discomfiting proximity of two gestures: the elegy that begins "there is a willow grows askaunt the brook" and the impotent, lyrical pointing toward a death that cannot be averted, "There, on the pendant boughs her crownet weeds/Clamb'ring to hang, an envious sliver broke."

Gertrude's speech is thus perhaps also about our impotence in the face of theatrical spectacle: We can no more save Ophelia than Gertrude can. (To intervene on her fate could be only to interrupt the play.) For Stanley Cavell in his great reading of *King Lear*, registering this impotence is, in its acknowl-edgment of the limits of human action, the beginning of human love. Regis-tering, with our helplessness to take on others' suffering, our solitude, the autonomy of other minds, and thereby puncturing our illusions of omnipo-tence (and depriving ourselves of the consolations of certain forms of self-aggrandizing guilt), is the beginning of finding what we can do, and of letting ourselves be seen.[28] Lear might not be so different from most of us, Cavell hu-manely suggests, but Lear is larger than life in the stage he gives to his all-too-human evasion, his lethal avoidance of love. Not coincidentally, then, *King Lear* likewise recurs to moments of self-reflexivity that, isolating us, also con-found inside and out—of the play, of consciousness—and bring the frailty of human speech (movingly embodied by Lear's increasingly impotent speech acts) into contact with the terrible efficacy of theatrical spectacle. The mo-ments in Wordsworth, Oppen, Glück, and Strand, heterogeneous as they are in many other respects, perhaps draw us toward a similar point where the po-em's gesture toward its outside (toward reference, toward its own making) is scarcely to be distinguished from an abyssal self-reflexivity. "There is."[29] These moments are in that sense prior to the distinction between literal and figural language, and linked to what, elsewhere in this book, I explore as language's reflection on its own constitution—in Welty's rendering of "gesture," for ex-ample, in Stevens's consideration of origin, or in the reflections, in George Eliot and Charles Dickens, on novelistic beginning and the emergence of character. "In Homer," notes Oren Izenberg, "the dead have no language— only an inarticulate batlike squeaking."[30] To speak I tried and forthwith spake: The thematic connections among the texts I have discussed here link that reflection to a fundamental—fundamentally productive, and perhaps even originary—"frailty" (in Welty's terms) of human beings who speak. For Adam as for the child in Freud's game of fort/da, this is the solitude of human speech. Mortals alone can divine it where it lies in each other and prick it in all its peril, with an instrument made of air.

9

Etiology, Solitude, and Queer Incipience

In the late poems, Wallace Stevens confronts mortality by returning to questions of beginnings: the confrontation, in the starkest of terms, of consciousness with its inception, and with the world that shapes it and that, paradoxically, thus shaped, it brings into being. For some queer people, or for this particular queer person, if the act of coming out has continued to be of interest, it is partly because what had long seemed like a resolved question—one, it seemed at the moment of crisis, of dissolving the fascination of a single, tedious, reiterated question of identification, recognition, and knowledge—has started to seem less so, has started to resonate with more generalized experiences of becoming and human temporality. Anachronistic, belated, old, even, in extreme moments, posthumous: an increasing dissonance between one's consciousness as it is shaped by desire and the name that continues to be given to those who ostensibly share it has made coming out seem relevant again, not, this time, as the threshold of knowledge about a self, but as a way of conceptualizing some of the consequences of living in time. To return to the question of queer beginnings, then, may be a way not of finding out what one is, not to resolve causation (whether to bestow credit and assign blame, or simply to know) but of thinking about consciousness as embedded in time and in the world, and as a structure of becoming.

At various moments in *Inceptions*, the questions of origination, inception, and beginning in literary creation have come together with the question, most broadly termed, of art and life: in what Henry James calls revision, for example, or in the body made articulate by gesture, or in the exploration of time and embodiment that Stevens ranges under his consideration of origin. Similar questions are raised by accounts of queer etiology, understood, most generally, as the confrontation between embodied desire and the literary or aesthetic forms that lend it coherence: queer origins, these, insofar as they chart the inception of subjects that disappear in the forms that give them birth. Foucault might call these "infamous lives";[1] they are lives of "gesture," and the potentiality of literary form is productively to be linked, I think, to queer incipience and various kinds of proto-sexuality.

Yet the question of the causes or origins of queer identities and desires is vexed, and writers in queer theory have, with very few exceptions, been reluctant to touch it.[2] Eve Kosofsky Sedgwick, though much of her work turned on questions of gay "incipience"—and was energized, ethically and affectively, by invocations of proto-gay kids—spelled out reasons to steer clear of the etiological questions that preoccupied many early advocates of gay liberation: in "How to Bring Your Kids Up Gay," she suggested that, whether turning to nature or nurture, etiologies of homosexuality are difficult, if not impossible, to insulate from a fantasy of eliminating gay people from the world.[3] As Ellis Hanson pithily put it, "'Why are you queer?' is less a question than a challenge to one's civil rights";[4] phrased in the second person, the question, however neutrally intended, has perlocutionary effects potentially assaultive to a gay addressee (echoing the unanswerable taunts of adolescence—which make one doubly contemptible: abject not merely for being gay but for having chosen that abjection, for having elected to embody a fate that no one would voluntarily choose). Current doxa, at least among the housetrained, does not so much refrain from asking the question as presume that it has been definitively resolved; to suggest that gay people become gay is taken to imply that they might become (or have become) something else. Gay people are "born that way," and to assert that homosexuality is not a "choice" is now shorthand for sexual tolerance. No doubt there is a story to tell about how that happened; one consequence is that certain strands of sexuality theory have become less legible. Claims about performative identity *de rigueur* in the 1990s are hard for millennial ears to distinguish from a homophobic sense that gay people, invested with the power of choice, should comply by choosing otherwise; whole swaths of gay-affirmative writing now seem potentially homophobic to readers schooled in the New Tolerance—so that Adrienne Rich's "lesbian continuum," for example, and her injunction to all right-minded feminists to choose lesbianism, now alike appear to subvert the lesbian desire she sought to inculcate.[5]

There is much to be criticized in contemporary studies of sexual etiology—studies that, more or less incoherently, provide the ballast for our sureties that sexuality is a biological given. To judge from accounts for non-specialists, the doxa about biological or genetic causation comes with other retrograde assumptions: assumptions about gender, for example (all human desire is heterosexual, and sexual inversion is the underlying cause of homosexuality), and a curiously literal-minded Darwinism. It's the literal-mindedness that is perhaps the problem; Proust's elaborations of the consequences of its logic show, among other things, some of the capacious possibilities of inversion framed in relation to evolutionary logics. Contemporary accounts are, needless to say, less agile. As Marlene Zuk notes, there is no reason for evolutionary motivation to entail direct causation. "Of course ultimately everything is about reproduction," she writes; traits need to be passed on or else they will disappear, and in that sense foraging, keeping warm, and maintaining one's blood pressure are "about" reproduction. "But if keeping warm is about sex, none of us expects to get pregnant every time we put on a sweater."[6] Viewed from the perspective of direct causation, homosexuality is an ineffectual route toward gene preservation; luckily, evolutionary biologists have found need for babysitters and non-competitive guardians of the gene pool, younger brothers who will take care of the kids, or at least stay out of the way as their elder brothers disseminate their shared genetic material.[7] (Perhaps, too, gay people are necessary to keep post-menopausal women company—another category of persons more literal-minded evolutionists have trouble accommodating, since human women, on average, outlive their reproductive usefulness by a much larger margin than other animals.)

Simon LeVay's Gay, Straight, and the Reasons Why, for instance, is a relentless, largely humorless reiteration of the thesis that homosexuality is a form of gender inversion—dour, mostly joyless reading, in spite of some anecdotal diversion: A "study" of identical twins separated at birth, for instance, attempts to draw conclusions about the genetic basis of homosexuality from twelve people (eight women and four men) where one pair of twin brothers was also an incestuous couple.[8] Were one to take as representative that group too infinitesimal even to call it statistically negligible, it is still unclear whether one could generalize as "homosexuality" whatever one might call that specialized form of eroticism. Yet homosexuality is in some sense itself also a confining category; as Foucault wrote of "sex," homosexuality groups together, in "an artificial unity, anatomical elements, biological functions, conducts, sensations, and pleasures" and enables one "to make use of this fictitious unity as a causal principle."[9] If gender inversion models of sexual identity presuppose what they proceed to find,[10] the entire enterprise is perhaps blind to a more basic presupposition: that homosexuality, qua sexual "orientation," names a discrete object that can be isolated and investigated. Etiological research thus begs a fundamental question by presupposing the existence of its object of study. As Valerie Rohy, in her smart and agile consideration of etiology, puts it, "Science will never find the biological cause of homosexuality, not because there is no biological cause but because there is no homosexuality: what that term names is too heterogeneous to totalize" (14).

For Sedgwick in "How to Bring Your Kids Up Gay," the homophobia of the etiology question seems anecdotal or contingently contextual (which isn't to say that the potential damage is trivial or ineffectual): It's the inescapabilty of homophobia in our society that makes the question dangerous (framed as it is by scientists who, after all, cannot stand aloof from their culture):

> If I had ever, in any medium, seen any researcher or popularizer refer even once to any supposed gay-producing circumstance as the proper hormone balance, or the conducive endocrine environment, for gay generation, I would be less chilled by the breezes of all this technological confidence. As things are, a medicalized dream of the prevention of gay bodies seems to be the less visible, far more respectable underside of the AIDS-fueled public dream of their extirpation. (164)

Rohy shows a structural homophobia unacknowledged in current assumptions that gay people are "born that way." Others, she remarks, have noted that various efforts to identify a biological etiology of homosexuality reinforce stereotypes, assume a categorical difference between homosexuality and heterosexuality, implicitly or explicitly dismiss lesbians and bisexuals, conflate gender identity and expression with object choice, naturalize heterosexuality, and overlook the synchronic and diachronic variety of gay experience, omitting the places and times in which same-sex desire has taken markedly different forms (Rohy, 41).

Rohy's analysis makes explicit that even ostensibly gay-affirmative turns to biological explanation install homophobic presumptions in their account of gay genesis. Denying the possibility of "choice" not only reduces cultural and environmental influences to an absurdly impoverished voluntarism and not only denies the possibility of seduction or influence; it also presupposes, as Sedgwick also pointed out, that such seduction or influence would be a bad thing, leavening tolerance with a hidden sense of pathos—it isn't a choice because no sane person would choose to be gay. (It is easy to tolerate a person who displays what one would fain eliminate—if the culpable party can plead that the offensive characteristic is not his fault. Such pity can, in fact, bolster homophobia even as it tolerates individual gay people.) Further, locating homosexual genesis in (aberrant) heterosexuality, it also denies gay people the possibility of reproducing. (If there is a "gay gene," one of its remarkable qualities is that those who have it are unable to pass it on.) For Rohy, the current talk of "born that way" shelters within it vulgarized evolutionary logic, leaving homosexuals, ostensibly tolerated, at once sterile and monstrously fecund.

(Or their implicit sterility in these biological accounts seeks to contain a monstrous fecundity: homosexuality's power to seduce, influence, and corrupt.) Persuasively, Rohy argues for the need to claim the power of seduction and indoctrination, the fecundity of "homosexual reproduction" attributed to it; if by being gay, or by talking about it, one could make more people gay, that, brave new world, would be a consummation devoutly to be wished.

In this, Rohy follows the lead of Sedgwick's powerful avowal of gay affirmation (no less bracing now, in our world of ostensible toleration). Sedgwick's essay might give one pause in too quickly embracing the natural or given as shelter from homophobic fantasies (or it may be practices) of intervention, and it is still worth emphasizing how far short avowals of tolerance fall, and even how destructive they can be, and to admire, therefore, Sedgwick's polemical argument for a "strong, explicit, *erotically invested* affirmation of some people's felt desire or need that there be gay people in the immediate world" (164). Yet the eschewing of questions of origin is not merely pragmatic; the essay's peroration protects gay incipience by subjecting it to a horizon that resolves it in an identity—those gay people we want to people our immediate world. Sedgwick's redemptive or reparative account would seem to have two objects at least nominally at odds: the proto-gay child in a state of suspension or potentiality (what Kathryn Bond Stockton calls the "interval" of the queer child)[11] and the gayness that seeks to emerge from that potentiality, and, in emerging, to dissolve it. That tension is perhaps visible throughout her work—as, perhaps, in queer theory more generally, especially when it comes closest to the antihomophobic commitments that animate it. To dwell on questions of queer origin, I will suggest, offers a way to sustain that "proto-gay" thread of potentiality, even within the actualization that makes it retrospectively legible—and to link it with questions of literary creation.

Sedgwick notes the particular biases that reflexively cast gay emergence in terms of deficiency or mistake; her insistence on her "felt desire or need that there be gay people in the immediate world" is also a defense of gay incipience. Yet the powerful critique of ego psychological models targets their identarian premises: assumptions that equate psychological health, reified egos, identities, and gendered identities (assumed in turn to be isomorphic with biological sex, however tendentiously conceived). Hence, Sedgwick notes, to be tolerated by these psychologists, gay men must be grown up, already gay, and recognizably masculine. For all that I share (at least on good days) Sedgwick's desire that there be more gay people in my immediate world and think it a necessary counter-weight to the homophobia secreted away in the tolerance that, then and now, remains only tolerance, the affirmation risks converging with the potentiality-negating logic of "born that way." Thus, while one could show fractures in discourses of sexual etiology, from the simplest (LeVay, for example) to the most complex (in Freud, as one traverses the transferential complexities of the case histories and the particular theories of sexual emergence he presents, the challenge is to derive a coherent theory of *heterosexual* etiology; the question, it often seems, is not how anyone turns out gay but how anyone doesn't),[12] such is not my focus here. Instead, I would like to dwell on incipience—on questions that emerge as texts consider queerness before it is named (or perhaps even felt) as such. The texts I consider contrive to remain suspended within a moment of queer inception—by confronting, mostly implicitly (though in one case explicitly) the risky question of gay origins. In the very risk that the proto-gay might not, after all, become gay, the "etiology question" brings into view the threshold of becoming that divides any identity from itself—a queerness inherent to human consciousness to the degree that it cannot originate itself.

The emphasis on the performative in queer theory—from *Epistemology of the Closet* to *Gender Trouble* and *Bodies That Matter*, among other examples—has become, in shorthand, a critique of identity, and of identity politics. But it is also a querying of origin: "coming out," as a defiant political gesture is also, in its performative dimension, an enactment of the recursive structure of origination. I am gay because I say I am, and, by saying it, I bring my visible identity into line with the condition my utterance retrospectively constitutes. The various ways that such a groundless structure is distinguished from voluntarism (people reading quickly might be forgiven for thinking, as many did, that Judith Butler was suggesting that sexuality and gender were personal choices) likewise brings to the fore the way that this "self-reflexivity" of origination deprives the self of any voluntary ground to stand on. Considering queer etiology in the context of literary inception, quite apart from whatever doctrinal distinctions one might want to make about whatever theoretical arguments seem pressing at any given historical moment, brings out ways that queer theory leads one to confront fundamental questions of a life suspended within the imponderable inception of literary creation.

The previous chapter, and the chapter on *Robinson Crusoe*, confronted a radical, even originary, solitude of human speech. To this solitude, I would now counterpoise a solitude of a different order: the solitude of the queer, or, as Sedgwick phrased it, the "proto-gay" child. That solitude has various determinants: the formative social isolation that, in D. A. Miller's account, installs solitude at the heart of queer articulations of belonging;[13] the "interval" of queer becoming that, for Kathryn Bond Stockton, means that the gay child cannot coincide with itself, can "be" itself only in retrospect; the experience of social stigma and isolation that led Radclyffe Hall to call her mortifying novel *The*

Well of Loneliness; an isolation that is built into the mysterious lines of transmission that structure queerness (most queer people do not have queer parents and therefore cannot view their sexuality as replicating a given social world); and even a more anecdotal or psychological sense of exceptionality and stigma (why was I chosen for this unwonted and unwanted gift?), which are flip sides of the same encounter with, in some cases, statistical rarity, and, in others, social invisibility. The solitude, in short, of queer origins: what might the solitude of speech have to tell us about texts of queer origination or emergence?

One possibility for thinking about the relation of solitude to queer origination is to stress the relation, in, for example, the account of Michel Foucault, between individuation and the invention of homosexuality. He offers a condensed version of this argument in a talk given in English and first published in the *London Review of Books* in 1981 entitled "Sexuality and Solitude."[14] Published in the period between the first two volumes of the *History of Sexuality*, it offers one articulation of the movement in Foucault's thinking between those two volumes. To analyze "the genealogy of the subject in Western civilization," Foucault writes, by way, he notes, of "a kind of auto-critique" of his previous tendency to over-emphasize discipline, "one must take into account not only techniques of domination but also techniques of the self" (177). Contrasting passages from Artemidorus (a third-century pagan philosopher) and Augustine, Foucault finds in Augustine the dawning of a new conception of desire, one where sexuality becomes solitary:

> Real purity is not acquired when one can lie down with a young and beautiful boy without even touching him, as Socrates did with Alcibiades. The monk was really chaste when no impure images occurred in his mind, even during the night, even during dreams. The criterion of purity does not consist in keeping control of oneself even in the presence of the most desirable people; it consists in discovering the truth in myself and in defeating the illusions in myself, and cutting out the images and thoughts of my mind continuously produces. The main question of sexual ethics has moved from relations to people, and from the penetration model to the relation of oneself and the erection problem: I mean to the set of internal movements that develop from the first and nearly imperceptible thought to the final but still solitary pollution. However different and eventually contradictory they were, a common effect was elicited: sexuality, subjectivity, and truth were strongly linked together. (183)

Masturbation becomes a problem for sexual ethics when sexuality becomes a relation to oneself, and through that relation, a relation to truth.

In "Ardent Masturbation," Leo Bersani, beginning with Cartesian certainty and moving then to Proust and Freud, traces a self-doubling that, central to modern thought, begins with gestures of self-isolation—where the division between self and world is as if internalized.[15] (Descartes and Proust alike stop up their ears and try to block out the external world.)[16] This mechanism, Bersani suggests, evokes masturbation:

> Descartes shutting his eyes and conversing with himself, Proust stopping his ears and shutting out all ideas extraneous to his self-concentration, Freud's attentiveness to the associations that accompany his memory of a dream, associations guiding him to the store-rooms deep within his mind—all three are moving toward what we might call sublimated climaxes (the certainty of being for Descartes, the present presence of the past for Proust, and the operations of the unconscious for Freud), but the preparations for these discoveries curiously resemble preludes to an activity of considerably less historical significance. (14)

Bersani has often returned to an impasse in psychoanalytic thought that baffles formulations of non-agonistic belonging or relationality. In my understanding of Bersani's essay, masturbation allows him to frame that impasse in relation to a fundamental structure in modern thought—and then to suggest ways to move beyond it, to find, paradoxically, a kind of sociality within masturbation itself. (In this it rhymes with Bersani's turn to forms of sameness as a way of escaping various agonisms of difference.)

For my purposes here, I would dwell on how this conclusion is prepared for by Bersani's reading of Freud's "A Special Type of Object Choice Made by Men."[17] This case, Bersani writes, "may be considered as a *mise en abîme* of the self-analysis that is the precondition for philosophical and psychological knowledge in Descartes, Proust, and Freud, as well as for their relation with the world" (8). "*Mise en abîme*," I think, not only because the "implicit reduction of the many to the one, the identity of the individuating with the universal," becomes "a certain paradigm for erotic desire" where "introspection is enacted . . . as a folding-in of desire onto the self" (8), but also because of the way the tortured logic of Freud's analysis enacts the processes he describes. Schematically, a form of desire that involves a proliferating cast of characters—men who desire women who are "taken" (men who need there to be an "injured third-party" [Freud 166], who desire women of low repute, who value women who are like prostitutes, and who fantasize about "rescuing" their objects of desire [Freud 168])—and that often produces a series of similar love objects, is reduced by Freud, first, to the three-person drama of the family romance and then to a one-man show where the desiring man takes all the parts.[18] That contraction is, as it were, both the form and the content of the "ardent masturbation" of teenaged life, where this fantasy, for Freud, becomes fixated.[19] The underlying fantasy, notably, is one of self-origination:

> Astonishingly, this type of object-choice, in which objects of love seem to multiply indefinitely, realizes the *causa sui* project, that of being the origin and cause of oneself. The mother is the vessel, the necessary but perhaps incidental instrument for this extraordinary working out of a fantasy of self-creation. (Bersani, 11)

This fantasy, Bersani notes, moves toward a dizzying (and hilarious) *mise en abîme* when it is extended to a fantasy of fathering one's own father:

> Not only, then, does the son become his own father, he can also become his father's father. This pushes further than the son's fantasy of identification with the father. The latter has become the creation of the former. In a dizzying conflation of being, the self-fathered son is also the son's father. And why not continue this multigenerational oneness? The new son (who was the original father) can fantasize not only giving birth to himself but also fathering *his* father (who originally was his son, before that son had him as a son), and there is no reason for this fantasmatic process not to continue indefinitely. The crowd of loved ones we began with . . . is, so to speak, more than compensated by this potential future army of one. Except for the nearly dismissible (if, obviously, indispensable) woman through whom all these self-replicas must pass, the psychic logic of this indeed very special type of object-choice culminates in a fantastical multiplication of sameness. (11–12)

Freud's analysis, Bersani notes, enacts the illogic of the unconscious, and this in a sense bodies forth the inadequacy of language to psychoanalysis:

> Language comes too late; it depends on distinctions and intervals of which the fundamental subject of psychoanalysis, as well as the psychoanalytic subject, are ignorant. The heroically impossible project of psychoanalysis is to theorize an untheorizable psyche, and the exceptional nature of Freudian (and, I would add, Lacanian) texts in the history of psychoanalysis is that they allow unreadable pressures to infiltrate the readable, thus creating a type of readability at odds with how we have been taught to read while also accounting for that which, in the psychic structure, is anterior to all readable accounting for. The Freudian text performs the blockages, the mergings, the incoherence inherent in the discipline Freud invented. (13)

Pointing to semantic discontinuities in the movement from the rescue fantasy to the fantasy of self-origination it ostensibly discloses, Bersani points to a paired set of blockages (Freud's intellectual blockage and subsequent self-rescue, and the boy's thwarted desire), and here emerges masturbation:

> But something else has been emphasized between the Oedipal solution and Freud's reading of the rescue fantasy, something that, it seems to me, will provide the pressure necessary for the incongruous link between rescuing the mother and giving birth to oneself through her. Freud has said that under the sway of the Oedipus complex, the boy, blocked in his desire for the mother by his sense that she is being unfaithful to him with his hated rival, the father, finds his only outlet for his desires in masturbation, masturbation accompanied by fantasies of the mother's infidelity. Masturbation also allows for revenge against the father; it is accompanied by images of the mother being unfaithful with the boy himself, a boy idealized as a man equal to or like the father. The "ardent masturbation" practiced in puberty . . . helps to fixate the fantasies that go along with it, fantasies that, having become fixated during puberty, are realized later on by the type of object-choice that has been the essay's subject. (13–14)

The elaboration of this particular object-choice enacts—on several levels—the mechanism of self-isolation that Bersani traces in Descartes and Proust. Thus does masturbation take on a curious centrality and importance.

I would also highlight something that Bersani does not mention—the temporal dimension that emerges here. That is what makes it "ardent masturbation" or "masturbation assiduously practiced" (*die eifrig geübte Onanie*). The first is Joan Riviere's translation; the second is the Standard Edition's, by Alan Tyson.[20] If the emphasis is the lack of an external object, or (for many, anyway) the sexual intensity that precedes any experience of one, one might prefer, as Bersani does, the former phrasing. *Ardent* captures the solitary yearning. Questions of temporality, however, might lead one to prefer the latter translation, which conveys not just the power of absorbed concentration that links masturbation and thought (and that, as English professors, among others, often volubly regret, vanishes—for some—with age, from one's practice of reading, too), but also the repetition through which it "helps to fixate the fantasies that go along with it" to emerge later, in "the type of object-choice that has been the essay's subject." Practice makes perfect; like a docile, self-training duckling, the libido imprints on the objects of this assiduous practice. For here, too, is another kind of self-origination, where the "origin" is a temporal structure of repetition: masturbation assiduously practiced in puberty produces the fantasy structure (to which it would also seem to respond). Another *mise en abîme*, it delineates origins unfathomable by dint of their recursivity, lost therefore in the quandaries of erotic inception.

Earlier in this essay, Freud gives a startlingly literal (and lurid) image for an analogous kind of imprinting—there, for the way "maternal characteristics remain stamped on the love objects that are chosen later": "The comparison with the way in which the skull of a newly born infant is shaped springs to mind at this point: after a protracted labor it always takes the form of a cast of the narrow part of the mother's pelvis" (Freud, 169).[21] As in masturbation, psychic mechanisms enact, or follow from, a literalized imprinting that, moreover, takes place in time—"protracted labor" or "masturbation assiduously practiced." (In the former case, one can hardly seek a more lurid figure for the marking of the subject by the maternal body.) Cartesian certainty would seem to be linked to a willed obscuring of one's origins elsewhere, a willed act of self-creation—which, therefore, cannot help miring the would-be autonomous subject in time, and in a world that shapes him. What Bersani calls "the sustaining sensuality of our *failure to be*" (16) is perhaps also the rupture introduced by the fact of origin itself.

The emphasis in early queer theory on the performativity in coming out brought to the fore, above all, the contingency of identity—and the arbitrary nature of the authority that presumes to bestow it. "Coming out," colloquially, names both this moment of emergence and the more or less extended period of deliberation that produces it; among the possible effects of returning to the question of origin is to bring into view a temporal dimension of coming out, and of homophobia, that perhaps disappears when they are viewed solely in relation to knowledge—to epistemology or to the identity of the one who knows or is known. (The "proto-gay" person is in a liminal temporal state that precedes, for however extended a period, the declaration of identity, if that latter ever arrives.) The various models of solitude I have explored might thus lead us back to more explicit questions of queer origin. Hannah Arendt differentiates between solitude and loneliness (and between these and isolation), making that psychic condition central to one's sense of the political form of totalitarianism.[22] Understood sociologically, queer origins are often both isolated and lonely. To what extent can they be thought of as solitary, and therefore of making manifest something more general about inception?

If there is an emblem for gay loneliness, it is perhaps Radclyffe Hall's *Well of Loneliness*; the experience at the heart of that unbearable novel is perhaps irredeemable because it is perceived, relentlessly, from the perspective not of becoming, but of the identity that will experience its development as a prelude to its isolation. Against Heather Love's brilliant reading of the novel,[23] one might suggest that it is not its willingness, like Lot, to look back that makes it so painful, but the redemptive movement of the text—its quest to redeem not the affective quality of the experience, which is unremittingly desolate, but the trajectory of that experience toward a future identity, and the desire that reveals that no element of experience can fail to add up, even if that adding up must be, of necessity, of the bleakest consolation. If the novel does not transcend its negativity, it also, it seems to me, does not transcend the urge to discipline its developmental divagations, to make them amount to a finished identity. Thus, relatedly, there is loneliness but not solitude; that separates Hall from other queer *Bildungsromane*.

Some of the most insightful renderings of queer development are texts that are, at least arguably, not explicitly about homosexual desire. In Carson McCullers's *The Member of the Wedding*,[24] for example, while there are plenty of clues about what Frankie's desire will become, what's legible as queerness is almost formal: her falling in love with a wedding describes an internalization of exclusion that will only later take on a particular content. In her misunderstanding of the phrase "member of the wedding"—she understands it on the model of the club that excludes her and so thinks that she can "join" it—she in effect marries herself to her exclusion. "They," as she phrases it, "are the we of me" (497); on the first page of the story, she describes her sense of exclusion as feeling "unjoined" (461). ("We," as Benveniste points out, can both include and exclude an addressee, the "you" to whom it is said, just as it might, in reverse form, exclude or include a "they." "We" can mean "you [singular or plural] and me" but also "we [and *not* you]." Here, the various possible parsings of the genitive in "of me"—appositive or partitive, for example—mean the phrase can shift among a number of possibilities: the "we" that is me, that I somehow possess, or that represents [but possibly does not include] me.)[25] As in *The Well of Loneliness*, the exclusion is relentless, and in this text, radiates outward: strikingly, it is not just the cruelty of the other girls, or the heedlessness of her family about her particular predicament, but also Frankie's striking inability to register the compelling community she already has with Berenice and John Henry West. The disturbingly grotesque death from meningitis of her small cousin—in many ways a more explicitly queer child than Frankie—marks, as Pamela Thurschwell astutely notes, a sacrifice that perhaps allows room for Frankie's "sideways growth" (for him, too, if he is sacrificed, that also means he will not have to grow up) and (relatedly) marks a movement toward the specification of desire.[26] It also makes distressingly literal what I have to imagine is a not uncommon source of regret for some who grew up in a homophobic world: regret for the queer communities we didn't know we shared among people whose private fears

and desires we couldn't know rhymed with our own and that we hence sacrificed, before we knew to cherish them, to homophobic imperatives or to the
first possibilities of desire we found.

However that may be, the community Frankie fails to register also points
to some of the ways that the novella is a text of anti-*Bildung*. Thus, for example, Berenice tries to caution her against having a "crush" on the wedding,
and warns her, from her own unhappy effort to recover, from part objects, her
lost love, about the staying power of first loves; Frankie can no more avoid reenacting that fate than such a story can provide an exemplum with which
another could identify. Strikingly, and compellingly, Frankie doesn't learn; perhaps even more than the logic of sacrifice it makes explicit, her strange non-
reaction to John Henry's agonizing death marks not just the heedless selfishness
of youth (and her single-minded focus on the girl on whom she now has a
crush) but her failure to register her own experience, and hence to know her
loss. That structure is visible elsewhere in the story, perhaps most notably in
its thwarting of expectations: The encounter with the sailor doesn't, as one
dreads it will, lead to rape or murder, and the central event of the story (the
wedding itself) is an anti-climax narrated only briefly, and in retrospect. The
narrative itself is like the unfinished melodies and scales that Frankie hears as
she walks around the town; Frankie is herself just such an unfinished scale.
For if the novella finally has her arrive at an epiphany, the realization is never
specified:

> but she recalled the silence in the hotel room; and all at once a fit in a
> front room, the silence, the nasty talk behind the garage—the separate
> recollections fell together in the darkness of her mind, as shafting
> searchlights meet in the night sky upon an aeroplane, so that in a
> flash there came in her an understanding. There was a feeling of cold
> surprise; she stopped a minute, then went on toward the blue moon.
> (598)

"I was never the same after that summer," remarks the satirically minded anti-
heroine of *The Opposite of Sex*, thus parodying the contentless production of
"difference" that structures many a coming-of-age tale.[27] Such texts presume
we know what that difference is or means (and it generally means emergence
into heterosexual sociality, which is to say the social as such). *The Member of
the Wedding* does not presume, and we do not know. The epiphany is perfunc-
tory, unspecified, and seemingly purely formal. Frankie doesn't dwell on it,
and neither does the novella. The text might be called an anti-*Bildungsroman*
because the promised development never arrives; the epiphany repeats, rather
than resolves, the terms of non-specification that, from one angle, make the

text so queerly evocative. Hence, the sense of exclusion that she cannot name at the beginning remains unnamed:[28] "strange words were flowering in her throat and now was the time for her to name them" (563), but "F Jasmine could not speak the unknown words" (565).

Notably, this third-person narration limits itself to Frankie's point of view. John Henry's death is narrated in retrospect, and at second-hand, and the text—unlike the other characters—quietly adopts the series of names that Frankie gives herself (Frankie, F Jasmine, and Frances). What ultimately makes the text such a powerful rendering of queer development is its refusal to narrate development, to tame the exorbitance of queer childhood by framing it in relation to the "finished" adult who will come to know what "it" was. It thus takes one back to a moment before one had names (queer, gay, or otherwise) to give one's intuited sense of queerness; it is a painful but illuminating text because it refuses to subordinate that experience to the identity that will consolidate it, and thus, in the very confusion of that primordial state, bodies forth the ghostly existence of what one was, in what Kathryn Bond Stockton calls the "interval" of the queer child—before a globalizing voice arrives to name, in retrospect, the child that has ceased to be.

The text's depiction of queer childhood—happier, one might also say, than the more redemptive *The Well of Loneliness*—is evocative for its rendering of queer solitude, not only because of its canny representation of the isolation of beginnings but also because of its refraining to name a cause for it. This suspension of naming brings to the fore the primordial condition of language that writers on solitude ask one to confront. Arguably, some of the best readings of queer texts manage to capture this suspension—in what might be called a contradiction in their own arguments. I'm thinking, for instance, of the accusation of illegitimate specification that can dog any reading that attempts to bring out queer energies where they are not explicitly named. The best of these readings refuse to resolve the contradiction inherent in the recognition at stake; their naming of a desire also puts in question naming. Eve Kosofsky Sedgwick's famous reading of James's "The Beast in the Jungle" makes clear that this contradiction follows from the strictures determining the relation of homosexuality to naming, a relation she explains through the trope of periphrasis and preterition. Homosexual meaning, Sedgwick notes, particularly in homophobic contexts, is often named through an explicit withdrawal of reference: "the love that dare not speak its name," as Lord Alfred Douglas put it, or, in legal terms, the "detestable and abominable sin, amongst Christians not to be named."[29] Such speech acts designate through the withdrawal of designation; in childhood, we learned quickly to recognize references to "that" kind of person, and learned, too, the perils of betraying any such canny skills of reading—long before we even knew what "that" apparently unnamable thing was. This suspension is not *only* homophobic; the source of a kind of queer pleasure, it is also true to the structure of inception. In a different register, then, Sedgwick's reading enacts this dimension of homosexual possibility: It is at once a misreading of James's story and a reading so astute that, once read, one can hardly see another narrative in the tale. And its claims for a specific narrative are played out against Sedgwick's contention that the reifying effects of preterition are, if anything, more "damaging" than the obliterative ones—and against the knowing, playful willfulness of the essay's identificatory mode of reading (her frank identification with May Bartram) (Sedgwick, "Beast," 204).

More recently, when one perceptive writer (reading, as it happens, in the context of Stockton's theories) refers in passing to Joel's "acceptance" of his homosexual desires at the end of Truman Capote's *Other Voices, Other Rooms*, the bravura point is that the "acceptance" remains, of course, entirely between the lines.[30] The text says no such thing. Instead, it says this: "'I am me,' Joel whooped. 'I am Joel, we are the same people.' . . . Joel slipped down from the tree; he had not made the top, but it did not matter, for he knew who he was, he knew that he was strong." And then, at the very end of the text: "No magic had happened; yet something had happened; or was about to . . . unafraid, not hesitating, he paused only at the garden's edge where, as though he'd forgotten something, he stopped and looked back at the bloomless, descending blue, at the boy he had left behind."[31] However recognizable, after the fact, to some, the realization is left as empty as Frankie's is in McCullers. Context, experience, various more or less tangible signs in the text lead one to translate the blank assertion of *Bildung* into something queer. "I am Joel, we are the same people," also suggests that self-acceptance, if that is what this is, presents a consolidation of identity that is difficult to distinguish from a dispersion. "They are the we of me," as Frankie puts it (McCullers, *Member of the Wedding*, 497); perhaps all affiliations with a group encrypt a secret residue of exclusion—and of suspended identity. Queer affiliations nearly always do, to my mind, and queer readings have clandestine ways of registering that fact. Such readings need to be considered not only in their explicit claims (which do translate, and perhaps too quickly, incipience into terms of identity) but also in their performative force, and in their own context. Such readings, too, can be read as enacting the kind of paradoxical consolidation given voice by Joel. By risking the reification of what isn't named, the reading itself enters the place of queer potentiality.

Su Friedrich's remarkable film *Hide and Seek* (1996) does something like this by weaving together a narrative film about a young girl named Lou with

interviews with lesbians (speaking for the most part about their girlhoods) and
footage from scientific and educational films such as might once have been
seen in school classrooms.[32] As in *The Member of the Wedding*, there are various clues in the narrative that suggest a lesbian future for Lou: often oblique
glances or expressions, as when she watches other girls touching each other,
or when she hears a rumor about a lesbian teacher, or when she gazes, in apparent rapture, at a girl reciting a poem or singing. There are likewise codes,
for those of us used to attending to them: her interest in animals and veteri-
nary medicine, or in African exploration—or the particular way her various
friendships are curiously, and unreasonably, vexed, as she makes waves seemingly out of all proportion to the particular occasion (with boys, around gender
identity, and with girls, around obscure hurts). More or less subtle observations,
they no doubt belong in many an anthology of mid-to-late-twentieth-century
proto-gay childhood experience. A detailed account of the film might dwell
on some of these moments, and on what they suggest about its understanding
of incipient lesbian desire.

Yet what makes us sense that Lou will become gay also in certain respects
withdraws the possibility of certainty: a montage effect, or the superimposition
of the documentary aspects of the film on its narrative ones. The documentary
footage on the one hand literalizes the connection of the narrative film to its
referential "outside"—and with it, to the lesbian future Lou might someday
learn to long for. (The acting in the narrative film is notably, and one has to
conclude, self-consciously, wooden; the interviews with grown-up lesbians,
with all their idiosyncratic modes of expression, come to "life" in the contrast.)
The interviews with these thoughtful, witty, and charismatic women with compellingly articulate capacities for self-reflection, at once overlap with the narrative
film (at moments, we hear the interviews over the narrative) and are explicitly
removed from Lou's kenning: The appealing lives of these women are what Lou,
at the moment of the film, cannot imagine, for herself, or for anyone. Nor can
we be certain, finally, that she will eventually know a world like it. The filmic
superimposition brings to the fore the gap between the two worlds by making
clear that their contact is a matter of formal juxtaposition; at such moments,
Lou's world feels, if anything, more sealed off than not from a lesbian future.[33]

The film explicitly thematizes formal juxtaposition in various ways—
perhaps most notably in its soundtrack. One of the most moving moments
occurs as Lou lies in bed as her more sociable (and unambiguously heterosexual) older sister chatters away and—as if enacting a Doris Day film—paints
her toenails. On the soundtrack, we hear the song "Dream Lover" (Bobby
Darin, 1960), and gaze at Lou's hauntingly unreadable face ("I want a dream
lover, so I don't have to dream alone"). In that moment, we glimpse a com-

plex identification—across, as it were, the sister—an exorbitant, and to my mind, highly recognizable yearning (for love, for belonging) whose pathos (and dangerously seductive appeal, then, and in memory) also depends on the knowledge of foreclosed hope (nothing but dream lovers for you, or even your dream lovers won't be represented here). It scarcely matters whether anyone actually has an unthwarted access to such yearned-for belonging and love; one doesn't need to have been a queer teenager to recognize the outlandish hopes and forms of self-pity expressed by such a sentimental song. Nevertheless, this scene allows some of us to recognize something more complex, a seductive exclusion we may have failed to recognize at the time. (The closet houses treacherous forms of rapture, too, that can mark a life with the long shadow of its loneliness; Berenice warns Frankie of the dangers of a similar seduction.) The point, in other terms, is the doubt about whether this pain recognizes itself—narratively, in this instance, whether Lou knows what her face expresses. The film doesn't let us know, and its refusal of specification no doubt contributes to the effects of identification or recognition. At the end of the film, the Supremes singing "You Can't Hurry Love" (Edward Holland, Lamont Dozier, and Brian Holland, 1966) seems simpler, as if supplying a gloss for Lou's non-coming-out and implying, perhaps, that she will have to wait for a love that will nevertheless eventually come. Resignifying the song's heterosexual context, it states not so much lesbian emergence as lesbian incipience—joining, therefore, Lou's world with the world of the interviews in a future that, nevertheless, the film withholds from us. (At the same time, the affect of joy isn't only in the adumbrating of a lesbian future; as we part ways with Lou, she is also consigned to a more general girlhood in which her specific difference does not, for the moment, stigmatize her.)

Yet such effects of superimposition are even more unruly than this preliminary account might suggest. One of the wittiest scenes in the film gives older women's speculations about gay emergence (about a gay gene, for example)[34] while we see an old scientific film of people raising a chimpanzee as a child (feeding it next to a child, or trying to teach it to read). An implicit account of the scientific discourses underlying contemporary understandings of sexual identity, and an implicit account, too, of the way that such discourses filter in to our consciousness (through scarcely remembered filmstrips in school, for example), it also reminds us of earlier in the film, when we saw shots of a girls' school while hearing the theme song to the Monkees' television show. That song, in turn, is seemingly motivated by one of the stories that Marie (one of the interview subjects) tells about an early lesbian experience. She and her friend, learning that it was "wrong," invented a cover story based on the television show:

Oh yea, after I found out that it was wrong, there had to be a reason to do it, you had to develop a story around it because you couldn't just do it anymore and it couldn't just happen: we had to develop a story. So The Monkees was the one we attached ourselves to, and we used to pretend to be one of the Monkees and his girlfriend.

And I had learned that much: that there were boyfriends and girlfriends and that they did things. And they went away for weekends and it was always filthy. They never did nothin' else, just were filthy together.

So we used to go up to her room and I'd pack a plastic bag and she'd pack a plastic bag—which were our weekend cases—and we'd go up to her room and we'd say how we were making an appointment to have this room for the weekend and I was Davy Jones and this was Patricia Canny, or I was Marie Honan and this was Davy Jones. And we'd get the key, you know, we had all this ritualistic stuff we used to do and we'd lock the door. And then she'd say, "Well, Davy, it's time to go to bed," And we'd pull back the covers and get into bed. And then we'd just rub off each other frantically. Take off our clothes sometimes. We stopped taking off our clothes after a while because we had to get ready to leap out in case anyone came. And that was part of it—listenin' for someone coming. And so we'd do that for ages and then we'd get up and pack our plastic bags and go home in our car. (*Hide and Seek*, 2)

The association linking Davy Jones to mid-century psychology seems at once profound—the same *Weltanschauung* produced both—and purely contingent, and the echoes across various layers of the film (moving up toward the most important, linking Lou's story to the stories we hear in the interviews) become equivocal, both "meant" and accidental. The inexact echo—Monkee, monkey, chimp—and its different modes of semantic or homographic connection embodies, as it were, the contingent effects in both meaning and sexual interpellation.

In another sequence, we hear a series of interviews about moments of confused or incipient identification: moments where the older women realize, in retrospect, that they had failed to recognize the same-sex desire (even the propositions) of other children, or where they detail the curious, oblique forms of recognition in remembered stories or myths about lesbians, evoking that stigmatized sense of incipient address from nevertheless outlandish forms that thwarted recognition even as they called for it. ("But I'll never forget—rumors started flying around about this public high school in the neighborhood. They were saying bulldaggers—I remember that word—were just terrorizing the women in the school. No, now that I think back, I remember my mother even talking about it, everybody knew about this. And what they would do is they'd hang out in the girl's bathroom and so the women who'd come in, you know, they'd attack them. And now that I think, this must have been bull shit, it must have just been, but, you know, with broomsticks, the whole bit" [*Hide and Seek*, 19].)[35] The more or less explicit subject in many of the stories we hear is the period of non-recognition that might characterize Lou's state in the narrative film. ("The idea of a lesbian for me," says Kelly, one of the interview subjects, "was some kind of shadowy, evil thing; it was definitely tied to this idea of a perverse girl. I didn't identify it at all with what I was" [*Hide and Seek*, 19]; for Cindy, on the other hand, "Oh, I really loved my childhood. I think the fact that I didn't know I was a lesbian helped a lot to have fun" [*Hide and Seek*, 20].)

As we hear these tales, we see an old psychology filmstrip ("What's in Your Mind?") showing us two people listening to "A SAMPLE STORY INVOLVING. . . . PAIN." "The purpose of this film," says an initial voiceover, "is to help you judge the emotional reaction of others. You will see these two people . . . reacting to stories they have been told to believe are true" (ellipsis in the script, marking an interval in the audio, not an omission of words) (*Hide and Seek*, 19). The stories of the interviewed lesbians take the place of these stories, and thus the filmstrip couple figures a viewer's empathetic reaction to the interviews—even as we fully realize that these are not the stories the filmed couple is responding to. Thus, the superimposition at once figures a responding audience and makes that reaction purely formal, or in any event, remote from any particular content. Their empathetic reactions are not coordinated with the stories we hear, and we are made acutely aware that we do not know the occasions for their expressions. Those other stories, also involving pain, are utterly lost to us. The moment thus figures a series of contradictory dynamics. First, it mimes, or anticipates, a viewer's response to the lesbians' stories even as it brings to the fore the gap separating the story told and the story heard (the gap between the unrendered stories in the excerpted film and the stories we hear thus figuring the gap between such stories and their reception). Second, in so doing, it also makes the viewer's reaction the object of the spectator's gaze, and we notice that the children in the lesbians' stories are, in a sense, spectators: What they tell is their remembered (and more or less uncomprehending) reactions to stories that no doubt involved pain. The subject of the stories, in other terms, could in several cases be said to be empathy and its capacity to elicit a clandestine form of identification.

Thus, third, at stake is a second-order, mimetic sympathy (as we potentially feel empathy for people in the absence of any motivating content: we don't

hear the stories, and know that they are stories "they have been told to believe
are true"—but might not be, or even are likely not to be). A rendering of fiction's
power to exact empathetic reactions, it also highlights the capacity of that
spectacle, in turn, to elicit a mirroring response. That reaction is undercut
(because it is purely "formal," taking place in reaction to unheard stories)
while also constituting an oblique relation to the lesbian stories: across, as it
were, superimposed images, one identifies with the girls' own distanced,
oblique, at-the-time possibly unrecognized identifications. Our relation to the
film thus doubles the proto-lesbian's relation to herself. Fourth, that tag (stories "they have been told to believe are true") could also belong to documentary more generally; whether as a contrast to the interviews we see (thereby
shored up in their purchase on reality) or as a figure for it (throwing into question their reality), an equivocal connection is established between the documentary and the psychological genre here incorporated. Fifth, in question here
is surely also what a psychologizing or quasi-scientific perspective fails to see,
or distorts through its very framing: It's not at all certain that "stories involving pain" is an adequate placard for tales of proto-lesbian childhood, or that
empathy for pain is an adequate (or even appropriate) response to hearing about
it. Relatedly, too, the excerpted film announces that its purpose is "to help you
judge the emotional reaction of others"—as if it were a kind of handbook for
the autistic or for emotional prosopagnosiacs; by not giving us the story that
occasions the expressions, we are given emotional reactions in the absence of
their cause (and there are many different ways for stories to "involve" pain).
Sixth, there is probably also a less tangible effect of historical distance: Among
the other things that we feel in the excerpted film is the historicity of gestures—
the facial expressions are not only severed from what occasioned them, but
also look noticeably dated. Something of the same possibility is implicit in the
stories of proto-lesbian childhood; the backdrop of the earlier psychological
film makes us aware of the ticking of time consigning these stories, too, to a
similar remove. Regard the freedom of seventy years ago.

"Synchronization" only begins to describe the complexities of these moments, which, in various ways, stand in for the relations among the different
layers of this film. Lou's non-coming-out—you can't hurry love—is only the
most explicit of the ways that the film attempts, like McCullers's *Member of
the Wedding*, to evoke queer incipience in its own right, without submitting it
to the perspective that will, retrospectively, make it the anticipation of queer
identity to come. Even the documentary presence of lesbians talking about
their desires and histories renders more uncertain whether the proto-gay existence represented in the narrative film will someday look back on a childhood
that portended a gay future. The making sense of lesbian childhood—linking

its proto-forms of desire to the identities and desires that will emerge from its chrysalis—thus becomes a mode of suspending it, of sustaining, in the very forms of juxtaposition through which the film makes the connection, the potentiality of that prior state.

At the end of James Baldwin's *Go Tell It on the Mountain*, the story of gay emergence is, on the one hand, legible:[36] The religious awakening that forms the story of the text is a sexual awakening, of John Grimes, who may or may not know that he is in love with Elisha. A detailed account of the novel might dwell on the complex way that faith functions in the text; among the complexities of existence for young John is the fact that religion *isn't* exactly a form of sublimated desire, and isn't in any clear way a substitution for desires that he cannot avow. Rather, his religious fervor is an experience of intensified embodiment that is not in any easy way to be separated from the particularities of his desire. Nor is that desire separable from the complex ways that ambivalence toward desire in ostensibly heterosexual contexts (in his stepfather's, mother's, and aunt's stories) is bound up not only with religion, but with race, class, and the history of America, slavery, and migration. In terms of John's desire (however artificially that is to isolate it), it is more or less explicit that John is in love with Elisha, although it is apparently more than possible for readers to miss it. That "revelation" is never given but appears in various narrative "clues" that point to his desire,[37] and, as in *The Member of the Wedding*, in a conspicuous form of non-specification:

> "I was mighty glad," said Elisha soberly, "to see little Johnny lay his sins on the altar, lay his *life* on the altar and rise up, praising God."
> Something shivered in him as the word *sin* was spoken. Tears sprang to his eyes again. (252)

> Then John was silent, wanting to put the question another way. (253)

> He wanted to stop and turn to Elisha, and tell him . . . something for which he found no words. (254, ellipsis in original)

> John, starting at Elisha, struggled to tell him something more—struggled to say—all that could never be said. (255).

There would be various ways to read these moments of pointed non-specification, and—though it would certainly be reductive to equate this "something more" with same-sex desire—I think that it could hardly be contentious at this point to assert that the secret of desire here "speaks." (Part of what's moving about such moments is the way it forces one to relive everything that exceeded gay desire in the secret it constituted for one, in what Baldwin elsewhere calls "that gasping and trembling, freezing and burning time.")[38] Read in epistemological terms, the novel then becomes the story of the closet— John's, perhaps, or even Baldwin's, who does not, in his first novel, name the homosexuality that will become explicit in his later texts.

I might also read these moments in a different context, which would be to ask why—if one focuses on the question of John's desire—so much of the novel is taken up with others, with the stories of his aunt, (step-) father, and mother. Part of the reason, I have stated, is the larger social context of John's awakening, and the novel is a profound exploration of the lived experience of embodiment that follows from ostensibly abstract social conditions. John's story intersects a more complex depiction of development and influence. The virtuoso second section of the novel ("The Prayers of the Saints") moves between the present tense of the prayer meeting where John will be "saved" and these characters' memories of their lives. That alternation produces a form of insight that, however ambiguous in particular instances, is structured by a kind of telos: the memories track the development of the people these characters will have become by this evening. However effective a device for the depiction of character psychology, and for a rendering of the complex narratives and conflicts that structure the world in which any child comes to consciousness, it also produces a striking structural asymmetry when, in the final section of the novel ("The Threshing Floor"), we turn to John. This may be another way of expressing why we aren't told, explicitly, that John desires Elisha; we don't know what the older John will make of his experience. His centrality forecloses the narrative development afforded the characters who raise, and, more intimately, form him. Our stories become complete—and thus become the basis of *Bildung*—only when the central story is someone else's. (This, one notes, is the structure in Proust's *Recherche*, where it is a basis for the first-person narration: Proust makes this explicit by dividing the central figure into two functions [character and narrator] and by making prominent the dissonances between the two roles. Proust's experiment [in this isolated sense] may differ in degree rather than kind from earlier instances—a similar structure is legible, for example, in *Great Expectations*.) Partly because the formative event coincides with the "present" from which the events in the other sections are remembered, there is no end from which the experience is told, no later realization beyond the immediacy of the present time.

Or rather, that interval is no longer placed between two narrative times; it is internal to the writing itself. We are suspended in the "proto-" state of queer emergence. I take this to be one reason for the very beautiful use of deixis referring to the present within a past-tense narration, which appears, perhaps most notably, when the final section returns to John. The bulk of the chapter is devoted to John's experience on "the threshing floor," his thoughts as he moves from death to salvation. After that, several short sections follow, moving among the various groups of people walking home after Church, and in a sense tying up some of the threads of the histories of Elizabeth, Florence, and Gabriel. It ends, then, with John and Elisha: "Now the long, the silent avenue stretched before them like some grey country of the dead" (249). The structural relation between remembered and remembering times is here the gap, internal to the narration, expressed by the collocation of "now" with a past tense verb form that is possible only in narrative fiction.[39] Notably, at this particular moment, that collocation also brings together the two "scenes," as well as the two "times," of the final section—"the long, the silent avenue," or the "external" scene, and the "country of the dead," or the "internal" one where John goes through his experience of salvation, and the time "before" and "after" that salvation. Unlike *The Well of Loneliness*, this novel does not avow its gay desire; unlike Hall, too, Baldwin does not subordinate queer development to the ending that will have made it queer. Baldwin, Friedrich, and McCullers raise the question of whether a beginning is still a beginning when it doesn't (yet?) begin anything in particular—if, remaining in latency or potential, it must await the name, conferring a meaning that will, in that conferral, dissolve it. That is the problem Sedgwick raises in speaking of the "proto-gay," and one might call it, too, the predicament—though it is also the thrill—of queer youth.

Yeats's "foul rag and bone shop of the heart" no doubt partakes of a dualism that is the most immediate context of the poem: pure mind versus the material or bodily refuse out of which it is made.[40] But it also raises the question of beginnings. "A mound of refuse or the sweepings of a street": the forlorn objects—"old kettles, old bottles, and a broken can"—address the question "out of what began?" That is to say, it may be moving too quickly if one assumes that they *answer* that question; the images that have grown in "pure mind" have a beginning that cannot be assimilated to them, that remains, to the very degree that it is initiating, unassimilated to the meaning it creates. The beginnings are "refuse," then, not because of any quality in themselves, nor even because of the material nature of the dying body to which a transcendent heart is fastened; they are "refuse" because the beginning is, of necessity, heterogeneous to the form it shapes. Something in beginnings remains, like the leavings on a street, unredeemed or unshaped by the forms that, retrospectively, they can be said to foretell. At the same time, I take Yeats's point to be that this inception is also not to be grasped. For why is everything old when we go back to where the ladders start? No doubt it is partly because the beginnings are, at this point, so far away, and the smiling public man, old clothes upon old sticks to scare a bird. But the repeated term also captures our attention as a repeated term, apart, in other words, from its meaning; these are images, too, one need hardly add, that pure mind might adduce for its material roots. They affect one as pure images to the very degree that they evoke what in fact escapes them. And thus they also stay with one because of the metrical patterning into which "old" may ultimately seem to disappear. Gay etiology raises these questions with particular economy—by seeking to trace the source and cause of a totality that does not exist, tracing a horizon that ever recedes from us, a groundless positing that we can grasp only as a form that exceeds us. Proto-gay kids embody what, could we see it, remains forever unformed within us, the potentiality that, sheltered within our ostensibly finished forms, is the heritage of our beginnings. To tell of proto-gay kids is also to pose the question of inception as such, and our queer origins abide in us as secret miracles, as the solitude, and the potentiality, of creatures who speak.

Acknowledgments

Remaining silent about the debts inevitably incurred in the writing of a book has at least the virtue of admitting that they are not to be discharged by the mere naming of them. Like Pip and Herbert's memoranda in *Great Expectations*, such lists, by substituting the clerical satisfactions of bookkeeping for the more bracing sacrifices of actual repayment, also risk the further fault of delusory self-congratulation, enjoying both the borrowed funds and (in advance) the self-regard earned by their repayment. It is tempting to think that, because one's desk is neat, one's accounts are in order; the debts will remain, however, even after the final quietus puts one beyond any feeling of them. In the meantime, therefore, like Pip and Herbert, I will continue to make the memoranda, and to leave a margin.

Earlier versions of several chapters were presented at the Mahindra Center at Harvard University, at Tufts University, at the University of Connecticut, at Williams College, and at panels at NAVSA and ACLA. Thanks to the organizers and audiences there for the invitations and their generous responses and questions, especially Amanda Claybaugh, Theo Davis, Jess Keiser, Rob Lehman, John Lurz, George Moore, Joe Rezek, Steve Tifft, Audrey Wasser, and the 2019–20 Williams College Class of 1960 scholars. Tyler Bradway, Anna Fishzon, and Emma Lieber also responded, in different contexts, to the chapters on James and Welty. For her help with Latin, I am grateful to Maria Kakavas. Thanks, once again, to Richard Morrison, and, also at Fordham University Press, to John Garza and to the two anonymous readers who gave unusually comprehending, thoughtful, and helpful advice on the manuscript. I am grateful to the Cornell Society for the Humanities for the fellowship during which many of the chapters were finished, and to Boston College for allowing me the year off I needed to accept it—and, more generally, for their unfailing support of my research. Thanks, furthermore, to Dean Greg Kalscheur and the university for the material support they have provided the book's publication.

I owe thanks to many friends who, knowingly or not, helped me during the writing of this book. At the Cornell Society for the Humanities, Tim Murray and the other fellows in my cohort, especially Pamela Gilbert, Alicia Imperiale, Gloria Kim, Karman MacKendrick, and Daniel Smyth. In Boston, New York, Ithaca, Williamstown, and elsewhere: Henry Russell Bergstein, Ti Bodenheimer, Cynthia Chase, Derek David, Chris Deluca, Andy Donnelly, Steve Fix, Cameron Freer, Ellis Hanson, Kristin Imre, Sandra Lim, John Lurz, Andrew Miller, John Morrison, Joe Nugent, Ianna Hawkins Owen, Jake Russin, Eric Savoy, Leah Shafer, Anita Sokolsky, Ken Stuckey, Oleg Tcherny, Steve Tifft, Georgia Warnke, Audrey Wasser, and Nell Wasserstrom. I owe a special debt to friends who read chapters and whose responses helped me revise the book, in large ways and small: Mary Crane, Rob Lehman, John Limon, Ellen McCallum, Laura Tanner, and James Uden.

The past couple of years have given me multiple chances to feel how much I rely on Ash Anderson, John Anspach, Katherine Biers, Theo Davis, Amy Foerster, Hollis Griffin, Niko Kolodny, and Joe Rezek. Thanks, perennially, to my parents and brother: Dee, Jim, and Kolin Ohi. Without them, there would have been no beginnings. João Marcos Copertino arrived on the scene too late for the inception of this work; ergue-te amigo que dormes nas manhãs frias—though let's spare the sleeping branches, and the birds. Several months during which I was writing this book were unusually difficult for me; David Kurnick helped me to think through the experience of disappointment and loss, and thereby to find my way back to new sources of interest and joy. There can be no margin left for such a debt. Nor, once again, can I do more than acknowledge the first and last reader of every page I write, Daniel Heller-Roazen, without whom I might never write at all, and certainly would never have written this particular book. Of aid less directly, and perhaps less substantively intellectual, were Milly and Seymour Bergstein, who, canine, consoling, utterly absorbing small creatures, are the (in their way, devoted) companions of my days.

Stanzas from W. B. Yeats, "The Circus Animals' Desertion," from *The Poems: Revised*, edited by Richard J. Finneran (New York: Macmillan Publishing Company, 1989) appear with the permission of A P Watt at United Agents on behalf of Caitriona Yeats.

Lines from Elizabeth Bishop's "The Imaginary Iceberg" appear with the following permissions. In the UK and Commonwealth: From *Complete Poems of Elizabeth Bishop* by Elizabeth Bishop. Published by Vintage. Reproduced by permission of The Random House Group LTD © 1970. In the US and the rest of the world: Excerpt from "The Imaginary Iceberg" from *POEMS* by Elizabeth Bishop. Copyright © 2011 by the Alice H. Methfessel Trust. Introduction and compilation copyright © 2011 by Farrar, Straus and Giroux. Reprinted by permission of Farrar, Straus and Giroux.

Lines from Jack Spicer's "Orfeo" from *My Vocabulary Did This to Me: The Collected Poetry of Jack Spicer* © 2008 by The Estate of Jack Spicer. Published by Wesleyan University Press. Used with permission.

Notes

Exordium

1. Giorgio Agamben, "The End of the Poem," *The End of the Poem: Studies in Poetics*, trans. Daniel Heller-Roazen (Stanford: Stanford University Press, 1999). Jean-Claude Milner, "Réflexions sur le fonctionnement du vers français," *Ordres et raisons du langue* (Paris: Le Seuil, 1982), 283–391. In Daniel Heller-Roazen's gloss of the Milnerian thesis, "poetry can be defined as that discourse in which it is possible to oppose a syntactical limit, such as the end of the phrase, to a phonological limit, such as the end of the line." Heller-Roazen, "Speaking in Tongues," *Paragraph* 25, no. 2 (2002): 92–115, 104. Future references to the essays by Heller-Roazen and Agamben will be given parenthetically.

2. R. Murray Schafer, *The Soundscape: Our Sonic Environment and the Tuning of the World* (Rochester, Vt.: Destiny Books, 1994), 262. (Reprint of *The Tuning of the World* [New York: Alfred Knopf, 1977].)

3. Recent critical considerations of form include: Jonathan Kramnick and Anahid Nersessian, "Form and Explanation," *Critical Inquiry* 43 (Spring 2017): 650–69; Caroline Levine, *Forms: Whole, Rhythm, Hierarchy, Network* (Princeton, N.J., Princeton University Press, 2014); and Robert S. Lehman, "Formalism, Mere Form, and Judgment," *New Literary History* 48 no. 2 (2017): 245–63.

4. On how the formal "gimmick" of time signatures works and on the details of how the dances fit together, see Wye Jamison Allanbrook, *Rhythmic Gesture in Mozart: Le Nozze di Figaro & Don Giovanni* (Chicago: University of Chicago Press, 1983), 283–4. Future references will be given parenthetically.

5. *Mozart's Don Giovanni: Complete Italian Libretto* (libretto by Lorenzo Da Ponte [uncredited in this edition]) (New York: Dover Publications, 1985), 64, my translation. Allanbrook notes that Zerlina's scream precipitates "harmonic and rhythmic chaos" (285).

6. Gilles Deleuze, Seminar of March–June, 1981: *La Peinture et la question des concepts*, part 3 of May 19, 1981. Transcription (by Binak Kalludra) online at *La Voix de Gilles Deleuze en Ligne*, http://www2.univ-paris8.fr/deleuze/article.php3?id _article=61 (my translation).

7. *OED Online*, s.v. "Inception (*n.*)," last modified September 2020, www.oed .com/view/Entry/93402.

8. See Maurice Platnauer, *Latin Elegiac Verse: A Study of the Metrical Usages of Tibullus, Propertius & Ovid* (Hamden, Conn., Archon Books, 1971). I discuss the second line of *The Metamorphoses* in greater detail in Chapter 6.

9. Joseph Brodsky, "On 'September 1, 1939' by W. H. Auden," in *Less Than One: Selected Essays* (New York: Farrar, Straus and Giroux, 1986), 304–56, 308. Daniel Heller-Roazen pointed me to this passage in Brodsky—and to the metrical issues of the *Amores* and the *Metamorphoses*.

10. Hannah Arendt, *The Origins of Totalitarianism* (Cleveland and New York: Meridian Books, 1958), 478–9. Arendt intends "freedom," I think, in what she understands to be the Greek sense—"to be free . . . meant neither to rule nor to be ruled" (32). The contemporary "social" world consigns man to a purely private existence (one of tending to biological necessity, among other things) and thus deprives him of the freedom that would be exercised in the political realm.

11. Hannah Arendt, *The Human Condition*, 2nd edition (Chicago: University of Chicago Press, 1958), 178.

12. Edward W. Said, *Beginnings: Intention and Method* (New York: Columbia University Press, 1975).

13. See Augustine, *Confessions*, Book XI. Saint Augustine, *Confessions*, trans. R. S. Pine-Coffin (New York: Penguin Books, 1961), 253–80. Future references will be given parenthetically.

14. William Wordsworth, *The Prelude: 1799, 1805, 1850* (1805 Prelude, II.234–8), ed. M. H. Abrams, Stephen Gill, and Jonathan Wordsworth (New York: Norton, 1979).

15. John Milton, *Paradise Lost* (VIII.249–50), ed. Gordon Teskey (New York: Norton, 2005). Future references will be given parenthetically as *PL* followed by the book and line numbers.

16. Charles Dickens, *David Copperfield*, ed. Nina Burgis (Oxford: Oxford University Press, 1981), 1. Future references will be given parenthetically. I discuss this structure and its consequences for the text in greater detail in "Autobiography and *David Copperfield*'s Temporalities of Loss," *Victorian Literature and Culture* 33 (2005): 435–49. For the contrast between *David Copperfield*, where the closing address to Agnes (or at least, to her "face") in a sense closes the gap between narrator and character, and *Great Expectations*, where that gap is never closed, see Chapter 5.

17. Émile Benveniste, "The Correlations of Tense in the French Verb," *Problems in General Linguistics*, trans. Mary Elizabeth Meek (Coral Gables, Fla.: University of Miami Press, 1971), 205–15. I am indebted to Daniel Heller-Roazen for pointing me to the exceptional status of *je naquis*.

18. On this opposition, see "Relationships of Person in the Verb," *Problems in General Linguistics*, 195–204.

19. Perhaps more precisely, the *passé simple* excludes a scenario of address, or communication. According to Ann Banfield, "the *passé simple*, contrary to Benveniste's claim that it cannot co-occur with the first or second person, *often appears with the first person, but never with the second.*" Banfield, "Where Epistemology, Style, and Grammar Meet Literary History: The development of represented speech and thought," in *Reflexive Language: Reported Speech and Metapragmatics*, ed. John Lucy (Cambridge, UK: Cambridge University Press, 1992), 339–64, 358. For Banfield, the E of narration may or may not contain a speaker, but it has no addressee/hearer; spoken, represented thought or speech may be, like the *passé simple*, but, insofar as it is spoken to no one, it does not thereby constitute a speaker.

20. William Shakespeare, *The Tempest*, ed. Stephen Orgel (New York: Oxford University Press, 1987), I.2.49–50.

21. There is also an extended consideration of ethics and potentiality in *Karman: A Brief Treatise on Action, Guilt, and Gesture*, trans. Adam Kotsko (Stanford: Stanford University Press, 2018). In question, most generally, is the effect of potentiality on the category of the will—the aporias that Agamben uncovers in the ascribing of will (and of imputable action) to a subject. ("The goal of rendering human beings masters of their actions and guaranteeing to them the paternity of their acts and their knowledges," Agamben writes of Megarians' reading of Aristotle, for example, "thus has the consequence of a fracture of their capacity to act, which is now constitutively split into potential and impotential, being able to do and being able not to do" (45).

22. Kevin Ohi, *Innocence and Rapture: The Erotic Child in Pater, Wilde, James, and Nabokov* (New York: Palgrave Macmillan, 2005); *Henry James and the Queerness of Style* (Minneapolis: University of Minnesota Press, 2011); *Dead Letters Sent: Queer Literary Transmission* (Minneapolis: University of Minnesota Press, 2015).

23. See the *Confessions*, Book IX, Chapter 12. There, the shame at his grief (death, for a man of faith, should not be the occasion of grief, and one suspects, too, a lingering classical sense of shame at immoderation—he fears, in any event, that the grief will compromise him, and his faith, in the eyes of non-believers) is assuaged by the hymn, which reconciles him to the losses of mortal life in part by giving them expression. The hymn gives him rest, and allows him to weep, in his sight and God's. The hymn is Ambrose's "Evening Hymn": *Deus Creator omnium*. For the text of the hymn, and a translation (by J. D. Chambers), see Augustine, *Confessions*, 202. See also Augustine, *On Music*, Book VI. Augustine, *On Music*, in *The Fathers of the Church: A New Translation*, vol 4, trans. Robert Catesby Taliaferro (Washington, D.C.: The Catholic University of America Press, 2002), 167–379 (for Book VI, see 324–79). (Thanks to Daniel Smyth for his advice about Augustine.)

24. On "tick-tock," see Frank Kermode, *The Sense of an Ending: Studies in the Theory of Fiction* (London and Oxford: Oxford University Press, 1966), 44–6. Future references will be given parenthetically.

25. In addition to Nuttall and J. Hillis Miller, see James Phelan, "Beginnings and Endings: Theories and Typologies of How Novels Open and Close," *Encyclopedia of the Novel*, vol. 1 (A–L), ed. Paul Schellinger (Chicago: Fitzroy Dearborn Publishers, 1998), 96–9; Brian Richardson, "Beginnings and Ends. Introduction: Openings and Closure," *Narrative Dynamics: Essays on Time, Plot, Closure and Frames*, ed. Brian Richardson (Columbus: Ohio State University Press, 2002), 249–55; Peter Rabinowitz, "Reading Beginnings and Endings," in *Narrative Dynamics*, ed. Richardson, 300–13; and Brian Richardson, ed., *Narrative Beginnings: Theories and Practices* (Lincoln: University of Nebraska Press, 2008)—perhaps especially Niels Buch Leander, "To Begin with the Beginning: Birth, Origin, and Narrative Inception," 15–28; Melba Cuddy-Keane, "Virginia Woolf and Beginning's Ragged Edge," 96–112; and James Phelan, "The Beginning of *Beloved*: A Rhetorical Approach," 195–212. See also Victor Brombert, "Opening Signals in Narrative," *New Literary History* 11, no. 3, On Narrative and Narratives (Spring 1980): 489–502; Matthew Beaumont, "Beginnings, Endings, Births, Deaths: Sterne, Dickens, and *Bleak House*," *Textual Practice* 26 (5) (2012): 807–27; Steven G. Kellman, "Grand Openings and Plain: The Poetics of First Lines," *SubStance* 6/7, no. 17 (Autumn 1977), 139–47; Trevor Dean, "How Historians Begin: Openings in Historical Discourse" *History* 95, no. 4 (320) (October 2010): 399–417; and Catherine Romagnolo, *Opening Acts: Narrative Beginnings in Twentieth-Century Feminist Fiction* (Lincoln: University of Nebraska Press, 2015). For a different sort of argument—which I don't take up here—see George Steiner, *Grammars of Creation: Originating in the Gifford Lectures for 1990* (New Haven: Yale University Press, 2001). Likewise, there are many accounts of the openings of particular novels, their importance for the texts they commence, and their relevance to the larger oeuvre of the writer. Perhaps the preeminent example is Ian Watt, "The First Paragraph of *The Ambassadors*: An Explication," *Essays in Criticism* 10, no. 3 (1960): 250–74.

26. Roland Barthes, "The Discourse of History," trans. Stephen Bann, *Comparative Criticism: A Yearbook*, ed. E. S. Shaffer (Cambridge: Cambridge University Press, 1981), 7–20, 8.

27. "It is to the extent that he *knows* what has not yet been told that the historian, like the actor of myth, needs to double up the chronological unwinding of events with references to the time of his own speech."

28. Ernst Robert Curtius, "The Muses," *European Literature and the Latin Middle Ages*, trans. Willard R. Trask (Princeton: Princeton University Press, 1953 [Bollingen Series XXXVI]), (second edition with minor corrections, 1967), 228–46, 234. At the end of this chapter, Curtius writes: "In any case a Christian poet makes himself ridiculous when he troubles pagan deities who have long since been dethroned. Nothing is more chilling and absurd than for a modern to invoke the Muses. Better—as Samuel Butler did in his *Hudibras* (1663)—to invoke a jug of beer. . . . the attempt to save the Muses by transplanting them to the Arctic or the Tropics shows only that they have been retired. Their music, which once was the harmony of the spheres, has ceased to sound" (245–6). In my reading of this chapter, Curtius does not much emphasize the turn

toward an internal muse; highlighting it here is my extrapolation to account for what strikes me as a structural principle in Nuttall. A. D. Nuttall, *Openings: Narrative Beginnings from the Epic to the Novel* (Oxford: Oxford University Press, 1992).

29. It also occurs to me to note the link this suggests between inspiration and free indirect style or represented thought in the tradition of the novel—as if the *invocatio* had moved, unspoken, inside the very mechanism of the novel's narration, leaving traces, in that third-person non-voice, of the Muses. This question emerges, obliquely, in various ways, in some of the readings here. On represented thought as (literally, or grammatically) unspeakable (and hence *not* a rendering of a voice), see Ann Banfield, *Unspeakable Sentences: Narration and Representation in the Language of Fiction* (New York: Routledge, 1982).

30. For the famous line in Horace, see the *Ars Poetica*, in *Horace: Satires, Epistles, The Art of Poetry*, trans. H. Rushton Fairclough, Loeb Classical Library 194 (Cambridge: Harvard University Press, 1926), 462–3 (full text: 442–90). (I briefly discuss the complexity of this famous line later in the book; see the endnotes to Chapter 4.) Nuttall writes: ""We begin to sense in the history of European literature an enormous tension between (say) 'In the beginning God created the heaven and the earth' and "hardly out of sight of Sicilian soil they were joyfully setting sail', that is, between a natural and a formal beginning" (27). Niels Buch Leander shows ways that this opposition between the "natural" and the "artificial" is untenable. Niels Buch Leander, "To Begin with the Beginning: Birth, Origin, and Narrative Inception," in *Narrative Beginnings: Theories and Practices*, ed. Brian Richardson (Lincoln: University of Nebraska Press, 2008), 15–28 (especially 26).

31. Leander suggests that an inside/out distinction is more productive than one between artifice and nature (26). It seems to me that the former might be implicit in Nuttall's opposition. Nuttall's discussion of Dante turns on a reading of Auerbach, "Figura," *Scenes from the Drama of European Literature*, trans. Ralph Manheim (Minneapolis: University of Minnesota Press, 1984), 11–76. I do not fully grasp Nuttall's understanding of this essay.

32. The nine invocations are listed by Robert Hollander: Dante, *The Inferno*, trans. Robert Hollander and Jean Hollander, with notes by Robert Hollander (New York: Anchor Books, 2000), 35–6 (note to *Inferno* II.7–9).

33. Gordon Teskey, "On the Origin in *Paradise Lost*," in *The Poetry of John Milton* (Cambridge: Harvard University Press, 2015), 340–69.

34. I discuss my sense of the importance of potentiality (in particular as it is set out by Giorgio Agamben) for literary reading in the introduction to *Dead Letters Sent: Queer Literary Transmission* (Minneapolis: University of Minnesota Press, 2015). See also Chapter 1 of the present volume, on James's prefaces.

35. Frank Kermode, *The Sense of an Ending*. This mistake is perhaps also related to what Paul de Man calls "aesthetic ideology." See also Cynthia Chase, "Trappings of an Education toward What We Do Not Yet Have," *Responses: On Paul de Man's Wartime Journalism*, ed. Werner Hamacher, Neil Hertz, and Thomas Keenan (Lincoln: University of Nebraska Press, 1989), 44–79.

36. I think this is one way to understand Melba Cuddy-Keane's astute observation that an *in medias res* opening, even though it shuffles the order of exposition, does not, on that account, challenge the boundaries of the *text*. She is led thereby to turn to what she calls the "ragged edge" of certain modernist texts: this "ragged edge, by contrast, harkens back to voices and experiences never to be explained or articulated in the narrative to come. The ghostly presence of voices always prior and outside the text means that narrative is never ultimately traceable to a point of origin, for there is no single, absolute point of origin to which narrative could be traced. . . . As opposed to a tale with beginning and ending, narrative is an always ongoing process to which the reader, as it were, tunes in" (98). Cuddy-Keane, "Virginia Woolf and Beginning's Ragged Edge," in *Narrative Beginnings: Theories and Practices*, ed. Brian Richardson (Lincoln: University of Nebraska Press, 2008), 96–112. It seems to me, however, that the gap between the "inside" and "outside" of the text on which her distinction is premised also means that the edge of *every* text is "ragged," that the specificity she finds in Woolf is but an explicitation of a generalizable textual structure.

37. Vladimir Nabokov, *Pale Fire* (New York: Vintage, 1962). I was led to think about this line in these terms by a conversation with David Kurnick.

38. D. A. Miller, *Narrative and Its Discontents: Problems of Closure in the Traditional Novel* (Princeton: Princeton University Press, 1981), ix. Future references will be given parenthetically.

39. "The project of these novelists seems curiously perverse, as though each had chosen the vehicle (narrative) least suited to its desired tenor (propriety, transcendence, erotic intensity). Their narratives stubbornly reach after what, as narratives, they seem intrinsically prevented from being. Accordingly, each novelist raises a problem far more radical than the specific problems furnished by the actual narrative: the problem of there being a narrative at all" (Miller, *Narrative and Its Discontents*, x).

40. J. Hillis Miller, "Beginnings," *Reading Narrative* (Norman: University of Oklahoma Press, 1998), 57–60, 57. Future references will be given parenthetically. One recognizes the Derridean discussion of the "hors-texte" (and his discussion of the "preface" in Hegel). See "Outwork; Hors d'oeuvre; Extratext; Foreplay; Bookend; Facing; Prefacing," in *Dissemination*, trans. Barbara Johnson (London: Athlone Press, 1981), 3–59.

41. Paul de Man, "Shelley Disfigured," in *The Rhetoric of Romanticism* (New York: Columbia University Press, 1984), 93–123, 117–18.

42. On the "lap" of sense, see Agamben's discussion of Dante's use of this term in *Vulgar Eloquence* ("End of the Poem," 110–11).

1. Revision, Origin, and the Courage of Truth: Henry James's New York Edition Prefaces

1. Gordon Teskey, "On the Origin in *Paradise Lost*," in *The Poetry of John Milton* (Cambridge: Harvard University Press, 2015), 340–69, 358–9. Future references will be given parenthetically.

2. All quotations from the New York Edition prefaces are from the Library of America edition: *Henry James: Literary Criticism, Volume Two: French Writers, Other European Writers, Prefaces to the New York Edition*, ed. Mark Wilson and Leon Edel (New York: The Library of America, 1984). Throughout the chapter, parenthetical references are to this edition.

3. See Henry James, *The Golden Bowl* (New York: Oxford University Press, 1999), 138–9.

4. Gilles Deleuze, *Proust and Signs: The Complete Text*, trans. Richard Howard (Minneapolis: University of Minnesota Press, 2004).

5. See Kevin Ohi, *Henry James and the Queerness of Style* (Minneapolis: University of Minnesota Press, 2011), 55–7. As I note there, my notice of the uncanny "figure with a pair of eyes, or at least with a field-glass" is indebted to Sheila Teahan.

6. "I must decidedly have supposed, all the while, that I was acutely observing— and with a blest absence of wonder at its being so easy" (1058); "Trying to recover here, for recognition, the germ of my idea, I see that it must have consisted not at all in any conceit of a 'plot,' nefarious name, in any flash, upon the fancy of a set of relations, or in any one of those situations that, by a logic of their own, immediately fall, for the fabulist, into a movement . . ." (1071); "What I make out from furthest back is that I must have had from still further back, must in fact practically always have had, the happy thought . . ." (1103); "Let it pass that if I am so oddly unable to say here, at any point, 'what gave me my idea,' I must just a trifle freely have helped myself to it from hidden stores" (1232).

7. See *Henry James and the Queerness of Style*, 46–8 and 188–9n19 (which cites other critical discussions of "as if" in James [for instance, by Leo Bersani], and notes its importance for William James as well). See also Katherine Biers, *Virtual Modernism: Writing and Technology in the Progressive Era* (Minneapolis: University of Minnesota Press, 2013).

8. There is a group of cognates and related terms—seed, virus, grain, especially. This metaphor also appears in William James. In Dora Zhang's summary, "to have acquaintance with something is thus only 'a very minimum of knowledge,' and although our own sensory experience always remains the ground of all knowledge for [William] James, cognition proceeds outwards from acquaintance to 'knowledge-about' like the 'germ' to the 'developed tree.'" Dora Zhang, "Naming the Indescribable: Woolf, Russell, James, and the Limits of Description," *New Literary History* 45, no. 1 (Winter 2014): 51–70, 57. She cites William James, *The Meaning of Truth* (Cambridge: Harvard University Press, 1975), 17.

9. "I instantly became aware, with my 'sense for the subject,' of the prick of inoculation; the *whole* of the virus, as I have called it, being infused by that single touch" (1140).

10. "The germ, wherever gathered, has ever been for me the germ of a 'story,' and most of the stories straining to shape under my hand have sprung from a single small seed, a seed as minute and wind-blown as that casual hint for 'The Spoils of Poynton' dropped unwitting by my neighbour, a mere floating particle in the stream

of talk. What above all comes back to me with this reminiscence is the sense of the inveterate minuteness, on such happy occasions, of the precious particle—reduced, that is, to its mere fruitful essence. Such is the interesting truth about the stray suggestion, the wandering word, the vague echo, at touch of which the novelist's imagination winces as at the prick of some sharp point: its virtue is all in its needle-like quality, the power to penetrate as finely as possible. This fineness it is that communicates the virus of suggestion, anything more than the minimum of which spoils the operation. If one is given a hint at all designedly one is sure to be given too much; one's subject is in the merest grain, the speck of truth, of beauty, of reality, scarce visible to the common eye—since, I firmly hold, a good eye for a subject is anything but usual" (1138).

11. "The Birthplace"—one of James's most explicit (and complex) considerations of the relation of the author to his work, which casts the drive to discover the personal traces of the author as a kind of desecration—figures the author's own origin as the empty husk of a seed: "The Holy of Holies of the Birthplace was the low, the sublime Chamber of Birth, sublime because, as the Americans usually said . . . it was so pathetic; and pathetic because was—well, really nothing else the world that one could name, number or measure. It was as empty as shell of which the kernel has withered, and contained neither busts nor prints nor early copies contained only the Fact—*the* Fact itself—which, as he stood sentient there at midnight, our friend, holding his breath, allowed to sink into him." Henry James, "The Birthplace," *The Novels and Tales of Henry James: New York Edition*, Volume XVII (New York: Charles Scribner's Sons, 1909), 131–213, 153–4.

12. In an essay on James's *Notebooks*, Maurice Blanchot suggests that James's repeated charting out of plans that nearly always diverge from the realized texts they imagine point to his terror of beginning, and mark an effort to see the reverse side of the canvas, the pure potentiality that precedes writing—which can reach that desired plane only by unwriting itself. Blanchot, "The Turn of the Screw," in *The Book to Come*, trans. Charlotte Mandel (Stanford: Stanford University Press, 2003), 126–33.

13. John Milton, *Paradise Lost* (I.13–16), ed. Gordon Teskey (New York: Norton, 2005). Future references will be given parenthetically as *PL* followed by the book and line numbers.

14. Gen. 1:14: "And God said, Let there be lights in the firmament of the heaven to divide the day from the night; and let them be for signs, and for seasons, and for days, and years" (Authorized King James Version).

15. For instance, Ezekiel 1:24: "And when they went, I heard the noise of their wings, like the noise of great waters, as the voice of the Almighty, the voice of speech, as the noise of an host: when they stood, they let down their wings." Or Ezekiel 10:5: "And the sound of the cherubims' wings was heard *even* to the outer court, as the voice of the Almighty God when he speaketh." Thanks to Zach Forsberg-Lary for these references. And thanks to Peter Grudin for reminding me of the moment in *Jane Eyre*. In *Parade's End*, Ford Madox Ford quotes (or, according

to Sara Haslam, slightly misquotes) John Bright's 1855 comments on the Crimean War: "It appeared to him queer that they should be behaving like that when you could hear . . . oh, say: the wings of the angel of death. . . . You can 'almost hear the very rustling of his wings' was the quotation." Ford, *A Man Could Stand Up*, vol. 3 of *Parade's End*, ed. Sara Haslam (Exeter, U.K.: Carcanet Press Limited, 2011), 101 (ellipses in original).

16. Henry James, "Introduction to *The Tempest*," in *Henry James: Literary Criticism*, vol. 1, *Essays on Literature, American Writers, English Writers* (New York: Library of America, 1984), 1205. Originally published in Sidney Lee, ed., *The Complete Works of William Shakespeare*, vol. XVI (New York: George D. Sproul, 1907). I discuss this torment in greater detail in "Hover, Torment Waste: Late Writings and the Great War," in *Henry James and the Queerness of Style*, 109–47.

17. *Shakespeare's Sonnets*, edited with an analytic commentary by Stephen Booth (New Haven: Yale University Press, 1977), 64–7. Booth notes that these lines echo the traditional burial service: "earth to earth, ashes to ashes, dust to dust" (262n7).

18. Virginia Woolf, "The Method of Henry James," in *The Essays of Virginia Woolf, Volume Two: 1912–1918*, ed. Andrew McNeillie (San Diego: Harcourt Brace Jovanovich, 1987), 346–9, 348. I learned of this passage in Andrew H. Miller, "The One Cake, The Only Cake," *Michigan Quarterly Review LI*, no. 2 (Spring 2012): 167–86, 175. Miller also recalls the passage from "A Sketch of the Past" describing her father's "perfect lesson": She could fish if she wanted, he said, but he didn't care to see fish caught. Her "passion for the thrill and tug" was slowly "extinguished." "But from the memory of my own passion I am still able to construct an idea of the sporting passion. It is one of those invaluable seeds, from which, since it is impossible to have every experience fully, one can grow something that represents other people's experiences. Often one has to make do with seeds; the germs of what might have been, had one's life been different." Woolf, "A Sketch of the Past," in *Moments of Being: A Collection of Autobiographical Writing*, ed. Jeanne Schulkind (San Diego: A Harvest Book, 1985), 64–159, 135.

19. Henry James, *A Small Boy and Others: A Critical Edition*, ed. Peter Collister (Charlottesville: University of Virginia Press, 2011). Future references will be given parenthetically.

20. "Present to me still is the fact of my sharper sense, after an hour or two, of my being there in distress . . . ; present to me above all the strange sense that something had begun that would make more difference to me, directly and indirectly, than anything had ever yet made. I might verily, on the spot, have seen, as in a fading of day and a change to something suddenly queer, the whole large extent of it. I must have thus, much impressed but half scared, have wanted to appeal; to which end I tumbled, all too weakly, out of bed and wavered toward the bell just across the room. The question of whether I really reached and rang it was to remain lost afterwards in the strong sick whirl of everything about me, under which I fell into a lapse of consciousness that I shall conveniently here treat as a considerable gap" (James, *Small Boy*, 329–30).

21. J. Hillis Miller, *The Ethics of Reading: Kant, de Man, Eliot, Trollope, James and Benjamin* (New York Columbia University Press, 1987).

22. That logic, which also guides the discussion of the Coburn frontispieces, distinguishes illustration (forbidden) from a "generalized" vision of elements in the text; the images were to be "expressions of no particular thing in the text, but only of the type or idea of this or that thing" (1327). Generalization turns illustration into rereading—what James calls "re-representation" (1329). A mediated, indirect view is opposed to "the mere muffled majesty of irresponsible 'authorship.'" Notably, too, the photographs were "to seek the way, which they have happily found, I think, not to keep, or to pretend to keep, anything like dramatic step with their suggestive matter" (1327).

23. For a different (and persuasive) account of "freedom" and ethics in relation to revision in James, see Leo Bersani, "The Jamesian Lie," in *A Future for Astyanax: Character and Desire in Literature* (Boston and Toronto: Little, Brown and Company, 1969), 128–55. For Bersani, James's freedom is a freedom from "a crippling notion of truth" (130)—truth of character (as psychological depth), and a certain model of realism, the correlation of fiction to a pre-existing reality: his "freedom" is that of "inventions so coercive that they resist any attempt to enrich—or reduce—them with meaning" (132). Testing out, in various ways, the artist's power to shape the world (with all the "strenuous responsibilities" that follow from that power [Bersani, 133])—thus tracing the consequences of the artwork's autonomy, an aestheticism that he takes to its limit—James, in Bersani's account, moves toward an idea of revision that removes the artwork from the realm of the interpretable (from meaning, from the intervention of criticism). The metafictional quality of *The Golden Bowl* then marks both the final realization of the novel as a genre and its destruction. Maggie's terrible ascendency at the end of James's masterpiece, he suggests, joins the artwork's eternity—its placid disregard for the various interpretations that will, in failing to capture it, simply wither away—with the particular self-sacrificial mode of empowerment displayed by (for example) Milly Theale: "a sacrifice so lovingly and so tyrannically devoid of specific claims that in order to accept it he must imitate it" (153). James's aestheticism is, Bersani concludes, ethically ambiguous: "Thus we see the inescapable ambiguity of a fiction so utterly released from the comfortable superstition of truth. The strength of James's uncompromising ethic of fiction finally requires a renunciation of that faculty to see (to criticize and to subvert) which, after all, protects us—and not simply in relation to art—from the tyranny of any community united in its assent to a single, insistent passion" (155).

24. "The linking together of words or ideas in speech or thought"; "Consecutiveness, continuity or coherence of ideas"; "a connecting passage, word, or particle"; the condition of being related to something else by a bond of interdependence, causality, logical sequence, coherence, or the like; relation between things one of which is bound up with, or involved in, another." ("Connection, n.," *OED Online*, last modified September 2020, www .oed.com/view/Entry/39356.)

25. Henry James, "Is There a Life after Death?" in *Henry James on Culture: Collected Essays on Politics and the American Social Scene*, ed. Pierre A. Walker (Lincoln: University of Nebraska Press, 1999), 115–27.

26. Michel Foucault, "Parrēsia," trans. Graham Burchell, *Critical Inquiry* 41, no 2 (Winter 2015): 219–53, 240, 244. See also *The Courage of Truth: The Government of Self and Others II, Lectures at the Collège de France, 1983–1984*, ed. Frédéric Gros, trans. Graham Burchell (New York: Palgrave Macmillan, 2011); and *Fearless Speech*, ed. Joseph Pearson (Los Angeles: Semiotext(e), 2001). Future references to all three texts will be given parenthetically.

27. For an account that—offering a critique of certain trends in queer theory, and particularly of the work of Lee Edelman—pursues the question of "revolution" in Foucault (and thus aims to separate a potential for revolution within queer critique from particular ["non-normative"] identities or acts), see Drucilla Cornell and Stephen D. Seely, "There Is Nothing Revolutionary About a Blowjob," *Social Text* 119, vol. 32, no. 2 (Summer 2014): 1–23. They turn especially to the "care of the self" and form of life articulated by truth-telling in the late writing. (One might find the essay very compelling, especially in its account of Lacan, while demurring from certain details in the critique of Edelman, and its rendering of Edelman's argument.) For an account of the linking of questions of ethics and politics in Foucault by way of the question of "conduct" and "counter-conduct," see Arnold I. Davidson, "In Praise of Counter-Conduct," *History of the Human Sciences* 24, no. 4 (2011): 25–41. ("The ethical and political impact of counter-conduct is also at the heart of Foucault's last courses, concerned with the practice of *parrhesia*, and is especially prominent in his discussion of the apex of philosophical counter-conduct, namely Cynic *parrhesia* and the Cynic way of life" [38].) Future references to Davidson will be given parenthetically.

28. For Davidson ("In Praise of Counter-Conduct"), the turn to parrhēsia offers a contrast to the way that "regimes of veridiction" can absorb counter-conduct (one example is masturbation—see 34–7) into forms of scientific knowledge or regulations of normality.

29. This connection is implicit in Ed Cohen's account of "psychagogy" in the movement from the politically framed parrhēsia of *The Government of Self and Others* to that of *The Courage of Truth*. Cohen writes: "Thinking troubles life itself insofar as it evinces a tension within life between the life that is and the life that could be. Thinking becomes 'live thinking' when it evokes the capacity of life to live otherwise, to gesture toward the 'other life' that it contains—and that contains it" (Cohen, "Live Thinking, or the Psychagogy of Michel Foucault," *differences: A Journal of Feminist Cultural Studies* 25, no. 2 [2014]: 1–32). See also Tim Dean, "The Biopolitics of Pleasure," *The South Atlantic Quarterly* 111, no. 3 (Summer 2012): 477–96. Dean cites Foucault's comments about writing in the first preface to *The Use of Pleasure*: "it would probably not be worth the trouble of making books," Foucault writes, "if they failed to teach the author something he had not known before, if they did not lead to unforeseen places, and if they did not disperse one

toward a strange and new relation with himself. The pain and pleasure of the book is to be an experience" (Foucault, "Preface to *The History of Sexuality*, Volume Two," in *The Essential Works of Michel Foucault, 1954–1984*, vol. 1, *Ethics, Subjectivity and Truth*, ed. Paul Rabinow, trans. Robert Hurley [New York: New Press, 1994], 205).

30. Giorgio Agamben, *The Fire and the Tale*, trans. Lorenzo Chiesa (Stanford: Stanford University Press, 2017), 94/98, translation modified. Future citations will be given parenthetically. Here and hereafter, where there are two page references, the first is to the English translation, and the second, to the Italian text: *Il fuoco e il racconto* (Rome: Nottetempo, 2014). In modifying the translations, I have also consulted *Le feu et le récit*, trans. Martin Rueff (Paris: Éditions Payot & Rivages, 2015).

31. "La Voix de Gilles Deleuze en Ligne": http://www2.univ-paris8.fr/deleuze/article .php3?id_article=453; http://www2.univ-paris8.fr/deleuze/article.php3?id_article=454; and http://www2.univ-paris8.fr/deleuze/article.php3?id_article=455. My translations.

32. One might consider in this regard Foucault's comments in *The Courage of Truth* on the Cynics—who represent for him a limit case of a life marked by truth. (Despite having "little importance in the history of doctrines," they have "considerable importance in the history of arts of living and the history of philosophy as a mode of life" [315n].) Thus Foucault marks a bifurcation—between courage of truth or care of the self that leads to metaphysics (and questions of truth) and that which leads to a form of life. "Metaphysical experience of the world, historico-critical experience of life: These are two fundamental cores in the genesis of European or Western philosophical experience" (315). Foucault presents this schematically as an opposition between the *Laches* and the *Alcibiades*: "When we compare the *Laches* and the *Alcibiades*, we have the starting point for two great lines of development of philosophical reflection and practice: on the one hand, philosophy as that which, by prompting and encouraging men to take care of themselves, leads them to the metaphysical reality of the soul, and, on the other, philosophy as a test of life, a test of existence, and the elaboration of a particular kind of form and modality of life. Of course, there is no incompatibility between these two themes of philosophy as a test of life and philosophy as a knowledge of the soul. . . . I think nevertheless that we have here the starting point of two aspects, two profiles, as it were, of philosophical activity, of philosophical practice in the West. On the one hand, a philosophy whose dominant theme is knowledge of the soul and which from this knowledge produces an ontology of the self. And then, on the other hand, a philosophy as test of life, of *bios*, which is the ethical material and object of an art of oneself. These two major profiles of Platonic philosophy, of Western philosophy, are fairly easily decipherable when we compare the dialogues of the *Laches* and the *Alcibiades* with each other" (127). He also schematizes this as a structural opposition between two questions: of the "other world," which he traces (again) to the *Alcibiades*, and an "other life," which he traces to the *Laches*: "the two great themes, the two great forms, the great limits within which Western philosophy

has constantly developed" (245). He then goes on to restate the opposition between the two legacies of Socratic parrhēsia: metaphysical truth (Platonists and neo-Platonists) and a form of life (Cynics).

33. See also Agamben's comments on the thought of thought in Aristotle—in "Bartleby, or, On Contingency," in *Potentialities: Collected Essays in Philosophy*, ed. and trans. Daniel Heller-Roazen (Stanford: Stanford University Press, 1999), 243–71.

34. In *Karman*, Agamben writes of the Greek term *ergon* (etymologically linked to *erdō*, to do), "like the Latin *opera* with respect to *opus*, it indicates first of all the operation and only secondarily its result" (*Karman: A Brief Treatise on Action, Guilt, and Gesture*, trans. Adam Kotsko [Stanford: Stanford University Press, 2018], 63. Future references will be given parenthetically). The context for Agamben's comment is his critique of the understanding of "action" in Hannah Arendt's *The Human Condition*. More generally, the consideration in *Karman* of action, guilt, and will, though beyond the scope of this chapter, would be illuminating for thinking about James's sense of "connection" at the end of the *Golden Bowl* preface, and for considering James's repeated use of the term *freedom*.

35. See also Giorgio Agamben, "*Se*: Hegel's Absolute and Heidegger's *Ereignis*," in *Potentialities*, 116–37. James Lee links the ethics in late Foucault to the "sublime turn" in Neil Hertz's reading of Longinus (writing about Sappho). Taking issue with those accounts of late Foucault that emphasize a freedom of self-fashioning (as if it were the self-invention of a dandy), Lee suggests that the fragmentation and reassembly of the body in a passage through a written text (which he spells out by way of Hertz) offers a way to understand how the ethical subject in Foucault constitutes itself (as other) by objectifying itself in writing. Lee, "Ethopoiesis: Foucault's Late Ethics and the Sublime Body," *New Literary History* 44, no. 1 (Winter 2013): 179–98. ("For Foucault, the transformation of the body into an aesthetic object serves as the basis of the ethical definition of the subject" [195].) His account of this ascesis or aesthetics of writing draws on an extended reading of Michel Foucault, "Self Writing," in *Ethics: Subjectivity and Truth*, ed. Paul Rabinow, trans. Robert Hurley and others (New York: The New Press, 1997), 207–22. For Hertz on Longinus, see Neil Hertz, "A Reading of Longinus," in *The End of the Line: Essays on Psychoanalysis and the Sublime* (New York: Columbia University Press, 1985), 1–20.

36. In the 1984 seminar on the Courage of Truth, Foucault at one moment speculates on the etymology of a series of terms that he has invoked for the care of the self and of others: "There is the word *melō*, which you find above all in the impersonal form *melei moi* (I care about; or more precisely, it concerns me, since it is impersonal), and then a whole series of other words: the noun *epimeleia*, the verb *epimelein* or *epimeleisthai*, the adjective *amelēs* (careless), the adverb *amelōs* (carelessly), and the noun *epimeletēs* (the person who cares for, who looks after, and which often has a fairly precise meaning in Greek institutions: it is a quasi-official responsibility of being the supervisor of something; at any rate [the term] may refer to a precise responsibility). Where does this series of words come from?" (117–18).

Foucault reports that he turned to Georges Dumézil for help; the Indo-European root is clearly *mel*, and (Dumézil said, Foucault reports) one might think of *melos*, found in *melōdia* ("song, rhythmic singing, music"). Dismissing the possible link initially, Dumézil apparently came back to it, thinking of "it appeals to me [*ça me chante*]"—though as an appeal of duty instead (as would be idiomatic) of freedom and pleasure. "But nevertheless," Foucault continues, still ventriloquizing Dumézil, I think, "we may very well conceive of an 'it appeals to me' which would refer instead to something in your head, which gets into your head, stays in your mind, obsesses you up to a point, and which appeals to you, but in the form of an order, an injunction, a duty to be performed." Adding another series of examples from Latin, Foucault then reports a further conversation with Paul Veyne, who pointed out that *melos* is also the call (*chant d'appel*)—for example, of a shepherd singing to call back his flock, or to signal other shepherds. "Consequently, *melei moi* would mean something like, not exactly 'it appeals to me in my head,' but: it appeals to me in the sense that it calls out to me or summons me." There might be, he suggests, "a musical secret, a secret of the musical appeal in this notion of care" (118–19). (The editors of the seminar report that P. Chantraine [in *Dictionnaire étymologique de la langue grecque* (Paris: Klincksiek, 1983), 683] finds this link "very doubtful" [139n1].)

37. This tension is the subject of the final chapter of this book, on queer incipience.

38. Eve Kosofsky Sedgwick, "Shame, Theatricality, and Performativity: Henry James's *The Art of the Novel*," in *Touching Feeling: Affect, Pedagogy, Performativity* (Durham, N.C.: Duke University Press, 2003), 35–65.

39. Elias Canetti, *Crowds and Power*, trans. Carol Stewart (New York: The Noonday Press of Farrar, Straus and Giroux, 1962).

40. For another account critical of queer theoretical uses of shame, see John Limon, "The Shame of Abu Ghraib," *Critical Inquiry* 33, no. 3 (Spring 2007): 543–72. Leo Bersani is also critical of the way that queer theory's use of shame produces a claimed innocence—which projects all unseemly forms of violence outward on to a persecuting social. Bersani, "Aggression, Shame, and Almodóvar's Art," in *Is the Rectum a Grave? and Other Essays* (Chicago: University of Chicago Press, 2010), 63–82, esp. 68.

41. See Leo Bersani, "Shame on You," in Leo Bersani and Adam Phillips, *Intimacies* (Chicago: University of Chicago Press, 2008), 31–56.

42. Agamben, *The Fire and the Tale*, 134; Agamben cites only the lines about happiness (not those about obligation or absolution). Foucault, *Speech Begins After Death*, ed. Philippe Artières, trans. Robert Bononno (Minneapolis: University of Minnesota Press, 2013), 64. Future references will be given parenthetically. Translated from Foucault, *Le Beau Danger. Entretien de Michel Foucault avec Claude Bonnefoy* (1968), Paris, EHESS, 2011, 56. Agamben cites an Italian translation: Foucault, *Il bel rischio*, trad. It di A Moscati (Napoli: Cronopio, 2013), 49: "Non è la scrittura che è felice, è la felicità di esistere che è sospesa alla scrittura, il che è un po' diverso." "Sospesa," here translating "*suspendu*,"

which Bononno renders as "attached," is also the word Agamben also often uses to describe the way that potentiality and impotentiality are maintained within the actualization that ostensibly resolves them.

43. Agamben does not cite these lines. Foucault later remarks: "This type of suppression, of self-mortification in the transition to signs, is, I believe, what also gives writing its character of obligation. It's an obligation without pleasure, you see, but, after all, when escaping an obligation leads to anxiety, when breaking the law leaves you so apprehensive and in such great disarray, isn't obeying the law the greatest form of pleasure? To obey an obligation whose origin is unknown, and the source of whose authority over us is equally unknown, to obey that—certainly narcissistic—law that weighs down on you, that hangs over you wherever you are, that, I think, is the pleasure of writing" (*Speech Begins After Death*, 68).

44. Seity: the term Chiesa chooses for seità, a nominalization of a reflexive pronoun lacking in English (*sé* in Italian; *se* or *soi* in French—or *sē*, the accusative and ablative form of the third-person reflexive pronoun [singular and plural] in Latin); the French translator has "seité." Perhaps it is common enough as a technical term; "self-ness," one might say, but only if one withdrew the usual meanings of self and perceived it only as the suffix indicating a reflexive relation—"-self," or perhaps "oneselfness"? Just before the assertion (quoted earlier) that the ethical subject is a contradiction in terms, Agamben highlights Michel Bréal's claim that the word *ethos* is formed from the reflexive pronoun—the *e* of the Greek reflexive pronoun followed by the suffix "-*thos*"—and concludes that ethos means, "simply and literally 'seity,' which is to say the manner in which each person experiences a self." This implies, he concludes, that the "idea of an ethical subject is a contradiction in terms" (133/136 [translation modified]).

45. In Agamben's terms at the close of this essay: "The form-of-life is where the work on an opus and the work on oneself perfectly coincide. The painter, the poet, the thinker—and in general anyone who practices an 'art' or an 'activity'—are not the appointed sovereign subjects of a creative operation and of an opus: they are, rather, anonymous living beings who, by contemplating and making inoperative, each time, the works of language, of vision, and of bodies, try to experience the self [*fare esperiencza di sé*] and to maintain themselves in relation to a potentiality, that is, to construct their life as a form-of-life. It is at this point, and this point only, that opus and Great Opus [the work and the masterwork?], gold and philosopher's gold, can at last be identified without residue" (138/142 [translation modified]).

46. Henry James, "The Middle Years," in *The Novels and Tales of Henry James: New York Edition*, Volume XVI (New York: Charles Scribner's Sons, 1909), 75–106. Future references will be given parenthetically.

47. Teskey, *The Poetry of John Milton*, 354, quoting from *Paradise Lost* IX.834–5.

48. I was thinking of Robert Alter's translation of Genesis, which James obviously could not have read. (Alter, *Genesis: Translation and Commentary* [New York: Norton, 1997]): "*When God began to create heaven and earth, and the earth then was welter and waste and darkness over the deep and God's breath hovering over the waters, God*

said, 'Let there be light.'" But the language does appear in a hymn by Bishop
William Walsham How: "O'er the shoreless waste of waters/In the world's primeval
night,/Moved the quickening Spirit, waking/All things into life and light./So,
Lord, in Thy new creation/Light in Thine own Light we see,/By the water and the
Spirit/Born again to life in Thee" (http://www.historichymns.com/HymnPage.aspx
?HymnalNumber=31&Hymn_Number=268&TextID=2206).

2. "First Love": Gesture and the Emergence of Desire in Eudora Welty

1. Kathryn Bond Stockton, *The Queer Child, Or Growing Sideways in the
Twentieth Century* (Durham, N.C.: Duke University Press, 2009).

2. For a brilliant reading of the story—and a very different consideration of "first
love"—see Sigi Jöttkandt, "In the Self's Temporary Lodgings: Eudora Welty," in *First
Love: A Phenomenology of the One* (Melbourne, Australia: re.press, 2010), 59–84.

3. Eudora Welty, "First Love," in *Collected Stories of Eudora Welty* (Orlando:
Harvest Books, 1980), 153–68, 168. Future references will be given parenthetically.

4. I do not take up a perhaps more obvious sense in which gesture might be relevant
for the story: sign-language. (I do not, however, see clear evidence that Joel signs.) For
an account of the speechless pantomime *Enchanted Island* (a Soviet production at the
deaf Theater of Mimicry and Gesture in Moscow) that might offer a way to link the
terms in which I explore "gesture" with effects of performance, see Anastasia Kayiatos,
"Silent Plasticity: Reenchanting Soviet Stagnation," *WSQ: Women's Studies Quarterly*
40, nos. 3 and 4 (Fall/Winter 2012): 105–25. Another possibly relevant connection I do
not take up here is the hysterical symptom—and the conversion whereby "speech"
becomes legible on the body. In her fascinating essay "The Gender of Sound," Anne
Carson makes the connection to sign language, which Alexander Graham Bell
apparently found "pernicious." Carson, "The Gender of Sound," in *Glass, Irony and
God* (New York: New Directions Books, 1995), 119–42, 128–9.

5. "F comme Fidelité," *L'abécédaire de Gilles Deleuze*, with Claire Parnet,
produced and directed by Pierre-André Boutang (Editions Montparnasse [DVD],
2004; film copyright held by Sodaperanga). My transcription and translation.

6. Kevin Ohi, *Henry James and the Queerness of Style* (Minneapolis: University
of Minnesota Press, 2011).

7. For an account that invokes a similar alternation in style, see D. A. Miller, *Jane
Austen, Or the Secret of Style* (Princeton: Princeton University Press, 2003).

8. Werner Hamacher, "The Gesture in the Name: On Benjamin and Kafka," in
Premises: Essays on Philosophy and Literature from Kant to Celan, trans. Peter
Fenves (Cambridge: Harvard University Press, 1996), 329–30. Hamacher continues:
"Just as the horse Bucephalus, whose function was to carry Alexander, remains after
the warrior is gone, just as the reader is left over from the text, gesture is left over
from language, from its law. This gesture carries the mere possibility of language
and at the same time holds back its actual arrival" (330).

9. Giorgio Agamben, "Kommerell, or On Gesture," in *Potentialities: Collected Essays in Philosophy*, ed. and trans. Daniel Heller-Roazen (Stanford: Stanford University Press, 1999), 77–85, 77. Future references will be given parenthetically.

10. Agamben, "Kommerell," 78, emphasis in original. Agamben quotes from Max Kommerell, *Dichterische Welterfahrungen* (Frankfurt am Main: Klostermann, 1952), 153. Translation by Heller-Roazen.

11. As Daniel Heller-Roazen writes, "Agamben, following Kommerell, defines 'gesture' as that dimension of language that is not exhausted in any communication of meaning and that, in this way marks the point at which language appears in its mere capacity to communicate" ("Editor's Introduction: 'To Read What Was Never Written,'" in *Potentialities*, 22). Future references will be given parenthetically.

12. Giorgio Agamben, "Notes on Gesture," in *Means Without Ends: Notes on Politics*, trans. Vincenzo Binetti and Cesare Casarino (Minneapolis: University of Minnesota Press, 2000), 59. Future references will be given parenthetically. See also the further discussion of this essay in the penultimate note to the current chapter.

13. Giorgio Agamben, "The Author as Gesture," in *Profanations*, trans. Jeff Fort (New York: Zone, 2007), 61–72. Future references will be given parenthetically. For Artaud, too, gesture leads him to "pure theater" (Antonin Artaud, "On the Balinese Theater," in *The Theater and Its Double*, trans. Mary Caroline Richards [New York: Grove Press, 1958], 53–67, 53); the "animated hieroglyphs" of the Balinese theater, turning, in gesture, bodies to signs, render *"matter as revelation"* (59): "In this theater all creation comes from the stage, finds its expression and its origins alike in a secret psychic impulse which is Speech before words" (60). "One senses in the Balinese theater," he writes, "a state prior to language and which can choose its own: music, gestures, movements, words" (62).

14. Daniel Heller-Roazen, "Speaking in Tongues," *Paragraph* 25, no. 2 (2002), 92–115. Future citations will be given parenthetically.

15. Heller-Roazen, "Speaking in Tongues," 93. He cites Agamben, "Preface," to *Infancy and History: The Destruction of Experience*, trans. Liz Heron (London: Verso, 1993), 3–10.

16. See Giorgio Agamben, "The End of the Poem," in *The End of the Poem: Studies in Poetics*, trans. Daniel Heller-Roazen (Stanford: Stanford University Press, 1999), 109–15, and Heller-Roazen, "Speaking in Tongues," especially 104. I discuss both of these texts in greater detail in the introduction ("Exordium").

17. Heller-Roazen, "Speaking in Tongues," 103. The account of the *aleph* here appears, in modified form, as a beautiful chapter of Daniel Heller-Roazen's *Echolalias: On the Forgetting of Language* (New York: Zone Books, 2005).

18. Eudora Welty, *One Writer's Beginnings*, in *Eudora Welty: Stories, Essays, and Memoir* (New York: The Library of America, 1998), 847. Future references will be given parenthetically.

19. "There was a kind of dominion promised in his gentlest glance. When he first would come and throw himself down to talk and the fire would flame up and the reflections of the snowy world grew bright, even the clumsy table seemed to change

its substance and to become a part of a ceremony. He might have talked in another language, in which there was nothing but evocation" (159). (Jonathan Foltz pointed out to me that one of the striking aspects of Burr's trial is that he was not among those apprehended in any apparent workings of the plot; he was accused of seducing others to perform actions in which he was not to take part.)

20. In *The End of the Poem*, Giorgio Agamben writes of Pascoli's reflections on the relation between poetry and "dead language" (his "dictation," a term, Agamben writes, "which we take from the vocabulary of medieval poetics, but which has never ceased to be familiar to the Italian poetic tradition" and which refers "to the originary event of speech itself" [63]), the "onomatopoetics" and "phono-symbolism," the uninterpretable words that, presenting "pure phonemes," punctuate his writing. "It is therefore not truly a matter of phono-symbolism, but rather a matter of a sphere so to speak beyond or before sound, a sphere that does not *symbolize* anything as much as it simply *indicates* an intention to signify, that is, the voice in its originary purity. This is an indication that has its place neither in mere sound nor in signification but rather, we might say, in pure *grammata*, in pure letters . . ." Agamben, "Pascoli and the Thought of the Voice," in *The End of the Poem*, 62–75, 67.

21. See Cynthia Chase, "Giving a Face to a Name: De Man's Figures," *Decomposing Figures: Rhetorical Readings in the Romantic Tradition* (Baltimore: Johns Hopkins University Press, 1986), 82–112.

22. On a basic plot level, there is the further mystery of what Burr is plotting with Blennerhassett, for it would seem that he has already been caught before the story begins. Whether there is an unmarked telescoping of time, whether they are planning his defense at his upcoming trial, or whether they are plotting an escape, time seems out of sync.

23. Cavell writes: "The fullest image of absolute isolation is in Dreyer's *Joan of Arc*, when Falconetti at the stake looks up to see a flight of birds wheel over her with the sun in their wings. They, there, are free. They are waiting in their freedom, to accompany her soul. She knows it. But first there is this body to be gone through utterly." Stanley Cavell, *The World Viewed: Reflections on the Ontology of Film: Enlarged Edition* (Cambridge: Harvard University Press, 1979), 159.

24. It is possible that this is a Biblical reference: "Ask now the beasts, and they shall teach thee; and the fowls of the air, and they shall tell thee: Or speak to the earth, and it shall teach thee: and the fishes of the sea shall declare unto thee" (Job 12:7–8, Authorized King James Version). I also thought of *Paradise Lost*:

Myself I then perused and limb by limb
Surveyed and sometimes went and sometimes ran
With supple joints as lively vigor led.
But who I was, or where, or from what cause
Knew not. To speak I tried and forthwith spake:
My tongue obeyed and readily could name
Whate'er I saw. "Thou Sun," said I, "fair light,
And thou enlightened Earth so fresh and gay,

Ye hills and dales, ye rivers, woods, and plains,
And ye that live and move, fair creatures, tell,
Tell if ye saw how came I thus, how here." (VIII.267–77)
(Milton, *Paradise Lost*, ed. Gordon Teskey [New York: Norton, 2005])

I discuss this passage in greater detail in Chapter 8; Joel's awakening—to desire and to loss—recalls Adam's.

25. Later on, the figure of the raft returns, this time with Blennerhassett and his wife: In Joel's room before she begins playing the violin, "they stood looking at each other there in the firelight like creatures balancing together on a raft" (163).

26. *OED Online*, s.v. "working (*n.*)," last modified September 2020, www.oed.com/view/Entry/230236; "work (*v.*)," www.oed.com/view/Entry/230217; "momentous (*adj.*)," www.oed.com/view/Entry/121015.

27. As Joel watches a sleeping Burr, another moment evokes Joel's desire to speak and hear: "Joel thought, I could speak if I would, or I could hear. Once I did each thing . . . Still he listened. . . . and it seemed that all that would speak, in this world, was listening. Burr was silent; he demanded nothing, nothing. . . . A boy or a man could be so alone in his heart that he could not even ask a question" (165, ellipses in original).

28. If Sigi Jöttkandt's reading of the story is one of the best readings of the story I have come across, that is because (among other reasons) it is an unblushingly figurative or allegorical reading: She reads the story as an allegory of Lacanian love. Locating itself in that register, its lucid and persuasive account of Lacan also allows it to perceive unexpected aspects of Welty's text.

29. "Inaccurate replications" appears in many of Bersani's works, and in his writings with Ulysse Dutoit. See, for example, Bersani, *Thoughts and Things* (Chicago: University of Chicago Press, 2015); and Bersani and Dutoit, *The Forms of Violence: Narrative in Assyrian Art and Modern Culture* (New York: Schocken Books, 1985); *Arts of Impoverishment: Beckett, Rothko, Resnais* (Cambridge: Harvard University Press, 1993); "'One Big Soul' (*The Thin Red Line*)," in *Forms of Being: Cinema, Aesthetics, Subjectivity*" (London: BFI, 2004), 124–85.

30. Walter Flavius McCaleb, *The Aaron Burr Conspiracy: A History largely from original and hitherto unused sources* (New York: Dodd, Mead, and Company, 1903). Annette Trefzer suggests that this coincidence points to the likelihood that Welty used this book as a source for the historical details (such as they are) in the story. Annette Trefzer, "Tracing the Natchez Trace: Native Americans and National Anxieties in Eudora Welty's 'First Love,'" *Mississippi Quarterly* 55, no. 3 (2002): 419–40, 436. (Trefzer also notes that Welty departs from this source in her depiction of Burr's escape from Natchez.)

31. For Adams, Burr's plan of creating "a Western Confederacy in the Valley of the Ohio," or a "new Empire in the Mississippi Valley," united a "scheme of disunion" with a pre-existing plot to free Mexico from Spanish rule, leveraging a liberation of New Orleans (impatient of U.S. rule) to split the United States in three (the new state formed by the plot would compel Eastern and Southern states to

separate, leaving three countries). Henry Adams, *History of the United States of America During the Administrations of Thomas Jefferson* (New York: The Library of America, 1986), 576, 754, 757, 763. Future references will be given parenthetically. (In the words of Daniel Clark [in a letter of September 7, 1805, cited in General James Wilkinson's Memoirs]: "The tale is a horrid one if well told. Kentucky, Tennessee, the State of Ohio, the four territories on the Mississippi and Ohio, with part of Georgia and Carolina, are to be bribed with the plunder of the Spanish countries west of us to separate from the Union" (757). (Adams's quotation is from Wilkinson, *Memoirs of My Own Times*, vol. 2 [Philadelphia: Abraham Small, 1816], 648.) Also in this letter, Clark seems to warn Burr of someone named "Minor," who has become Burr's friend in Natchez and in whom Clark fears Burr has confided too much of their conspiracy.

32. Adams sides with Jefferson, who asserted that Burr's plans were treasonous, an effort to split the fledgling Union into three parts. (For Adams, Burr destroyed his own "insane" plot with his indiscretion [Adams, 858, 758].) McCaleb takes Burr's side, suggesting that the treasonous designs were in fact a (seemingly patriotic) ruse to enlist the support of France and England against the Spanish in Mexico.

33. Agamben ends an earlier essay on gesture—the beautiful, oblique "Notes on Gesture"—with this assertion: *"Politics is the sphere of pure means, that is, of the absolute and complete gesturality of human beings"* (59, italics in original). The essay's penultimate section moves toward this conclusion by way of Varro's distinction between "making" and "enacting," which, for Agamben, follows from that between "action" and "production" in Aristotle's *Nicomachean Ethics*. Gesture is neither: "if producing is a means in view of an end and praxis is an end without means, the gesture then breaks with the false alternative between ends and means that paralyzes morality and presents instead means that, as such, evade the orbit of mediality without becoming, for this reason, ends" (56). *"Gesture,"* he goes on to write, *"is the exhibition of a mediality: it is the process of making a means visible as such.* It allows the emergence of the being-in-a-medium of human beings and thus it opens the ethical dimension for them" (57, emphasis in original). The political dimension Agamben invokes at the end of the text would seem to emerge in a turn toward potentiality (see also the final paragraph of Daniel Heller-Roazen's introduction to *Potentialities*: [Heller-Roazen, "Editor's Introduction," 80]), which we might link to Joel's muteness. In Agamben's essay:

> if we understand the "word" as the means of communication, then to show a word does not mean to have at one's disposal a higher level (a metalanguage, itself incommunicable within the first level), starting from which we could make that word an object of communication; it means, rather, to expose the word in its own mediality, in its own being a means, without any transcendence. The gesture is, in this sense, communication of a communicability. It has precisely nothing to say because what it shows is the being-in-language of human beings as pure mediality. However, because being-in-language is not

something that could be said in sentences, the gesture is essentially always a gesture of not being able to figure something out in language; it is always a *gag* in the proper meaning of the term, indicating first of all something that could be put in your mouth to hinder speech, as well as in the sense of the actor's improvisation meant to compensate a loss of memory or an inability to speak. . . . The Wittgensteinian definition of the mystic as the appearing of what cannot be said is literally a definition of the *gag*. And every great philosophical text is the *gag* exhibiting language itself, being-in-language itself as a gigantic loss of memory, as an incurable speech defect. (Agamben, "Notes on Gesture," 58–9)

Agamben returns to the question of action (*poesis* vs. *praxis*) and then to gesture as pure mediality in *Karman: A Brief Treatise on Action, Guilt, and Gesture*, trans. Adam Kotsko (Stanford: Stanford University Press, 2018). See "Beyond Action," 60–85 (especially 82–5).

34. This lesson returns just before he witnesses Burr's gesture: "Perhaps he was saved from giving a cry by knowing it could be heard. Then the gesture one of the men made in the air transfixed him where he waited" (157).

3. *Robinson Crusoe* and the Inception of Speech

1. Jorge Luis Borges, "The Secret Miracle," in *Collected Fictions*, trans. Andrew Hurley (New York: Penguin Books, 1998), 161–2. Future references will be given parenthetically. See also Foucault's discussion of this story in an essay he wrote on Blanchot: "Language to Infinity," in *Language, Counter-memory, Practice: Selected Essays and Interviews*, ed. Donald F. Bouchard, trans. Bouchard and Sherry Simon (Ithaca, N.Y.: Cornell University Press, 1977), 53–67, 56–7.

2. Walter Pater, "Conclusion," to *The Renaissance: Studies in Art and Poetry (the 1893 text)*, ed. Donald L. Hill (Berkeley: University of California Press, 1980), 190. Pater here cites Victor Hugo (in *Han d'Islande* [1823]) in order to paraphrase a moment in Rousseau's *Confessions*. He continues by citing Milton and *Psalms*: "We have an interval, and then our place knows us no more" (see *Paradise Lost* VII.144–5: God says that Satan "into fraud / Drew many whom their place knows here no more" [*Paradise Lost*, ed. Gordon Teskey (New York: Norton, 2005)]). Or Psalms 103:15–6 (Authorized King James Version): "As for man, his days are as grass: as a flower of the field, so he flourisheth. / For the wind passeth over it, and it is gone; and the place thereof shall know it no more." Future references to *Paradise Lost* will be given parenthetically as *PL*, followed by book and line numbers.

3. Eudora Welty, "First Love," in *Collected Stories of Eudora Welty* (Orlando: Harvest Books, 1980), 153–68, 165.

4. Daniel Defoe, *Robinson Crusoe* [*The Life and Strange Surprizing Adventures of Robinson Crusoe, Of York, Mariner: Who Lived Eight and Twenty Years all alone in an un-inhabited island on the Coast of America, near the Mouth of the Great River of Oroonoque; having been cast on Shore by Shipwreck, where-in all the Men perished*

but himself. With An Account how he was at last as strangely deliver'd by Pyrates. Written by Himself. (1719)] (London: Penguin English Library, 2012), 60. Future references will be given parenthetically.

5. Moving toward the questions that interest me in *Robinson Crusoe*, I am of course drastically simplifying what is at stake in the history of character in relation to interiority. See, among many other texts, Deidre Shauna Lynch, *The Economy of Character: Novels, Market Culture, and the Business of Inner Meaning* (Chicago: University of Chicago Press, 1998), and Alex Woloch, *The One vs. the Many: Minor Characters and the Space of the Protagonist in the Novel* (Princeton: Princeton University Press, 2003).

6. Samuel Richardson, *Clarissa, Or, The History of a Young Lady*, ed. Angus Ross (New York: Penguin Classics, 1986), 382. Emphasis in original.

7. Virginia Woolf, "Robinson Crusoe," *The Common Reader: Second Series*, in *The Essays of Virginia Woolf, Vol V: 1929–32*, ed. Stuart N. Clarke (Boston: Houghton Mifflin Harcourt, 2010), 376–82, 379. Here is Ian Watt's version of this diagnosis: "Indeed, if we, perhaps unwisely, attempt to draw a general conclusion from Crusoe's life on the island, it must surely be that out of humanity's repertoire of conceivable designs for living, rational economic behavior alone is entitled to ontological status" (Ian Watt, "*Robinson Crusoe* as Myth," in *Robinson Crusoe*: A *Norton Critical Edition*, 2nd edition, ed. Michael Shinagel [New York: Norton, 1994], 288–306, 291). Future references to both texts will be given parenthetically.

8. See Barbara Johnson, "They Urn It," in *Persons and Things* (Cambridge: Harvard University Press, 2008), 61–82.

9. Watt, "*Robinson Crusoe* as Myth," 297.

10. Gilles Deleuze, "Desert Islands," in *Desert Islands and Other Texts: 1953– 1974*, ed. David Lapoujade (Los Angeles: Semiotext(e), 2004), 9–14, 12. Translation modified. (Translation of "Causes et Raisons des Îles Desertes," *L'Île Deserte: Textes et Entretiens 1953–1974*, ed. David Lapoujade [Paris: Les Éditions de Minuit, 2002], 11–17.) Future references (to the English translation) will be given parenthetically.

11. "The mythical recreation of the world from the deserted island has given way to the reconstitution of everyday bourgeois life from a reserve of capital. Everything is taken from the ship. Nothing is invented. It is all painstakingly put in place and used [*appliqué*] on the island. Time is nothing but the time necessary for capital to produce a benefit as the outcome of work. And the providential function of God is to guarantee a return [*le revenu*]. God knows his people, the hardworking honest types [*les honnêtes gens*], by their beautiful properties, and the evil doers [*les méchants*], by their poorly maintained, shabby property. Robinson's companion is not Eve, but Friday, docile towards work, happy to be a slave, and too easily disgusted by cannibalism. Any healthy reader would dream of seeing him finally eat Robinson" (Deleuze, "Desert Islands," 12).

12. Elizabeth Bishop, *The Complete Poems 1927–1979* (New York: Farrar Straus and Giroux, 1983), 162–6; William Wordsworth, "I Wandered Lonely as a Cloud," in *Norton Anthology of Poetry*, Fifth Edition, ed. Margaret Ferguson, Mary Jo Salter, and Jon Stallworthy (New York: Norton, 2005), 801. See also the discussion of

solitude and silence in invocations of Crusoe by George Oppen (and Bishop) in Oren Izenberg, "Oppen's Silence, Crusoe's Silence, and the Silence of Other Minds," in *Of Being Numerous: Poetry and the Ground of Social Life* (Princeton: Princeton University Press, 2011), 78–106.

13. Jean-Jacques Rousseau, *Emilius and Sophia: or, a New System of Education*, trans. William Kenrick (1762). Quoted in the Broadview edition of *Robinson Crusoe*: Defoe, *Robinson Crusoe*, ed. Evan R. Davis (Peterborough, Ontario, Canada: Broadview Press, 2010), 361–2. Future references to this edition will be given parenthetically (as "Broadview"). The more famous discussion is in *Émile, or On Education*. "Since we absolutely must have books, there exists one which, to my taste, provides the most felicitous treatise on natural education. This book will be the first that my Emile will read. For a long time it will alone compose his whole library, and it will always hold a distinguished place there. It will be the text for which all our discussions on the natural sciences will serve only as a commentary. It will serve as a test of the condition of our judgment during our progress; and so long as our taste is not spoiled, its reading will always please us. What, then, is this marvelous book? Is it Aristotle? Is it Pliny? Is it Buffon? No. It is *Robinson Crusoe*." Rousseau, *Emile, Or On Education*, ed. and trans. Allan Bloom (New York: Basic Books, 1979), 184.

14. The quotation is from Coleridge's marginal notes in his copy of *Robinson Crusoe*. Cited in Broadview edition, 367n11; quoted from Pat Rogers, ed., *Defoe: The Critical Heritage* (London: Routledge and Kegan Paul, 1972), 81.

15. Michael McKeon writes, in a very different context, that "Defoe gives to the notion of true history so intimate and introspective a form that it comes close to looking more like self-creation." ("Defoe and the Naturalization of Desire," in *The Origins of the English Novel: 1600–1740*, Fifteenth Anniversary Edition [Baltimore: Johns Hopkins University Press, 2002], 337.)

16. Henry James, Preface to *The Wings of the Dove*, in *Henry James: Literary Criticism, Volume Two: French Writers, Other European Writers, Prefaces to the New York Edition*, ed. Mark Wilson and Leon Edel (New York: The Library of America, 1984), 1287–303, 1288.

17. Quoted in the *Norton Critical Edition*, 274. Quoted from John Forster, *The Life of Charles Dickens* (Philadelphia, 1874), 3n135.

18. Nigel Dennis, *Jonathan Swift: A Short Character* (New York: The Macmillan Company, 1965), 125.

19. The rebellious angels, overcome in battle, are said to be "astonished": "They, astonished, all resistance lost, / All courage; down their idle weapons dropt" (*PL* VI.838–9)—anticipating lines that are, to my mind, among the most beautiful in the poem, when Adam encounters Eve just after she has eaten the apple, and drops the garland he has been weaving for her: "On the other side Adam, soon as he heard / The fatal trespass done by Eve, amazed, / Astonied stood and blank, while horror chill / Ran through his veins, and all his joints relaxed; / From his slack hand the garland wreathed for Eve / Down dropt, and all the faded roses shed: / Speechless he stood and pale, till thus at length / First to himself he inward silence broke"

(*PL* IX.888–95). Teskey notes the allusion to Book I of the *Aeneid*, when Aeneas faces the storm stirred by Aeolus: "Immediately Aenesas's limbs were dissolved with cold" (*Extemplo Aeneae solvuntur frigora membra*) [Aeneid, I, 92; Teskey, *Paradise Lost*, 221, note.] "'Astonishment,'" Barbara Johnson writes, "which I first assumed had some 'stony' etymology, comes from 'thunder'—to be astonished is to be thunderstruck" (Barbara E. Johnson, *Persons and Things* [Cambridge: Harvard University Press, 2010], 38–9). I had suspected this from reading Milton (after pursuing the same initial intuition as Johnson) and verified it from a source (possibly the same one as Johnson's, though she does not give a citation) that I can no longer find. The word, in any event, seems to come from a compound of *ex-* (out) and *-tonare* (to thunder). *Astonied*, which the *OED* suggests "various writers have apparently fancied" to be a derivative of "stony," is now archaic, and seems to be a version of "astonished" ("astonied [*adj.*]," *OED Online*, last modified September 2020, www.oed.com/view/Entry/12165).

20. Hugh Kenner, *The Counterfeiters: An Historical Comedy* (Baltimore: Johns Hopkins University Press, 1985 [reprint of 1968 edition by Indiana University Press]), 82. Whether the footprint is literally Friday's perhaps doesn't matter; structurally, it is, as it is that of the second man.

Kenner puts this in different, but related terms—the implicit self-reflexivity of forgery in relation to the emergence of the novel (and thus of the quandary that follows if one begins to think of *Robinson Crusoe* as a "forged" life): "Crusoe also saw a footprint, but could not usefully assume that it was forged, since to postulate a forger is still to postulate a second man. The reader is meant to respond to Crusoe's book exactly as Crusoe responded to Friday's footprint. He is to assume that the system of reality accessible to him contains one more man than he had previously surmised" (82).

21. J. M. Coetzee, *Foe* (London: Penguin Books, 1986), 141. Future references will be given parenthetically.

22. Jean-Claude Milner, "Être seul," in *L'universel en éclats: Court traite politique 3* (Paris: Éditions Verdier, 2014), 131–52. All translations from this text are mine. Future references will be given parenthetically.

23. Maurice Blanchot, "The Death of the Last Writer," in *The Book to Come*, trans. Charlotte Mandell (Stanford: Stanford University Press, 2003), 218–23.

24. For Milner's understanding of the consequences of the speaking subject's being turned to a thing, see *La Politique des Choses* (Paris: Verdier, 2011).

25. See, perhaps, the comments both of Gustave Flaubert ("Madame Bovary, c'est moi"—Madame Bovary is me) and Arthur Rimbaud ("je est un autre"—I is another). The remark from Rimbaud appears in a letter of May 13, 1871 (to Georges Izambard); it seems that Flaubert's comment might be apocryphal.

4. The Clock Finger at Nought: *Daniel Deronda* and the Positing of Perspective

1. George Eliot, *Daniel Deronda*, ed. Graham Handley (Oxford: Clarendon Press of Oxford University Press, 1984), 3. Future references will be given parenthetically.

There is also an epigraph or "motto" for the entire book, which appeared in the eight-volume edition of 1876 but was omitted in the corrected single-volume edition of 1877. Most modern editions appear to print the initial epigraph. Graham Handley explains his decision to follow the text of the 1876 edition (instead of editions Eliot revised in 1877 and 1878) in his introduction to the Clarendon Press edition.

2. For a more specific and informed account of the "science" at issue in George Eliot (and in this passage), see Sally Shuttleworth, *George Eliot and Nineteenth-Century Science: The Make-Believe of a Beginning* (Cambridge: Cambridge University Press, 1984).

3. Andy Donnelly taught me the bodily basis of the word *fathom*.

4. For an articulation of a related problem in nineteenth-century thought, see Christopher Herbert, *Culture and Anomie: Ethnographic Imagination in the Nineteenth Century* (Chicago: University of Chicago Press, 1991).

5. On *Middlemarch* and the difficulty of knowing where significance stops, see Andrew Miller, "*Middlemarch*: January in Lowick," in *A Companion to George Eliot*, ed. Harry Shaw and Amanda Anderson (London: Wiley-Blackwell, 2013), 153–65. "Wagers on," and attempts to secure a foundation, or a grounding for knowledge; there would, of course, be varying ideas of whether the novel succeeds in this project, and, if it does, whether success is desirable. Some of the best readings of the novel—for example, by Cynthia Chase, Irene Tucker, David Kurnick, Neil Hertz, and Amanda Anderson—might be said, in their very different idioms and very different arguments, to highlight ways that the text is (often laudably) unable to move seamlessly from the particular, localized view to a globalizing perspective—even if that is, in some sense, an ambition of Eliot's "sympathy."

6. From the *OED*: Greek ἐπιγραφή inscription, < ἐπιγράφειν to write upon, < ἐπί upon + γράφειν to write. In French *épigraphe*. *OED Online*, "Epigraph (*n.*)," last modified September 2020, www.oed.com/view/Entry/63381.

7. Ellis Hanson pointed out to me that Eliot's use of epigraphs derives from Walter Scott and Ann Radcliffe. There is no doubt a story to be told about the novel genre at this historical moment—its claiming of authority, its relation to history, and so on. Something of this very compelling project is being undertaken by Amelia Hall, currently a PhD student at Cornell. See Amelia Hall, "Epic-graphic Proportions in George Eliot's *Middlemarch*," forthcoming in *SEL: Studies in English Literature 1500–1900* 60, no. 4 (2020).

8. On form in George Eliot, see David Kurnick's consideration of Eliot's "Notes on Form in Art" at the beginning of his chapter on Eliot in *Empty Houses: Theatrical Failure and the Novel* (Princeton: Princeton University Press, 2011), 67–8. Future references will be given parenthetically. I do not have any particular axe to grind in relation to recent polemical debates about form. Jonathan Kramnick and Anahid Nersessian make the liberating suggestion that we do not, after all, have to agree on a meaning for the term *form*, that, as in any viable discipline, this central term can have a range of meanings that are context-specific: "We might thus say

that a literary critic who uses the word form is already in possession of formal concepts and therefore of a working concept of form itself. . . . Form, like cause— perhaps like any useful and compelling term—is not a word without content but a notion bound pragmatically to its instances" (661). For them, the range of meanings of the term point to the health of the discipline (rather than its frequently announced state of crisis): "our exploration of form leads us to conclude that the inconsistency with which the term is used gives criticism a solid justification for remaining the way it is . . . The record inspires confidence, insofar as it has tacitly allowed a methodological and discursive pluralism to count as a testament to rigor, much as it does for other fields and forms of knowledge" (668–9). Kramnick and Nersessian, "Form and Explanation," *Critical Inquiry* 43 (Spring 2017): 650–69. For an influential recent account of form, see Caroline Levine, *Forms: Whole, Rhythm, Hierarchy, Network* (Princeton: Princeton University Press, 2014).

9. Epigraphs are also in some sense ornamental; among many other things that they do, they point—to themselves (as passages in another text, as epigraphs) and to elements in the text that follows them, saying "attend to this." For a beautiful consideration of some of the complex ways that the concept of the ornamental might shift our sense of the function and operation of poetic language (within a different literary tradition), see Theo Davis, *Ornamental Aesthetics: The Poetry of Attending in Thoreau, Dickinson, and Whitman* (Oxford: Oxford University Press, 2016).

10. Gérard Genette, *Paratexts: Thresholds of Interpretation*, trans. Richard Macksey (Cambridge: Cambridge University Press, 1997).

11. Alex Woloch makes a related observation in "*Daniel Deronda*: Late Form, or After *Middlemarch*," in A *Companion to George Eliot*, ed. Harry Shaw and Amanda Anderson, (London: Wiley-Blackwell, 2013), 166–77: "One fairly discrete example of this disruptive effect is the over-and-under principle through which Eliot weaves many of her seventy chapter epigraphs so that what appears in one context as a putatively stabilizing frame for a section of the narrative gets submerged, at another point, into the narrative proper. Not only are we prompted to 'relate' the varied epigraphs to one another—as these allusions (real or invented) trigger abundant resonances and cross-currents between themselves—we're also often confronted with frames that reappear within the composition itself, or alternatively, tropes and points of reference within the story that suddenly leap out as epigraphs (and thus mediating devices)" (169–70). Future references to Woloch's essay will be given parenthetically.

12. I owe this observation about Goethe to someone else, but I no longer remember where I read it.

13. The passage in Horace to which Eliot refers is itself far less simple than its appearance as a generalized dictum would make one think: "Not smoke after flame does he plan to give, but after smoke the light, that then he may set forth striking and wondrous tales— . . . Nor does he begin Diomede's return from the death of Meleager, or the war of Troy from the twin eggs. Ever he hastens to the issue, and

hurries his hearer into the story's midst, as if already known, and what he fears he cannot make attractive with his touch he abandons; and so skillfully does he invent, so closely does he blend facts and fiction, that the middle is not discordant with the beginning, nor the end with the middle." Horace, *Ars Poetica*, in *Satires. Epistles. The Art of Poetry*, trans. H. Rushton Fairclough, Loeb Classical Library 194 (Cambridge: Harvard University Press, 1926), 462. Future references given parenthetically. (Non fumum ex fulgore, sed ex fumo dare lucem / cogitat, ut speciosa dehinc miracula promat, / [. . .] / nec reditum Diomedis ab interitu Meleagri, / nec gemino bellum Troianum orditur ab ovo; / semper ad euentum festinat et in medias res / non secus ac notas auditorem rapit, et quae / desperat tractata nitescere posse, relinquit, / atque ita mentitur, sic veris falsa remiscet, / primo ne medium, medio ne discrepet imum. [463]) To state only what is most obvious, the eschewing of causal sequence ("not smoke after flame" [*Non fumum ex fulgore*]) shifts its ground, and "fire" seems to become figural—so that sequence can entail another sort of logic: "but after smoke the light" (*sed ex fumo dare lucem / cogitat*). Fire as cause is displaced and becomes the illumination effected by the striking and wondrous tale. That excitement seems a function, again, of a positing: of the "as if already known." The importance of the line from Horace is well-known. Genette writes of the "anachrony" at the beginning of the *Iliad*: "We know that his beginning *in medias res*, followed by an expository return to an earlier time, will become one of the formal topoi of the epic, and we also know how faithfully the style of novelistic narration follows in this respect the style of its remote ancestor, even in the heart of the 'realistic' nineteenth century." Gérard Genette, *Narrative Discourse: An Essay in Method*, trans. Jane E. Lewin (Ithaca: Cornell University Press, 1980), 36.

14. For an account immersed in the details of nineteenth-century astronomy, see Anna Henchman, "George Eliot and the Sweep of the Senses," in *The Starry Sky Within: Astronomy and the Reach of the Mind in Victorian Fiction* (Oxford: Oxford University Press, 2014), 158–95. Henchman is particularly interested in the way that Eliot's narrative makes readers "viscerally experience radical shifts in position, scale, and texture"; juxtapositions of scale and the jolting of one out of an immersion in particular experience are linked, for her, to the text's highlighting of the ways that "scientists and novelists alike observe the world from an embodied perspective" (164). On the epigraph, see 162–4.

15. The greatest reading of the narrative structure of the text is perhaps that of Cynthia Chase, "The Decomposition of the Elephants: Double-Reading *Daniel Deronda*," in *Decomposing Figures: Rhetorical Readings in the Romantic Tradition* (Baltimore: Johns Hopkins University Press, 1986), 157–74. In another passage, Eliot herself compares the displacement of egotism by a more capacious view of the world to the transition to a heliocentric solar system.

16. David Kurnick notes the retrospective attribution of this paragraph to Daniel and suggests that, initially, it seems to enact the mechanism of interiorization (displayed both in the logic of the questions—there is no doubt about Gwendolen's

outside, he asserts; the question, rather, is "was she beautiful *inside?*" [Kurnick, *Empty Houses*, 95]—and in the constitution of the free indirect style) that, in most accounts of Eliot (and the novel genre more generally), marks a turn away from theatrical forms and collectivities to psychological interiority. Yet here "the interiorizing agenda encounters static": The delay in the attribution of these observations introduces a "stutter into the machinery of the interiorizing imagination" (95). Kurnick then emphasizes how tenuous is the "psychological coherence" achieved in the opening pages, as the perspective ravels out into the gathered collectivity of the gambling hall.

17. Andrew H. Miller, *The Burdens of Perfection: On Ethics and Reading in Nineteenth-Century British Literature* (Ithaca, N.Y.: Cornell University Press, 2010), 91.

18. On the (figuring and disfiguring) "pulse" of chance in the novel, see Neil Hertz, *George Eliot's Pulse* (Stanford: Stanford University Press, 2003).

19. Woloch, 171. He continues: "The sealed quality of this circuit simply literalizes the way in which larger units of narrative in *Daniel Deronda*—building blocks for the inter-connected totality toward which Eliot aspires—so often can stand out or turn in on themselves, creating heightened aesthetic effects that simultaneously put pressure on the dynamic unfolding of the narrative as a whole."

20. For a detailed account of the movement through the room in this opening, see Kurnick, *Empty Houses*, 94–6.

21. Tucker, "Writing a Place for History: *Daniel Deronda* and the Fictions of Belief," in *A Probable State: The Novel, the Contract, and the Jews* (Chicago: University of Chicago Press, 2000), 33–121, 83. Future references will be given parenthetically. For Tucker, the temporal scrambling is important, among other reasons, because of the model of reading that the novel articulates—a model not unrelated to the question of beginning. In an argument too intricate to reproduce here, Tucker traces the book's different (and often disjunctive) temporalities: the shuffling of narrative chronology in the *récit* mirrors such other temporalities in different registers of the text, such as that of perception, realization, identity, history, and the phenomenology of reading. With the end of *Daniel Deronda*, Tucker writes, "Eliot invites her readers to imagine a world that she has not yet *written*. In concluding her novel so many times that effectively it fails to conclude at all, Eliot redefines what it means to 'read' a novel. . . . As *Daniel Deronda* ends we are invited to imagine a place that does not yet exist and about which no words, no common language, have been written. Reading is thus converted from the imaginative acts that turn words on a page into a visible world as they are understood to the imagining of alternative worlds that the reader is impelled to produce as a *consequence* of having read" (119–20). For Tucker, this mode of reading implicitly critiques the notion of a "common culture" that is there to be found: "Only by representing a literary culture in an unevenly overlapping, embattled, and finally *changing* relation to forms of commonness organized around language, land, and the authority of the state does Eliot invest the vision of textual culture offered by *Daniel Deronda* with the potential to make social relations anew" (121).

22. I do not mean to imply that Deronda's and Gwendolen's modes of apprehending the world are the same. Their difference is, of course, a central element of the text. On their different modes of reading (and Gwendolen's in contrast to Grandcourt's), see Tucker, 84.

23. Rather than "dramatic," Kurnick might say her "novelistic" body. In his witty rendering, "Gwendolen's humiliating failure to succeed as an actress and singer is a central concern of the novel, which brutally tracks her transformation from a 'Vandyke duchess' (558) into a penitent widow who literally learns to appreciate 'kindness, even from a dog, as a gift above expectation' (795). But this trajectory is only a narrative elaboration of a defeat Gwendolen suffers by virtue of her existence as a novelistic heroine. Her awakening to Daniel's moral teaching might simply be described as the aspiring actress's realization that she has wandered into the world of the novel" (Kurnick, *Empty Houses*, 96; he cites the reprint of the 1876 edition: [London: Penguin, 1995]).

24. David Kurnick reminded me of the crucial discussion of this boy in Joseph Litvak, *Caught in the Act*. Litvak in turn reminds us that Catherine Gallagher has drawn our attention to the resemblance between this little boy and Daniel as a boy, as we later learn of him (Gallagher, "George Eliot and *Daniel Deronda*: The Prostitute and the Jewish Question," in *Sex, Politics, and Science in the Nineteenth-Century Novel: Selected Papers from The English Institute, 1983–84*, ed. Ruth Bernard Yeazell [Baltimore and London: Johns Hopkins University Press, 1986], 39–62, 53). Litvak writes: "For the image of the 'melancholy little boy' is in some sense a defensive projection of a certain 'exhibitionist' potential that, as we will learn, Daniel has good reason to fear in himself." (Litvak, "Poetry and Theatricality in *Daniel Deronda*," in *Caught in the Act: Theatricality in the Nineteenth-Century English Novel* (Berkeley: University of California Press, 1992), 147–94.

25. My sense of this painting (and my reason for thinking of it here) is shaped by Foucault's reading of it. Michel Foucault, "Las Meninas," in *The Order of Things: An Archeology of the Human Sciences*, trans. Alan Sheridan (New York: Routledge, 1991), 3–16. See also Anne Carson, "Symbolon," in *Eros the Bittersweet* (Normal, Ill.: Dalkey Archive Press, 1998), 70–6.

5. Proto-Reading and the Positing of Character in *Our Mutual Friend*

1. Jesse Oak Taylor, "Realism After Nature: Reading the Greenhouse Effect in *Bleak House*," in *The Sky of Our Manufacture: The London Fog in British Fiction from Dickens to Woolf* (Charlottesville: University of Virginia Press, 2016), 21–43.

2. Charles Dickens, *Bleak House*, ed. Stephen Gill (Oxford: Oxford University Press, 1998), 11.

3. See Kevin Ohi, "Autobiography and *David Copperfield*'s Temporalities of Loss," *Victorian Literature and Culture* 33 (2005): 435–49.

4. Charles Dickens, *David Copperfield*, ed. Nina Burgis (Oxford: Oxford University Press, 1983), 1.

5. Charles Dickens, *Great Expectations* (New York: Vintage Classics, 2012), 3. Future references will be given parenthetically.

6. Alex Woloch notes that the novel might be said to emerge from a minor character in *Great Expectations*, the "Jack" whom Pip encounters during the attempt to secure Magwitch's escape: "Suddenly we can see the next triple-decker novel emerging out of this most peripheral character in *Great Expectations.*" Woloch, *The One vs. the Many: Minor Characters and the Space of the Protagonist in the Novel* (Princeton: Princeton University Press, 2003), 236. Future references will be given parenthetically.

7. Charles Dickens, *Our Mutual Friend*, ed. Adrian Poole (New York: Penguin, 1997), 13. Future references will be given parenthetically.

8. This passage provides Robyn Warhol an instance of what she calls "disnarration"—(where a "narrator tells something that did not happen, in place of saying what did" [231]). "'What Might Have Been Is Not What Is': Dickens's Narrative Refusals," in *Counterfactual Thinking—Counterfactual Writing*, ed. Dorothee Birke, Michael Butter, and Tilmann Köppe (Berlin: Walter de Gruyter GmbH & Co, 2011), 227–39. See 233–4.

9. On indefinite (and "infinite") names formed by negations, see Daniel Heller-Roazen, *No One's Ways: An Essay on Infinite Naming* (New York: Zone Books, 2017). On negation's central place in the establishing of realism (where the reality effect comes from a subtraction rather than an addition), see Roland Barthes, *S/Z: An Essay*, trans. Richard Miller (New York: Hill and Wang, 1974).

10. Rosemarie Bodenheimer, "Dickens and the Identical Man: *Our Mutual Friend* Doubled," *Dickens Studies Annual* 31 (2002): 159–74, 168. Future references will be given parenthetically.

11. James Phelan, "The Beginning of *Beloved*: A Rhetorical Approach," in Brian Richardson, ed., *Narrative Beginnings: Theories and Practices* (Lincoln: University of Nebraska Press, 2008), 195–212, 195.

12. Ann Banfield, "No-narrator theory," *Routledge Encyclopedia of Rhetorical Theory*, ed. David Herman, Manfred Jahn, and Marie-Laure Ryan (New York and London: Routledge, 2005), 396–7. See also Ann Banfield, *Unspeakable Sentences* (London: Routledge and Keegan Paul, 1982), and Ann Banfield, *Describing the Unobserved and Other Essays: Unspeakable Sentences after Unspeakable Sentences*, ed. Sylvie Patron (Newcastle upon Tyne, UK: Cambridge Scholars Publishing, 2019).

13. Andrew H. Miller, *The Burdens of Perfection: On Ethics and Reading in Nineteenth-Century British Literature* (Ithaca, N.Y.: Cornell University Press, 2008), 92–119. He invokes "what we now only rarely call casuistry, the practical reasoning that considers whether a particular act fits within an ethical paradigm and allows each—act and paradigm—to modify the other" (94).

14. In Lizzie's first oblique confession of love for Eugene Wrayburn, she invokes a generic love story of a higher class and then seeks, in a moment of self-forgetting, to be put in it: "Her heart—is given him, with all its love and truth. She would joyfully

die with him, or, better than that, die for him. She knows he has failings, but she thinks they have grown up through his being like one cast away, for the want of something to trust in, and care for, and think well of. And she says, that lady rich and beautiful that I can never come near, 'Only put me in that empty place, only try how little I mind myself, only prove what a world of things I will do and bear for you, and I hope that you might even come to be much better than you are, through me who am so much worse, and hardly worth the thinking of beside you'" (344). Whatever one might say about the class and gender determinants of this speech—and about why this particular form of desire is valorized over, for example, Bradley Headstone's—also notable is the way (typical in the novel) that a character's internal state is not only described but seemingly experienced as an impersonal form or convention into which the character is then placed: only put me in that empty place. (Wrayburn's is perhaps the most extreme form of this—his utter detachment from himself is hyperbolized as a near-complete form of self-alienation.) Harmon-Rokesmith's soliloquy returns that structure to the most primordial instance not just of affect but of its conditions of possibility. If, famously, *Our Mutual Friend* has a "Postscript in lieu of a preface," that structure—the structure that I am trying here to show—also involves a substitution of places (or *lieux*).

15. Gilles Deleuze, "Immanence: A Life," in *Pure Immanence: Essays on a Life,* trans. Anne Boyman (New York: Zone Books, 2001), 25–34. See also Garrett Stewart, "Lived Death: Dickens's Rogue Glyphs," in *Dickens's Style,* ed. Daniel Tyler (Cambridge: Cambridge University Press, 2013), 231–52. The moment with Riderhood also recalls the famous episode in Rousseau's fifth reverie, where the wandering philosopher, knocked down and badly injured by a Great Dane, comes to—and then only later comes back to himself: "je ne me sentais que par là. Je naissais dans cet instant à la vie, et il me semblait que je remplissais de ma légère existence tous les objets que j'apercevais" (Jean-Jacques Rousseau, *Les Rêveries du Promeneur Solitaire,* ed. S. de Sacy [Paris: Éditions Gallimard, 1972], 61). (On this episode, see Daniel Heller-Roazen, "To Myself; or, The Great Dane," in *The Inner Touch: Archeology of a Sensation* [New York: Zone Books, 2007], 211–18; and Neil Hertz, *George Eliot's Pulse* [Stanford: Stanford University Press, 2003], 45–9.)

16. Bodenheimer remarks: "The substitution of housekeeping for sexuality, as well as the expression of acceptable sexuality through housekeeping, is a peculiarity of Dickens's imagination whose origins can only be guessed at." Rosemarie Bodenheimer, *Knowing Dickens* (Ithaca, N.Y.: Cornell University Press, 2007), 141.

17. "Love at first sight is a trite expression quite sufficiently discussed; enough that in certain smouldering natures like this man's, that passion leaps into a blaze, and makes such head as fire does in a rage of wind, when other passions, but for its mastery, could be held in chains. As a multitude of weak, imitative natures are always lying by, ready to go mad upon the next wrong idea that may be broached—in these times, generally some form of tribute to Somebody for something that never was done, or, if ever done, that was done by Somebody Else—so these less ordinary natures may lie by for years, ready on the touch of an instant to burst into flame"

(*Our Mutual Friend*, 336). Headstone is, of course, tormented by what it means to be "somebody." On Bradley Headstone, see Frances Ferguson, "Envy Rising," *ELH* 69, no. 4 (2002): 889–905.

18. Chapter IX of Book IV is called "Two Places Vacated."

19. When Wrayburn, just before this, knows he has defeated Lizzie's reserve, it, too, is presented as a confrontation of faces: "He looked full at her handsome face, and in his own handsome face there was a light of blended admiration, anger, and reproach, which she—who loved him so in secret whose heart had long been so full, and he the cause of its overflowing—drooped before. She tried hard to retain her firmness, but he saw it melting away under his eyes. In the moment of its dissolution, and of his first full knowledge of his influence upon her, she dropped, and he caught her on his arm" (677).

20. Paul de Man, "Autobiography as De-Facement," in *The Rhetoric of Romanticism* (New York: Columbia University Press, 1984), 67–82; Cynthia Chase, "Giving a Face to a Name: De Man's Figures," in *Decomposing Figures: Rhetorical Readings in the Romantic Tradition* (Baltimore: Johns Hopkins University Press, 1986), 82–112; Neil Hertz, "Lurid Figures," in *The Ends of Rhetoric: History, Theory, Practice*, ed. John Bender and David E. Wellbery (Stanford: Stanford University Press, 1990), 100–124; Hertz, "More Lurid Figures," *Diacritics: A Review of Contemporary Criticism* 20, no. 3 (1990): 2–27; Kevin Ohi, "The Beast's Storied End," in *Dead Letters Sent: Queer Literary Transmission* (Minneapolis: University of Minnesota Press, 2015), 156–74. Future references to Chase's essay will be given parenthetically.

21. "I must be sore disfigured. Are you afraid to kiss me?" asks Betty Higden, as, close to death, she sees Lizzie hovering over her (506). (In this scene, too, we experience her death from both inside and out—both hear Betty's thoughts and speech and experience her bafflement as Lizzie repeatedly fails to understand her. Thus we also experience significant signs, as if from the "inside," that *fail* to become meaningful.)

22. Some instances of this we have already seen. I would include the descriptions of Boffin's miserliness: "A kind of illegibility, though a different kind, stole over Mr Boffin's face. Its old simplicity of expression got masked by a certain craftiness that assimilated even his good-humour to itself. His very smile was cunning, as if he had been studying smiles among the portraits of his misers" (467). In retrospect, it appears that the craftiness here is not his scheming to make money so much as his scheming to appear scheming. Making feigning and hapless transparency curiously indistinct, and thus making his craft but another mode of his sincerity, Dickens creates in Boffin here the perplexity of an instance that needs to be read twice—or read in light of the novel's end. For the first-time reader is no less duped, I think, than Bella is.

23. Wrayburn points to this in his characteristically wry and distanced way: "(By-the-by, that very word, Reading, in its critical use, always charms me. An actress's Reading of a chambermaid, a dancer's Reading of a hornpipe, a singer's Reading of a song, a marine painter's Reading of the sea, the kettle-drum's Reading of an instrumental passage, are phrases ever youthful and delightful)" (532).

6. Ovid and Orpheus

1. Thanks to James Uden—whom I will have more than one occasion to thank in the course of this chapter—for pointing me to the textual controversy. Any subsequent errors are, of course, my own.

2. Ovid, *Metamorphoses: Books 1–8*, ed. Jeffrey Henderson, third edition (Cambridge: Harvard University Press, 1977), 2. The Loeb translation of these lines (by Frank Justus Miller, revised by G. P. Goold) reads: "My mind is bent to tell of bodies changed into new forms. Ye gods, for you yourselves have wrought the changes, breathe on these my undertakings, and bring down my song in unbroken strains from the world's very beginning even unto the present time" (3).

3. *The Metamorphoses of Ovid*, trans. Allen Mandelbaum (San Diego: A Harvest Book, 1993), 3. Hereafter, unless otherwise noted, all citations of the poem refer by page number to this translation.

4. *Ovid's Metamorphoses: The Arthur Golding Translation of 1567*, ed. John Frederick Nims (Philadelphia: Paul Dry Books, 2000), 3.

5. Giles, The Late Rev Dr., *The Metamorphoses of Ovid*, Books I–IV, Construed Literally and Word for Word (London and Dublin: Cornish and Sons, n.d.), 5. Downloaded from https://www.textkit.com/learn/ID/154/author_id/71/. It is no doubt clear that Giles's source text is different than the Loeb Latin text I have cited. The text doesn't provide information on its Latin source.

6. P. Lejay, *Morceaux choisis des Métamorphoses d'Ovide* (Paris, 1894); cited in David Kovacs, "Ovid, Metamorphoses 1.2," *The Classical Quarterly* 37, no. 2 (1987): 458–65, 458. Kovacs had to rely on the 4th edition (Paris, 1911), where the discussion of the relevant line is on page 67. Future references will be given parenthetically.

7. E. J. Kenney, "Ovidius Prooemians," *Cambridge Classical Journal* 22 (1976): 46–53. Future references will be given parenthetically.

8. According to William Anderson, the word (in the plural) "became a familiar word for poetic 'beginnings' after Vergil." *Ovid's* Metamorphoses, Books 1–5, ed. with introduction and commentary by William S. Anderson (Norman: University of Oklahoma Press, 1997), 150. Future references will be given parenthetically. See Virgil's First Georgic, line 40, *The Georgics of Virgil: Bilingual Edition*, trans. David Ferry (New York: Farrar, Straus and Giroux, 2005), 6.

9. See Kovacs for further arguments against "illas."

10. Kenney, "Ovidius Prooemians," 46. He cites *P. Ovidi Nasonis Metamorphoseon*, ed. A. G. Lee, Liber I (1953) (Reprint: Cambridge University Press, 1968). (Kenney does not supply a reference for Housman.)

11. R. J. Tarrant points out that the reading of Lejay and Kenney is not a "modern conjecture" but a "medieval variant," attested in two manuscripts from the twelfth or thirteenth centuries (351). R. J. Tarrant, "Review Article: Editing Ovid's Metamorphoses: Problems and Possibilities," *Classical Philology* 77, no. 4 (October 1982): 342–60. The review is of Anderson's edition of the text. Future references will be given parenthetically.

12. William S. Anderson, "Form Changed; Ovid's Metamorphoses," in *Roman Epic*, ed. A. J. Boyle (London and New York: Routledge, 1993), 108–24, 109. Future references will be given parenthetically.

13. In Anderson's more extended description of the drama of this moment: "The parenthesis completes the hexameter. For a first-time audience of the poem, however, this would be a unique moment. Never before had they experienced a poem by Ovid which consisted of continuous hexameters: he was the greatest master of the elegiac metre alive in Rome, and he had been unchallenged for fifteen or twenty years, since Propertius stopped writing verse. What Ovid in fact made a caesura would normally, in his elegiac couplets, have functioned as the break between the halves of the *pentameter*. Thus, as the admiring audience start to sit back to another elegant Ovidian performance in elegiacs, they suddenly hear a metrical conclusion to the line, emphasized by the many long syllables of the spondees, which transforms their expectations and the poetic form from elegiacs into hexameters. And that meant that, incredibly or at least paradoxically, the world's most successful elegiac poet was suddenly an epic poet. Could he, with the help of the gods, really carry through this transformation, no matter what it demanded of him?" (Anderson, "Form Changed," 109). Peter E. Knox makes a similar point: "the parenthesis fills the second half of the second hexameter, precisely the point where the reader of a new work by Rome's most celebrated elegist will first notice that this is not an elegiac couplet. At the end of the line most manuscripts and editors read *illas*, which spoils the point. The case for reading *illa*, a reference to Ovid's poetic endeavors, has been made elsewhere, and it ought now to be accepted into the text." Knox, *Ovid's "Metamorphoses" and the Traditions of Augustan Poetry* (Cambridge: Cambridge Philological Society [Cambridge University Press], 1986), 9.

14. The spirit, mind, or soul of *animus* may or may not have a possessive pronoun. It isn't explicitly given in the text, but Latin sometimes leaves such pronouns implicit.

15. *Metamorphoses*, Books 1–5, ed. Anderson, 150.

16. James O'Hara notes Ovid's inconsistencies in his accounts of origins: "We have seen cases in which Ovid presents more than one explanation for something, most notably the creation of man, and most oddly the two possible reasons for why Ino and her child jumped off a cliff and became sea deities. In terms of both style and content, these passages resemble the multiple explanations of cultural practices and especially natural phenomena common in aetiological and didactic poetry" [123].) James O'Hara, "Inconsistency and Authority in Ovid's *Metamorphoses*," in *Inconsistency in Roman Epic: Studies in Catullus, Lucretius, Vergil, Ovid and Lucan* (Cambridge: Cambridge University Press, 2006), 104–30. Future references will be given parenthetically.

17. I am indebted to Sean Keilen for leading me to think about the beginning of the poem.

18. Deleuze, "Causes et Raisons des îles desertes," in *L'île deserte et autres textes: textes et entretiens 1953–1974*, ed. David Lapoujade (Paris: Les éditions de Minuit, 2002), 11–17, 16–17.

19. "Perpetuum . . . carmen" [continuous song or poem] could also mean, simply, that the poem is an epic; Ovid's playful claim, then, is that he will write an epic about changing forms. Cf. *Metamorphoses*, Books 1–5, ed. Anderson, 151.

20. Thanks to Sean Keilen for pointing me to this passage, and for suggesting that I think about it in the context of the poem's repeated beginnings.

21. Rilke's *Malte Laurids Brigge* puts forward Byblis as an ideal of the "woman in love"—the unrequited woman. See Rainer Maria Rilke, *The Notebooks of Malte Laurids Brigge*, trans. Michael Hulse (New York: Penguin, 2009), 151.

22. For an account of "inconsistency" in Ovid's narrative of creation (its orderly, "philosophical" account, for example, undone by "passion"), see O'Hara, "Inconsistency and Authority in Ovid's *Metamorphoses*," esp. 108–14. "Skepticism or doubt is encouraged," he writes, "particularly when aetiology incorporates irreconcilable mythological variants, so that multiple, mutually exclusive explanations are offered for the same phenomenon" (124). O'Hara also notes of the proem that Ovid begins by claiming his own power to inspire his work (*"In nova fert animus . . ."*) before, in the parenthesis in line 2, he then appears to credit the (unnamed) gods. For an account of Ovid's relation to aetiological poetry, see K. Sara Myers, *Ovid's Causes: Cosmogony and Aetiology in the "Metamorphoses"* (Ann Arbor: University of Michigan Press, 1994).

23. Frederick Ahl, *Metaformations: Soundplay and Wordplay in Ovid and Other Classical Poets* (Ithaca, N.Y.: Cornell University Press, 1985), 104. Future references will be given parenthetically. On some of the other fascinating wordplays Ahl finds in this episode, see pages 104–23.

24. For a beautiful account of Io and the birth of writing, see Daniel Heller-Roazen, "The Writing Cow," in *Echolalias: On the Forgetting of Language* (New York: Zone Books, 2005), 121–7. See also Ahl, 144–66.

25. The "central myth of Etruscan prophecy," the wise child Tages springs from the freshly plowed earth and reveals the rules of *Etrusca disciplina*; the story is also cited in Cicero (*De div* 2:23), in Johannes Lydus (sixth century) *De ostentis* 2.6 B, and in Verrius Flaccus (as epitomized by Festus (second century), in *De significatu verborum*, 359:14. These sources are given in Nancy Thomson de Grummond, "Prophets and Priests," in *The Religion of the Etruscans*, ed. Nancy Thomson de Grummond and Erika Simon (Austin: University of Texas Press, 2006), 27 (on Tages, see 27–30). In Cicero and Lydus, after the plowman cuts the furrow, the child emerges from the ground and begins singing.

26. For a beautiful, speculative novelistic account of Ovid's own confrontation with forms of inception in the exile that closed his life, see David Malouf, *An Imaginary Life* (New York: Vintage International, 1996) (originally published in 1978).

27. Thomas K. Hubbard, ed., *Homosexuality in Greece and Rome: A Sourcebook of Basic Documents* (Berkeley: University of California Press, 2003), 269, 287–88. Future references will be given parenthetically.

28. For other general overviews of the history of the Orpheus myth, see George Segal, *Orpheus: The Myth of the Poet* (Baltimore: Johns Hopkins University Press, 1989) and John Warden, ed., *Orpheus: The Metamorphosis of a Myth* (Toronto: University of Toronto Press, 1982). On the myth in twentieth-century art, see Judith E. Bernstock, *Under the Spell of Orpheus: The Persistence of a Myth in Twentieth-Century Art* (Carbondale: Southern Illinois Press, 1991). On Orpheus in

Shakespearean Romance, see David Armitage, "The Dismemberment of Orpheus: Mythic Elements in Shakespeare's romances," *Shakespeare Survey* 39 (1987): 123–33.

29. Thanks once again to James Uden, for remarking to me that Orpheus is said to have taught this "practice" to the Thracians, not to the Romans.

30. For a lucid and subtle overview of this post-Foucauldian understanding of Roman sexuality, see Kirk Ormand, "Impossible Lesbians in Ovid's *Metamorphoses*," in *Gendered Dynamics in Latin Love Poetry*, ed. Ronnie Ancona and Ellen Greene (Baltimore: Johns Hopkins University Press, 2005): 79–110. Ormand also takes up some important arguments against this view: major critics find evidence of homophobia, and of Romans' conceiving of same-sex desire, at least to a limited extent, and within the framework of a gendered opposition of activity to passivity, in identitarian terms—perhaps most notably in what animadversions on lesbian desire reveal about Roman understandings of it. (These critics include Amy Richlin, Judith Hallett, and Bernadette Brooten.) Reading the episode of Iphis and Ianthe in Book IX of the *Metamorphoses*, Ormand suggests that the would-be lover's plaint directed at an unnatural desire, which has often been taken as a denunciation of lesbianism, decries, instead, the love's impossibility. Iphis seems to think that (as a girl) her love for another girl is not forbidden but impossible. ("Hers is not the love that dare not speak its name; it is a love that has no Roman name to speak" [102].) Ormand also compellingly locates the Ovidian episode in relation to the literary topoi of love poetry that it evokes. For a modern variation on the Iphis myth, see Ali Smith, *Girl Meets Boy: The Myth of Iphis* (Edinburgh: Canongate, 2007). See also Amy Richlin, "Not Before Homosexuality: The Materiality of the Cinaedus and the Roman Law Against Love Between Men," *Journal of the History of Sexuality* 3, no. 4 (1993): 523–73; Amy Richlin, "Reading Ovid's Rapes," in *Pornography and Represen-tation in Greece and Rome*, ed. Amy Richlin (New York: Oxford University Press, 1992), 158–79; Judith Hallett, "Female Homoeroticism and the Denial of Roman Reality in Latin Literature," *Yale Journal of Criticism* 3, no. 1 (1989): 209–27; Bernadette Brooten, *Love Between Women: Early Christian Responses to Female Homoeroticism* (Chicago: University of Chicago Press, 1996); and Kirk Ormand, *Controlling Desires: Sexuality in Ancient Greece and Rome*, 2nd edition (Austin: University of Texas Press, 2018).

31. Craig A. Williams, *Roman Homosexuality*, 2nd edition (Oxford: Oxford University Press, 2010): 178. According to Williams, these are the verbs:

	Insertive	Receptive
Vaginal	futuere	crisare
Anal	pedicare	cevere
Oral	irrumare	fellare

Thanks to James Uden to pointing me to Craig Williams—and to Kirk Ormand and others on Roman sexuality (and on *The Metamorphoses* more generally). Uden also alerted me to the work of Holt Parker; some people will know why he cautioned me to weigh the implications of citing him. My decision to do so is mine alone; in my view, the scholarship should be judged on its own terms, and, moreover, whatever the publicity, one should, I think, be cautious about taking sides in sexual (and other) scandals. I do not presume to know the details of the case—and haven't found it relevant to my reading of the essays to try to find them out.

32. See, among other texts, K. J. Dover, *Greek Homosexuality (Updated, with a new postscript)* (Cambridge: Harvard University Press, 1989); Michel Foucault, *The History of Sexuality, Volume 2: The Use of Pleasure*, trans. Robert Hurley (New York: Vintage, 1990), esp. 185–215; H. I. Marrou, "Pederasty in Classical Education," in *A History of Education in Antiquity*, trans. George Lamb (Madison: University of Wisconsin Press, 1956), 26–35; Jesper Svenbro, *Phrasikleia: An Anthropology of Reading in Ancient Greece*, trans. Janet Lloyd (Ithaca, N.Y.: Cornell University Press, 1993); John Addington Symonds, *A Problem in Greek Ethics: Being an Inquiry into the Phenomenon of Sexual Inversion Addressed Especially to Medical Psychologists and Jurists* (London, 1908 [Privately Printed for the Αρεοπαγιτιγα Society]).

33. For a fascinating consideration of this question—as well as a concise, lucid formulation of a related understanding of Roman sexuality—see Holt Parker, "The Teratogenic Grid," in *Roman Sexualities*, ed. Judith P. Hallett and Marilyn B. Skinner (Princeton: Princeton University Press, 1997), 47–65. Parker has a slightly different graph from that of Williams, and he doesn't include *crisare* and *cevere*. Parker's innovation, when it comes to his rendition of the sexual roles formulated by Williams and others, may be in his reading of cunnilingus as the "passive" analogue of vaginal penetration; the cunnilictor is "penetrated" by an "active" woman. Leaving aside the details of terminology and the "grid" that he spells out for normative and pathological sexual acts (according to what we can decipher of Roman sexual ideology), his central polemical point is that there is, of course, no position for "homosexual" or "heterosexual"—because, anatomical specification notwithstanding, the terms are indifferent to gender (being determined instead by sexual role).

34. For J. D. Reed, on the contrary, "unlike attraction to women, paiderastia is problematized here—it requires an origin and an explanation—at least for Thrace, if not for other places . . . or among the gods." Ovid, *Metamorphoses*, trans. Rolfe Humphries, annotated by J. D. Reed (Bloomington: Indiana University Press, 2018), 462, note to p. 236 [10.83–5]. Future references will be given parenthetically.

35. This account is derived from John Block Friedman, *Orpheus in the Middle Ages* (Cambridge: Harvard University Press, 1970), 287–8. On Henryson's use (and rewriting) of Ovid—and for a lucid account of the allegorical rendering of the Orpheus myth by Boethius, whose *Consolation of Philosophy* was translated by Chaucer—see Jennifer N. Brown, "Cosmology, Sexuality and Music in Robert Henryson's *Orpheus and Eurydice*," in *Sexuality, Sociality, and Cosmology in Medieval Literary Texts*, ed. Marla Segol and Jennifer N. Brown (New York: Palgrave Macmillan, 2013), 145–58. Thanks to Brown for sharing this essay with me, and to Julie Orlemanski for putting me in touch with her. For an account of how

the homoeroticism of Ovid's Orpheus appears in two early modern "epyllia," *Orpheus and his Journey to Hell* (1595), by "R.B. Gent," and the *Legend of Orpheus and Eurydice*, appended to the anonymous *Of Loves Complaint* (1597), see Jennifer Ingleheart, "The Invention of (Thracian) Homosexuality," in *Ancient Rome and the Construction of Modern Homosexual Identities*, ed. Jennifer Ingleheart (Oxford: Oxford University Press, 2016), 56–73.

36. "[The Epistle]," *Ovid's Metamorphoses: The Arthur Golding Translation of 1567*, ed. John Frederick Nims (Philadelphia: Paul Dry Books, 2000), 411 (ll.213–15). Thanks to Liza Blake for pointing me to this passage.

37. Bruce W. Holsinger, *Music, Body, and Desire in Medieval Culture: Hildegard of Bingen to Chaucer* (Stanford: Stanford University Press, 2001), 309. Future references will be given parenthetically.

38. Lydgate's *Fall of Princes*, he writes, "is the clearest medieval precedent for a small but rich strand of English humanistic poetry centering upon the homoerotic possibilities of the Orpheus narrative" (339). Holsinger also gives a brief account of some of the early modern references to Orpheus (340–2).

39. Kaja Silverman emphasizes the misogyny that is part of this tradition. (See, for example, Poliziano's *Orfeo* [which was translated into English by John Addington Symonds] for a defense of sodomy [a misogynistic defense, among other things].) In an argument that complements the work of Leo Bersani, Silverman adumbrates a tradition privileging sameness and connection (as against difference and its hypostatizing of identity); suggesting that mortality is perhaps the ultimate realization of this sameness (as well as what most threatens identity), she sees in Orpheus's turning back a refusal of mortality (rather, a violent projection of it onto others as a denial of it in oneself) that she also links to misogyny (seemingly reading back from the tradition of readings of the myth that marginalize Eurydice [seeing it as his drama rather than hers]) to the myth itself. She thus offers this suggestive, but I think highly tendentious, summary of the episode in Ovid: "Orpheus descends to Hades to plead for her life, but when he arrives, he seems less interested in her than in conquering death. He is so eloquent that the gods of the underworld allow him to take Eurydice back to earth . . . [but] he is overwhelmed by the desire to see her and turns around. Eurydice is immediately transported back to Hades, and Orpheus is terrified by her sudden disappearance, which makes death real to him. He attempts to rid himself of his mortality by feminizing it, and since this projection renders women repugnant to him, he transfers his desire to young men." There is little in Ovid to justify the psychological reading, or the rendering of homosexual desire as misogyny; the misreading, though, allows for an interesting rewriting of the tradition of Orpheus with Eurydice as its central figure. Her terms make his death redemptive—and, in passing, turn erotic neglect of women into "misogyny." (Many critics refer in passing to Orpheus's erotic neglect of women as "misogyny," which is far from obvious to me. In "The Beast in the Closet: James and the Writing of Homosexual Panic," Eve Kosofsky Sedgwick makes the important point that misogyny is rooted less in the failure to desire women than in the compulsion to do

so. [Sedgwick, "The Beast in the Closet: James and the Writing of Homosexual Panic," in *Epistemology of the Closet* (Berkeley: University of California Press, 1990), 180–212.] There may be other moments that can legitimately be called misogynist. In Plato's *Republic*, Orpheus's soul hates women because they killed him [in some ways a not entirely unreasonable reaction to his experience]; my sense of Ovid is that "misogyny" before his death is harder to maintain [*Republic* 620a].) In Book XI, Silverman says, Orpheus is "killed and dismembered by a group of women, who resent his misogyny, and death transforms him." Returning to Hades, he clasps Eurydice in his arms "and acknowledges her ontological equality." Silverman, *Flesh of My Flesh* (Stanford: Stanford University Press, 2009), 4–5. (Silverman gives further justification for her summary of the tale in Ovid in the next chapter of the book. See *Flesh of My Flesh*, 49–50.) Future references to Silverman will be given parenthetically. According to J. D. Reed, in Orpheus's death "Ovid combines two traditions: that of the Hellenistic poet Phanocles . . . in which Orpheus is killed for rejecting sex and love with women and promulgating that with males, and that he is torn apart by Maenads . . . for dishonoring the god, which originates in Aeschylus's lost tragedy *Bassarids*; in Ovid's version his killers are angry at his refusal to marry." Reed adds that the detail of Orpheus's head floating to Lesbos is also there in Phanocles (and not in Virgil's *Georgics*). (*Metamorphoses*, trans. Humphries, 469, note to 259–61 [XI.1–66].)

40. For a brief account of uses of Orpheus from the Middle Ages through *Totem and Taboo*, see Silverman, *Flesh of My Flesh*, 52–58. See also Fausto Gisalberti, "Medieval Biographies of Ovid," *Journal of the Warburg and Courtauld Institutes* 9 (1946): 10–59; Simone Viarre, *La survie d'Ovide dans la littérature scientifique des XIIe et XIIIe siècles* (Poitiers: Publications du CESCM, vol. 4. [Université de Poitiers, 1966]); and Jane Chance, *Medieval Mythography* (3 volumes) (Gainesville: University Press of Florida, 1994).

41. Mark D. Jordan, *The Invention of Sodomy in Christian Theology* (Chicago and London: University of Chicago Press, 1997).

42. This is the claim of Kaja Silverman in *Flesh of My Flesh*, though her focus is primarily on the gender implications of this (more appealing) foundation myth: "The myth of Orpheus and Eurydice is one the ur-narratives of Western subjectivity—equal in importance to, and perhaps even more important than, the one recounted by Sophocles in *Oedipus Rex*. The latter myth is cloyingly familiar, but few of us could recount what happens in the former. This does not mean, though, that we have ceased to live it. There is an Orpheus inside every Oedipus, and it is *he* who will determine our future" (58).

43. For an account of queer history that explores the potential of looking back, see Heather Love, *Feeling Backward* (Cambridge: Harvard University Press, 2007).

44. "For the Greek *META-MORPHosis* is itself changed into the Latin *MUTatas* . . . *FORMas* in Ovid's first line. *FORMa* is a cross-language anagram of *MORPHEe*, and *MUTatas* even echoes the consonant patterns of the Greek. But Ovid does not stop here. Between *MUTAtas* (changed) and *FORMAs* he inserts the

word *dicere* (speak of): this addition suggests the Latin *MUTus* (silent) as well as the idea of change. Ovid gives voice to forms that cannot speak for themselves. In so doing he is animating nature as *ORPHeus* had done. *ORPHeus'* audience, after all, is as *metamORPHosed* as is the backdrop to his narrative of metamorphosis" (Ahl, *Metaformations*, 59). Ahl then notes that Morpheus, god of sleep, first appears in Book XI of the *Metamorphoses*, and "true to the etymology of his name, he generates shapes that somehow come to life. Nature is the artist imitating art. Sleep, in Latin, is proverbially the brother of death, *MORs*, and as Ovid's Myrrha suggests, *metaMORphosis* lies somewhere between life and death. If there is a song to be sung about it, then, Orpheus is surely the appropriate singer: as *IGNIS* [fire] in *lIGNIS* [wood], so *ORPHEUS* is in *MORPHEUS*" (60).

45. *Ovid's metamorphoses in fifteen books. Translated by the most Eminent Hands. Adorn'd with Sculptures*, trans. John Dryden, et al. (London: Printed for Jacob Tonson [etc.], 1717). Downloaded from English Poetry, Second edition: http://gateway.proquest .com/openurl?ctx_ver=Z39.88-2003&xri:pqil:res_ver=0.2&res_id=xri:ilcs-us&rft_id =xri:ilcs:ft:ep2:Z400439643:4. Future references will be given parenthetically.

46. Jack Spicer, "Orpheus in Hell," *My Vocabulary Did This to Me: The Collected Poetry of Jack Spicer*, ed. Peter Gizzi and Kevin Killian (Middletown, Conn.: Wesleyan University Press, 2008), 18. See also "Love Poems," where Spicer superimposes the trips to the underworld of Odysseus, Aeneas, and Orpheus—and, conflating Cerberus, guarding hell, with Sandy, the dog of Little Orphan Annie, and with Artemis's dogs, who devour the hart that Achteon becomes, Spicer also links the dog to his own heart, which won't give up its desire. "Love Poems," *My Vocabulary Did This To Me*, 382–6. Orpheus is a recurrent figure in Spicer's poetry.

47. In Samuel Croxall's translation:

Oh Father! Father! she would fain have spoke,
But the sharp Torture her Intention broke;
In vain she tries, for now the Blade has cut
Her Tongue sheer off, close to the trembling Root.
The mangled Part still quiver'd on the Ground,
Murmuring with a faint imperfect Sound:
And, as a Serpent writhes his wounded Train,
Uneasy, panting, and possess'd with Pain;
The Piece, while Life remain'd, still trembled fast,
And to its Mistress pointed to the last.
(*Metamorphoses*, trans. Dryden, et al., VI:835–44)

48. One might compare the passage about the death of the Greek gods in *La Tentation de Saint Antoine*—a passage that recalls Orpheus's visit to the underworld in both Ovid and Virgil. (From Pluto: "La vautour qui mange les entrailles de Titos releva la tête, Tantale eut la lèvre mouillé, la roué d'Ixion s'arrêta . . . Le jour des hommes a pénétré le Tartare!" [193].) Gustave Flaubert, *La Tentation de Saint Antoine* [text of 3rd edition (1875)], ed. Claudine Gothot-Mersch (Paris: Éditions

Gallimard, 1983). William Anderson suggests that the image of Sisyphus sitting on his stone marks the tone of this moment as ironic or comical (in contrast to Virgil's seriousness: "Ovid exuberantly amuses himself and us with the effects of Orpheus's song upon the damned: he cannot be taken seriously when he even apostrophizes Sisyphus sitting on his stone [44: the alliteration is Ovid's!]"), *Ovid's Metamorphoses, Books 6–10* (Norman: University of Oklahoma Press, 1972), 476.

49. Other stories present similar conflicts between different orders of unification. The story of Myrrha, for instance, is narratively justified because her incestuous passion leads to the birth of Adonis, who is the audience for Venus's speech, and the object of transformation at its end. Conceptually, the logic seems bumpier, although it, too, is a tale of unhappy love and loss, as well as (in incest itself) an enactment of a form of reflexivity as enchantment that could be traced through the rest of the book—and could be linked to those moments where poetry or song becomes difficult to separate from the absorption it inspires, or from the subjects about which it sings.

50. Paul de Man, it is worth noting, suggests that Rilke's affinity for the Orpheus story derives from the centrality of reversal in it (which he ties to the trope of chiasmus). See "Tropes [Rilke]," in *Allegories of Reading: Figural Language in Rousseau, Nietzsche, Rilke, and Proust* (New Haven: Yale University Press, 1979), 20–57. See also Werner Hamacher, "The Second of Inversion: Movements of a Figure Through Celan's Poetry," in *Premises: Essays on Philosophy and Literature from Kant to Celan*, trans. Peter Fenvres (Cambridge: Harvard University Press, 1996), 337–87 (on Rilke, see 342–44).

51. One also thinks of the repeated moments of erotic monologue (in the forms of soliloquies detailing internal moral debates) in the poem (Byblis [309]; Myrrha [339]; Medea [209]) and of recurrent figures of apostrophe (for example, Narcissus [94]).

52. In Addison's translation: "That Tongue, for this thy Crime, / Which could so many subtle Tales produce, / Shall be hereafter but of little use. / Hence 'tis she prattles in a fainter Tone, / With mimick Sounds, and Accents not her own" (*Metamorphoses*, trans. Dryden, et al., III:467–71).

53. "And as his head, cut off from his beautiful neck, / Was tumbling down the rushing course of Hebrus, / His voice and tongue, with his last breath, / cried out, 'Eurýdicé! O poor Eurýdicé!' / And the banks of the downward river Hebrus echoed, 'O poor Eurýdicé! Eurýdicé!'" Virgil, Fourth Georgic, *The Georgics of Virgil: Bilingual Edition*, trans. David Ferry (New York: Farrar, Straus and Giroux, 2005), 181. Silverman discusses this echo in *Flesh of My Flesh* (48).

54. Percy Bysshe Shelley, "Orpheus," http://gateway.proquest.com/openurl?ctx _ver=Z39.88-2003&xri:pqil:res_ver=0.2&res_id=xri:ilcs-us&rft_id =xri:ilcs:ft:ep2:Z300484238:3.

55. The hyacinth is given two different origins in *The Metamorphoses*. As James O'Hara writes: "When both Hyacinthus, the doomed beloved of Apollo, and the blood of the suicidal hero Ajax turn into the hyacinth flower, Ovid provides explicit cross-references. Hyacinthus dies in Book 10, and a flower grows, and the apparent

letters AI on the flower are said to spell out Apollo's cry of woe as he laments Hyacinthus. But Apollo at this time also predicts Ajax's death: 'that time will come, when the bravest hero will add himself to this flower and be read on the same leaf' (*tempus et illud erit, quo se fortissimus heros | addat in hunc florem folioque legatur eodem*, 10.207–8). In Book 13, Ajax's blood causes the hyacinth to grow—the hyacinth that was born from the wound of the Oebalian's Hyacinth (*Oebalio . . . de vulnere*, 396)—and the letters inscribed in the plant are now ambiguous, referring both to Apollo's lament for Hyacinth and to the name Ajax: *littera communis mediis pueroque viroque | inscripta est foliis, haec nominis, illa querellae* ('letters common to the boy and the man—to the name of the latter and the lament for the former—are written on the inner leaves,' 13.397–8). It is hard to say with confidence what is being said in these passages. . . . Something odd is going on here." (O'Hara, 125)

7. Wallace Stevens and the Temporalities of Inception and Embodiment

1. Wallace Stevens, "The Rock," in *The Collected Poems of Wallace Stevens* (New York: Vintage, 1982), 525–8. Future references to Stevens's poetry will be to this edition, and will be given parenthetically by page number. J. Hillis Miller notes that another possible reference here is Whitman: "I believe the soggy clods shall become lovers and lamps." (J. Hillis Miller, "Stevens' Rock and Criticism as Cure," *Georgia Review* 30 [1976]: 5–31, 22.) Future references will be given parenthetically.

2. Although I do not take up this possibility here, this structure could be examined by way of the relation of humankind to objects charted by Elaine Scarry in *The Body in Pain*, an "arc" that relieves people of the burden of sentience by projecting it outwards, onto things, which sentience then returns (by way of a lever or fulcrum, in her metaphor) to reshape the creating consciousness. See *The Body in Pain: The Making and Unmaking of the World* (New York: Oxford University Press, 1985). For Douglas Mao—in his rich account of Stevens's relation to modernist understandings of the object (and the ethics and politics of production and consumption)—Stevens comes increasingly to give value to perception (even as fleeting, which for Mao is also tied to Stevens's lack of interest in poetry as itself an object or artifact, and to his placidity [unusual, Mao suggests, among modernists] about human reshapings of the material world). Douglas Mao, *Solid Objects: Modernism and the Test of Production* (Princeton: Princeton University Press, 1998.) Future references will be given parenthetically. Mao also notes that, unlike William Carlos Williams, Stevens did not think that the mind could have access to the thing itself—an assumption that underlies the late poems' valuing of perception, even in the face of the "sheer priority" of the material world (234–5). The placidity of the late poems perhaps derives (according to Mao) from a shift whereby the inaccessibility and priority of the material world that earlier on inspires a valorized desire comes instead to point toward a valuing of perception, where, for the material traces of those perceptions, as Stevens writes in "The Planet on the Table," "It was

not important that they survive." See also Charles Altieri, *Wallace Stevens and the Demands of Modernity: Toward a Phenomenology of Value* (Ithaca, N.Y.: Cornell University Press, 2013); and Simon Critchley, *Things Merely Are: Philosophy in the Poetry of Wallace Stevens* (London: Routledge, 2005).

3. *Shakespeare's Sonnets*, edited with an analytic commentary by Stephen Booth (New Haven: Yale University Press, 2000), 84–7. The opposition between presence and representation is, as Booth points out in his commentary (317–21), Platonic in origin. For Booth's explanation of "summer's story," see pages 319–20.

4. For perhaps the most compelling critical account of this "secondariness," see Charles Altieri, "Aspect-Seeing and Stevens' Ideal of Ordinary Experience," *Wallace Stevens Journal* 36, no. 1 (Spring 2012): 78–93. In my possibly reductive understanding, aspect-seeing, which Altieri takes from Wittgenstein, describes a shift in perception (most famously, in Wittgenstein's rabbit-duck) where the object is "changed" (from a rabbit to a duck, for instance) by a shift in the subject even as there is, explicitly, no change in objective reality. In Altieri's terms, "one feels power as a subject to determine a world even though the object given for perception is fixed and stable" (81); for Altieri, this means "we are justified in questioning the standard view of Stevens's fascination with subject-object relations as epistemically driven—that is, as involving questions about truth and falsity in relation to things presented as charged by artifice" (83). This structure also allows Altieri to articulate what is potentially consoling about Stevens's vision, even within his unblinking gaze at the desolations of human experience: poems that show the world to be "a source of unrelenting pain and disappointment, lit by moments of grace" challenge readers to find "acceptance and even affirmation that is neither the will to pleasure nor the will to power" (*WSJ*, 89). A later version of Alteri's essay appears as "Aspect-Seeing and Its Implications in *The Rock*," in *Wallace Stevens and the Demands of Modernity: Toward a Phenomenology of Value* (Ithaca, N.Y.: Cornell University Press, 2013), 202–32. For a helpful account of Altieri's book—more philosophically informed than mine—see Oren Izenberg's review, *Wallace Stevens Journal* 37, no. 1 (Spring 2013): 108–10. For another exploration of related problems, see Scarry, *The Body in Pain*.

5. Marjorie Perloff suggests that the green plant is inside: "The glaring plant is part of the 'harsh reality,' but, ironically, its green is not the green of spring renewal; it is 'barbarous green' because the indoor plant, artificially cultivated, is really less, not more, alive than the dying autumn foliage. As the plant's 'reality' impinges upon the narrator's mind, a strange transformation takes place: the ugly outdoor scene becomes a 'legend' into which the plant cannot enter; the 'wrecked umbrellas' become a 'forest,' and 'red' and 'yellow' become the more refined 'maroon' and 'olive.' The 'effete vocabulary of summer' does say something after all." "Irony in Wallace Stevens's 'The Rock,'" *American Literature* 36, no. 3 (November 1964): 327–42.

6. On this property of the language in "The Rock," which he discusses in relation to catachresis, see J. Hillis Miller, "Criticism as Cure."

7. For a suggestive reading of verbs of being in Stevens—which comes up against, at several moments, related questions of positing—see Roger Gilbert, "Verbs of

Mere Being: A Defense of Stevens' Style," *Wallace Stevens Journal* 28, no. 2 (Fall 2004): 191–202. On the question of the relation of the "seen" and the "unseen" in Stevens (and Eliot) that discusses Stevens's interest in the possibility (as Stevens puts it in a letter about "Notes Toward a Supreme Fiction") "to believe in something that we know to be untrue," see Douglas Mao, "The Unseen Side of Things: Eliot and Stevens," in Rosalyn Gregory and Benjamin Kohlmann, eds., *Utopian Spaces of Modernism: British Literature and Culture, 1885–1945* (London: Palgrave Macmillan, 2012), 194–213. (Quotation is from 198; Mao quotes from *Letters of Wallace Stevens* [Berkeley: University of California Press, 1996], 443.) Mao links this "will to believe" to William James, and sees in both Eliot and Stevens a reaction to nineteenth-century utopian thought.

8. For an account of Stevens's particularly "modern" relation to Romanticism, see Robert S. Lehman, "Abstract Pleasures: Romanticism and Finitism in the Poetry of Wallace Stevens," *Modern Philology* 111, no. 2 (November 2013): 308–28. Future references will be given parenthetically. Stevens is "modern," Lehman suggests, because he repeatedly returns to "one of modernity's central traumas" (315), a founding gesture of Romantic aesthetics whereby the constitutive finitude of Kant's Copernican revolution first appears, in Baumgarten, "as an effect of a distinction between" philosophical and poetic language and "of the irreducibility of the latter to the former" (314). In this break, in other terms, "the theme of finitude" is derived "from the experience of literary language" (315); finitude ("the human subject, limited by space and time, may perceive the 'plain sense of things' but never the thing-in-itself"), Lehman writes, "is at the origin of what Stevens calls poetry" (308). Stevens, read in the context of this detailed account of Romanticism, makes evident how "a version of finitude reasserts itself as an absolute limit within Romanticism"; "one can recognize in Stevens's verse an immanent break in the romantic project, an interruption of the movement between the sensual and the ideal" (309). This break, Lehman suggests, "indicates the persistence of a preromantic remainder within Stevens's romanticism, one that can be followed back to the aesthetic revolutions of the eighteenth century, when the complicated relationship between literary language and the philosophical theme of finitude first presented itself" (310).

9. Andrew Marvell, "To His Coy Mistress," in *The Norton Anthology of Poetry*, 5th edition, ed. Margaret Ferguson, Mary Jo Salter, and Jon Stallworthy (New York: Norton, 2005), 478–9, 479.

10. William Shakespeare, *Hamlet*, ed. Frank Kermode, *The Riverside Shakespeare*, vol. 2, 2nd edition, ed. G. Blakemore Evans and J. J. Tobin (Boston and New York: Houghton Mifflin, 1997), IV.vii.166. Future references will be given parenthetically. "Ophelia," writes Anne Carson, "takes sexual appetite into the river and drowns it amid water plants." Anne Carson, *The Albertine Workout* (New York: New Directions Poetry Pamphlet #13, 2014), 11. Originally printed as "The Albertine Workout," from *London Review of Books* 36, no. 11 (June 5, 2014), 34–5. On Ophelia, see also Chapter 8 of the present book.

11. The central statement of this aesthetic ideal in aestheticism is Walter Pater, "The School of Giorgione," in *The Renaissance: Studies in Art and Poetry, The 1893*

Text, ed. Donald Hill (Berkeley: University of California Press, 1980), 102–22. Future references will be given parenthetically. For a detailed aesthetic genealogy of related questions, see Lehman, "Abstract Pleasures." On Stevens's relation to aestheticism, particularly as it is filtered through George Santayana, see Mao, *Solid Objects*.

12. *OED Online*, s.v. "sacrament (*n.*)," last modified September 2020, www.oed .com/view/Entry/169523.

13. This pun was pointed out to me by Andy Tareila. Many of the thoughts pursued in this chapter are indebted to conversations with him while I advised his senior thesis on Stevens and aestheticism.

14. Walter Pater, "The School of Giorgione," 106, italics in original. As he writes later in the essay, "art, then, is thus always striving to be independent of the mere intelligence, to become a matter of pure perception" (108).

15. The questions here, like many of the concerns of my argument, could be recast in terms of skepticism, or of verifying subjective impressions of an external world (something that is addressed, one might argue, by Stevens's projecting of perception outwards, "into" things): "though hardly unusual among the philosophically inclined in accepting that there is no grasping of the thing undistorted by the mind's associations, peculiarities, and memories, Stevens is perhaps unique among poets in the extent to which his achievement is generated from the poetic possibilities of this impossibility" (Mao, *Solid Objects*, 221).

16. William Shakespeare, *A Midsummer Night's Dream*, ed. Anne Barton, *The Riverside Shakespeare*, vol. 2, 2nd edition, ed. G. Blakemore Evans and J. J. M. Tobin (Boston and New York: Houghton Mifflin, 1997), V.i.210. Future references will be given parenthetically by act, scene, and line number.

17. Stevens's *momentary* in the conclusion of the poem may also derive from *A Midsummer Night's Dream*. Condoling with Hermia about some of the many ways that "The course of true love never did run smooth," Lysander remarks, "Or if there were a sympathy in choice, / War, death, or sickness did lay siege to it, / Making it momentany as a sound, / Swift as a shadow, short as any dream, / Brief as the lightning in the collied night, / That, in a spleen, unfolds both heaven and earth; / And ere a man hath power to say 'Behold!' / The jaws of darkness do devour it up; / So quick bright things come to confusion" (I.i.134, 141–9). (*Momentany*, now obsolete, means "Relating to the moment, momentary; transitory; evanescent" (*OED Online*). The first folio has "momentarie" (Riverside Shakespeare, 281).

18. Kevin Ohi, "The Consummation of the Swallow's Wings: A Zoo Story," *The South Atlantic Quarterly* 110, no. 3 (Summer 2011) ("Digital Desire," edited by Ellis Hanson), 715–43. On Stevens, see especially 726–9. Future references will be given parenthetically.

19. William Wordsworth, "Ode: Intimations of Immortality from Recollections of Early Childhood," in *Poems, Poets, Poetry: An Introduction and Anthology*, 3rd edition, ed. Helen Vendler (Boston: Bedford/St. Martin's, 2010), 635–41, 639. I discuss Wordsworth's poem in greater detail in Chapter 8.

20. I was led to think about the effect of sound in this passage (and its power to persuade) by (again) Andy Tareila.

21. For a very different reading of this poem (and the volume in which it appears)—in the context of Stevens's relation to the political developments of the '30s—see Mao, *Solid Objects*, 216–7. "*Ideas* does not so much raise questions about the subject's impositions on the object world as lend the authority of natural process to both the masses' desire *for* shape and the leader's desire *to* shape" (217).

22. On this structure of surrogate voice, see Sean Keck, "Dark Muse: Paramour and Encounter in the Poetry of Wallace Stevens," *The Wallace Stevens Journal* 33, no. 2 (Fall 2009): 177–90.

23. J. Hillis Miller reads these lines as a figure for a *mise en abyme*. (See "Criticism as Cure," 25–6.)

24. "The creative and regulative power which is conceived of as operating in the material world and as the immediate cause of its phenomena" (*OED Online*).

25. Helen Vendler, *Last Looks, Last Books: Stevens, Plath, Lowell, Bishop, Merrill* (Princeton: Princeton University Press, 2010). For Vendler, the first section of "The Rock" is the primary example of a redemption that she finds in late Stevens—a movement from a desolating and despairing confrontation with death to a revival of consciousness from a remote and "almost posthumous state" (46). "There is no better example in lyric poetry," she writes, "of the recapturing of kindled emotion as one relives the sense of being loved and being in love" (46). I share the sense of redemption in this section, and in the poem as a whole; I hope I have made clear my different sense of its terms. For Vendler, this transformation seems to depend on understanding the poem as an autobiographical confession (which, needless to say, it might have been) and on making the clods (and the "two figures") "male" and "female." The redemption, she notes, depends on "the sun's cosmic sponsorship of marriage" (44). For a characteristically oblique discussion of the autobiographical, see Wallace Stevens, "Effects of Analogy," in *Collected Poetry and Prose*, ed. Frank Kermode and Joan Richardson (New York: The Library of America, 1997), 707–23, 717.

26. For a deconstructive account of why the poem resists being read as autobiography—because the self in the poem is just one of a series of figural constructs, none of which can, finally, be made the literal "ground" of the others—see J. Hillis Miller, "Criticism as Cure," especially 20–25. "Self in the sense of individual personality is one of the major illusions dissolved by the poem" (25). More generally, Miller notes, in helpfully schematic terms, that the poem "contains at least four distinct linguistic 'scenes,'" each with its own vocabulary: a scene of love or of human life, a geometrical diagram, a natural scene (cycles of the seasons, night and day, growth and decay), and "a theory of poetry." The question, he writes, "is which of these scenes is the literal subject of the poem, the real base of which the others are illustrative figures" (17). That each register is, on examination even of its surface vocabulary, contaminated by the others, is perhaps the simplest reason that this question is undecidable. For Miller, "*mise en abyme*" might allow one to visualize the figural structure of the poem, for which "catachresis" might be the most apt term.

27. *OED Online*, s.v. "illusion (*n*.)," last modified September 2020, www.oed.com /view/Entry/91565.

28. I make this last point in "The Consummation of the Swallow's Wings," 739.

29. For an (ultimately, Levinasian) reading of this tension between the general and the particular—in ethics and in literary reading—in relation to Stevens (among others), see Jon Kertzer, "The Course of a Particular: On the Ethics of Literary Singularity," *Twentieth Century Literature* 50, no. 3 (Autumn 2004): 207–38.

30. *OED Online*, s.v. "particular (*adj.*, *n.*, *adv.*)," and "gross (*adj.* and *n.4*)," last modified September 2020, www.oed.com/view/Entry/138260 and www.oed.com/view /Entry/81765.

31. *Gross* can also mean what is left over—the dregs; in that sense, it is not unlike the "culls," at least in one sense of that word.

32. This use of *gross* derives, ultimately, from Matthew and the parable of the sower, where Jesus explains why he speaks in parables: "Therefore speak I to them in parables: because they seeing see not; and hearing they hear not, neither do they understand. And in them is fulfilled the prophecy of Esaias, which saith, By hearing ye shall hear, and shall not understand; and seeing ye shall see, and shall not perceive: For this people's heart is waxed gross, and *their* ears are dull of hearing, and their eyes they have closed; lest at any time they should see with *their* eyes and hear with *their* ears, and should understand with *their* heart, and should be converted, and I should heal them" (Matthew 13:13–15, Authorized King James Version).

33. *OED Online*, s.v. "cure (*v.2*)," last modified September 2020, www.oed.com /view/Entry/46007.

34. *OED Online*, s.v. "cure (*v.1*)," last modified September 2020, www.oed.com /view/Entry/46006.

35. B. J. Leggett (in a critique of J. Hillis Miller's account of the poem) suggests that we read "cure of the ground" as possessive (as the cure offered by the ground): "if the particular experiences of living in the world are fruitful and if we 'feast' on life—if we devour it so that it becomes a part of us—this could be seen as a cure of nothingness or meaninglessness offered by the earth, as opposed to a cure that *we* contrive, the other possible cure the poem considers" (107). "Reconstructing 'The Rock': Stevens and Misreading," in *Late Stevens: The Final Fictions* (Baton Rouge: Louisiana State University Press, 2005), 93–112.

36. Theo Davis, *Formalism, Experience, and the Making of American Literature in the Nineteenth Century* (Cambridge: Cambridge University Press, 2007), 46.

37. Later in Section II, these seasons are also coordinated with (it seems) human procreation: "They bloom as a man loves, as he lives in love. / They bear their fruit so the year is known" (527). J. Hillis Miller notes a reference to Genesis and Milton: "in the day ye eat thereof, then your eyes shall be opened, and ye shall be as gods, knowing good and evil" (Genesis 3:5 [Authorized King James Version]; Hillis Miller, 16).

38. *OED Online*, s.v. "icon (*n*.)," last modified September 2020, www.oed.com /view/Entry/90879.

39. The "eye" is also the enclosed space in a letter—in *d*, *e*, or *o*, and so on. (*OED Online*).

40. Rob Lehman has suggested a more likely reading: "Vivid sleep" is the sleep of the living, in contrast to the sleep of death.

41. John Milton, *Paradise Lost*, ed. Gordon Teskey (New York: Norton, 2005), IX.872–85. Future references will be given parenthetically as *PL* followed by the book and line numbers. Odious also appears in Book Six, in the description of the first night of the battle in Heaven—when there is a respite from "the odious din of war" (*PL* VI.408). And it appears, too, in Sin's description of Death: "At last this odious offspring whom thou seest/Thine own begotten breaking violent way/Tore through my entrails, that with fear and pain/Distorted, all my nether shape thus grew/Transform'd: but he my inbred enemy/Forth issued . . ." (*PL* II.781–5).

42. I owe my parsing of this line to Daniel Heller-Roazen.

43. Complaining to God of his solitude, Adam (in *Paradise Lost*) says he cannot turn animals into human companions: "I by conversing cannot these erect/From prone, nor in their ways complacence find" (*PL* VIII.432–3).

44. *OED Online*, s.v. "adduce (*v*.)," last modified September 2020, www.oed.com /view/Entry/2225.

45. I do not know whether Stevens knew that a mango's rind contains the same chemical compound as poison ivy, and that it can therefore produce a severe allergic reaction in people who touch it. The "mango's rind" is thus not a "cull" that we could safely eat—or, in any case, we would have to eat the colorings without touching the rind.

8. "Epitaph, the Idiom of Man": Imaginings of the Beginning

1. Eudora Welty, "Circe," in *The Collected Stories of Eudora Welty* (Orlando: Houghton Mifflin Harcourt, 1980), 531–37. Future references will be given parenthetically.

2. Gerard Manley Hopkins, "Spring and Fall: To a Young Child," in *Selected Poetry*, ed. Catherine Phillips (Oxford: Oxford World's Classics, 2008), 137. Future quotations of the poem are from this page of this edition.

3. This is Paul Doherty's reading of the poem: "The speaker in the poem does not see beyond the Fall. But his view is a partial one, limited by his own nature (he sees the Golden-grove's shedding its leaves not as a part of a natural cycle, but a 'blight'), and by the particular experience which he undergoes. The reader, whose perspective is greater, can see both fall and spring, the full cycle of death and rebirth" (143). Paul Doherty, "Hopkins' 'Spring and Fall: To a Young Girl,'" *Victorian Poetry* 5, no. 2 (Summer 1967): 140–3.

4. In *Seven Types of Ambiguity*, William Empson notes the ambiguity of "And yet you will weep and know why": "*Will weep* may mean: 'insist upon weeping, now or later,' or 'shall weep in the future.' *Know* in either case may follow *will*, like *weep*, 'you insist upon knowing, or you shall know,' or may mean: 'you already know why you weep, why you shall weep, or why you insist upon weeping,' or thirdly, may be

imperative, 'listen and I shall tell you why you weep, or shall weep, or shall insist upon weeping, or insist upon weeping already'" ([London: Chatto and Windus, 1949], 148). Empson notes that this ambiguity was pointed out by I. A. Richards (in *Practical Criticism* [83]), who, however, considered "that the ambiguity of *will* is removed by the accent which Hopkins placed on it." Doherty develops the consequences of this ambiguity in relation to the split or ironized voice inherent in the dramatic monologue.

5. See Jesper Svenbro, *Phrasikleia: An Anthropology of Reading in Ancient Greece*, trans. Janet Lloyd (Ithaca, N.Y.: Cornell University Press, 1993). Briefly, because ancient readers would not have read silently—would have read the epitaphs out loud—the *I* thus spoken marks an appropriation of the (live) reader's voice by the dead: the first people to give voice to a written *I* did it on behalf of the dead, and by having their voices taken over by a voice not their own. I explain my sense of some implications of these claims in *Dead Letters Sent: Queer Literary Transmission* (Minneapolis: University of Minnesota Press, 2015), 12–14. In the comic speech of Aristophanes in Plato's *Symposium*, the threat, after Zeus has cut overweening humankind into halves, is that he will do it again: "there's a danger that if we don't keep order before the gods, we'll be split in two again, and then we'll be walking around in the condition of people carved on gravestones in bas-relief, sawn apart between the nostrils, like half-dice." Plato, *Symposium*, trans. Alexander Nehamas and Paul Woodruff (Indianapolis: Hackett Publishing, 1989), 29. Another form of prospective epitaph, this, as legible within the wry, parodic story of the fundamental dissatisfaction and maladaptation at the origins of desire.

6. My thinking throughout this chapter is indebted to Daniel Heller-Roazen, *Echolalias: On the Forgetting of Language* (New York: Zone Books, 2005). I was inspired, especially, by "The Lesser Animal," pp. 128–47.

7. Anne Carson, *Eros the Bittersweet* (Normal, Ill.: Dalkey Archive Press, 1998), 76.

8. John Milton, *Paradise Lost*, ed. Gordon Teskey (New York: Norton, 2005). Future references will be given parenthetically as *PL* followed by the book and line numbers.

9. "First, it is true that from the deserted island it is not creation but re-creation, not the beginning but a re-beginning that takes place. The deserted island is the origin, but a second origin. From it everything begins anew. The island is the necessary minimum for this re-beginning, the material that survives the first origin, the radiating seed or egg that must be sufficient to re-produce everything. Clearly, this presupposes that the formation of the world happens in two stages, in two periods of time, birth and re-birth, and that the second is just as necessary and essential as the first, and thus the first is necessarily compromised, born for renewal and already renounced in a catastrophe. It is not that there is a second birth because there has been a catastrophe, but the reverse, there is a catastrophe after the origin because there must be, from the beginning, a second birth. . . . The second moment does not succeed the first: it is the reappearance of the first when the cycle of other moments has been completed. The second origin is thus more essential than the

first, since it gives us the law of repetition, the law of the series, whose first origin gave us only moments. . . . The second origin of the world is more important than the first: it is a sacred island. Many myths recount that what we find there is an egg, a cosmic egg. Since the island is a second origin, it is entrusted to man and not to the gods. . . . In the ideal of beginning anew there is something that precedes the beginning itself, that takes it up to deepen it and delay it in the passage of time. The desert island is the material of this something immemorial, this something most profound. (Gilles Deleuze, "Desert Islands," in *Desert Islands and Other Texts: 1953–1974*, ed. David Lapoujade [Los Angeles: Semiotext(e), 2004], 9–14, 13–14. [Translation of "Causes et Raisons des Îles Desertes," in *L'Île Deserte: Textes et Entretiens 1953–1974*, ed. David Lapoujade (Paris: Les Éditions de Minuit, 2002), 11–17.])

10. One might also compare Eve's apostrophes to the apple in Book IX ("Great are thy virtues, best of fruits, / Though kept from man, and worthy to be admired" [*PL* IX.745–6]) and to the tree ("O sovereign, virtuous, precious of all trees / In Paradise" [*PL* IX.795–6]).

11. He continues: "For none I know / Second to Me or like, equal much less. / How have I then with whom to hold converse / Save with the creatures which I made, and those / To me inferior, infinite descents / Beneath what other creatures are to thee?" (*PL* VIII.406–11)

12. My sense of Milton's use of "subtle" is indebted to Gavin Alexander, "Prosopopoeia; the Speaking Figure," in *Renaissance Figures of Speech*, ed. Sylvia Adamson, Gavin Alexander, and Katrin Ettenhuber (Cambridge: Cambridge University Press, 2007), 97–112, especially 107.

13. William Wordsworth, "Ode: Intimations of Immortality from Recollections of Early Childhood," in *Poems, Poets, Poetry: An Introduction and Anthology*, 3rd edition, ed. Helen Vendler (Boston: Bedford/St. Martin's, 2010), 635–41, 640. Future references will be given parenthetically.

14. *Metamorphoses: Ovid's Metamorphoses: The Arthur Golding Translation of 1567*, ed. John Frederick Nims (Philadelphia: Paul Dry Books, 2000), 168. Thanks to Mary Crane, who, when I asked her about the echo in Wordsworth, Milton, Shakespeare, and Ovid, suggested to me that Golding's Ovid is the likely source here.

15. William Shakespeare, *The Tempest*, ed. Stephen Orgel (Oxford: Oxford University Press, 1987). Future references will be given parenthetically (by act, scene, and line number), and are to this edition. Another possible source is Psalms: "Praise ye the Lord. Praise ye the Lord from the heavens: praise him in the heights. / . . . Praise the Lord from the earth: ye dragons and all deeps. / Fire, and hail, snow, and vapour: stormy wind fulfilling his word: / Mountaines and all hille: fruitful trees, and all cedars. / Beasts and all cattle: creeping things, and flying fowl: / Kings of the earth, and all people: princes, and all judges of the earth: / . . . Praise ye the Lord" (Psalms 148:1, 7–11, 14, Authorized King James Version). Very similar language also appears in Marlowe's "The Passionate Shepherd to His Love": "Come live with me and be my love, / And we will all the pleasures prove / That

valleys, groves, hills, and fields,/Woods or steepy mountains yields." *The Norton Anthology of Poetry*, fifth edition, ed. Margaret Ferguson, Mary Jo Salter, and Jon Stallworthy (New York: Norton, 2005), 256.

16. Ohi, "Forgetting *The Tempest*," in *Dead Letters Sent: Queer Literary Transmission* (Minneapolis: University of Minnesota Press, 2015), 49–65. On the citation of Ovid, see pp. 61–2.

17. On this, see Gordon Teskey, *The Poetry of John Milton* (Cambridge: Harvard University Press, 2015), 334–5. Teskey's larger point here is that Milton's poem is on the threshold of the modern world—"the last major work of European literature in which the act of creation is centered in God and the first major work of European literature in which the act of creation begins to find its center in the human." This displacement "of divine Creation by human creativity . . . is important to understanding how the subject of *Paradise Lost* is in large measure the excitement of an epic being made" [333].) Here is William Empson's tart response to this moment in Milton: "When I was a little boy I was very afraid I might not have the courage which I knew life to demand of me; my life has turned out pretty easy so far, but, if some bully said he would burn me alive unless I pretended to believe he had created me, I hope I would have enough honour to tell him that the evidence did not seem to me decisive." William Empson, *Milton's God* (London: Chatto and Windus, 1961), 89; quoted in Michael Wood, *On Empson* (Princeton: Princeton University Press, 2017), 185–6. Future references to Wood will be given parenthetically.

18. I am indebted to Mary Crane for this formulation.

19. An obliquely related poem is perhaps William Empson's "A Note on Local Flora," which begins: "There is a tree native in Turkestan,/Or further east towards the Tree of Heaven." *Collected Poems* (New York: Harcourt, Brace, 1949), 56. ("For blissful Paradise/Of God the garden was by him in th' east/Of Eden planted" [*PL* IV.208–10]). See Michael Wood's commentary on the poem, *On Empson*, 78–81.

20. George Oppen, "The Image of the Engine," in *New Collected Poems*, ed. Michael Davidson (New York: New Directions, 2008), 40–2, 40. Future references will be given parenthetically.

21. Louise Glück, "The Wild Iris," in *The Wild Iris* (New York: Echo Press, 1992), 1. All future quotations are taken from this page in this edition.

22. Mark Strand, "Elegy for My Father," in *New Selected Poems* (New York: Alfred Knopf, 2009), 71–77, 76. Future references will be given parenthetically.

23. Thomas Gray, "Elegy Written in a Country Churchyard," ll.53–4, in *The Norton Anthology of Poetry*, 669–72, 670.

24. *Hamlet*, ed. Frank Kermode, in *The Riverside Shakespeare*, vol. 2, 2nd edition, ed. G. Blakemore Evans and J. J. M. Tobin (Boston and New York: Houghton Mifflin Company, 1997). Future references will be given parenthetically (by act, scene, and line number).

25. I am indebted here to Mary Crane—who suggested to me that it might be a mistake to push too hard on the psychological verisimilitude of Shakespearean characters.

26. Marcel Proust, *In Search of Lost Time*, vol. 2, *Within a Budding Grove*, trans. C. K. Moncrieff and Terence Kilmartin, revised by D. J. Enright (New York: The Modern Library, 1992), 371–2. ("comme dans certaines scènes de Molière où deux acteurs monologuant depuis longtemps chacun de son côté à quelques pas l'un de l'autre, sont censés ne pas s'être vus encore, et tout à coup s'aperçoivent, n'en peuvent croire leurs yeux, entrecoupent leurs propos, finalement parlent ensemble, le choeur ayant suivi le dialogue, et se jettent dans les bras l'un de l'autre" A *l'ombre des jeunes filles en fleurs*, À *la recherche du temps perdu*, Tome 1, ed. Pierre Clarac and André Ferré [Paris: Bibliothèque de la Pléiade, Éditions Gallimard, 1954], 694.)

27. For an account of distraction and absorption in the play that details some of the paradoxes that attend the subject's effort to found itself, see Christopher Pye, "Dumb *Hamlet*," in *The Vanishing: Shakespeare, The Subject, and Early Modern Culture* (Durham, N.C.: Duke University Press, 2000), 105–29.

28. Stanley Cavell, "The Avoidance of Love," in *Must We Mean What We Say? A Book of Essays: Updated Edition* (Cambridge: Cambridge University Press, 2002), 246–325. (Originally published in 1969.) Future references will be given parenthetically.

29. I do not propose to address here the extended philosophical consideration of "there is"—starting with Heidegger and "*es gibt*," and moving into, among others, Blanchot, Levinas, Foucault, and Deleuze. For an account of the syntax of "il y a" whose terms are relevant for my argument here, see Ann Banfield, "The Name of the Subject: The 'Il'?," *Yale French Studies* 93 (The Place of Maurice Blanchot) (1998): 133–74. For a discussion of the two sorts of "there is"—one that is demonstrative, pointing to a present object, and another that is existential, asserting the existence of something (in French, *voici* vs. *il y a*)—see Banfield, "Describing the Unobserved: Events Grouped Around an Empty Center," in *The Linguistics of Writing; Arguments between Language and Literature*, ed. Nigel Fabb, Derek Attridge, Alan Durant, and Colin MacCabe (Manchester, UK: Manchester University Press, 1987), 265–85, especially 269 and 276–7. Her rendering of the empty center of represented thought and speech invokes the temporal vanishing in the phrase she takes from Barthes's study of photography: "*this was now here*" (Banfield, 279).

30. Oren Izenberg, *Of Being Numerous: Poetry and the Ground of Social Life* (Princeton: Princeton University Press, 2011), 166.

9. Etiology, Solitude, and Queer Incipience

1. See Michel Foucault, "Lives of Infamous Men," in *Essential Works of Foucault, 1954–1984*, vol. 3: *Power*, ed. James D. Faubion, trans. Robert Hurley et al. (New York: The New Press, 2001), 157–75; and Giorgio Agamben, "The Author as Gesture," in *Profanations*, trans. Jeff Fort (New York: Zone Books, 2007), 61–72.

2. As will be evident in this chapter, among the exceptions is Valerie Rohy, *Lost Causes: Narrative, Etiology, and Queer Theory* (Oxford: Oxford University Press, 2014). Future references will be given parenthetically.

3. Eve Kosofsky Sedgwick, "How to Bring Your Kids Up Gay: The War on Effeminate Boys," in *Tendencies* (Durham, N.C.: Duke University Press, 1993): 154–64. Future references will be given parenthetically. Some of the material in this paragraph and the three following it is adapted from my review of Valerie Rohy's *Lost Causes: Ohi*, "*Res Ipsa Loquitur*," *Papers on Language and Literature* 52, no. 1 (2016): 91–102.

4. Ellis Hanson, "The Telephone and Its Queerness," in *Cruising the Performative: Interventions into the Representation of Ethnicity, Nationality, and Sexuality*, ed. Sue-Ellen Case, Philip Brett, and Susan Leigh Foster (Bloomington: Indiana University Press, 1995): 34–58, 52.

5. Adrienne Rich, "Compulsory Heterosexuality and Lesbian Existence," *Signs* 5, no. 4 (1980): 631–60.

6. Marlene Zuk, *Sexual Selections: What We Can and Can't Learn about Sex from Animals* (Berkeley: University of California Press, 2003), 172.

7. For less depressing anti-homophobic "evolutionary" accounts of homosexuality—which see diversity itself as a desirable outcome—see Bruce Bagemihl, *Biological Exuberance: Animal Homosexuality and Natural Diversity* (New York: Stonewall Inn Editions, 2000), and Joan Roughgarden, *Evolution's Rainbow: Diversity, Gender, and Sexuality in Nature and People—Tenth Anniversary Edition* (Berkeley: University of California Press, 2013). See also Timothy F. Murphy, "Scientific Accounts of Sexual Orientation," from *Gay Science: The Ethics of Sexual Orientation Research* (New York: Columbia University Press, 1997), 13–48.

8. Simon Levay, *Gay, Straight, and the Reason Why: The Science of Sexual Orientation* (Oxford: Oxford University Press, 2011), 166.

9. Michel Foucault, *The History of Sexuality. Volume One: An Introduction*, trans. Robert Hurley (New York: Vintage Books, 1990), 154. Future references will be given parenthetically.

10. See Georgia Warnke, "Sex and Science," in *After Identity: Rethinking Race, Sex, and Gender* (Cambridge: Cambridge University Press, 2008): 121–52.

11. Kathryn Bond Stockton, *The Queer Child, Or Growing Sideways in the Twentieth Century* (Durham, N.C.: Duke University Press, 2009). See also "Eve's Queer Child," in *Regarding Sedgwick: Essays in Queer Culture and Critical Theory*, ed. Steven M. Barber and David L. Clarke (New York: Routledge, 2002), 181–200.

12. In her reading of one of Freud's lesbian case histories, Mary Jacobus notes in passing that "If the psychogenesis of homosexuality and of sexuality in general can be traced back to maternal fixation, the wonder is that all men aren't homosexual, and all women, too" (48). Jacobus, "Russian Tactics: Freud's 'Case of Homosexuality in a Woman,'" in *First Things: The Maternal Imaginary in Literature, Art, and Psychoanalysis* (New York: Routledge, 1995), 43–59.

13. D. A. Miller, *Place for Us: An Essay on the Broadway Musical* (Cambridge: Harvard University Press, 1998). (I discuss how Miller's texts raises this question of social isolation [as the possible—paradoxical—ground of social communion] in *Dead Letters Sent*.)

14. *London Review of Books* (3:9) (May 21–June 5, 1981): 3, 5, 6. My citations are to the reprinting of the essay in Paul Rabinow, ed., *Ethics: Subjectivity and Truth (Essential Works of Michel Foucault, 1954–1984, Vol. 1)* (New York: The New Press, 1998), 174–84. Future references will be given parenthetically.

15. Leo Bersani, "'Ardent Masturbation' (Descartes, Freud, and Others)," *Critical Inquiry* 38, no. 1 (Autumn 2011): 1–16. Future references will be given parenthetically. There would be any number of other contexts through which to explore this particular question. It would be one way to phrase Stanley Cavell's preoccupation with skepticism (which is not solely his preoccupation, of course). It would also be one way to describe Elaine Scarry's project in *The Body in Pain*, where pain provides the perhaps exemplary instance of the problem of the self's relation to the world.

16. On solitude in Descartes, see also Jean-Claude Milner, "Être seul," in *L'universel en éclats: Court traité politique 3* (Paris: Éditions Verdier, 2014), 131–52, 142–3. I discuss Milner's text in detail in Chapter 3.

17. Sigmund Freud, "A Special Type of Choice of Object in Men" (1910), in *The Standard Edition of the Complete Psychological Works of Sigmund Freud*, ed. and trans. James Strachey, 24 vols. (London, 1953–74), 11:163–75. Future references will be given parenthetically.

18. For his description of the unfolding of Freud's analysis, see Bersani, 8–9.

19. "A Special Type of Object Choice Made by Men," *Sexuality and the Psychology of Love*, ed. Philip Rieff, trans. Joan Riviere (New York, 1963), 46.

20. For *die eifrig geübte Onanie*, both Alan Tyson's "masturbation assiduously practiced" (in the *Standard Edition*, Freud 172) and Joan Riviere's "ardent masturbation" are cited in Bersani, 14. (Bersani, however, gives the page number for the *Standard Edition* as 166).

21. It is not my focus here, but it would not be difficult to imagine a reading that would be more attentive to the ways these quandaries of origin point to an obscured maternal power of origination.

22. Hannah Arendt, *The Origins of Totalitarianism* (Cleveland and New York: Meridian Books, 1958), esp. 474–8. Another artifact of the same period: David Riesman, *The Lonely Crowd: A Study in the Changing American Character* (New Haven: Yale University Press, 1950).

23. Heather Love, "Spoiled Identity: Radclyffe Hall's Unwanted Being," in *Feeling Backward: Loss and the Politics of Queer History* (Cambridge: Harvard University Press, 2007), 100–28.

24. Carson McCullers, *The Member of the Wedding*, in *Complete Novels* (New York: Library of America, 2001), 461–605. Future references will be given parenthetically.

25. See Émile Benveniste, "Relationships of Person in the Verb," in *Problems in General Linguistics*, trans. Mary Elizabeth Meek (Coral Gables, Fla.: University of Miami Press, 1971), 195–204 (esp. 202). On the appositional and the partitive, see Otto Jespersen, *Essentials of English Grammar* (Tuscaloosa: University of Alabama Press, 1964), 145–6. An instance of a partitive *of* is "some of us"; Jespersen gives as an

appositional *of* "that clever little wretch of a Rebecca" (146) (from Thackeray's *Vanity Fair*).

26. Pamela Thurschwell, "Dead Boys and Adolescent Girls: Unjoining the *Bildungsroman* in Carson McCullers's *The Member of the Wedding* and Toni Morrison's *Sula*," *ESC: English Studies in Canada*, vol. 38, no. 3 (2012): 105–28.

27. *The Opposite of Sex*, dir. Don Roos, Rysher Entertainment and Sony Pictures Classics, 1997.

28. These terms of non-specification recur throughout the text—from the beginning when the text doesn't tell us why "she was afraid" (466) through the wedding and the end of the text: "there was something about this wedding that gave Frankie a feeling she could not name" (462); "she did not know why she was sad, but because of this peculiar sadness, she began to realize she ought to leave the town" (479); "And it was as though a question came into her heart, and the sky did not answer. The things she had never noticed much before began to hurt her" (480); an "unnamable connection" (507); "there was an uneasy doubt that she could not quite place or name" (521).

29. Eve Kosofsky Sedgwick, "The Beast in the Closet: James and the Writing of Homosexual Panic," in *Epistemology of the Closet* (Berkeley: University of California Press, 1990), 180–212. Future references will be given parenthetically. Lord Alfred Douglas, "Two Loves," in *The Penguin Book of Homosexual Verse*, ed. Stephen Coote (New York: Penguin, 1986), 262–4, 264. Edward Coke, *The Third Part of the Institutes of the Laws of England* (London, 1644), 58, quoted in Alan Bray, *Homosexuality in Renaissance England* (New York: Columbia University Press, 1995), 61. I discuss Sedgwick's reading in greater detail in "The Beast's Storied End," *Dead Letters Sent: Queer Literary Transmission* (Minneapolis: University of Minnesota Press, 2015), 156–74.

30. Andy Donnelly, unpublished manuscript.

31. Truman Capote, *Other Voices, Other Rooms* [1948] (New York: Vintage International, 1994), 227, 230–1.

32. Written by Friedrich and Cathy Nan Quinlan; directed by Friedrich. Friedrich has posted the script on her website: http://sufriedrich.com/PDFs /PDFs%20of%20English%20scripts/Hide_and_Seek.pdf. (All quotations from the film are taken from this source, and will be cited parenthetically as *Hide and Seek*.)

33. For Patricia White, the film's refusal of coming out makes it part of what she calls—following (loosely) from Deleuze and Guattari and their study of Kafka—"lesbian minor cinema." Grouping *Hide and Seek* with films by Sadie Benning and Jennifer Montgomery, White writes, "These works help define lesbian minor cinema in terms of format (the short or short feature shot on 16 mm, 8 mm, or analogue video), a 'de-aestheticization' (black-and-white or hand-processed) comparable to [Chantal] Akerman's minimalism, and the inchoate sexual and gender identities of their young female-bodied protagonists. These films and tapes do not belong to a 'coming out' genre; although they deal with the interstitial moments between childhood and adolescence or adolescence and adulthood, they

are inconclusive and liminal, youth is not universalized, lesbianism is not affirmed" (419). Patricia White, "Lesbian Minor Cinema," *Screen* 49:4 (Winter 2008), 410–25.

34. "Maybe there is this gene that makes you gay. Maybe it is like eye color or hair color or something like that. I don't really know, I don't really think too much about it. I just know that I feel better this way and I spent so much of my life thinking about why am I gay and why am I this way and is it okay, is it not okay. It's like, I'm forty-three years old now and I gave it up. I don't really want to know, I don't care anymore" (*Hide and Seek*, 5).

35. There is a humor here, too, about the kinds of stories one hears in the context of gay bonding—surely recognizable to anyone who has heard them, where the punchline is often the same ("then years later it turns out she's a lesbian"; or "'She's a lezzie. You don't want to hang out with her' And it wasn't, I mean, she wasn't, she was very . . . well, it turned out later she was, but at the time she wasn't and she didn't understand it and we didn't understand it" [*Hide and Seek*, 20; ellipsis in original].)

36. James Baldwin, *Go Tell It on the Mountain* [1954] (London: Penguin Classics, 2001). Future references will be given parenthetically.

37. Just for example, at the end of the first section of the novel, we read (from John's point of view): "What were the thoughts of Elisha when night came, and he was alone where no eye could see, and no tongue bear witness, save only the trumpet-like tongue of God? Were his thoughts, his bed, his body foul? What were his dreams? . . . The Lord was riding on the wind to-night. What might that wind have spoken before the morning came?" (Baldwin, *Go Tell It on the Mountain*, 70).

38. James Baldwin, *Another Country* [1962] (New York: Vintage, 1993), 237.

39. See Ann Banfield, *Unspeakable Sentences: Narration and Representation in the Language of Fiction* (London: Routledge, 2015), 103–8. (Reprint: originally published by Routledge and Kegan Paul in 1982.)

40. W. B. Yeats, "The Circus Animals' Desertion," in *The Poems, Revised*, ed. Richard J. Finneran (New York: Macmillan, 1983), 346–8.

Index

KEVIN OHI is Professor of English at Boston College. He is the author of three previous books, including, most recently, *Dead Letters Sent: Queer Literary Transmission*.

CPSIA information can be obtained
at www.ICGtesting.com
Printed in the USA
LVHW031959230221
679754LV00006B/527